Terrorism and the Politics of Fear

Terrorism and the Politics of Fear

Second Edition

David L. Altheide

ROWMAN & LITTLEFIELD
Lanham • Boulder • New York • London

Executive Editor: Dhara Snowden
Associate Editor: Mary Malley
Marketing Manager: Deborah Hudson
Production Editor: Elaine McGarraugh
Cover Designer: Chloe Batch

Credits and acknowledgments of sources for material or information used with permission appear on the appropriate page within the text or in the credit section on page XXX.

Published by Rowman & Littlefield
A wholly owned subsidiary of The Rowman & Littlefield Publishing Group, Inc.
4501 Forbes Boulevard, Suite 200, Lanham, Maryland 20706
www.rowman.com

Unit A, Whitacre Mews, 26-34 Stannary Street, London SE11 4AB

Copyright © 2017 by Rowman & Littlefield

British Library Cataloguing in Publication Information Available

Library of Congress Cataloging-in-Publication Data

Terrorism and the Politics of Fear
Library of Congress Cataloging-in-Publication Data

Names: Altheide, David L.
Title: Terrorism and the politics of fear, 2nd ed. / David L. Altheide.
Description: Lanham : Rowman & Littlefield, 2017. | Revised edition of the author's Terrorism and the politics of fear, c2006. | Includes bibliographical references and index.
Identifiers: LCCN 2017008445 (print) | LCCN 2017012113 (ebook) | ISBN 9781442274525 (ebook) | ISBN 9781442274501 (cloth) | ISBN 9781442274518 (pbk.)
Subjects: LCSH: Mass media--Social aspects--United States. | Mass media and public opinion--United States. | Terrorism in mass media. | Fear--United States. | Propaganda--United States. | Social control--United States.
Classification: LCC HN90.M3 (ebook) | LCC HN90.M3 A47 2017 (print) | DDC 302.230973--dc23.
LC record available at https://lccn.loc.gov/2017008445

♾ ™ The paper used in this publication meets the minimum requirements of American National Standard for Information Sciences Permanence of Paper for Printed Library Materials, ANSI/NISO Z39.48-1992.

Printed in the United States of America

For our Grandchildren

—Karl, Aksel, Kyla, and Davin—

may they live without fear.

Contents

Preface

This book is about social power and the role that the mass media play in constructing social life. Fear is a scary topic. Most people have experienced fear, but few really understand it, especially how it supports anxiety and anger. After some twenty-five years of research on the topic, I understand how others use and exploit fear for their own agendas. That is my topic: the origin, use, and consequences of fear and propaganda for social life. This is very important for me because I have grandchildren, who deserve a future that is free from the politics of fear. By the politics of fear, I mean decision makers' promotion and use of audience beliefs and assumptions about danger, risk, and fear in order to achieve certain goals.

Much has happened since the first edition in 2006. My basic thesis is that the politics of fear that were promoted by mass media communication and entertainment formats after the 9/11 attacks paved the way for Donald Trump's presidential victory in 2016. This victory was a kind of natural experiment on the blending of social media with the politics of fear. Trump's election is a testimonial to the significance of the ecology of communication, or the impact of news information technologies and communication formats on social action, routines, and social institutions. His actions to "keep America safe" within the first weeks of office included a failed attempt—blocked by federal judges—to close U.S. borders to immigrants and refugees, including green card holders, who have already been cleared to live and work in the United States. Continued support from his minions shows that fear fueled by social media has no limits.

I have written several books about fear and the media. The first one, *Creating Fear: News and the Construction of Crisis* (2002), was in the final stages of production when hijacked aircraft carried death and destruction to New York, Pennsylvania, and Washington, D.C. That work demonstrated that use of the word *fear* is widespread in American life, and increasingly, throughout much of Europe as well. This pervasive use of *fear* is part of the social construction of reality in the modern age. By this I mean that the meanings and frameworks that are used to make sense out of events are created. I was able to add the following to the preface of that book as it went to press: "The entertainment format, use of visuals, emerging icons of fear, slogans, and especially the emphasis on the fear frame and 'evil' provide many examples of how these attacks contributed to the expansion of the discourse of fear into more attempts at social control."

That sentence set my research agenda for the next fifteen years; this edition of *Terrorism and the Politics of Fear* reports what I discovered across three presidents' terms of office, and how the social construction of terrorism as a condition helped produce our surveillance society. The following pages give an account of how fear is socially constructed, packaged, and presented through the mass media by politicians and decision makers to protect us by offering more control over our lives and culture. Fear entertains us and helps others control us. But the politics of fear continue even when the specific fears subside; programs that are enacted to protect us at one point in time endure to influence other social action. This process has expanded and accelerated with our entertainment-oriented popular culture as we are constantly given more things to fear, which tend to accumulate, socially hibernate for a time, but then are reawakened by the next crisis. They then provide audiences with a context and interpretative frameworks for believing that "here we go again," and that the latest crisis is merely an extension of the fear stuff that gave us the others. And so on.

My approach to this work is informed by previous conceptual developments in symbolic interaction and the social construction of reality as well as media logic and the ecology of communication. Regarding the former, power can be defined as the ability to apprise a situation for self and others. As for media logic, the mass media are a major source of audience's definitions of fear and issues. Extensive work over forty years shows how information technology and communication formats shape information, on the one hand, while also guiding audience members to use and interpret social meanings on the other hand (see *The Media Syndrome*, 2016). The rise of social media, dealt with in my book *Media Edge* (2014), enables users to become their own sources and objects of fear.

This edition of *Terrorism and the Politics of Fear* illustrates how symbolic meanings about safety, danger, and fear can lead to major institutional changes and even war. The following chapters illustrate how media representations inform audience's and decision makers' perspectives and understandings. The politics of fear is built on audience perceptions and beliefs about the nature and source of fear. Fears associated with beliefs and statements by powerful claims makers can be tracked over time using qualitative document analysis (Altheide & Schneider, 2013).

Acknowledgments

Understanding the politics of fear has been a long-term project. In pursuing this project I have conducted original research; examined thousands of documents, including TV news reports, documentaries, movies, novels, Internet URLs, and numerous scholarly books and articles; as well as many conversations and correspondence with scholars throughout the world working on similar issues. Graduate seminars, assistance from graduate assistants, and helpful suggestions from colleagues inform the materials in this book. In particular, students in the seminar Justice and the Mass Media (JUS 588) collaborated on course projects that provided insights and information that were particularly relevant for the material in chapter 4.

Several of the projects reported in this book benefited from graduate student contributions, including Chris Schneider, Michael Coyle, Kimber Williams, Ray Maratea, and Jennifer Grimes. Simon Gottschalk, Norman Denzin, and Enric Castello were helpful and encouraging editors, who inspire and promote new ideas. Many colleagues contributed valuable ideas, critiques, and suggestions: the late Arthur Vidich, Gray Cavender, Pat Lauderdale, Annamarie Oliverio, John Johnson, the late Richard Ericson, Aaron Doyle, Frank Furedi, Gary Marx, Jeff Ferrell, Erich Goode, Maximiliano Korstanje, Klaus Schoenbach, Ray Surette, Lance Bennett, John Hall, and John Hofer.

I am also indebted to several conference organizers, who invited presentations that contributed to this volume.

- University of Missouri faculty members Jay Gubrium, Clarence Lo, Peter Hall, and Charles Davis, for providing an intellectual forum to present some of my ideas, which were subsequently improved with comments from Joel Best, another speaker (2003).
- I must also thank Professor Gabrio Forti (Professore ordinario di Diritto penale e Criminologia nella Facoltà di Giurisprudenza dell'Univeristà Cattolica del S.C. di Milano), who organized an exceptional seminar at the Catholic University in Milan for scholars investigating crime and the mass media (2003). Steve Chermak, Martin Innes, Paul Mason, and Aaron Doyle were among the participants who provided helpful suggestions.

- Jordi Farre Coma, who organized two major presentations on communication and risk at Universitat Rovira i Virgili, Tarragona, Spain, in 2010 and 2011.
- Andrea Salvini's kind invitations to the University of Pisa (2008, 2010, 2016) supported conceptual integration of media studies, document analysis, and symbolic interaction.
- Janet Chan and the law faculty at the University of New South Wales (2012) provided an opportunity to examine cross-cultural currents in criminology, surveillance, and cultural studies.
- Marion Adolf and Nico Stehr are kindly acknowledged for arranging my visit as a Fulbright Specialist (2012) to Zeppelin University in Friedrichshafen, Germany.
- My appreciation for comments by Stig Hjarvard, Andreas Hepp, Friedrich Krotz, and conference organizer, Caja Thimm, for the exceptional international conference on Media Logics in Bonn in 2015.
- I am also grateful to Beth McLin and Vancouver Island University for the invitation to present a keynote address, "The Media Syndrome and Contemporary Crises," at the 2016 Couch Stone Symposium.

My longtime colleague, Robert Snow, who helped develop our original formulations about media logic and the power of communications formats, remains an inspiration even in retirement. My brother, Duane, provides many examples of power and resistance. My wife and love, Carla, still believes in my work, forgives my inattentiveness when I draft papers in my head, and provides more love and understanding than anyone deserves. I am most fortunate.

Portions of several of the chapters appeared elsewhere:

Chapter 3: *Handbook of Symbolic Interactionism.* Rowman & Littlefield (AltaMira Press).
Chapter 4: *La Televisione del Crimine.* 2005.
Chapter 5 and Chapter 7: *Symbolic Interactionism.* 2004.
Chapter 6: *Cultural Studies: Critical Methodologies.* 2005.
Chapter 8: *The Sociological Quarterly.* 2005.

ONE

Introduction

It was the lightest tap on my door that I've ever heard in my life. . . . I opened the door and I seen the man in the dress greens and I knew. I immediately knew. But I thought that if, as long as I didn't let him in, he couldn't tell me. And then it—none of that would've happened. So he kept saying, "Ma'am, I need to come in." And I kept telling him, "I'm sorry, but you can't come in."
—Paula Zasadny when she learned that her nineteen-year-old daughter, Holly McGeogh, had been killed by a bomb in Kirkuk, Iraq. From the HBO documentary *Last Letters Home* and Herbert, 2004.

This is a book about power and how power is communicated: Paula Zasadny felt like the loved ones of more than 1,500 dead American soldiers (2016, 4,400) and an estimated 100,000 dead Iraqi civilians (2016, 500,000), although we never heard any of the Iraqi stories. Paula Zasadny had very little power; neither did the hundreds of thousands of Mexican immigrants who would be deported or imprisoned by the Bush and Obama administrations during the next twelve years. Ms. Zasadny and thousands of other parents who sent their loved ones off to war believed that their government told them the truth and was doing the right thing. While one is tempted to blame zealous politicians for the death and destruction that has occurred in Iraq, it is not that simple. Of course, politicians' decision making played a big part in the Iraq War, but they also depended on propaganda and a willing U.S. Congress and American public. This book is also about the politics of fear and the war-making process that killed Holly McGeogh, launched fifteen years of invasions of Middle Eastern countries, sent hundreds of unmanned drone attacks that killed thousands of civilians, and launched an epoch of governmental surveillance and propaganda that systematically frightened and angered millions of Americans to such an extent that they elected Donald Trump,

1

who vowed to prevent Muslims from entering the United States and ultimately to "Make America Great Again."

The war in Iraq was partly the result of an expanding politics of fear, or decision makers' promotion and use of audience beliefs and assumptions about danger, risk, and fear in order to achieve certain goals. Political leaders rely on fear to promote the social control of citizens. The mass media are the most important source of information and social control because they have helped make fear a part of our life, our language, and our point of view. This messy enterprise was partly constructed with media formats.

The impact of media and social media on the politics of fear in the United States can be illustrated with three major events since the Vietnam War ended: the 9/11 attacks; the election and reelection of President Barack Obama in 2008 and 2012; and the election of Donald Trump as president of the United States in 2016. My argument is that there is a direct line from the aftermath of the falling twin towers in New York to the election of Donald Trump, arguably the least prepared presidential candidate in the history of the United States. Furthermore, this election occurred as a result of intended and unintended consequences of a decade of propaganda and information manipulation about threats, fear, and strategies for political victory. The fundamental change was how these events were defined and given meaning. This was part of a complex process that involved emerging social media that were instantaneous, visual, and personal. Each of these events was based on a series of decisions, but most importantly for our purposes, a communication process that relied on new information technologies, and particularly the emergence of social media that promoted targeted information delivery.

The following pages examine how entertaining news and popular culture meshed well with two decades of fear of crime and eventually terrorism. This new edition, written in 2016—ten years after the first edition, and twelve years after Holly's death—fills in how a decade of Middle Eastern wars and other maladies have fueled fear in the United States and throughout much of the world. A spiral of fear has been unleashed by new media that can easily morph numerous threats into the deadly inevitability of doom, which in turn can only be deterred through massive social control, regulation, and surveillance efforts. During this time refined information technologies and digital media provided social media that are instantaneous, visual, and personal. These developments have expanded the communication sphere and have spawned sophisticated marketing, surveillance, as well as hideous propaganda and recruitment efforts by newfound enemies of the Western world such as the Islamic State in Iraq and Syria (also known as ISIS or ISIL), whose deadly ideological zeal has escalated inhumane wars in Syria and other parts of the Middle East into an epic slaughter of civilians that sparked the most massive refugee movement since World War II. The pressure put on borders throughout the Western world—especially Europe—has shifted political discourse to the right as leaders have emerged to protect the "homeland(s)" from non-Western immigrants, many of whom are Muslims. Thousands of refugees have drowned at sea as a result of unsafe escape routes mainly from Syria and Iraq, and the European Union has partly dissolved as the once-open borders between its members have become hardened with guards, barbed wire, and alarmed citizens. Indeed, Great Britain's departure (also known as Brexit) from the European Union was spearheaded by politicians denouncing the current and anticipated hordes of Muslims.

The United States seemed to easily shift away from cherished values of nondiscrimination and relative openness as many politicians decried the potential terrorist threats from Muslim immigrants. This, of course, redoubled the exclusionary rhetoric for strengthening the southern border of the United States, and building more fences, to keep control of the American way of life while also keeping citizens safe. One of the most noticeable voices of doom and despair was Donald Trump, who emerged from a blustery brief career as a reality TV persona and gained notoriety by challenging President Obama's birth certificate as an American citizen and eligibility to be president of the United States. Trump steamrolled through the 2016 presidential campaign and dominated most primary elections, and he emerged as the Republican nominee for president of the United States. Trump played to fear and insecurity fueled by social media that rebroadcast his numerous tweets insulting political opponents, women, disabled people, and minorities. His promise to build a wall on the U.S. southern border, ban most Muslims from entering the United States—and monitor those who were already in the United States—resonated with millions of citizens. This was directly fueled by the mass media and the politics of fear that were promoted after the 9/11 attacks.

There have been more terrorist attacks at home and abroad, including particularly grotesque attacks in Paris and Amsterdam, as well as numerous frightening videos of ISIS terrorists beheading captives. And there have been serious illness outbreaks identified as Ebola and Zika; the former is nearly deadly upon contact, while the latter is devastating for unborn children's brains and mental development. There have been many consequences of how the mass media hype and social media have constructed a fearscape of daily life (Vasterman, 2005). Authorities promote fear among citizens because they know that concerns for personal safety will tempt even the most cynical observer to hand over their lives for protection. This chapter sets forth a basic argument and an overview of the rest of the book. My basic thesis is that fear as entertainment informs the production of popular culture and news, generates profits, and enables political decision makers to control audiences through propaganda. This process is referred to as the politics of fear.

PLAYING TO FEAR

This is a story about fear, dread, death, terror, and entertainment. One way to illustrate the connection between entertainment and fear is to liken it to a baseball game. There is the history of baseball that fans know and appreciate, the key players, the particular season and rivals, and the consequences of a particular game. As all fans realize, the outcome of a particular game is of interest, but it is always contextualized by the previous considerations. The context is what is important for baseball, fear, and war. All of these are brought to us by the mass media and popular culture.

Let me locate myself in this story. I was at an Arizona Diamondbacks baseball game on May 1, 2003, watching batting practice just prior to the first pitch while mindless advertisements played on the jumbotron to entertain early arrivals, who were not really baseball fans but had become accustomed to visual action and entertainment. As I enjoyed a beer and followed the flight of big-league smashes landing in the outfield seats, a hurried voice interrupted the promo about an upcoming concert and urged the fans to watch live coverage of the president of the United States, who was about to make an important announcement. Field activity stopped. Sluggers took off their batting gloves and directed their eyes to the massive screen in Bank One Ballpark.

Jerry Colangelo, a local politician, who took pride in escaping Hell's Kitchen, parlayed some street smarts and good breaks into landing the Phoenix Suns basketball team—and eventually the Arizona Diamondbacks—into a fortune. He and the owners of other major league baseball teams went along with the political propagandists to have fans sing "God Bless America" during the seventh-inning stretch, prior to "Take Me Out to the Ball Game." He saw nothing at all wrong with interrupting America's pastime with a political stunt; after all, the difference between mass media fantasy and political reality had long since disappeared. So we stared at the jumbotron as President George W. Bush, costumed like a fighter pilot, landed on an aircraft carrier, the *Abraham Lincoln*. He had his picture taken with sailors in front of a banner that read, "Mission Accomplished." He told the sailors and the media representatives, who had been assembled for this ultimate photo opportunity, that "major combat operations in Iraq have ended." The president grinned, the sailors cheered on cue, the fans cheered the jumbotron—but I booed—and soon the game began.

Private Jess Givens did not see the presidential charade before he was killed that day in Iraq. This is how his wife reacted to the news of his death:

> Melissa Givens was told by a chaplain that her husband, Pfc. Jesse Givens, who was 34, had drowned when his tank fell into the Euphra-

tes River. Distraught, she insisted that the chaplain was lying. But she said that was O.K., because she would never tell anyone that he had lied. She said he could walk away and she would just forget about the whole thing. (Herbert, 2004)

The mission was not accomplished; the war had barely begun and would greatly expand for the next fifteen years.

The hijacking of sports for propaganda and to promote various wars gained considerable strength over the next fifteen years. Sports-wars–military connections were tightened through the impetus of the Bush administration, and were strengthened during the newly elected (2008) Obama administration. As will be discussed in more detail in later chapters, professional and college teams not only placed American flags on their uniforms but also adopted "camo" (i.e., camouflage) uniforms, hats, and other sports paraphernalia to support the military — which were also sold to fans, as well as adding commercials and on-the-field banners and displays that in some cases were paid for by the military. Military families were honored in various ways, including "10% off ticket prices," and actual swearing-in inductions of new volunteers were held between innings.

Packaged patriotism is cheap; authentic patriotism is priceless. The Iraq War gave us more of the former. In the seventh inning, some fans sang "God Bless America," but I did not. I never do. I only sing "Take Me Out to the Ball Game." Most major league baseball players follow their instructions and also pause during the seventh inning to participate in what an astute sports columnist referred to as "patriotic packaging." Not all players play the patriotic game. Carlos Delgado, a Toronto Blue Jays slugger from Puerto Rico, preferred to sit in the dugout and tried to avoid standing with hat in hand. He, along with some other Puerto Rican notables, has tried unsuccessfully for several years to stop the U.S. naval testing off the island of Vieques. Of course, Delgado was chastised by some fans for his independence.

Delgado's protest was political rather than musical. The Puerto Rican slugger objected to America's Iraq policy — "the stupidest war ever," he calls it — and he has chosen "God Bless America" to register his dissent. Though he continued to stand for both the American and the Canadian national anthems, Delgado declined to participate this season in the seventh-inning solemnity that baseball introduced after the terrorist attacks of September 11, 2001:

"I'm not trying to get anyone mad," Delgado told *The New York Times* this week. "This is my personal feeling. I don't want to draw attention to myself or go out of my way to protest. If I make the last out of the seventh inning, I'll stand there. But I'd rather be in the dugout." (T. Sullivan, 2004)

The war in Iraq raged for several more baseball seasons even though some Bush supporters and generals acknowledged that most goals of the war had not been met. Indeed, it continues unabated in 2017, even though the American force has been considerably reduced and twenty-three thousand Special Operations "advisors" and "contract" soldiers (aka mercenaries) operate in the Middle East (http://time.com/4075458/afghanistan-drawdown-obama-troops/). Since President Bush played aviator, nearly seven thousand Americans have died and more than nine hundred thousand were injured (http://www.huffingtonpost.com/h-a-goodman/6845-americans-died-and-9_b_6667830.html), along with an estimated 250,000 civilian and military Iraqis; (https://www.iraqbodycount.org/).

> The United States has likely reached a grim but historic milestone in the war on terror: 1 million veterans injured from the fighting in Iraq and Afghanistan . . .
> All that can be said with any certainty is that as of last December more than 900,000 service men and women had been treated at Department of Veterans Affairs hospitals and clinics since returning from war zones in Iraq and Afghanistan, and that the monthly rate of new patients to these facilities as of the end of 2012 was around 10,000. Beyond that, the picture gets murky. In March, VA abruptly stopped releasing statistics on non-fatal war casualties to the public. (http://time.com/4075458/afghanistan-drawdown-obama-troops/)

The Middle East is more fragmented and alien from the Western world than at any other time in the past fifty years, and the United States is hated throughout the First, Second, and Third worlds. Yet politicians would continue to play to fear as other crises would be contextualized and informed by the Iraqi experience.

Toughness plays well in a climate of fear. President Bush started the war with ample assistance from Congress, a compliant news media, and an embarrassingly uninformed American electorate. Chapter 8 explains how this war was actually planned in 1992 by a group called the Project for a New American Century (PNAC), which included future Bush cabinet members (e.g., Dick Cheney, Colin Powell, and Paul Wolfowitz) and influential publishers such as William Kristol, who had been former vice president Dan Quayle's chief of staff. Most Americans never heard of this group because the compliant news media did not want to be critical of the Bush agenda after the infamous 9/11 attacks, and with a few exceptions they refrained from even mentioning it until after Bush played fighter pilot. Indeed, Bush was reelected despite incontrovertible evidence that he and his administration misled the American people about the reasons and necessity to go to war.

His competition, Senator John Kerry, tried to sound tougher and more bellicose than the incumbent. Kerry argued that Bush was wrong in the rationale for going to war, had done a miserable job of guiding the war effort, and had enacted draconian domestic surveillance programs (e.g., the USA Patriot Act) that threatened the civil liberties of all citizens. (In later chapters, it will be noted that journalists referred to people concerned about civil liberties, especially government surveillance, as "privacy advocates.") Kerry proclaimed that he would be tougher on terrorists, would "track down and kill Osama bin Laden," and would make America stronger—brutal words for a presidential candidate. He did not say that we would bring bin Laden to "justice" or that he would have bin Laden judged by the world; he simply said that he would kill him. Kerry also vowed to protect us more by patrolling our borders. Kerry knew that the mood of the country was following the tone of countless newspaper and television news reports about the horrendous bin Laden and his loose-knit organization, al Qaeda. Popular culture and network television news, particularly Fox News, presented U.S. audiences with ample propaganda about the horrors of Afghanistan and Iraq. Until he was forced to resign in a sexual harassment scandal in 2016, Roger Ailes, former media consultant for Richard Nixon, Ronald Reagan, George Bush, and corporate giant Philip Morris, headed Fox News.

Congress was aware of the media and political mood about "taking it to the enemy," so at the start of the war it did not pay much attention to how the nearly $4 billion a month being spent on these military ventures was distributed to a handful of contractors (e.g., Halliburton, whose previous chief executive officer [CEO] was Dick Cheney) without any bidding, even though a whistleblower, Bunnatine Greenhouse, had complained a month before the start of the war that Halliburton inappropriately received a five-year contract instead of a one-year deal (Zagorin & Burger, 2004). The corruption eventually became so blatant that the FBI, Congress, and the Pentagon opened investigations. Vice President Cheney objected to being asked about some blatant improprieties and argued that these investigations into contractual improprieties were "political." Indeed, on June 22, 2004, he told Senator Patrick Leahy, who was involved in hearings about Halliburton's improprieties, "to fuck yourself." More tough talk.

Street-level discourse is permissible in a world of fear. It sounds tough, and within the discourse of fear toughness trumps intelligence and sophistication. Recall that former president Reagan drew on his acting background, and when faced with possible plans for tax increases that he would oppose he quoted the gun-toting character in the movie *Dirty Harry*, to "make my day." Part of the propaganda hype for the first Gulf War in 1991 starred the elder President Bush proclaiming to members of Congress that "Saddam Hussein was going to get his ass kicked" (*Los Angeles Times*, March 6, 1991, E1). Numerous T-shirts, bumper stickers, and street signs added to the lingo of fighter pilots about "kicking ass." One notable T-shirt read, "Hussein—I'll Kick Your Ass and Take

Your Gas" (*Washington Post*, October 21, 1990, F2). The younger George Bush also knew a good street slogan and used it after sixty-five soldiers had died following his jet ride to the aircraft carrier. When told that Iraqi fighters would be attacking American troops, Bush replied, "Bring it on" (*USA Today*, July 2, 2003). This phrase became very popular throughout the campaign and was used by several Democratic challengers as well. The tough talk became more common some twelve years later, so commonplace that Republican presidential nominee Donald Trump told Fox News's Greta Van Susteren in 2016:

> I do know what to do and I would know how to bring ISIS to the table or, beyond that, defeat ISIS very quickly. And I'm not gonna tell you what it is tonight. . . . If I win, I don't want the enemy to know what I'm doing. Unfortunately, I'll probably have to tell at some point, but there is a method of defeating them quickly and effectively and having total victory. . . . All I can tell you is that it is a foolproof way of winning the war with ISIS and it will 100%—at a minimum they'll come to the table and actually they'll be defeated very quickly. (https://www.aei.org/publication/trump-finally-reveals-his-top-secret-foolproof-plan-to-defeat-isis/)

Numerous Trump messages resonated with fear and uncertainty not only about terrorists but also about political intrigue at home. He echoed the false claim made by numerous conservative politicians over the last two decades that voter fraud was rampant and voter ID (identification) laws should be passed. In August 2016, prior to a primary election in Pennsylvania, Mr. Trump stated:

> "The only way we can lose, in my opinion—I really mean this, Pennsylvania—is if cheating goes on," Mr. Trump said at a rally on Aug. 12 in Altoona. A local Republican official introducing Mr. Trump was more specific, pointing to Philadelphia, a city with a large African-American population. That came days after Mr. Trump told a rally in Wilmington, N.C., that without strict voter identification laws, people would be "voting 15 times for Hillary." (http://www.nytimes.com/2016/08/22/us/politics/donald-trump-a-rigged-election-and-the-politics-of-race.html?_r=0)

Numerous studies show that voter fraud is virtually nonexistent in the United States, especially "voter impersonation"—the only kind of fraud that could be captured with voter ID checks. Yet nearly half of American voters think that it is quite common. This is due to constant repetition by mainly Republican politicians who are trying to suppress minority-group voting.

> As study after study has shown, there is virtually no voter fraud anywhere in the country. The most comprehensive investigation to date found that out of one billion votes cast in all American elections between 2000 and 2014, there were 31 possible cases of impersonation

fraud. Other violations—like absentee ballot fraud, multiple voting and registration fraud—are alsoexceedingly rare. (http://www.nytimes. com/2016/09/20/opinion/the-success-of-the-voter-fraud-myth.html? emc=edit_th_20160920&nl=todaysheadlines&nlid=27364645)

Unfortunately, voter ID laws, now operating in thirty-four states, discourage minority group members, young people, and newly registered voters from voting and suppress a large number of U.S. citizens from voting (http://www.ncsl.org/research/elections-and-campaigns/voter-id. aspx). And there is evidence that these efforts are intentional.

> In 2012, a former Florida Republican Party chairman, Jim Greer, told *The Palm Beach Post* that voter ID laws and cutbacks in early voting are "done for one reason and one reason only"—to suppress Democratic turnout. Consultants, Mr. Greer said, "never came in to see me and tell me we had a fraud issue. It's all a marketing ploy." (http://www.ncsl. org/research/elections-and-campaigns/voter-id.aspx)

Fearful messages have strong effects on the political process partly because leaders can tap the emotional churning from audiences' basic concerns about safety for themselves and their families. Indeed, fear is such a basic emotion that humans probably could not survive without it. There is clearly a biological and psychological component of fear; there are physical responses to fear, including adrenaline charges that provide the bursts of energy and strength that become part of personal heroics and historical lore. In addition to fearful messages about "false voters," the psychological dimension of fear may be tapped by propaganda about threat and death. These images and feelings can be generated not only by real, immediate threats, such as one's child being hurt, but also by skillful use of symbols and language, including photos. Psychologists who study this aspect of fear report profound changes in people who are confronted by scenes and images of death, including the following: (1) having more favorable evaluations of people with similar religious and political beliefs and more unfavorable evaluations of those who differ on these dimensions; (2) being more punitive toward moral transgressors and more benevolent to heroic individuals; (3) being more physically aggressive toward others with dissimilar political orientations; and (4) striving more vigorously to meet cultural standards of value (Pyszczynski, Greenberg, & Solomon, 2003; Solomon, Greenberg, & Pyszczynsk, 2004).

Moreover, the researchers examined how people responded to different scenarios and types of leaders (Solomon et al., 2004). They found that when asked to think about the events of 9/11 and their own death, support for President Bush increased noticeably. The researchers argued that part of this can be explained by the associated images of the destruction of 9/11 plus the often-repeated slogans about combating an evil enemy. They conclude,

We also do not mean to imply that all support for President Bush is necessarily a defensive reaction to concerns about death. And although it is a matter of public record that President Bush's re-election campaign has been carefully crafted to emphasize the war on terrorism and domestic security, the strategic use of fear to advance political agendas has a long history in American politics (all politics for that matter) and is by no means confined to the Republican Party.

However, the fact that a subtle, brief manipulation of psychological conditions (asking people to think about their own death or the events of 9/11) produced such striking differences in political preferences (for charismatic leaders in general and President Bush in particular) suggests that close elections could be decided as a result of non-rational terror management concerns. We'd like to think that Americans across the political spectrum would agree that this is antithetical to the democratic ideal that voting behavior should be the result of rational choice based on an informed understanding of the relevant issues. National elections are no guarantee against totalitarian outcomes. (Solomon et al., 2004, 15)

The politics of fear, then, is central to the psychology of fear. Leaders learn to promote fear in their media messages. For example, the artful use of terrorist attacks was an explicit strategy during the presidential campaign of 2004:

Republican leaders said yesterday that they would repeatedly remind the nation of the September 11 attacks as their convention opens in New York City today. (*New York Times*, August 30, 2004)

The Bush campaign followed the guidelines, especially in three ads that ran in sixteen critical states:

All three ads are designed to highlight President Bush's leadership amid economic uncertainty and national security challenges. Two of the new spots show fleeting images of the World Trade twin towers' collapse, with an American flag flying over the debris and firemen working in the smoldering wreckage. Closing the images is the tagline: "President Bush: Steady Leadership in Times of Change." (*On Line News Hour*, March 5, 2004;http://www.pbs.org/newshour/updates/white_house-jan-june04-bush-ads_03-05/)

So offensive were the ads to the families of those killed in the 9/11 attacks that one organization, Sept. 11 Families for Peaceful Tomorrows, asked candidates and political parties not to use the images. A few comments illustrate the depth of feeling:

But to show the horror of 9/11 in the background, that's just some advertising agency's attempt to grab people by the throat.

One of the ads, titled "Safer, Stronger," which also includes a Spanish version, features a one-second shot of firefighters removing the flag-draped remains of a victim from the twisted debris. Both ads showcase ground-zero imagery with shots of two firefighters.

> "It's as sick as people who stole things out of the place," said firefighter Tommy Fee of Queens Rescue Squad 270. "The image of firefighters at Ground Zero should not be used for this stuff, for politics."
>
> "It's a slap in the face of the murders of 3,000 people," Monica Gabrielle, whose husband died in the twin tower attacks, told the *New York Daily News*. "This is a president who has resisted the creation of the 9/11 Commission. . . . For anyone to use 9/11 for political gain is despicable." (*On Line News Hour*, March 5, 2004;http://www.pbs.org/newshour/updates/white_house-jan-june04-bush-ads_03-05/)

Later, Vice President Cheney urged voters to support President Bush and be safe: "If we make the wrong choice, the danger is that we will get hit again, that we'll be hit in a way that is devastating." As one undecided voter said of Bush, "He has conviction. . . . He's taking the fight to the terrorists. . . . I love my kids. I want my kids to be safe" (ABC affiliate, Phoenix, Arizona, October 13, 2004). The message about fear carried the day for many Americans. A CNN analysis of why people voted for Bush found that Bush supporters were more likely to be worried about terrorism and also believed that the Iraq War made them more secure. Bush won the election of 2004, the war raged, more people died, parents wept, and fear reigned. Bush's ill-planned invasions of Afghanistan and Iraq would later be blamed by many observers for helping to unsettle the fragile Middle Eastern region, including laying the groundwork for the demise of strong—but hardly benevolent—leaders in Libya, Egypt, and adding to the imploding chaos in Syria, where the rise of the brutal ISIS (aka ISIL) would usurp al Qaeda's viciousness.

Barack Obama won the presidency in 2008 by defeating Republican senator John McCain, and was reelected in 2012 (over former Massachusetts governor Mitt Romney), buoyed by the slogan of "Hope and Change" as an alternative to the politics of fear. He withdrew most of the U.S. troops from Iraq, but the timetable was stalled as failures by the Iraqi military permitted opposition forces to rally. A contributing negative force for the future of President Bush's predecessor, Barack Obama, was that the Iraqi leadership that was propped up by the United States was a strongly Shiite version of Islam, against their long-time—but very powerful—nemesis Sunnis, which were systematically prevented from participating in the new government. This proved to be an unwise political move since a large number of these people were experienced military leaders, many of whom would join a growing religious-based resistance to the new Iraqi leadership, as well as the United States. Thus was born in 2014 the Islamic State in Syria (ISIS, aka ISIL) and the resurgence of what amounted to a religious-based war that would ravage the region for many years.

ISIS is mysterious in part because it is so many things at once. It combines Islamic piety and reverence for the prophet and his companions with the most modern social-media platforms and encryption schemes; its videos blend the raw pornographic violence of a snuff film with the pious chanting of religious warriors; the group has the discipline of a prison gang (many of its recruits were indeed drawn from U.S.-organized prisons in Iraq), but also the tactical subtlety and capacity for deception of the most skilled members of Saddam Hussein's intelligence services, who were also pulled into the ISIS net. (Ignatius, 2015)

As we shall see in later chapters, President Obama also promoted strong security measures, including the deportation of several million undocumented people, while authorizing the corralling of more than thirty thousand undocumented people in for-profit immigration detention prisons while they awaited immigration hearings (http://www.latimes.com/nation/la-na-immigration-detention-20160906-snap-story.html). His legacy also includes calling for ten times the number of drone strikes by his predecessor, George W. Bush (five hundred versus fifty; http://www.globalresearch.ca/obama-ordered-ten-times-more-drone-strikes-than-bush/5475415). The terrorism-inspired bombings at home during the Boston Marathon on April 13, 2013, raised the fear specter and intensified nationalism and support to battle terrorists at home and abroad with all available weapons, including drones. The majority (58 percent) of Americans approved of this remote-controlled warfare even though it was condemned by the United Nations as unlawful assassinations, which often killed innocent civilians (http://www.people-press.org/2015/05/28/public-continues-to-back-u-s-drone-attacks/). At least two movies—*Good Kill* and *Eye in the Sky*—were made of the drone warfare decision making. Thus, the dramatization of fear about terrorism increased in news reports and popular culture, and it intensified through political discourse against Middle Eastern immigrants fleeing the hellfire of Syria. Republican presidential candidate Donald Trump would gain popularity, along with several aspiring leaders in Europe, for calling for tighter border controls and profiling and restricting Muslim immigrants, especially those from Syria. This rhetoric, along with several "homegrown" terrorist bombings by ISIS recruits, cultivated more fear and mistrust among his supporters, particularly when he stated in the third and final debate with Hillary Clinton that he might not accept the election results because the entire process, including the media coverage as well as illegal registered voters, was all corrupt and ultimately rigged against him. Opinion polls subsequently reported that as many as one-third of likely voters are either "not confident" or "not at all confident" that the election would be fair (http://www.politico.com/story/2016/10/poll-will-trump-accept-election-results-230291).

The argument in this book is not that fear is bad but that it is promoted and exploited by leaders for their own survival and policies rather than that of their audiences. The challenge is to recognize how fear is being used politically. The 2016 presidential campaign was a very good example of excessive fear being mobilized for political ends. I take note of a recommendation by psychologists who show how focusing on one's own mortality and death can influence political decision making:

> As a culture, we should also work to teach our children and encourage our citizens to vote with their "heads" rather than their "hearts." And it may also be helpful to raise awareness of how concerns about mortality affect human behavior. Hopefully, such measures will encourage people to make choices based on the political qualifications and positions of the candidates rather than on defensive needs to preserve psychological equanimity in response to reminders of death. (Solomon et al., 2004, 15)

AN APPROACH TO THE POLITICS OF FEAR

My approach to the study of the politics of fear is well grounded in sociological theory, mass communications research, and qualitative research methods. First, I start with a basic assumption that the most important thing that one can know about another person is what he or she takes for granted. What do people assume to be the order of things, the rock-bottom reality of how the world operates, the source of problems, and likely threats? Fundamental changes in the mass-mediated world cannot be understood without careful consideration of culture and symbolic construction of meanings that are produced by a few and shared by many. Second, I assume that it is the meaning of things that drives people to action or nonaction, and these meanings are derived through a communication process that involves symbols (e.g., language) and images. Third, the mass media and popular culture are the major sources of information for most people about events with which they do not have direct experience. These media involve television, radio, newspaper, magazines, movies, videos, video games, social media networks, and conversations with peers that are informed largely by these sources. Fourth, many of the experiences that we have with the mass media provide a language and perspective for viewing events in our daily lives. Fifth, many of the experiences that we have in everyday life tend to be consistent with our media messages.

These theoretical assumptions inform a basic methodological point: important symbolic messages can be studied by comparative systematic investigation of mass media publications over a period of time. This qualitative media approach has been well documented and used rather extensively by scholars in several disciplines (Altheide, 1996). Its specific application to the politics of fear involves "tracking discourse," or following certain issues, words, themes, and frames over a period of time, across different issues, and across different news media. Tracking discourse is a qualitative document analysis technique that applies an ethnographic approach to content analysis to new information bases, such as NEXIS, Vanderbilt Television News Index and Archive, Foreign Broadcast Information Service, and others, that are accessible through computer technology (Altheide, 1996; Altheide & Schneider, 2013; van Dijk, 1988; Grimshaw and Burke, 1994; Weiler and Pearce, 1992; Wuthnow, 1992). While there are many differences in some of the approaches, all share an assumption that symbolic representations are enmeshed in a context of other assumptions that are not stated as such. Our approach blends interpretive, ethnographic, and ethnomethodological approaches with media logic, particularly studies of news organizational culture, information technology, and communication formats. The capacity to examine numerous documents with specific conceptually informed search terms and logic provides a new way of "exploring" documents, applying "natural experimental" research designs to the materials, and retrieving and analyzing individual documents qualitatively. Moreover, because the technology permits immediate access to an enormous amount of material, comparative exploration, conceptual refinement, and data collection and analysis can cover a longer time period than other technologies can.

My basic argument is that the politics of fear trades on audience beliefs, expectations, and taken-for-granted meanings about social reality, threats, and the nature of those who pose the threats—namely, "outsiders" or "the other." We know from previous research that the entertainment media promote fear as a feature of entertainment, most commonly crime in the past thirty years. But there is more to it than merely repeating news reports night after night that crime is rampant, dangerous, and threatening to us all. The numerous crime shows, movies, and video games are also not enough to explain the rise of the politics of fear, but they do add a lot to the entertainment mix of experience that Americans have about the nature, appearance, and threat of the "other."

PLAN OF THE BOOK

After the publication of the first edition in 2006, I have provided more recent examples through 2016 of the way that media depictions of fear have contributed to an expansive foundation about risks and the necessity for urgent action to "save us." Much of this book's focus is on the war on terrorism that followed the death, destruction, and official government reactions to the September 11, 2001, crashing of hijacked airliners into the World Trade Center and the Pentagon and the downing of an aircraft that was reportedly destined for another target in Washington, D.C. The catastrophic attacks led to a massive propaganda campaign that would substantially defuse the presidential goals of Barack Obama, on the one hand, and propel the politics of fear that carried Donald Trump into the White House in 2016. Unlike some other books on the 9/11 attacks and subsequent reactions, such as expansive surveillance programs (Mueller & Steward, 2016), I try to place the position of the United States in a context of social control and change by focusing on how fear has become incorporated into political decisions, language, and much of everyday life. I wish to understand the reactions and definitions associated with these acts that gave special meaning to the deadly deeds by an outlaw organization and quickly came to mean an all-out war against "evil" that pitted the United States against most of the world, including numerous Middle Eastern countries, but also the United Nations and allies in Europe and beyond.

Much of the book examines how the mass media and popular culture contributed to the political use of fear. Chapter 2, "The Social Reality of Fear," provides some context, including an overview of the rise of the politics of fear, especially in the United States, and how this is experienced in everyday life. In addition to setting forth the context for the rise of Donald Trump in 2016, this chapter examines how fear relates to force and social control, and brief analyses are given of the significance and consequences of the politics of fear in recent wars; crime legislation; the drug war; the complicity of business, universities, and religion in playing to fear; and the growing acceptance of uniforms and the look of control.

Chapter 3, "The Mass Media as a Social Institution," offers an analysis of social institutions transformed through media in order to illustrate how the logic and forms of media perspectives have transformed much of the social stock of knowledge we share. Social media have become far more important during the last decade since the publication of the first edition. This includes the manner in which conventional mass media have incorporated elements of social media into their formats, as well as altered journalism work by stressing entertainment, visuals, and above all, speed and being first, often at the expense of accuracy as well as incomplete contextual understanding. A major thesis in this book is that terrorism and the politics of fear are constructed by media logic and the growing impact of mass media formats on our everyday lives and social institutions. The mass media are significant for our lives because they are both form and content of cultural categories and experience. As form, the mass media provide the criteria, shape, rhythm, and style of an expanding array of activities, many of which are outside the "communication" process. As content, the new ideas, fashions, vocabularies, and a myriad of types of information (e.g., politics) are acquired through the mass media, often accompanied by social media. For example, during the 2016 presidential campaign, it was common for Donald Trump, the Republican nominee, to send numerous tweets to his millions of followers that were inflammatory and often simply incorrect. Amplified by Internet commentary, these messages would be picked up and often rebroadcast by conventional media, to which Trump would respond through interviews and additional tweets. The cascading exchanges around questionable facts would amplify the original claims. This mediated political messaging transformed much of the public discussion during this campaign.

A discussion of media logic illustrates how news coverage from wars and political campaigns is ideological and reflects entertainment formats that promote fear. Media logic is defined as a form of communication and the process through which media transmit and communicate information. Elements of this form include the distinctive features of each medium and the formats used by these media for the organization, the style in which the information is presented, the focus or emphasis on particular characteristics of behavior, and the grammar of media communication. This logic, or the rationale, emphasis, and orientation promoted by media production, processes, and messages tends to be evocative, encapsulated, highly thematic, familiar to audiences, and easy to use. In a broad sense, media culture refers to the character of such institutions as religion, politics, or sports that develops through the use of media. Specifically, when media logic is employed to present and interpret institutional phenomena, the form and content of those institutions are altered.

Chapter 4, "Crime and Terrorism," discusses how news coverage of war reflects fear and closely resembles three decades of crime news. Crime in particular and fear in general have become a major part of the message as news media throughout the world have adapted "entertainment formats" to attract audiences. One consequence of this emphasis is to promote a discourse of fear, or the pervasive communication, symbolic awareness, and expectation that danger and risk are a central feature of everyday life. As this discourse becomes more common and taken for granted, it influences many aspects of everyday life, including the rapidly expanding popular culture. National and international priorities are influenced by this discourse, as in the United States, where "terrorism" reports are strongly influenced by a long history of crime reports.

Chapter 5, "Consuming Terrorism," describes the mass communications process that linked giving and spending to patriotism, domestic control, and a major foreign policy shift following the terrorist attacks on September 11, 2001. Analysis of news reports and advertisements suggests that popular culture and mass media depictions of fear, patriotism, consumption, and victimization contributed to the emergence of a "national identity" and collective action that was fostered by elite decision makers' propaganda and the military-media complex that was sustained for a decade as more surveillance programs were expanded to monitor the growth in social media. Initial declarations about recovery and retaliation to promote patriotism became a "war on terrorism" with no end in sight. Global policing that would justify a "first strike" against sovereign governments was socially constructed as commensurate with personal caring and a national identity. These findings are organized around three points: (1) fear supported consumption as a meaningful way for audiences to sustain an identity of substance and character; (2) consumption and giving were joined symbolically as government and business propaganda emphasized common themes of spending/buying to "help the country get back on track"; and (3) the absence of a clear target for reprisals contributed to the construction of broad symbolic enemies and goals.

Chapter 6, "Terrorism and the Politics of Fear," develops the argument that the terrorist attacks of 9/11 were socially constructed to have both a specific and a broad meaning. These attacks became the basic reference point to justify numerous national and international events involving the expansion of military action—the use of Special Ops and unmanned drones into other countries. The analysis examines how news reports about terrorism in five nationally prominent U.S. newspapers reflect the terms and discourse associated with the politics of fear. Data were analyzed with a qualitative content analysis method—"tracking discourse," which tracks words, themes, and frames over a period of time, across different issues, and across different news media. While some qualitative materials are presented, the emphasis in this chapter is on the changes in the extent of coverage in news reports linking fear with terrorism and victimization that occurred after 9/11. Examining the prevalence and meaning of the words *fear, victim, terrorism,* and *crime* eighteen months before and after the attacks of 9/11 shows that there was a dramatic increase in linking terrorism to fear, and that coverage of crime and fear persisted (but at a very low rate, and there was a large increase in news reports linking terrorism to victim). Later wars of the United States and other countries during the Bush and Obama administrations would operate with a more expansive terrorism narrative, which basically meant that any tactic could be used in fighting terrorism.

Chapter 7, "Mediated Interaction and the Control Narrative of the Internet," expands on how the politics of fear and the penchant for social control reaches well beyond a specific event to include some of the most basic communication processes in our culture. The control narrative refers to the relevance for the communication process and social action of actors' awareness and expectation that symbolic meanings may be monitored and used by diverse audiences for various purposes. Fear is used as a form of social control; fear of terrorism reflects a politics of fear that cuts through basic communication practices and information technologies as part of everyday life. Internet use promotes social control. This chapter addresses how a control narrative is becoming the story of the Internet, not only through expansive governmental and commercial surveillance to manipulate consumers but also for computer hackers, who seek to disrupt commerce, on the one hand, as well as steal identities for fun and profit. It is estimated that some fifteen million U.S. residents are victims of identity theft each year (http://www.identitytheft.info/victims.aspx).

The expansion of surveillance, monitoring, and control informs how people use the Internet and suggests changes in private and public communication. Organizational contexts and structures inform individual use as part of a "technological seam," the uneasy fit between everyday life routines and technological formats. Electronic formats and the visual nature of the Internet exemplify a surveillance culture that is fueled by a discourse of fear. Efforts to police the Internet are confounded by the paradox of Internet security that it requires violation and surveillance. Discussion of the implications of this expanding surveillance is informed by an analysis of "Internet filters," surveillance by business and police agents, and "Internet stings."

Chapter 8, "Propaganda of Fear, the Iraq War, and the Islamic State," addresses how the invasion of Iraq was justified to the American people by the most massive propaganda campaign since World War II. One objective of this chapter is to show how the members of the Project for a New American Century (PNAC) had been developing the rationale for the invasion as a "public conspiracy" for more than a decade. The second objective is to describe and clarify why the PNAC's plans for Iraq and for an imperialist foreign policy received very little news media coverage. The third aim of this chapter is to set forth a theoretical argument for analyzing modern propaganda campaigns as a feature of mass-mediated discourse crafted by media logic. Qualitative content analysis of news materials suggests that the news sources and news media shared a logic and perspective about "timely and entertaining news." The PNAC plan was not publicized by the major news media because it fell outside the focus of the Bush administration's propaganda campaign to demonize Iraq and its leader, Saddam Hussein, who was held to be responsible for attacks on the United States. One result of the current structure of policy and critique is now institutionalized and formatted as "war programming," which connects criticism within a narrative sequence, including critiques and reflections about journalistic failings. The scope of the action is so immense that it precludes and preempts its critique. Indeed, the military operations, and particularly the gruesome killings of Iraqi and Afghani civilians, is hardly tolerated, although political second-guessing of the initial decisions to invade foreign countries is more common. A new approach is needed to offer critique before the event. The implications of such a well-organized propaganda campaign for future news coverage of war are discussed, and material from other wars illustrates how a terrorism narrative justified additional military and political actions.

Chapter 9, "Constructing Heroes: Pat Tillman and Chris Kyle," focuses on how popular culture and propaganda socially construct two heroes fighting terrorism: Pat Tillman and Chris Kyle. Pat Tillman was a twenty-seven-year-old promising professional football player who walked away from a multimillion-dollar contract with the Arizona Cardinals to join the U.S. Army and serve as a Ranger in Afghanistan, where fellow Rangers killed him on April 22, 2004. Sports and nationalism are joined in popular culture through narratives, metaphors, language, and emotions. This is particularly true with wars. Audiences recognize and identify with individual athletes who are associated with familiar sports. Propagandists, such as government officials, seek to link athletes and others who are well known with values, causes, and justifications for a particular war.

Chris Kyle was a well-known sniper credited with several hundred "kills." He wrote a book about guns as well as another best-selling book about his military activities that was the basis for a successful movie, *American Sniper*, directed by Hollywood icon Clint Eastwood. An outspoken critic of President Obama's efforts to have background checks for gun buyers, Kyle was touted as not only a patriot but also as a defender of Middle Eastern wars. He and his wife established a foundation that was funded by movie and book royalties and that would support some military families. He advocated a kind of shooting therapy for soldiers suffering from PTSD, and tragically, he and a fellow instructor/counselor were shot dead at a shooting range on February 2, 2013, by a disturbed former soldier. His funeral, like Pat Tillman's, was attended by thousands and was widely discussed.

The connection is made through "heroism," as the dead individual(s) are deemed "heroes." The construction process provides a sociological glimpse into (1) organizations (e.g., the propaganda of the U.S. Army and the news media); (2) the political process in a mass-mediated age (e.g., how politicians link names and "faces" to international conflict as an emotional identifier for audiences—there is now a "face" to this war); (3) collective identity and symbolic commensuration (e.g., "he's still a hero" even if the enemy did not kill him); (4) value-enriching morality plays ("be worthy of the sacrifice made on our behalf"); and (5) contemporary popular and political usage of "hero."

Chapter 10, "Conclusion: Beyond the Politics of Fear," summarizes the effect of terrorism coverage on the politics of fear and links these media reports with the social construction of the Iraq War, subsequent U.S. invasions, and the origin of massive "blowback" and resistance by Middle Eastern factions throughout the region that destabilized established leaders (e.g., Egypt, Syria, and Lebanon) and helped create and galvanize opposition forces such as the Islamic State in Syria (aka ISIS). ISIS would terrorize toppled governments, on the one hand, while using social media to recruit thousands of fighters from throughout the world, including enticing horrendous terrorist acts in Europe, especially France and Belgium. Their recruiting efforts of American Muslims to commit terrorist acts will also be mentioned. The relevance of war programming (discussed in chapter 8) for future coverage of social issues will be discussed, along with noting key questions and topics that should be investigated in the future. Finally, the theoretical contribution of viewing the politics of fear from a mass communications perspective will be set forth.

TWO

The Social Reality of Fear

See something, say something.

— "The Social Reality of Fear"

A benefactor and key contributor to widespread fear in the United States was Republican presidential candidate Donald Trump, whose nationalistic, racist, and anti-immigrant rants earned him an Electoral College victory as president despite trailing Hillary Clinton by nearly three million votes. Trump's campaign rhetoric celebrated the politics of fear with the slogan "Make America Great Again" by building on fifteen years of propaganda campaigns and the discourse of fear that linked immigrants to terrorism and called for stricter border controls with Mexico to keep out potential threats to American safety. The not-subtle subtext was that immigrants, including Muslim refugees already in the United States as well as those admitted from the failed state of Syria, were degrading the United States, occasionally attacking it and planning extensive covert operations. After all, hadn't there been several domestic terror incidents, including the Boston Marathon bombing attack in 2013, the San Bernardino murders in 2015, and the Orlando nightclub shooting on June 13, 2016? Three days later, on June 16, 2016, presidential candidate Donald Trump began his campaign, stating:

> When Mexico sends its people, they're not sending their best. They're not sending you. They're not sending you. They're sending people that have lots of problems, and they're bringing those problems with us. They're bringing drugs. They're bringing crime. They're rapists. And some, I assume, are good people.

He added many statements about the expanding crime rate of undocumented people, and featured family members of a few people who had been killed by illegal border crossers—all Mexicans. It did not matter to

21

about half the country that supported his candidacy that the immigrant crime rate was lower than other groups in the United States. Facts were virtually unimportant in this election that floated on tweets and other social media–generated clichés, slogans, and vituperative personal attacks on other Republican candidates for the presidency, and particularly on his Democratic opponent Hillary Clinton, whom he pilloried with monikers like "Crooked Hillary"—even in traditional presidential debates—when he threatened to investigate alleged corruption and lock her up. A toxic brew of fear was seasoned with disdain and uncivility unknown in modern U.S. politics. Many supporters who attended his rallies sported highly visible T-shirts and placards with phrases like "Lock Her Up," "Trump the Bitch," and the jab at elected politicians, "Drain the Swamp." And the major media loved it because it fit the emerging entertainment format central to media logic: conflict, drama, emotional appeal, and with social media, instantaneous, personal, and visual. The CEO of CBS said of Trump's candidacy and the wild presidential election: "It may not be good for America, but it's damn good for CBS." In the first several months of his campaign Donald Trump received more than three times the coverage of his political opponents, worth an estimated $2 billion of free publicity. NBC's long-running news show *Meet the Press* would conduct telephone interviews with Trump while requiring all other guests to appear in person. Jeff Zucker, CNN president, admitted, "We put him on because you never knew what he was going to say." The entertainment pitch paid off: CNN beat its revenue estimates by $100 million (O'Neill & Grynbaum, 2016). How did we get to this point in political discourse?

The politics of fear is rampant in the United States. A New York Times/CBS (December 10, 2015) poll showed that Americans are more fearful of a terrorist attack than any other time since the 9/11 attacks. The cartoon character Pogo's statement "We have met the enemy, and he is us" captures popular culture's complicity in Donald Trump's antics, particularly when the Republican front-runner cranked up fear and gave terrorism a symbolic victory on December 7 by calling for a ban on Muslims entering the United States. But the blame goes beyond campaign harangues: the real culprit is our entertaining media culture that thrives on fear, confrontation, and conflict. And social media have extended the opportunity to be profane. Many of Mr. Trump's followers state that he says what they are feeling. And that is the problem: civility and maintaining a public order requires restricting dark, petty, and bigoted feelings to private spaces. This is why regulations about media content and appropriateness are as important as they are contentious. It was no accident that a debate between Democratic presidential hopefuls Hillary Clinton and Bernie Sanders was billed as "fight night." Jabs and knockouts appeal to our lesser selves, but public discourse and civility have taken a hit, a big hit.

The role of the media goes a long way in explaining major divisions in the United States today. Fear is the foundation of anger, and fear prompts people to take action and to speak their mind. My research shows that the politics of fear fits well with communication formats that are personal, instantaneous, and visual. We are barraged with dramatic and evocative messages that danger and threat are imminent even though numerous studies show that Americans face little danger from terrorist attacks. Politicos like Donald Trump have skillfully combined the politics of fear with personal attacks blaming opponents for permitting the danger, such as restricting gun sales and not restricting immigrants. This gets a lot of media attention as shown by a *New York Times* report (March 15, 2016) about the extensive amount of "earned"—or free—coverage Mr. Trump receives. The bombastic reality TV star clearly understands that the reaction and meaning of an event, such as the San Bernardino shootings or of disruptive protesters, is often as significant as the event itself. This presidential wannabe's hysterical bombshell about banning Muslims went global and validated the murderers' claims about the hatred of the United States against all Muslims. Many Americans agreed with Mr. Trump. The governors of some sixteen states said they would refuse to permit Syrian refugees from entering their states. And Americans did what they often do when fear increases: they buy guns, lots of guns. Several national gun retailers tripled their sales within two weeks of the San Bernardino killings. It is the rise and escalation of the politics of fear that draws our attention in this chapter.

Social media and entertaining formats account for much the widespread fear and vitriol. Social media that make communication instantaneous, visual, and personal are being used to promote fear of terrorism and support for war against ISIS. In 2001 it took an attack on the U.S. homeland and the deaths of nearly three thousand people—along with a strong propaganda campaign—for Americans to overwhelmingly support the invasions of Afghanistan and Iraq. In 2014 the global broadcast of the brutal killing of two American journalists apparently was enough to heighten public support for military action against ISIS, which President Obama officially announced within days of the second brutal snuff video viewed by thousands. How we communicate and get information has changed dramatically during this thirteen-year period. According to the Pew Research Internet Project, in 2000 about 46 percent of Americans had access to the Internet, while over 87 percent did so in 2014. Cell phone usage increased from 53 percent to 90 percent during the same period. And smartphone ownership—quite rare in 2000—soared to nearly 60 percent in 2014. These media provide direct access to audiences, who view and experience the material out of context and without reflection on what it all means.

Decades of sensationalized crime reporting set the baseline for the last two decades' emphasis on imminent dangers from immigrants and terrorism. These reports, along with countless popular culture images about dread and suffering, fuel the politics of fear that pervades both mass and social media today. This fear is being promoted by the same media dynamic that nurtures Donald Trump's harsh and derogatory comments about his Republican and Democratic opponents—impugning their integrity, intelligence, gender, and physical appearance—as well as minority groups, women, and even a disabled political reporter. Mr. Trump's diatribes played especially well with audiences that have long avoided conventional news sources such as the major American TV networks and established newspapers in favor of Internet blogs, social media, and alternative news sources with political and ideological agendas. Many of these are rife with reports about fear and impending danger, even governmental threats to personal and family security. Many Americans who rely on such sources believe that the 9/11 attacks were an "inside job," meaning that the U.S. government was actually behind the catastrophe. Other sites make similar allegations about the murder of children at Sandy Hook Elementary School in Newtown, Connecticut. Thus, when mass shootings occur, whether at Sandy Hook or in San Bernardino, a substantial baseline of mistrust, fear, and antigovernment sentiment is activated for many Americans.

Social media formats provoke an increasingly harsh and conflictual media culture. Civility suffers as crude and personal attacks become commonplace. The entertainment format of news, as well as reality TV shows such as Mr. Trump's *The Apprentice*, promotes conflict, shock, and harsh language and treatment to attract audiences. As the *New York Times* (January 9, 2016) columnist Frank Bruni stated, "Obnoxiousness is the new charisma." Nasty discourse was promoted and used for entertainment and effect throughout American history, but it has reached a new low in modern times with the attacks on President Obama. Congressional representatives have routinely attacked President Obama with nasty, personal, and often false (e.g., "birther," not a Christian) statements in order to get elected and to assure these constituents that they are representing their interests and would keep them safe. Republican Joe Wilson called President Obama a liar ("you lie") during an address to Congress on September 9, 2009. Indeed, several of the Republican candidates for president used uncivil rhetoric to their benefit in local and congressional campaigns. Voters were wooed with inflammatory statements and crude language in some state and regional campaigns over the last several years, and they became accustomed to the crude appeals that were made by Donald Trump in his presidential bid. Incivility went viral as the load of Republican presidential candidates repeatedly called opponents liars and even impugned and boasted about sexual prowess and physical characteristics. Ironically, establishment Republican candidates were undone by these polarizing tactics.

Fear, anger, and support for Mr. Trump was intensified with social media, especially brief tweets that affirm emotional positions and relationships. Voters who were angry with politicians were attracted because Mr. Trump's attacks resonated with what many people feel—anger and neglect—and enabled the bulk of his supporters to bask in the outrage against conventional politicians. Bigotry, racism, and economic backsliding fuel the search for blame. Many of Mr. Trump's supporters are on the underdog's side in a moral crusade to affirm their identity and pain. Thus, voting for Mr. Trump enables them to fight back and win the day, regardless of the outcome of the general election. An article in the *Washington Post* (December 10, 2015) pointed out that Republican media consultant Frank Luntz was blown away by the results of a focus group of people who had voted for Mitt Romney in the last election. He found that Trump's exaggerations, insults, and false statements actually made him a more attractive candidate. Luntz told reporters, "Normally, if I did this for a campaign, I'd have destroyed the candidate by this point." That hateful and distorted rhetoric would work on some audiences should not have surprised Luntz, who was the architect behind the evocative language and "talking points" for Republican opposition to many issues over the last several years, including substituting "death tax" for "estate tax." Perhaps even Pogo would be aghast at the benefits of such negative statements, but it all makes sense given our current birther.

The 2016 presidential campaign was the latest example of the impact of the media syndrome, which refers to the prevalence, impact, and significance of media logic, communication formats, and media content in social life. My research over forty years on numerous political and international events—ranging from Watergate to the Iraq War—reveal how misinformation often is shaped by the information technology and news routines employed at the time (Altheide, 2016). The old adage "you are what you eat" has a corollary with information: increasingly, "what we know is affected by how we know." And this has changed remarkably, particularly with digital media.

The real culprit of the uncivil campaigning is our entertaining media culture that thrives on fear, confrontation, and conflict. Entertainment boosted Donald Trump's ratings in the early part of his campaign. This was due to an expanding media logic that governs news decisions as well as audience expectations and preferences: media formats, especially TV, now emphasize visual imagery, drama and conflict, and emotional resonance with the audience. TV news, along with social media, is more instantaneous, personal, and visual. Donald Trump got much more media coverage than Hillary Clinton or his rivals because his tweeted tirades and attacks fit the entertainment format that governs much of the news media, and uncivil remarks that blasted away his more experienced challengers in the Republican primaries. According to the Harvard Kennedy School's Shorenstein Center on Media, Politics and Public Policy,

Trump's mainly positive media coverage through March 2016 was worth $55 million, which was $19 million more than his primary campaign rival, Jeb Bush.

Ironically, the entertainment format that elevated Mr. Trump on the public stage helped diminish his public appeal as he would interrupt his "on message" statements with insulting and confrontational asides and digressions. Potential newsworthy reports that may have focused on policy statements were replaced by continual "off message" dramatic missteps as the campaign wore on, including attacks on a Muslim Gold Star family whose son was killed in combat, audio tape of sexual boasts about groping women, and demeaning comments about the weight and appearance of a former Miss Universe. Trump disparaged reporters, even mocking one with a disability, and made numerous racist and sexist comments. He refused to let his tax returns be examined and boasted about not paying any income tax for fifteen years—"That makes me smart." And this was done with vitriol and hateful comments, particularly during the campaign, against his Democratic challenger, whom he derided as "Crooked Hillary" and had his minions chant, "Lock her up," which continued even after he won the election. Twitter's Chief Economic Officer (CEO), Jack Dorsey, refused an offer from the Trump campaign to develop an unflattering emoji of Clinton "that would show up on tweets during the second presidential debate anytime Twitter users used the hashtag #CrookedHillary." Journalists speculated that this refusal was the reason that he was not invited to attend a highly publicized postelection meeting with other technology industry leaders (Palazzo, 2016).

Each of these received more attention than the less evocative policy statements and critiques. However, despite being entertaining and getting attention, the vitriolic performances were less appealing to many citizens, whose distaste was amplified as the visuals of Donald Trump's missteps were rebroadcast, retweeted, and vilified throughout social media. And this affected his poll numbers, but supporters ultimately rallied around the politics of fear he spewed about minorities, immigrants, Muslims, and his rival, Secretary of State Clinton.

The impact of speed and entertainment formats on a well-informed citizenry is far reaching. Many journalists sidestepped conventional practices of checking and authenticating some of the more enticing reports. For example, NBC regularly reported on alleged emails about Hillary Clinton, adding that they had not been checked on or authenticated by NBC News. Yet they would put out the report. The competitive urge to be first, especially with a potentially important—and usually very entertaining—report underlies taking such shortcuts in the digital age.

Trump's successful campaign was cultivated by the explosions of fear that followed the 9/11 attacks and widespread propaganda campaigns that promoted the impending risk of not taking strong military action against our enemies abroad and to add more scrutiny to potentially hidden terrorist networks at home. This was consistent with the growth of surveillance and more information about threats to safety and livelihoods. Ulrich Beck (Beck, 1992) and others argued that modernity is associated with increased knowledge, globalization that has led to more concern about a predictable future and avoiding certain problems that have contributed to an awareness of impending risks ranging from environmental, health, and numerous sources of disaster, including terrorism. It seems to be a simultaneous longing for more control, yet with awareness that the control is elusive. This has produced a cultural shift to imagining, predicting, and trying to prevent risks. And this is directly and indirectly shared with audiences through risk communication (Beck, 1992; Ekberg, 2007; Ericson & Haggerty, 1997):

> "An interactive process of exchange of information and opinion among individuals, groups, and institutions." The definition includes "discussion about risk types and levels and about methods for managing risks. Specifically, this process is defined by levels of involvement in decisions, actions, or policies aimed at managing or controlling health or environmental risks." (National Public Health Service, 1995)

Risk communication may be hindering our safety and protection while eroding privacy and reshaping collective identities as people at risk and "potential victims." This counterintuitive argument hinges on how risk communication has been shanghaied by institutional and organizational communication rules and structures that often, essentially, promote self-serving propaganda and misinformation while carving issues and problems to be solved through consumption (commodified) of products, services, or policies that are not isomorphic (and barely parallel) to the nature and extent of the offending risk.

Donald Trump's election as president of the United States in 2016 was paved through skilled propaganda technique promoting the sense of risk to many voters. The president of a research group that studies global risks explained:

> You now have billions of people on the internet, and most of them are not that happy with the status quo. . . . They think their local government is authoritarian. They think they're on the wrong side of the establishment. They're aggrieved by identity politics and a hollowed-out middle class . . . "Through this new technology, people are now empowered to express their grievances and to follow people they see as echoing their grievances," Mr. Bremmer said. "If it wasn't for social media, I don't see Trump winning." (Manjoo, 2016b)

The politics of fear plays into this focus.

The politics of fear is exercised during times of conflict, but it accumulates and gradually informs policy and everyday life behavior, even if there are occasional bouts of resistance. The politics of fear does not imply that citizens are constantly afraid of, say, a certain enemy, day in and day out. The object of fear might change, but fear of threats to one's security is fairly constant. The context of control promotes this, as do numerous messages about menaces that justify general social control measures. This chapter examines how fear has informed political decisions that resulted in social control and the enactment of policies and programs that had long-term effects on social life. This overview includes crime control, previous wars, the expansion of surveillance, the role of business and universities in promoting fear, organized religion's complicity in playing to the politics of fear, and the importance of uniforms in communicating control in everyday life.

FEAR IN CONTEXT

Fear has been part of the game plan to control populations for centuries. Previous work has shown that fear abounds in the United States and western Europe (Altheide, 2002b; Furedi, 1997; Furedi, 2005; Glassner, 1999). As argued throughout this chapter, the expanding use of fear in everyday life has produced a discourse of fear. When fear becomes a familiar experience and expectation, then the symbolic environment is ripe for the politics of fear. The war in Iraq, terrorism, and concerns about crime have promoted the politics of fear. I wish to trace some of these developments in order to set forth an argument that fear is perpetuated by entertaining media that rely on fear, which in turn encourages political actors, like Donald Trump, to frame messages about fear in order to get the most public attention and gain support that they are looking out for the public's interest and well-being. There is a long history to the politics of fear in the United States, and I will touch on only part of it while paying the most attention to events in the United States since the 1970s. This history includes several decades of domestic crime hysteria (especially the "drug wars") as well as recent international wars, such as Grenada, Panama, and the first Gulf War, which were also occasionally justified as part of the drug war.

The politics of fear results when social control is perceived to have broken down and/or a higher level of control is called for by a situation or events, such as a "terrorist attack." But the politics of fear can key off other events as well. During the Cold War in the twentieth century, the United States was involved in numerous terrorist activities, but there were very few against us. Yet the politics of fear was rampant. As a child, I learned to get under my desk at school whenever we heard an air-raid siren. This was to protect us from a nuclear attack from the "Russians" and the "communists," but the real political purpose was to indoctrinate young children as well as our parents that we were threatened by a major enemy and that we had to rely on the U.S. government to protect us, even if the actions seemed reckless at the time. We were being taught a story about our lives, others, and trusting our leaders.

> Like most official stories, it was partly true, partly invention, and partly omission. The nuclear nightmare narrative was fueled by an interior ideological drama—a dangerous invention—that perpetrated mass fear in public forums, schools, churches, and civic groups. Its rhetoric touched every person and every institution in America, and, when combined with the domestic campaigns of the USIA, it demonstrated the power of fear and heightened anxiety in gaining acceptance for the basic political message. As Parry-Giles puts it, "the narrative repetition of the Cold War message from 1945 to 1960 helped normalize the Cold War ideology that resonates in the U.S. collective memory of that battle." (Goodall, 2004, 18)

Actions like the infamous McCarthy hearings on un-American activities in 1950 became a witch hunt against scores of Americans. Then, like during the enactments of the USA Patriot Act in 2002, individual civil liberties were suspended, spying was encouraged, and numerous lives were disrupted. Individuals were forced to testify and "name names" of communist sympathizers and collaborators. The chapters to follow devote some attention to new forms of social control (see chapter 7).

While a specific crisis might erupt suddenly, the politics of fear emerges gradually when there is a cumulative public definition of a crisis that will challenge political leadership, sovereignty, national identity, or ideology. Thus, not all international crises result in the politics of fear. Natural disasters can be a crisis, but not one that evokes the politics of fear. For example, the devastating loss of life of more than two hundred thousand in India, Sri Lanka, and Indonesia from a massive tsunami in December 2004 shocked the world into mobilizing for aid; countries seemed to want to "outbid" each other for offering money and relief. One survey estimated that nearly half of U.S. families had made private contributions to go along with several hundred million dollars in aid. This crisis did not generate fear, or negative action, which is usually violent and destructive. Rather, it marked a time of human suffering and called on people to empathize with millions of homeless people.

The critical point is how an event is defined. It is the way in which this definition is shaped and engineered that also requires some attention. Thus, not all wars evoke the politics of fear, although most are justified in terms of the basic framework noted previously (e.g., challenge political leadership, sovereignty, national identity, or ideology). The basic process of defining the situation and justifying the politics of fear involves propaganda, or the manipulation of information for a specific purpose. Several of the following chapters examine how propaganda has contributed to the politics of fear. Propaganda is very significant because the politics of fear is set in motion by appealing to audiences' emotions and stereotypes.

Stated differently, part of the problem is that audiences are systematically misinformed about events and policies, yet the ways in which information is presented—often by credible newspeople and respected leaders— misleads audiences. The problem, then, is partly what audiences think they know about the relevant policy or events. For example, after the 9/11 attacks, several neighbors told me that many people in Muslim nations hated the United States because of our freedom and quality of life. They had been told this by a number of news commentators and government spokespersons. There was no understanding of how our foreign policy— and that of several western European nations—might have contributed to perceived injustices for more than fifty years. A blue-collar worker I know told me that his niece came home from Europe "when Muslims began exploding car bombs in France or Spain or somewhere. Those guys think that if they die they'll see Allah or someone. They're crazy." He added that there are twenty-four thousand terrorists in the United States waiting for instruction. It is what this man "knows" that enables politicians, like Donald Trump, to gain leverage over his perception, values, votes, and tax dollars for various policies.

Our sense of reality is altered as we become more oriented to the visual, which, in the case of crime and crisis reporting becomes all too familiar, anticipated, and quickly merged with hundreds of other images intertwined from movies, news reports, documentaries, as well as numerous urban legends stressing mayhem, conflict, and danger—and fear about the potential risks that engulf our personal and social horizons. But it is entertaining, fun, and adventuresome, and if the TV and movie producers are correct, audiences crave it. Some mass media outlets (e.g., selected TV stations, broadcast networks, exceptional newspapers like the *New York Times*) are marked by the sharp contrast with the media universe they inhabit. The media edge has emerged from the way in which the media logic, formats, and "entertaining grab" have evolved on a platform of fear, danger, excitement, and risk.

The visual has been altered to fit the parameters and format of the screen:

> As a consequence of the screen's influence, we internalize a new experience of space and time. The screen alters the communication matrix, not by changing the structure of or reinventing the physiology of the ear but by providing a different sensory experience. . . . The screen links visual, auditory, and kinesthetic elements, altering one's experience of time, space, and duration in the process. One is both physically grounded with a particular horizon and yet not grounded. The consequence is a deep contradiction. With the advent of the screen, it is possible to experience a duration that is nothing like one's ordinary experience. To the extent that such an altered duration is internalized, the world is in us—is influencing us—in a very different way. (Waite, 2003, 159)

Fundamental media and information technology changes are responsible for the craziness that now defines American politics, our major institutions, and everyday life as it has been essentially organized since World War II. The window that has long presented information and constructed social reality for American audiences was smashed by technological changes in three ways: (1) technological changes and new formats; (2) sensational entertainment-inspired forecasts of doom and gloom, a kind of "disaster pornography; and (3) a fresh perspective for understanding the nature of our mass-mediated world. We can see how this has happened through fear.

Citizen beliefs often are constructed and then manipulated by those who seek to benefit. Fear does not just happen; it is socially constructed and managed by political actors to promote their own goals. The goal of such manipulators might be money, but more often than not it is political power and symbolic dominance: getting one's view of the world accepted opens the door to many other programs and activities to implement this view. This is where ideology comes to play a large part in the manipulation of fear. A key aspect of all ideology is the promotion of a mythology, a set of ideas or "stories" that explains things, organizes our view of the world, and puts people, places, and events in convenient categories (Davis, 1986; Kappeler, Blumberg, & Potter, 1999).

Mythology is promoted by misinformation and propaganda. This does not mean that everyone in the mass media lies, although that is certainly true of a number of politicians (e.g., Richard Nixon about Watergate, George W. Bush about Iraq and weapons of mass destruction, and Bill Clinton about sexual exploits). Rather, as pointed out in chapter 3, it is the emphasis on entertainment and making profits that leads to the major distortions. A good example is the uncivil but highly entertaining charges and insults by Donald Trump in the 2016 presidential campaign. While President Barack Obama, the nation's first black president, was ridiculed and cast as a Muslim and foreigner—many people still believe that he was not born in the United States—his campaigns against Republican challengers John McCain (2008) and Mitt Romney (2012) were quite civil by comparison. Indeed, it was Trump who pressed the "birther movement" for five years that President Barack Obama was not a U.S. citizen. This so-called birther movement was espoused throughout social media, particularly by Donald Trump, who, as late as 2016, repeatedly stated that President Obama was not born in the United States. Indeed, it was not until his bid for the presidency that Donald Trump acknowledged that President Obama was born in the United States, although he did not apologize for the years of erroneous claims, which by then had been accepted by about half of Republican voters. Many of these beliefs were reinforced through social media networks and numerous web pages that also questioned President Obama's commitment to protect the United States from terrorist attacks, especially by Muslims. This mattered since there had been several tragic incidents involving homegrown terrorists or recent immigrants who were Muslims. Indeed, former Arizona sheriff Joe Arpaio insisted as late as December 17, 2016—about five weeks before the end of Obama's second term—that there was still strong evidence that Obama was not born in the United States.

The critical point is that these blatantly false charges were carried by both major and social media, not because they were at all credible but because they were entertaining—controversial, dramatic, confrontational. There are many reports that are emphasized because of entertainment and fear. Candidate Trump did not disappoint: he bullied people during debates and chastised the Obama administration and former Secretary of State Clinton with failing the country, not keeping it safe, not caring about the exporting of jobs, and in general, making America weak and vulnerable. And the established media loved it. The major TV networks carried his daily spew and their ratings rocketed, giving them enormous profits from advertising revenue.

> All three major cable news networks had their largest audiences ever, thanks to the drawing power of the nonstop surprises of the 2016 White House campaign that culminated with the election of Donald Trump. Year-end numbers from Nielsen showed that the 21st Century Fox–owned Fox News Channel was the most-watched network in all of cable with an average of 2.43 million viewers in prime time, up 36% over last year. Only the four major broadcast networks had a larger audience.
>
> Both Fox News competitors finished in the top 10 among ad-supported networks, with Time Warner's CNN averaging 1.29 million viewers, up 77%, and NBC Universal's MSNBC seeing an 88% gain with 1.1 million viewers. (Battaglio, 2016b)

Fear helped Donald Trump become president of the United States. Donald Trump's astounding presidential victory over heavily favored Hillary Clinton surprised pollsters and the nation, and it has rattled global allies and partners. The foundation of this cataclysmic break with conventional politics was an expansive use of social media that is instantaneous, personal, and visual. Contrary to the widespread conclusion that economic insecurity led voters to abandon historical political alliances, I argue that jobs were but a small part of the upswing for Trump, and that the politics of fear promoted by media messages about terrorists, minority groups, immigrants, and civil liberties were more important. The 2016 presidential campaign was perhaps the most uncivil in U.S. history. Without ever having been elected to a public office, businessman Trump plowed through some sixteen primary challengers, and then attacked former U.S. Senator and Secretary of State Clinton with insults and monikers (Crooked Hillary, Corrupt Hillary) and threatened during a debate to appoint a special prosecutor to put her in jail. In addition to demeaning Muslim Gold Star parents, whose son was killed in combat, he made numerous categorical insults and threats to Mexican immigrants ("rapists and murderers") and Syrian refugees. He made sexual boasts about his physical prowess, and audio-recorded bragging about groping women was revealed. There were also promises to abandon a major health initiative—the Affordable Care Act—as well as withdrawing from significant international defense and trade treaties. He also threatened to abolish the Environmental Protection Agency as part of his disavowal that climate change is occurring and that it is all a big hoax. Still, many people voted for him because of their dislike and distrust of Hillary Clinton, and the belief that the vulgar candidate would calm down once elected.

The specific vote totals are relevant. Despite winning the popular vote by nearly three million votes, Clinton lost the Electoral College vote 232 to 304. Examining the vote totals in a few states that gave Trump enough electoral votes (270+) provides another indication of how close the election results were. Clinton lost the electoral votes of Pennsylvania (20), Michigan (16), and Wisconsin (10)—forty-six votes—by a popular vote of less than seventy-eight thousand, a margin smaller than a Rose Bowl football game crowd. Nevertheless, Trump won, Clinton lost. But that is not the end of the story, which calls for plausible explanations of how a candidate favored by most polls lost this important election.

I wish to examine several claims about why Donald Trump won the election and offer an alternative explanation. Many analysts have pointed out that people supported Trump because of job losses as well as an uninspired economy, especially in Pennsylvania, Michigan, Ohio, and Wisconsin. It has been widely proclaimed that his being an "outsider" won the day—someone who was not beholden to the corrupt and self-serving Washington establishment. His promise to "Make America Great Again" and to "Drain the Swamp" was consistent with his refrain that all of Washington was corrupt and that a bold businessman like him could solve problems and make America great again. But one of his loudest boasts was that he would abandon trade agreements, which he claimed had taken jobs from Americans and cast many into despair, while ruining many cities that in turn had turned the United States into a Third World country.

While there was undoubtedly a lot of voter anger, as there usually is during a presidential campaign, the emphasis on job loss and lowered standard of living that was attributed to the eight years of the Obama administration was especially profound. Many journalists interviewed workers—both employed and unemployed—about their economic woes, and how the politicians, and particularly the Democrats, had abandoned the white working class. This was a recurring theme in the postelection mortem with many spokespersons, media pundits, and even some political candidates arguing that the election was lost because not enough attention was paid to the economic and job situation of millions of working and unemployed Americans. Thus, it was jobs that mattered, or as a repeated cliché says, "It's the economy, stupid." This simple answer is appealing, but it is at best only part of the picture, and at worst it is wrong. This is why.

Most of Donald Trump's primary voters were employed and made a median income of $72,000, significantly more than the average American, and more than Democratic supporters (Klein, 2016).

> The idea that Trumpism arose as a response to a stalled economy collapsed as America experienced its longest sustained run of private sector job growth, and the highest single-year jump in median incomes, in modern history.
>
> The idea that Trump was a reaction to failed trade deals and heavy competition from immigrants slammed into data showing support for him showed no relationship to lost manufacturing jobs and was strongest in areas without immigrant labor.
>
> The idea that Trump is a reaction to historic disgust with American elites is at war with President Barack Obama's approval ratings, which have risen above 50 percent and now match Ronald Reagan's at this point in his presidency.
>
> The reality is that the patterns of Trumpism, the trends of the US economy, and the polls measuring the American mood have stubbornly refused to fit the comforting theory that this is an extraordinary candidacy that could only emerge in an extraordinary moment. Indeed, if this were a period as thick with economic pain and anti-establishment sentiment as the pundits pretend, Trump's victory would likely be assured. (Klinkner, 2016)

Now, let's not underestimate the importance of economic conditions, which have gradually worsened since the "Reagan Revolution" led to the busting of unions, lowering taxes for the most wealthy, and a declining standard of living for millions of Americans. And there can be no doubt that trade deals (e.g., NAFTA) contributed to the movement of jobs out of the country, but numerous analysis make it clear that much of declining industrial base in the United States owed more to technological changes and expanding globalization and improvement in world markets, which, ironically, the U.S. consumers have benefitted greatly from, including a large influx of new jobs (W. Williams, 2016).

Fortunately, data are available to sort out the relative unimportance of the economy per se, and jobs in particular. More documentation of the voting patterns for Donald Trump can be illustrated by challenging the strictly economic/jobs explanation. If jobs were the more important factor, then, presumably, states that voted for Trump would also have higher unemployment rates. However, Trump won several states with a large number of electoral votes that had relatively low unemployment rates. Moreover, the rates had been declining steadily since 2008 to 2009 when President Obama took office and faced the daunting task of putting

Americans back to work. This can be shown by a quick comparison of the unemployment rates over nearly a decade in selected states that gave Trump the Electoral College victory.

Employment, at least measured by unemployment data, was much better in 2016 than 2009 when many counties in the above states supported Barack Obama. However, during the campaign both candidates, and especially Donald Trump, repeated that the "forgotten people" had lost their jobs due to bad trade deals and a general uncaring on the part of politicians, including Hillary Clinton. Voters seldom heard much about the relatively good economic news. The Bureau of Labor Statistics (BLS) supports this view across the United States.

> On Friday, in the last economic snapshot before voters go to the polls, the government reported that the jobless rate fell to 4.9 percent in October, matching the level in February 2008. Today, though, most economic bellwethers are showing improvement. Particularly encouraging was the fact that hourly wages rose 2.8 percent compared with a year ago, the best gain in more than seven years. "The economy set three post-recession records this month," said Jed Kolko, chief economist at the online jobs website Indeed, citing solid wage growth, a drop in the number of discouraged and underemployed workers, and a return of prime-age men and women to the labor force. "These are all signs that the labor market continues to strengthen and is at its strongest point since the crisis," he said. (P. Cohen, 2016)

There are other indications that it was not the lousy economy that was unilaterally driving the voter anger and turn toward Trump in selected counties. For example, in Wisconsin two of three counties with the highest unemployment rate voted for Clinton. Moreover, nine or ten counties with the highest median income—more than $55,000—voted for Trump. And why voter anger about jobs would be more pronounced in Michigan is a mystery since the Obama administration and the federal government bailed out the auto industry in Detroit with loans of nearly $18 billion of TARP funds, and basically kept it alive until it rebounded in 2012 and

Table 2.1. Unemployment Rates in Selected States

State	2007	2009	2016
Florida	3.5	10.5	4.7
Michigan	7.0	13.6	4.6
North Carolina	4.7	10.6	4.7
Ohio	5.5	10.2	4.8
Pennsylvania	4.4	8.1	5.7
Wisconsin	4.9	8.5	4.1

paid back the government loans. It was estimated that 250,000 jobs were saved.

> Massachusetts governor Deval Patrick called him the president "who saved the American auto industry from extinction." The former CEO of the super-sized used car dealership CarMax, Austin Ligon, said the president's decisive action to restructure General Motors and Chrysler "helped prevent a domino effect that would have taken down everything in the auto industry, from the factories that manufactured auto parts to the dealers who sold the cars . . . The massive loss of jobs and the disruption to the network of auto parts suppliers did not happen. The shock that might have hit all car makers and the overall economy is not staring lawmakers in the face." (Greenberg, 2012)

Granted that Trump won Michigan by less than eleven thousand votes, but there is little evidence that the economy was the impetus for voters' change. And it wasn't only Michigan where other things were at work. During an NBC election report, veteran journalist Tom Brokaw stated:

> "This is our Brexit," said Brokaw, referring to the equally stunning vote by Britain to withdraw from the European Union. "People are not entirely sure about why they're . . . off. I was just out in Nebraska, South Dakota and Iowa—things are good. But they feel like they have to be . . . off." (Battaglio, 2016a)

Jobs were not the big factor that turned significant states against the Democratic candidate in 2016. The deal breaker was fear generated by invasive social media that focused on disdain for politicians who supported big changes in the United States involving terrorists, refugees, minorities, and exaggerated claims about the negative impact of globalization and trade. Results from the 2016 American National Election Study show clearly that the big factor was not economic worries per se, but rather reactions to terrorists and immigrants.

> You can ask just one simple question to find out whether someone likes Donald Trump more than Hillary Clinton: Is Barack Obama a Muslim? If they are white and the answer is yes, 89 percent of the time that person will have a higher opinion of Trump than Clinton. That's more accurate than asking people if it's harder to move up the income ladder than it was for their parents (54 percent), whether they oppose trade deals (66 percent), or if they think the economy is worse now than last year (81 percent). It's even more accurate than asking them if they are Republican (87 percent). (Klinkner, 2016)

The impact of technological change, and how robots were replacing assembly line workers in plants, was barely touched by the Republican challenger. Trump hit numerous fear buttons about the insecurity and downward slide of the nation, often by stating outright lies about crime by minorities and immigrants, the threats from refugees, the miserable state of the U.S. economy, and the growing impotence of our military and misdirection by leadership in foreign policy.

> Trump is especially good at tapping into fear, a particularly motivating emotion. Studies find when white people (any white people, even liberals) are reminded that minorities will eventually be the majority, their views tilt conservative. A recent experiment showed that this reminder increased support for Trump. Which doesn't mean all white people are racist: It means fear is an all-too-easy button to press. We fear, unthinkingly. It directs our actions. And it nudges us to believe the person who says they will vanquish our fears. Trump understands what many miss: people don't make decisions based on facts. (Belluz & Resnick, 2015)

Donald Trump's comments fueled racial antagonism, and many supporters agreed with him. Prejudice against minority and outsider groups is connected with fears about competition, intergroup relations—including marriage—as well as property value concerns. Hillary Clinton was cast as supportive of the Obama administration's concerns about improving police-community relations across the country with regard to racial discrimination and civil rights. President Obama was cautious in focusing on race as a social issue, but several egregious police shootings of unarmed youth, including Trayvon Martin (February 26, 2012) and Michael Brown (August 9, 2014) in Ferguson, Missouri, as well as the slaughter of nine black members at a prayer meeting at the African Methodist Episcopal Church by an avowed white supremacist on June 7, 2015, led him to urge more attention to police-community relations and more understanding about the significance of race in the United States. According to a *Frontline* documentary, those measured comments nevertheless led many people, and especially the right-wing Fox News and various talk radio hosts, to attack him as a racist and being unsupportive of the police   (http://www.pbs.org/wgbh/frontline/film/divided-states-of-america/).

Other researchers show how animosity toward minority groups informed Trump supporters' political action: people who thought that whites were treated unfairly compared to blacks were very likely to support Donald Trump (Tesler & Sides, 2016). It is well-established in research that white attitudes toward minority groups, and blacks in particular, influence whites' opinions on many issues (Tesler & Sides, 2016). The American National Election Study found:

> Those who express more resentment toward African Americans, those who think the word "violent" describes Muslims well, and those who believe President Obama is a Muslim have much more positive views of Trump compared with Clinton. (Klinkner, 2016)

Donald Trump led a national effort to discredit President Obama by claiming that he was not born in the United States, was not a citizen, and therefore was not eligible to be president of the United States. He continued this claim through 2015, and did not state publicly that President Obama was born in the United States until his 2016 campaign for president. More than half of Republicans still did not accept that President Obama was born in the United States (Velencia, 2016)!

Voter concern about jobs is easily linked to more expansive general fears about the future, especially when political opponents are simplistically blamed for complex economic phenomena, foreign trade, energy interdependence, and political alliances built from global connections.

> Even if it is out of sync with their personal situation, "people's perception of seemingly objective information is very much influenced by what they hear from their party candidates and leaders," said Thomas E. Mann, a resident scholar at the Institute of Governmental Studies at the University of California, Berkeley.
> "The more dystopian views that Republicans have is basically a consequence of what they're hearing from Donald Trump and other Republicans," Mr. Mann explained. As for Mrs. Clinton, he said, she wants to make clear that she is not ignoring the plight of people who are struggling. (Belluz & Resnick, 2015)

As noted previously, since Reagan sanctioned union busting in the 1980s, there has been increased pressure to get rid of organized labor. The rhetoric about wasteful union labor, along with the expanding power of Wall Street investment firms buying and then selling or simply closing plants for tax advantages, gradually added to a massive inequality of income between the top 1 percent of income brackets and everyone else. Democratic presidential hopeful Senator Bernie Sanders made much of this discrepancy in his unsuccessful bid for the nomination. All of this took a toll on the standard of living of many workers, but the explanation for why this was occurring were more complex and seldom discussed in the mass media, except during political campaigns. As one writer explained:

> How much of the shift [Democrat to Republican] took place because of trade is hard to tell: The job losses mostly took place during the first decade of this century, but the states did not flip to vote for a Republican until this year. And other issues were in play, including tensions over immigration, race and the presence of a woman on the Democratic ticket. (Kitroeff, 2016)

The development and widespread use of social media to connect people who shared similar views of problems accentuated the difficulty of meaningful political action. Propagandists know that simple is better, especially if it is repeated often enough and if clear culprits can be identified. An economic advisor for Donald Trump saw it this way:

> These workers were not necessarily scraping by—the average American with a factory gig made around $64,000 in 2015, BLS data

show. But in Ohio, Michigan and Pennsylvania, pay for manufacturing employees has declined or remained relatively flat since 2000, after adjusting for inflation, even as it inched up in the country overall. (Kitroeff, 2016)

An example is a worker who had been making $55,000 a year but due to plant closure had to take another job with a salary of $40,000. He did not appreciate hearing politicians talk about an economic recovery (since 2008). His account illustrates how fear and discontent create a space for scapegoating. He explained that he did not vote on race issues, but they were relevant:

> "Even if the progressives want to say we are progressing, we aren't really progressing. . . . More people are hating on white Americans than any other race or any other walk of life," he said. "I think white America is fed up with that."

This message was carried repeatedly as social media facilitated sharing frustrations and prejudices with others on Facebook, WhatsApp, WeChat, Instagram, Twitter, and widely accessible websites through Google. One student of social networks explained the consequences for civility:

> White was kept at bay because of pluralistic ignorance. . . . Every person who was sitting in their basement yelling at the TV about immigrants or was willing to say white Christians were more American than other kinds of Americans—they didn't know how many others shared their views. Thanks to the internet, now each person with once-maligned views can see that he's not alone. And when these people find one another, they can do things—create memes, publications and entire online worlds that bolster their worldview, and then break into the mainstream. The groups also become ready targets for political figures like Mr. Trump, who recognize their energy and enthusiasm and tap into it for real-world victories. (Manjoo, 2016b)

The foundation of this election outcome was a massive change in the ecology of communication that guided emotional communications through new formats that accompanied big changes in information technologies. Groups and organizations such as radical, right-wing white nationalists and neo-Nazis now have access to widely available communication networks, and this is happening globally. As one observer put it:

> The election of Donald J. Trump is perhaps the starkest illustration yet that across the planet, social networks are helping to fundamentally rewire human society. They have subsumed and gutted mainstream media. They have undone traditional political advantages like fundraising and access to advertising. And they are destabilizing and replacing old-line institutions and established ways of doing things, including political parties, transnational organizations and longstanding, unspoken social prohibitions against blatant expressions of racism and xenophobia. (Manjoo, 2016b)

The format changes in social media do more than alter how we send messages: for example, we are affected and our sense of what is appropriate changes when we're constantly exposed to brief tweets that demean, vilify, and use derogatory terms about political opponents. They alter the content as well. Violating this distinction has profound changes. Civilization turns on the distinction between what we may feel-say-and-do in private from what we say-and-do in public. Civil discourse lubricates everyday interaction as well as political discussions about contested issues. Just as adventure and dramatic movies continue to escalate special effects to build on the audience's changing baseline of tolerance and expectations—to make things more exciting!—so, too, does our range of what is "normal" and what is "shocking" and inappropriate change. For thirty years American TV audiences have been groomed by Fox News, Rush Limbaugh's radio commentary, and other sources for Donald Trump's hateful and personally demeaning attacks against his opponents, as well as women, military members, a disabled reporter, Mexican immigrants, Syrian refugees, and Muslims. He encouraged violence against protesters at political gatherings, told blatant lies about crime statistics and fraudulent voting, and demeaned generals as not knowing as much about planning and conducting military operations.

Donald Trump, building on the controversial legacy of public insults hurled at media outlets, provided bushels of sound bites for entertainment-oriented media, on the one hand, while personalizing the messages with hundreds of impromptu tweets, often in the middle of the night, to chastise and demean political opponents. These would be reported on the mainstream media, then Trump would reply—and often deny—what he had just tweeted as a miscommunication. This helped normalize harsh speaking and action, more people shared views on social media, and quickly a "new normal" appeared. This has consequences for social life.

Within hours of Trump's election, there were several hundred reports of attacks against minority groups, including black women, Mexican American students, and Muslim women. The Southern Poverty Law Center reported more than seven hundred attacks and harassment since Election Day (Yan, Sgueglia, & Walker, 2016). Many of the reports involved painted swastikas on churches, playgrounds, and schools. When told of the actions, Donald Trump asked that it be stopped. A few days later he appointed an advisor, Steve Bannon, who had run a website (Breitbart News) that supported white nationalists and anti-Semitism. Bannon had referred to the website as the "platform of the alt-right." A few days later handwritten letters were sent to several Islamic Centers in Southern California. Referring to Muslims as "vile and filthy people," the letter was addressed to "the children of Satan."

"Your day of reckoning has arrived," the letter states, according to CAIRLA. "There's a new sheriff in town—President Donald Trump.

He's going to cleanse America and make it shine again. And, he's going to start with you Muslims."

The letter, signed only by "Americans for a Better Way," said Trump was "going to do to you Muslims what Hitler did to the jews." (Branson-Potts, 2016)

The executive director of the Council on American-Islamic Relations requested police protection and expressed dismay with Donald Trump's rhetoric:

"I'm not saying [Trump] created racist people," he said. "He normalized it. While he might say he's not responsible, and I respect that, I remind President-elect Trump that he has a responsibility to act as a president for all Americans." (Branson-Potts, 2016)

The context of fear and hate that emerged and expanded with Trump's campaign is further attested to by the FBI report that gun sales hit an all-time high during the election cycle (Gutowski, 2016). The politics of fear carried through entertaining mass media and personally selected social media helped win the election, as well as establishing a new normal of incivility within the discourse of fear, especially since Mr. Trump's nominee for Attorney General, Jeff Sessions, expressed support for ongoing surveillance against Muslims, including establishing a database to keep track of them. Clearly, surveillance accompanies and promotes the politics of fear.

Surveillance Expansion

Consider the money, excitement, and intrigue associated with the massive expansion of surveillance in our lives. Surveillance represents one of the most intrusive changes in our everyday life and can be traced to the politics of fear. For example, surveillance was initially promoted to protect us from crime, particularly during the drug war of the past three decades (Kappeler et al., 1999; Marx, 1988; Staples, 2000).

New technologies and formats have altered the communication order while expanding surveillance through changing information technologies. Surveillance is complex: there are both risks and benefits. The key is to develop a framework for understanding what is at stake, what is gained, and what is lost. One of the top authorities on surveillance, Gary T. Marx, advises that surveillance must be accountable; the watchers must also be willing to be watched, or at least share criteria and justifications.

If it is correct that surveillance is neither good nor bad but context and comportment make it so, then a central task for analysts is to understand variations within and between contexts, while a central task for citizens is eternal vigilance. Cherished values are ever precarious, and freedom is indeed a constant struggle. (Marx, 2016, 320)

Many of these changes, particularly social media, contribute to negotiating social interaction within institutionally mediated contexts. Protesters in Cairo used social media in the Egyptian revolt in January 2011. An
official with Al Jazeera stated that the protests in Tunisia were

> broadcast to the entire world through Al Jazeera, so there was a sort of
> partnership between those people on the ground and Al Jazeera. In my
> opinion, this is a new ecosystem emerging in media, between the so-
> called traditional media and the new media. . . . And this new ecosys-
> tem is not based on competition and who is going to win, it's based on
> complementing each other. (Stelter, 2011)

Social media use and effectiveness varies by social and political contexts. Ironically, the media get mediated to adjust to social and political
contexts. It was noted earlier that eight years of Republican attacks
against President Obama through social media contributed to the acceptance of vulgar language by social media users, ultimately lowering the
nation's bar for civil political discourse during the 2016 presidential campaign.

A key aspect of surveillance is that it focuses on the "body" as an
object rather than as a subject, with feelings, emotions, rights, and, in
short, humanity. We can count bodies, photograph them, frisk bodies,
peak inside them with drug tests as well as various scanners, and capture
DNA information that contains the "truth." News media reports about
crime and terrorism (chapter 4) stressed the need for surveillance and
more cooperation between federal agencies. The "war on terrorism" promoted massive federal, state, and local surveillance policies, all of which
were guided by the USA Patriot Act, which legitimated a wide range of
technological intrusions on American citizens and the detaining of citizens and foreign nationals for extended periods of time without allowing
them access to an attorney. These developments are examined in later
chapters, but the important point for now is that surveillance becomes
institutionalized and promotes, often subtly, the notion that all of us are
under attack and need protection. In 2016 Donald Trump attracted millions of followers who were told repeatedly that their lives were in danger by Muslims, particularly foreign immigrants and refugees from Syria,
who were not being properly screened. His solution was to propose banning their entry altogether on December 7, 2016:

> Donald J. Trump is calling for a total and complete shutdown of Mus-
> lims entering the United States until our country's representatives can
> figure out what is going on. (http://www.cnn.com/2016/05/12/politics/
> donald-trump-muslim-ban/)

No major news commentator noted the irony that this statement occurred on the anniversary of the attack on Pearl Harbor (1941), which

drew the United States into World War II and led to the illegal incarceration of more than 110,000 Japanese Americans.

FORCE AND THE POLITICS OF FEAR

The politics of fear is not new to social life or to journalists, politicians, and social scientists who have studied politics and social order. Arendt's (1966) conceptualization of tyrannical terror and more recently Robin's (2004) elucidation of fear in political theory suggest that many intellectuals separated fear from politics, seeing terror as a weapon rather than as a lens for understanding social inequality and political partisanship.

My focus is on the modern application of fear in politics in a media age. We must make a distinction between the actual use of force, on the one hand, and mobilizing support with fear on the other. Force can kill, but fear can defeat. Fear is the meaningful side of force. Living in fear is not synonymous with the politics of fear, but the latter does promote the former. Force without fear is futile and will achieve nothing but eradication of some enemies and ultimately the resolve of those who wield the force. If people do not fear certain consequences—and if they cannot anticipate and visualize these—then force will be more cruel than effective. Without sufficient fear, however, more enemies will follow those who have been killed. Anyone familiar with the decades of feuds and hatred in the Balkans (e.g., Serbs and Croatians), the Middle East (e.g., Israelis and Palestinians), Rwanda (e.g., Tutsis and Hutus), and elsewhere can recognize the cycle of killing, hatred, and revenge. The U.S. invasion of Iraq dramatized this relationship between force and fear: many Iraqis volunteer for suicide missions because they believe that a martyred death is an opportunity for eternal life. One who does not fear death cannot be controlled by fear unless it is the source of their faith, their god. Zealous leaders of some nations, like the United States, have not considered this in their war plans. Thus, uninformed American war planners who planned the destructive bombing of Baghdad that began the Iraq invasion believed that Iraqi citizens and soldiers would be "shocked and awed" by the display, thus assuring a rather quick capitulation. This did not occur for the reasons noted previously; it was mere force and did not generate sufficient fear because the politics of fear were not meaningful to the Iraqis. This is perhaps even truer of ISIS, the sectarian fighting force that emerged during the Syrian conflict in 2014, whose routine strategy was to employ suicide bombers, as well as fighting to the death, with no surrender. Their use of social media showing callous executions of prisoners, including beheadings of Western hostages, promoted fear.

Leaders and politicians want to be fear effective. This requires manipulating symbolic meanings of actions and threats. This can be achieved through effective propaganda and the use of the mass media. Political leaders promote fear in order to ensure safety and, ironically, freedom. The very nature of political power and decision making entails an appreciation of the use of pressure, force, dominance, and a range of fearlike approaches. Observers for thousands of years have commented on the myriad ways to get power, maintain control, and exercise force to support one's goals. Indeed, political philosophers have offered numerous alternatives to the use of brute force to instill and sustain the governed. In a sense, analysts and advocates of "civilization" have grappled with alternatives to fear as a political weapon. Indeed, reason and the Enlightenment aspired to promote understanding and consensus through common logics so that consensus could be achieved. What is often forgotten is that this was, by and large, offered in opposition to brute force and fear. From a political standpoint, fear is negative, while reason and the aspiration to higher values were positive. One looks in vain to find any philosopher who argued that the highest order of civilization was force and intimidation, although many acknowledged that it may be necessary from time to time, or that there may be stages in social and historical development that rely on such force and fear.

Many scholars have examined how terrorism, which may be defined as "the purposeful act or threat of violence to create fear and or compliant behavior in a victim and or audience of the act or threat" (Lopez & Stohl, 1984, 4), is one dimension of force (Gale, 2002; Offe, 2002; Shirlow & Pain, 2003; C. Sparks, 2003; Thomaz, 1997; Yavuz, 2002). Studies of political oppression, torture, and random as well as targeted brutality reveal that fear is short-lived as a political weapon, partly because it cannot be sustained indefinitely, even with some compliance from the governed. As noted by Sparks (2003),

> Overly fearful governments can lurch into panoptic governance, undermining the world they seek to preserve. In such situations, citizens come to be seen as actual or potential enemies within, vigilantes prosper, civility withers and, ironically, the uncertainties and dangers that lurk within the society become its defining and potentially terminating features. (201)

Stated differently, fear needs to be understood against its opposite: predictability, certainty, and positive and sustaining action. In this sense, some segments of society live in perpetual fear yet may not be subject to the politics of fear. It is just that their everyday life routines operate so far below the comfort zone of their known contemporaries that daily living is tenuous and problematic. As the Belize Minister of Foreign Affairs stated at the 60th Session of the United Nations General Assembly, "What is often not recognised: that a person that is not free from want can only live in fear, and that the greatest evil, the most effective and consuming terrorism of our age is the terrorism of abject poverty, a poverty in which millions of people live in terror because they know that sooner rather than later they or their loved ones will die from hunger or preventable diseases" (http://www.un.org/webcast/ga/60/statements/beli050923eng.pdf).

This condition of fear is perceived to be a feature of indifferent others who wantonly seek to hurt or take advantage of them. While poverty and exploitation may provoke emotions and circumstances that cultivate the politics of fear, this is not an inevitable development.

People can live in circumstances that promote fear quite independently of the politics of fear. The politics of fear promotes fear through propaganda and symbolic manipulation. Donald Trump's campaign demonstrated that in contemporary Western countries like the United States, it is not abject poverty and want that sustains the politics of fear but rather collective support for leaders, ideologies, and policies that claim to protect people from losing what they have as well as maintaining opportunities for them to improve their lives and obtain more economic and social security and well-being.

The key point is that fear is constituted through interaction and meaning with others. Several of the following chapters examine how terrorism has been defined for political reasons. Simply having a building bombed does not constitute the politics of fear; it is the reaction of leaders to the act and especially how those reactions are communicated to the audiences they govern that do matter. Like many aspects of social life, fear is blamed on outsiders or others. Thus, we see that terrorism, especially following the 9/11 attacks, was cast as something that was done to the United States as barbaric, as unfair. A number of officials stated or implied that the United States, by contrast, did not engage in terrorist activities ever. Most official documents of the United States would support this claim. One searches massive news archives in vain to find any statements by elected officials—especially in high federal office—stating that the United States engages in terrorist activities. Yet other sources, including government documents, make it clear that the United States and many of our allies have engaged in assassinations, kidnapping, torture, civilian bombings, and so on. The United States, like most countries, provides rhetoric encased in certain narratives or complete stories of our history, character, and purpose:

> The omission element in the political construction of the propaganda message was equally powerful in shaping the war. It was an ideological battle to be sure, but it was fueled by secret international economic and trade interests, which meant that money and power were the secrets kept at the heart of Cold War fever. For this reason, nothing that risked exposing those secrets was anything less than "Top Secret"; and, it was the covert operations run by intelligence operatives and directed by members of the elite classes that were used to win the war against Communism that was also a war to protect their own, and their

wealthy friends', interests. To conduct this covert war, Presidents and CIA directors relied heavily on paying bribes; international money laundering; illegal arms trade; drug smuggling; the seduction, intimidation, and blackmailing of officials; carrying out the occasional murder, assassination, or attempted assassination of leaders; and other violent, illegal acts labeled by our opponents as "state-sponsored terrorism" or "acts of aggression." (Goodall, 2004)

American legislators learned from the experiences with centralized control in Nazi Germany and the Soviet Union that a police state not only operates on fear but is very coordinated as well. These lessons were renewed during the civil rights movement and anti–Vietnam War protests in the 1960s and 1970s when federal and state police agencies spied on U.S. citizens, conducted illegal wiretaps and surveillance, and committed burglaries and blackmail. Much of this came to a head during the Nixon administration with the infamous Watergate burglary at the national Democratic headquarters. The fallout from the Watergate investigation (e.g., Bob Woodward and Carl Bernstein's reporting for the *Washington Post*) and the cadre of Nixon operatives, also known as the "plumbers," revealed that they had ties to the FBI, the CIA, and several state-sponsored terrorist groups, including individuals involved with the unsuccessful Bay of Pigs invasion of Cuba in the 1960s. The Nixon administration claimed that these and other acts were warranted by "national security," a catchphrase that lost credibility and would not be used with the same fervor until the Iraq War in 2003.

The politics of fear, then, is made visible through various policy changes ranging from property forfeitures through RICO legislation to other abuses, like the federal government's violations of civil rights, the abuse of power in meddling in foreign affairs, and the breaking of the law. However, the legal and ethical violations become old news and are short-lived, seldom remembered when the next "crisis" warrants a rebirth of the soiled policy. This happened with centralized state control during the Cold War, when domestic spying was applied to innocent citizens. Surveillance operations were scaled back, and legislation was enacted to prohibit agencies from working together to harm American citizens. All of these criminal acts and violations of citizens' civil rights led Congress to pass strident legislation separating police powers and functions. This separation extended to lines of authority as well as limitations on interagency jurisdiction (e.g., the FBI and the CIA were not to work together to investigate U.S. citizens) and information sharing, and communication guidelines, including confidentiality rules, were intended to maintain some structural separation between agencies. Some officials did not like these limitations and, as we have seen throughout history, simply chose to break the law in order to pursue their own interpretation of what was needed. (Chapter 8 describes how a number of U.S. officials began planning the war with Iraq in 1992, ten years before bombs fell on Baghdad.) A good example was the Iran-Contra scandal that was coordinated by the Reagan administration in the 1980s (http://nsarchive.gwu.edu/nsa/publications/irancontra/irancon.html). The plan was to violate congressional and United Nations laws and sell arms to Iran, then involved in a bloody war against Iraq. The profits were then used to fund rebel forces, the "Contras," opposing an elected government in Nicaragua. Marine Colonel Oliver North oversaw this plan, and later became a conservative radio talk-show host and motivational speaker (http://premierespeakers.com/oliver_north/bio).

After the 9/11 attacks, proponents of centralized police authority and information bases negated the lessons learned and the civil rights violations by overwhelmingly passing the USA Patriot Act, which gave the federal government tremendous power over civil rights, including surveillance of personal records. The appeal was to work together against the nation's common terrorist enemies. Numerous members of Congress would later claim that they neither read the act nor were given time to do so. Action was called for to protect Americans from the enemy in "these times," now that the "world is different." The passage of this act symbolizes perhaps more than any other recent legislation the renewal of the politics of fear. Several Americans and numerous foreigners were detained without charges and were denied legal counsel (Walker, 2002). This did not happen solely because of the 9/11 attacks; the effort to focus central control against the "enemy" was relentlessly pursued by strong proponents of social control even after Watergate.

Most wars invoke the politics of fear to varying degrees. Unlike previous wars in the late twentieth century, such as Grenada, Panama, and the first Gulf War, the war against terror does not have an end in sight, partly because there is not a well-defined enemy or a clear objective, although in each case the enemy was appropriately demonized or else castigated as the personification of evil. Both Panamanian rulers Manuel Noriega and Iraqi president Saddam Hussein were apt targets for cartoons and tough street language (e.g., "kick your ass"). Noriega was also referred to as "pineapple face" because of an acne problem and was said to like men, women, voodoo, and pornography.

> The Ronald Reagan and George Bush administrations in the United States both used their War on Drugs to legitimize United States intervention in Latin American countries. The United States concluded that drug-trafficking and left wing social movements were closely related to each other. . . . The increasing cooperation in the world to curb drug trafficking made it feasible for the United States to use drug trafficking as an excuse to intervene in Panama, especially with Noriega's connection to drug cartels in Colombia. (Calderon, 2003)

The war with Iraq, which the administration claimed to be the nation's flagship war against terrorism (Afghanistan was secondary, even though it was the original bombing target), will end, and the United States will declare victory regardless of the government that is in place. But the war on terrorism is much more open-ended. Another battle or enemy will have to be discovered for the politics of fear to endure with terrorism. Indeed, U.S. military action increased throughout the Middle East during President Barack Obama's two terms (2008–2016) in the White House. The use of drones for surveillance and bombing became routine. At least five hundred drone strikes have been carried out in at least six countries against avowed enemy agents, as well as numerous civilians, as collateral damage:

> Obama's embrace and vast expansion of drone strikes against militants and terrorists will be an enduring foreign policy legacy. Whereas President George W. Bush authorized approximately 50 drone strikes that killed 296 terrorists and 195 civilians in Yemen, Pakistan and Somalia, Obama has authorized 506 strikes that have killed 3,040 terrorists and 391 civilians. (Using the average estimates provided by three nongovernmental organizations.) A technology developed and matured shortly before 9/11 to kill one individual, Osama bin Laden, became the default tactic for a range of counterinsurgency and counterterrorism missions outside of traditional battlefields. (M. Zenko, 2016)

And,

> "Between January 2012 and February 2013," The Intercept reported, "U.S. special operations airstrikes killed more than 200 people. Of those, only 35 were the intended targets. During one five-month period of the operation, according to the documents, nearly 90 percent of the people killed in airstrikes were not the intended targets." That's one campaign of many in just one country where drone killings happen. (Friedersdorf, 2016)

THE POLITICS OF FEAR IN CONTEXT

The politics of fear can exist independently of the actual fear level of the population. This paradox requires some conceptual attention. Social control is the key element and criterion of the politics of fear. Increased control is justified by appealing to citizens or their interest groups. Crime provides a good example. Opinion polls, letters to decision makers, and mass media emphasis on problems like gangs or drugs can amplify the problem and broadcast its consequences to a broader audience than the original groups that are most directly affected by the problem (Best, 1995; De Young, 2004; A. Hunt, 1997; Jenkins, 1998; Spector & Kitsuse, 1987; Walker, 2002). Thus, drugs became a societal issue that qualified as a moral panic, calling for strict action to save society from morally unraveling (Pfuhl & Henry, 1993). Citizens are also likely to support officials taking action to protect them if rationales are provided that emphasize citizen safety and the salvation of social order. This support is likely to be ensured if any actual or potential opposition to the expanded control is couched in negative language (e.g., "soft on crime," "liberals," or, in the case of terrorism, "unpatriotic"). Associating dissenters or the opposition with outsiders, deviants, or the "other" is a common propaganda technique that neutralizes the opposition. This suggests that any analysis of the politics of fear must be sensitive to the language of membership, particularly insiders and outsiders (Becker, 1973).

The politics of fear plays to the mass media–generated concerns of audiences, but it can continue long after the initial incidents have receded from public attention. As social control is increased, the state control agents that usually promote such efforts can simultaneously point to their efforts to ensure public safety as well as take credit for reducing the problem that prompted the expanded control. For example, the drug war is given credit for not only incarcerating thousands of offenders but also reducing the supply and use of illegal drugs, even though careful research shows that incarceration played little part in crime reduction or drug use. Nevertheless, the politics of fear sets the discourse for claims of its effectiveness. President George W. Bush's statement to the American Bar Association illustrates this claim. When asked his views about federal sentencing policy in view of growing evidence of the ineffectiveness of harsh sentencing, President Bush is reported to have replied,

> With respect to our overall sentencing policies, the United States is experiencing a 30-year low in crime. Nearly 27.5 million violent crimes were not committed in the last decade because of this reduction in crime. It is therefore hard to accept the claim that current sentencing policies are ineffective. Nor are they too costly when state prison budgets today account for less than 2 percent of state and local spending. Our crime rates are low because we are keeping violent, repeat offenders in prison and off our streets. (*ABA Journal*, 2004)

As noted in chapter 4, there was finally a turn against the massive U.S. incarceration rate around 2012, as skyrocketing costs led many politicians to agree with an expanding choir of police chiefs and academic research that locking up more than two million people for mainly drug offenses was also socially costly. The tone quickly changed from "tough on crime" to "smart on crime" (Altheide & Coyle, 2006). Indeed, Hillary Clinton's support of her husband's—President Bill Clinton—$30 billion Violent Crime Control and Law Enforcement Act in 1994, a euphemism for a harsh prison-sentencing bill, cost her some votes in black America when she ran for president in 2016.

The harsh sentencing guidelines remain after the initial media flurry about crime waves and drug wars have been replaced by newer threats to public order, such as terrorism. The public and policy response to fear-induced social control are interlocked with the latest societal threats. Various audiences are affected by the social control efforts and gradually take them for granted. For example, gated communities, security guards, and home security systems—complete with camouflaged landscaping and aesthetic ram-proof fences—are now part of what has been referred to as the architecture of fear (Ellin, 1997). The lesson, then, is that political enactments informed by fear can continue to communicate fear over a period of time. Indeed, enough time may lapse between fear-inspired events and dramatic media productions that some audiences may perceive that all the social control is no longer needed. However, most citizens will support the status quo and continue to cling to the prior definitions of fear-induced policies. The persistence of fear is illustrated by the actions of public schools.

THE HOMELAND SECURITY BUSINESS AND THE UNIVERSITY

The politics of fear is recognized during designated times of "crisis," such as occurred at the 9/11 attacks, but the foundation for these politics is far more basic, having begun much earlier. A key part of the politics of fear, as we discuss more in a later chapter, concerns crime, and the "crime entrepreneurs," mainly law enforcement agencies, play a large role in getting out the message about fear of crime through the local news media. Crime, after all, is the most common local news item. But city and municipal governments also play a large part in promoting fear by funding programs to deal with citizens' concerns about safety, such as establishing block watch programs and dozens of other citizen-involvement projects. Recall the previous discussion about how schools buy products and services. Many of the people working in these programs are businesspeople who, while community oriented, are also focused on the impact of crime and fear on business and products. These concerns inform a variety of routine and mundane decisions as well as policy directives.

The university researchers who studied crime, deviance, and illegal drug use helped fund the university with their research grants. Ironically, the very social sciences that had historically been the most critical of government efforts at social control were also enabling the control efforts by accepting government research grants. The universities were, then, in the social control business as well. Their research reports, while occasionally critical of certain criminal justice practices (e.g., police behavior), were nevertheless a key component in the politics of fear.

The penchant of universities for chasing large research grants continued following the 9/11 attacks, but now the emphasis has shifted from crime to terrorism. As with many institutions in the United States that pursued the multibillion-dollar largesse to "fight terrorism," universities ramped up their typically slow bureaucratic processes to approve new academic majors by adding terrorism and security to their repertoire.

The universities' most recent linkage to agencies perpetuates the framing of fear rather than offering alternative perspectives that may generate research questions to help uncover other takes on the problem. The politics of fear is self-sustaining, guiding even the "study of fear" along certain directions. Thus, these new programs were not oriented to such questions as, What do the 9/11 attacks (and other events) tell us about the place of the United States in the international order? Rather, the questions deal with reaction and adjustment within a fear framework:

> "All the students we have been involved with haven't seen this as a political issue, but as a way to come together for their country," said Melvin Bernstein, the director of university programs at the Department of Homeland Security. (Hoffman, 2004)

The politics of fear is effective because it joins basic emotional motivations with social structural contexts. The most effective politics of fear promotes extensive social control efforts that reflect audience fears and resonate with collective identity about the legitimacy of protecting "us" against "them." Leaders who provide such directions are validated by their constituents because they reflect that they are presumed to share the same deep feelings of their audiences.

> Social control takes many forms and generates resistance. Just as many students are rebelling against the imposition of uniforms today, students were protesting the politics of fear and its regulation of apparel more than forty years ago. During the 1960s, one of the organizational goals was to not have student protest. One of the first to gain public attention occurred in Des Moines, Iowa, in the 1960s, when three students, Mary Beth Tinker, John Tinker, and Chris Eckhardt, went to high school in Iowa wearing black armbands to protest the Vietnam War. The students were suspended. Some four years later in 1965, the U.S. Supreme Court, in *Tinker v. Des Moines*, ruled that students do not "shed their constitutional rights to freedom of speech or expression at the schoolhouse gate" and declared that "state-sponsored schools may not be enclaves of totalitarianism." (http://archive.aclu.org/features/f110499a.html)

Working together was promoted by appearing to be on the same team. The commonality of uniforms was enhanced when the American flag began appearing on numerous outfits in 1991 in support of the Gulf War. For the first time in U.S. history, athletic teams, along with police and fire departments, corrections officers, and private security operations, wore American flags on their uniforms. This was an important change that was sparked by supporters of the Gulf War, who reigned over numerous paramilitary organizations that were commensurate with military regimens. Other organizations that symbolized patriotic fervor and sought to demonstrate common values with their fans, such as professional athletics and the National Collegiate Athletic Association, would follow suit in the coming months. Soon, virtually all teams—athletic, police, and fire—wore American flags on their uniforms to symbolize that they belonged to the same team.

The patriotic uniform, especially in university and professional sports, steamrolled across the United States as terrorist acts at home and abroad received extensive media attention between 2010 and 2015. Teams such as baseball's San Diego Padres wore camouflage jerseys on Sunday games. Arizona State University's football team wore a special military-styled "salute-to-service" uniform honoring Pat Tillman, in a game against Oregon (October 2015; https://asunow.asu.edu/20161104-sun-devil-life-2016-salute-to-service-week-kicks-off). And the National Football League revealed in 2016 that the military had funded many patriotic themes during pregame and half-time shows.

The symbolic value of a uniform could also be measured monetarily. Firefighters who were killed when buildings collapsed as a result of 9/11 attacks were also described as "heroes" even though they were just doing their job. The monetary value of "heroism" on 9/11 was about $1 million. As part of a reported $38 billion paid to families and relatives of persons killed in the attacks, the largest payouts went to businesses, followed by disparate compensation for individuals who died. The funds available to those killed included the federal government's Victim Compensation Fund, various charities, and insurance payments:

> The families or loved ones of civilians killed on Sept. 11 received, on average, $3.1 million in government and charitable awards. The families of those who died in uniform that day—including police officers and firefighters—received more, their average compensation exceeding $4.2 million. . . . The Rand study determined that the families of the more than 400 uniformed men and women who died, out of a total of 2,976 victims, received a total of $1.9 billion. On average, the families received, in addition to a $250,000 death award for public safety officers, an average of $880,000 more in charitable awards than civilians with similar economic losses. (Chen, 2004)

The disproportionate attention to the 9/11 victims was influenced by the number of uniformed people who died that day. Police officers, especially firefighters, who entered burning buildings symbolized not only valor but also people doing their jobs. Most Americans, while saddened at the loss of any lives at the hands of the hijackers, were particularly upset with the deaths of uniformed personnel, partly because all Americans see representatives of police and fire departments in their own communities and most Americans actually know a police officer or firefighter. This made it very personal, much more than, say, wealthy stockbrokers. The class or group of firefighters and police officers was joined to the very meaning of the attacks and America's resolve to get revenge. These people, after all, were entrusted to protect us, but this implied a kind of contract with the universe: that these protectors would not themselves be harmed. If our protectors were harmed, then we were all more vulnerable to danger, and that was frightening. From a social-psychological standpoint, then, it made a lot of sense to continue the tradition of honoring men and women in certain uniforms, partly to symbolically resurrect our symbolic protection. This was further extended in 2016 when the U.S. Congress voted to approve the Justice Against Sponsors of Terrorism Act, or JASTA, legislation that would enable family members of those killed in 9/11 to sue Saudi Arabia, long thought to have enabled the aircraft hijackers. This bill basically violated an international agreement that prevented foreign governments from suing each other, which was very important for the United States with so many military personnel throughout the world. President Obama's veto was quickly overridden by a vote of 97–1, although several representatives began backpedaling within hours of the passage, concerned that this action would set a precedent for other nations to bring suits against the United States (Min Kim, 2016).

I stated that the politics of fear rests on a foundation of meanings and cultural symbols, practices, routines, and social institutions. It is helpful to look at the contributions of these factors for several conflicts over a period of years. While most of the remaining chapters examine the emphasis on terrorism and the politics of fear since 2001, none of this would have occurred without the foundation in narratives about crime that will be examined in chapter 4 or the previous wars that developed and packaged narratives about America's enemies. The mass media, especially news reports, play a major role in the propaganda process and in shaping audience perceptions of "us" and "them." The next chapter provides an overview of the operation and significance of mass media as a social institution.

THREE

The Mass Media as a Social Institution

> People were taking clues as to what kind of president he [Donald Trump] might be from a television show.
>
> —Jeff Greenfield, NBC reporter

Donald Trump's surprising election in 2016 was a victory for the politics of fear, which relies on a compliant mass media that will carry news reports and other popular-culture messages that promote fear. The politics of fear works best when the messages and meanings are part of the broader culture and are recognized and taken for granted by a mass audience. In general, this occurs as entertaining mass media reports about fear are selectively parroted—and often reedited—by self-serving Internet sites and social networks. Communication scholars have known for years that Hitler and his top propagandist, Joseph Goebbels, were correct in proposing that the "big lie" would be believed if it was reduced to very simple black-and-white terms and repeated often. Notwithstanding occasional efforts by journalists to correct the blatant lies of Trump and his minions, as noted in chapter 2, a coherent but largely false narrative about his candidacy and that of his opponents was reified and proved consequential for the election. This was enhanced by the decade-old political attack on facts-as-opinions that was preached in the United States by Fox News, as well as talk-radio stars such as Rush Limbaugh (Jamiesen & Capella, 2008).

The mass media refer to information technologies that permit "broadcasting" and communication to a large audience. The mass media are critical carriers and definers of popular culture. Traditionally, these media have included print (e.g., books, newspapers, magazines, and billboards) and electronic media (e.g., cinema, radio, and television), and, more recently, various computer communication formats, particularly the Internet. They also include personal communication devices (e.g., audio CD players and video games), as well as cell phones—especially smartphones when the latter are used for "broadcasting" of messages to social networks and Internet blogs and, in some cases, conventional media organizations.

Information technologies have made media content more accessible, personal, and visual, but they have also altered the content as well as socialized media consumers, especially on social media, to be less discerning and more accepting of information that confirm their values, emotions, and ideals. Fox News, owned by Rupert Murdoch, which also provided highly distorted news in the U.K., has found a large audience among more conservative Americans, who claimed to have been neglected by more liberal and established news media. Studies of news preferences among Democrats and Republicans in the United States suggest some unsettling trends in self-selection of information. The authors' concluding comment is prescient for understanding the trends in the ecology of communication for citizen information:

> One thing is certain. The importance of source labels to news consumption will only grow as technology diffuses and consumers increasingly customize their online news menus. As this trend progresses, there is the real possibility that news will no longer serve as a "social glue" that connects all Americans; instead, the very same lines that divide voters will also divide news audiences. (Iyengar & Morin, 2006)

The divisiveness of news became more apparent in the years following the election (2008) and reelection (2012) of President Barack Obama. As the Republican Party pursued Newt Gingrich's strategy in the mid-1990s of strongly promoting antigovernment stances among candidates for the House and Senate, Fox News provided the supportive coverage by emphasizing conflict and ultimate victory over the liberal and even "socialistic" Democratic candidates for the House and the Senate:

> As moderates came to believe that nothing was to be gained from cooperating with Democrats, they became more receptive to Mr. Gingrich's argument that the way to dislodge the entrenched majority was to polarize the electorate while attacking Congress as an irredeemable and illegitimate institution. And so the moderates propelled Mr. Gingrich into power. (McCoy, 2013)

My point is not just that Fox News is reactionary, but rather that it provided a self-serving news source for those audience members seeking validation of their preconceived views of politics, policy, and even morality. Moreover, this network, along with venomous right-wing radio talk shows (e.g., Rush Limbaugh), prepared audiences for the crude slogans and "one-liner" attacks that would come from Donald Trump in 2016 by promoting hate speech and uncivil discourse against minority groups and numerous politicians, and deriding scientific experts' views about various issues, including global warming.

Very few Republican incumbents or candidates receive negative or critical assessments from several commentators (e.g., Hannity, O'Reilly), even on the nature and impact of global warming, which Republican political strategist Frank Luntz—who conducts focus group research to identify emotionally charged words and phrases—recast as "climate change." As one focus group participant noted of climate change:

> "Sounds like you're going from Pittsburgh to Fort Lauderdale." While global warming has catastrophic connotations attached to it, climate change suggests a more controllable and less emotional challenge. (http://www.skepticalscience.com/print.php?r=326)

Fifty-five percent of the Republicans serving in the Senate and House of the 113th Congress denied that climate change is occurring, despite virtual unanimity among every world scientific organization and blue-ribbon committee charged with investigating this issue (Sierra, November/December 2013, 22). In 2012 Donald Trump stated that climate change was a hoax invented by the Chinese to gain an economic advantage: "The concept of global warming was created by and for the Chinese in order to make U.S. manufacturing non-competitive" (Wong, 2016).

Since either "climate change" or "global warming" suggests that an increase in carbon dioxide is causing important changes, including rising temperatures, melting of polar ice caps, and an increase in major weather events (e.g., hurricanes), social policies to combat this involve reducing carbon emissions by industrialized countries. A partial remedy is to reduce such emissions, but this could have an impact on fuel sources used by industry, as well as impinge on taxation of certain products sold by corporations. Accordingly, many industries oppose recognizing the concept of global warming, as well as any legislation to reduce the toxic emissions. Not surprisingly, the "climate deniers" in Congress receive more than 500 percent more in campaign contributions from "dirty energy" suppliers. There is very little news about the political context of this important issue.

Thus, while conventional news provided a semblance of a community viewing certain events—even if they may not share the same views—Fox News offered an alternative "network" approach for people who were schooled in conservative ideology and news frames (e.g., taxes in general as "burdens," estate taxes as "death taxes," the Affordable Care Act as "Obamacare," etc.), and this in turn promoted more political candidates seeking support from this network.

One well-known commentator is Rush Limbaugh, whose radio show is dedicated to all things ultraconservative—even to the point of bickering with Fox News, if they suggest that extreme reactionary radio can hurt some Republican candidates who are not far enough to the right. Limbaugh's radio career illustrates how entertaining and verbally aggressive political "talk" can fill a political niche, even as he has become a "personality" and occasional news source for mainstream media. Rush Limbaugh is the poster child of right-wing conservativism and is a regular news source for established news channels. Jamiesen and Capella's book documents Limbaugh's role in the conservative media industry:

> In this book we analyze the ways Limbaugh, Fox, and the editorial pages of the country's major conservative newspaper both have protected Reagan conservatism across a more than decade-long period and insulated their audiences from political persuasion from Democrats and the "liberal media." Specifically, we argue that these conservative media create a self-protective enclave hospitable to conservative beliefs. This safe haven reinforces the views of these outlets' like-minded audience members, helps them maintain ideological coherence, protects them from counterpersuasion, reinforces conservative values and dispositions. (Jamiesen & Capella, 2008, x)

With some fifteen million radio listeners, a widely read newsletter, and best-selling books, Limbaugh was credited with the 1994 Republican takeover of the House of Representatives, and was given honorary membership in this body by his newly elected admirers:

> "Rush Limbaugh did not take his direction from us," reported Republican House leader Tom DeLay; "he was the standard by which we ran. [He] was setting the standard for conservative thought . . . " In 1993 and 1994, he was the salvation of the conservative movement. (Jamiesen & Capella, 2008, 46)

His rise as a multimillion-dollar radio talk show host was aided by a news industry that used him for a news source, although Limbaugh's career is also tied to a wave of very popular right-wing personalities (e.g., Bill O'Reilly, Glenn Beck, and Hannity) associated with well-funded media organizations, including Fox News. This emergence is associated with established network television's embracing of entertaining news structured around conflict and fear.

Conservative media became more popular, and several more radio stations became mainstays for conservative politicians. Radio, plus the Fox Network, and a plethora of Internet and digital media connections and blogs, including widespread use of Facebook and Twitter, helped change the political landscape for extremely conservative politicians, particularly the aggressive attacks on President Obama and the Democrats after the passage of the Affordable Care Act. The media edge reduced audiences for established media and enhanced narrowly focused niche partisan media, such as Limbaugh's radio program, and popular Fox commenters like Bill O'Reilly, Glenn Beck, and Sean Hannity. The slightest edge of critical viewership was also diminished as self-selected information reinforced biases and prejudices.

> When confronted with discomforting information, humans readily find ways to reject it. Among other moves, they (and we) apply tests of

evidence to it that all but ensure its rejection. By contrast, information that shores up existing attitudes is welcomed uncritically. In short, selective exposure, selective perception, and selective retention pervade the process by which we make sense of who we are as political creatures. (Jamiesen & Capella, 2008, 75)

These media contributed handily to the success of the Tea Party's fear campaign about big government that was sparked by 2008 vice presidential candidate Sarah Palin's harangues against President Obama's effort to save the American economy by loaning money to major banks and the auto industry. This fear-based stance led to attacks against any Republican who even considered working with Democrats on legislation. Another propaganda coup was provided by Republican spin doctor Frank Luntz, who instructed his media minions to repeatedly refer to health care legislation as the "government takeover of health care," which appeared ninety times on House Speaker John Boehner's website (Adair & Holan, 2010). One of the most effective "Luntzisms" was "death panels" that would arbitrarily be in charge of life and death decisions after the government took it over! (Ray, 2015) The Tea Party contributed to the Republican gain of sixty-three seats in the House and six seats in the Senate in the 2010 midyear elections. Social media were very important to their campaigns in largely gerrymandered districts to help ensure their success. Ted Cruz, Michele Bachmann, and other ultraconservative leaders arose from these toxic symbols of fear and mistrust. The most significant impact of this campaign was to encourage "outsiders" to run for office on campaign pledges to adamantly oppose any piece of legislation that was not consistent with a narrow range of principals involving, essentially, states' rights, no governmental programs or regulations, and basic teachings consistent with evangelical beliefs. Reaching the supporters mattered, but over the next several years getting them to use Facebook and other social media became critical. As one blogger explained,

"It is your pissed off, anti-Obama, pro–Sarah Palin voters who are the most active online," Harris said. "Ted Cruz spoke to those people." (Friess, 2012)

These social media users were critical in electing Donald Trump.

Viewing Fox programs and reading numerous analyses of editorial policy as well as content analyses of programs (Hendershot, 2004; Jamiesen & Capella, 2008) shows that Fox's mantra is that most institutional news organs in the United States (e.g., NBC, CBS, ABC, CNN), including the "elite" press, such as the *New York Times*, are liberal and ultraprogressive, and are therefore biased and untrustworthy, as they publish materials that suggest moral and philosophical positions that are claimed to promote relativism and scientific investigations, and are critical of—or anti—Christian views and even have anti-American positions. This changing ecology of information in the digital age greatly enhanced the politics of fear and contributed to the further denigration of any concern with facts; entertainment and seeking confirming information came to matter most. Denial of basic facts contributed heavily to the widespread emergence of "fake news" during the 2016 presidential election campaign.

FAKE NEWS AND THE POLITICS OF FEAR

Fake news is produced typically on Internet and social media sites in order to promote certain points of view, but they are mainly to attract readers/viewers for advertising revenue. The information is blatantly false, made up, and usually absurd when viewed from any rational or semicritical perspective. In the 2016 presidential campaign fake news basically operated with a formula of promoting conflict and hateful diatribes against popular villains. Examples include reports that Hillary Clinton was a Satan worshiper, that the pope had endorsed Donald Trump, and that a Washington, D.C., pizzeria was a front for Clinton's child sex slave enterprise. All false! But believers seeking validation of views and opinions find it easily digestible.

> A BuzzFeed investigation found that of the Facebook posts it examined from three major right-wing websites, 38 percent were either false or a mixture of truth and falsehood. More discouraging, it was the lies that readers were particularly eager to share and thus profitable to publish. Freedom Daily had the most inaccurate Facebook page reviewed, and also produced the right-wing content most likely to go viral.
>
> Some of the people promoting these sites aren't even conservatives; they're foreign entrepreneurs trying to build websites that gain a large audience and thus advertising dollars.
>
> Alt-right and fake news sites for some reason have emerged in particular in Macedonia, in the former Yugoslavia. BuzzFeed found more than 100 sites about U.S. politics from a single town, Veles, population 45,000, in Macedonia. "I started the site for a easy way to make money," a 17-year-old Macedonian who runs DailyNewsPolitics.com told BuzzFeed.
>
> Facebook has been a powerful platform to disseminate these lies. If people see many articles on their Facebook feed, shared by numerous conservative friends, all indicating that Hillary Clinton is about to be indicted for crimes she committed, they may believe it. (Kristof, 2016)

Fake news, as will be discussed more in chapter 7, draws on prior news reports, and then simply exaggerates and distorts the information in order to draw viewers. A journalist who spent time with two fake news producers in Tiblisi, Georgia (not the state), and Vancouver, British Columbia, noted that they were only interested in the money they received from advertising, and were not really interested in politics at all. Their main goal "was to make money from Google ads by luring people off Facebook pages and onto his websites" (Higgins, McIntire, & Dance, 2016). The digital media make this possible:

> One window into how the meat in fake sausages gets ground can be found in the buccaneering internet economy, where satire produced in Canada can be taken by a recent college graduate in the former Soviet republic of Georgia and presented as real news to attract clicks from credulous readers in the United States. (Higgins et al., 2016)

One man explained how he first wanted to focus on fake news about Hillary Clinton:

> He realized what did drive traffic: laudatory stories about Donald J. Trump that mixed real—and completely fake—news in a stew of anti-Clinton fervor. [Another fake news producer] discovered that writing about Mr. Trump was a "gold mine." His traffic soared and his work, notably a story that President Obama would move to Canada if Mr. Trump won, was plundered by Mr. Latsabidze and other internet entrepreneurs for their own websites. "It's all Trump," Mr. Egan said by telephone. "People go nuts for it" . . . "My audience likes Trump," he said. "I don't want to write bad things about Trump. If I write fake [viz., unfavorable] stories about Trump, I lose my audience." (Higgins et al., 2016)

A big concern was having their material stolen by other fake news producers, prompting one fake writer to file a copyright suit against a competitor.

As people regularly use social media they become accustomed to the format, especially the ease with which they can copy or paraphrase what they've read and present it as their own. One of my colleagues told me about a student who had copied/plagiarized material from a website and presented it as his own work. The bewildered copier admitted doing so, but since he had claimed that he had copied it himself, it wasn't plagiarism! This is part of the challenge of new information technologies that intrude into daily activities. A *New York Times* columnist reflected on this trend:

> More than a decade ago, as a young reporter covering the intersection of technology and politics, I noticed the opposite. The internet was filled with 9/11 truthers, and partisans who believed against all evidence that George W. Bush stole the 2004 election from John Kerry, or that Barack Obama was a foreign-born Muslim. (He was born in Hawaii and is a practicing Christian.) (Manjoo, 2016a)

The politics of fear reflects important changes that have occurred in the mass media over the past fifty years. Popular culture provides the experiences and meanings for audiences about fear, social control, and scenarios for relying on the state to protect us. As chapter 2 stressed, formal agents of social control are often the source of many images and concerns as well as "news" updates about how well the policies are working. A large part of the politics of fear involves mass media formats to promote familiarity and repetitive images and slogans about crime, fear, and terrorism. This chapter examines the media logic that joins entertainment with reality.

Strange things change over time, and across communication formats. Imagine this. A posh English wedding, costing $35,000, was videotaped, but the wedding was reenacted because the mother of the bride was dissatisfied with the footage. "The video was dreadful. . . . There were no shots of the reception, and the video man missed the bride going up the aisle" (*Arizona Republic*, October 19, 1988). That seemed a bit strange in 1988, but less than twenty-eight years later things have gotten even more bizarre: in 2015 to 2016 presidential candidate Donald Trump—soon to be President Donald Trump—using Twitter to send short messages, even in the middle of the night, routinely attacked his opponents, calling them derogatory names, challenging their sexuality, demeaning women, and threatening challengers with jail terms: personal, instantaneous, and visual.

The election of reality TV host Donald Trump as president of the United States illustrates mass media are significant for our lives because they are both form and content of cultural categories and experience. As form, the mass media provide the criteria, shape, rhythm, and style of an expanding array of activities, many of which are outside the "communication" process. As content, the new ideas, fashions, vocabularies, and a myriad of types of information (e.g., politics) are acquired through mass media. This chapter offers an analysis of social institutions transformed through media to illustrate how the logic and forms of media perspectives have transformed much of the social stock of knowledge we share.

A medium is any social or technological procedure or device that is used for the selection, transmission, and reception of information. Every civilization has developed various types of media, transmitted through such social elements as territory, dwelling units, dress and fashion, language, clocks and calendars (Zerubavel, 1985), dance, and other rituals (Couch, 1984). But in the modern world, these types of media have been overshadowed by newspapers, radio, television, and more recently the Internet, and various mobile devices that constitute social media. Groups aspiring to power seek to gain leverage and legitimacy through media. In addition, select media promote a public portrayal of everyday life and political power according to the logic of the dominant institutions.

A PERSPECTIVE ON MEDIA

The mass media are enigmatic for social scientists. Traditional sociological analysis of mass media tend to treat them as a "separate institution" and regard them as just one "functioning" part of the other social institutions (DeFleur & Ball-Rokeach, 1982). The nature and impact of mass media in social life are difficult to discern because they are so much a part of culture (Comstock, 1991; Comstock & Scharrer, 1999). I consider mass media to be our most important social institution. I regard the "definition of the situation" as the key theoretical construct for the study of social life. Indeed, this is why I study mass media: they contribute to the definitions of situations in social life. Moreover, I regard social power as the capacity to define a situation for oneself and others. If the mass media contribute to social definitions, then they are also relevant for any attempt to understand "power in society."

A symbolic interactionist approach to mass media stresses interaction and context in understanding the social impact of new information technology (Maines and Couch, 1988; Surratt, 2001). Symbolic interactionism focuses on the origins of definitions and their enactment in interaction, and the consequences of such actions are rich theoretically and, most important for our analyses, grounded in the time, place, and manner of action. From this perspective, meanings are derived through a process of symbolic interaction between an actor and another (e.g., an audience), even between a television viewer and a program; mass media interaction is not "monologic" as poststructuralists assert but involves two-way (dialogic) and even three-way (trialogic) communication. Theory suggests that we exist as social beings in the midst of process. We don't own an "identity" but are featured and acknowledged as such in situations defined as such; we live in the identity process. The mass media are part of the identity process and thereby influence social interaction, everyday life, and social institutions.

Social power rests on information technology and communication. This includes symbol systems as well as assumptions about how, what, and when we communicate. Changes in information technology are rapidly altering social routines, assumptions, and social institutions. These changes constitute a "media edge" (Altheide, 2014a), which refers to a new relationship between the audience, the information sources (e.g., officials and organizational outlets), information technology (e.g., newspapers, television), and social action and routines.

> The essence of the media edge is that accounts of social reality reflect personal media and accompanying news formats and content, which are more relevant to everyday life than traditional/conventional mass media and corresponding news formats and content. It is a result of media logic, and the pervasive mediatization of social interaction. The previous chapters have examined how this works, how it is maintained, and what some of the implications are. The edge has been honed through substantive changes in technology and marketing. We are also at the edge of assumptions that have long defined the nature and process of mass communication. (Altheide, 2014a, 155–56)

A review of the major phases of media studies provides a foundation for clarifying how contemporary practices and criteria are intertwined. I draw on a previous discussions of communication phases (Altheide, 1995b, 2014a; McQuail, 1983, 176).

Phase 1. (1900 to late 1930s) The emphasis was on the ways that public opinion is shaped.

Phase 2. (1930s to 1960s) The focus turned to the nature of persuasion by film and other media, including some of the unintended consequences of media messages.

Phase 3. (1960s to 1980s) This was the period for the rise of "cultural studies" approaches (R. Williams, 1982), with emphasis on organizational production of messages, as well as media effects on beliefs, ideologies, and cultural patterns and investigating media impact on individual behaviors (e.g., voting, violence, prejudice). The nature and impact of institutionalized media forms as "media logic" (Altheide & Snow, 1979) was set forth, but it was largely ignored by researchers pursuing traditional media effects with positivistic methodology.

Phase 4. (1990 to 2000) While a number of investigators previously had emphasized a conception of "the social construction of reality," this perspective became more widely accepted. Toward the end of the twentieth century attention shifted to media and modes of representations as significant features of social life, and more research examined cultural logics, social institutions, and public discourse (Ferrarotti, 1988; Gronbeck, Farrell, & Soukup, 1991). The nature, logic, and impact of communication forms, formats, and media frames became more significant, including power, ideology, and influence. In this period, significant social analysis is inseparable from media analysis. The key concept is "reflexivity," or how the technology and logic of communication forms shape the content, and how social institutions that are not thought of as "media arenas"—such as religion, sports, politics, the family—adopt the logic of media and are thereby transformed into second-order media institutions. As media logic came to define the organizational meaning of news, journalists and those involved in the events being covered (e.g., news sources) shared perspectives about what was newsworthy and the traditional relationship between the journalist and the event was fractured, thus contributing to our "postjournalism" era. As we noted:

> The most significant media effect on social orders throughout the world is the folding in or media logic and perspectives into the daily routines and expectations of everyday life. (Altheide & Snow, 1991, 244)

Phase 5: (2000 to present [2017]). This phase is largely defined by the ecology of the communication process involving technology, formats, and social activities. Numerous researchers throughout the world adapted communication theories to cyberspace and the impact of digital media on personal identities, relationships, activities, and social institutions, including the ways in which government and finance have changed and are continuing to adjust and reflect the nonlinear and virtual features of digital media (Altheide, 2003, 2013; Kamalipour & Snow, 2004; Meyer & Hinchman, 2002; Norris, Kern, & Just, 2003). More researchers discovered, elaborated, and incorporated critical elements of media logic into emerging theories of a mediated communication order (Adolf, 2013; Couldry & Hepp, 2017; Farré Coma, 2005; Friesen, 2009; Hepp, 2011; Livingstone, 2009; Lundby, 2009).

The contemporary communication order reflects these phases of communication ecologies, yet remains grounded in several of these. There are three reasons for this: First, we have newer technologies (e.g., social media) that free audiences from being merely recipients of information from one source (e.g., a TV newscast); just as citizens are now both objects and agents of surveillance, the mediated citizen sends and receives images formatted and framed by entertainment, brevity, visual interest, and fleeting temporal and spatial relevance. Second, we are wedded to a theory of organizational truth grounded in immediate visual imagery. Third, most media users are grounded in entertainment logic that promotes idealized worldviews compatible with a variety of cultural narratives and ideologies, even if information sources include "fake news" or other sources (Wonneberger, Schoenbach, & Meurs, 2013). These considerations must be included as part of any theory of social change.

The media edge cuts through traditional social and institutional relationships, and therefore must be considered in any serious investigation of continuity and change. A key concept to emerge during this period is media logic. Media logic consists of a form of communication: the process through which media present and transmit information. Elements of this form include the various media and the formats used by these media. Format consists, in part, of how material is organized, the style in which it is presented, the focus or emphasis on particular characteristics of behavior, and the grammar of media communication. My focus is on the process and impact of this logic on other domains of social life. Formats of communication and control are central elements of this phase; communication modes are no longer regarded merely as "resources" used by powerful elements. Rather, communication formats become "topics" in their own right, significant for shaping the rhetoric, frames, and formats of all content, including power, ideology, and influence.

According to the media logic perspective, ideas, interests, and ideologies are clothed in communication logics and formats; it is the negotiability of the latter that enlivens the former. The research agenda for innovative work in mass communication will involve its "cultural reflexivity," including how "news codes," "entertainment codes," and mediated logics, styles, and rhythms have transformed our postmodern experiences through an "ecology of communication" that clarifies the complex relationships between information technology, new communication formats, and social activities. For example, research shows that significant "news sources," such as the police and politicians, now use the reflexive media logic and formats through which they have learned to "successfully communicate" via news media agencies to their various publics. Police agencies now routinely use social media to monitor public space and invite citizens to contact them about suspicious activities, as well as promote police and surveillance activities (Schneider & Trottier, 2013). The media increasingly control the negotiation process for setting the themes and discourse through which those agenda items are to be addressed (Ericson, Baranek, & Chan, 1989). These developments prompted the introduction of a more expansive view of communication in the social environment: the ecology of communication.

In its broadest terms, the ecology of communication refers to the structure, organization, and accessibility of information technology, various forums, media, and channels of information (Altheide, 1995b). Contemporary social life increasingly is conducted and evaluated on the basis of organizational and technological criteria that have contributed to the development of new communication formats that modify existing activities and help shape new activities. Social life is a communicated experience, but the rules and logics of communication have changed drastically in recent decades with the maturation of magnetic recording devices, television broadcasting, and information-processing machines (e.g., computers). Many of these points are particularly applicable to "postindustrial" societies where an increasing array of work and play involves symbols and symbolic manipulations. It is in this sense that our lives increasingly are mediated.

There are several points to consider when assessing the process and extent to which popular culture and communication formats contribute to the changing face of identity. First, the United States and many Western countries are deeply involved with media and the entire gamut of popular culture. Whether measured in terms of hours viewing television, movie attendance, music and CD purchases, popular brands of clothing, and so on, the experience, while far from uniform in our pluralistic society, is enormous (Comstock & Scharrer, 1999). Second, popular culture affords individuals a plethora of styles, personas, and potential role models. Third, popular-culture audiences are also participants, albeit in varying degrees. Fourth, the physical and symbolic environment reflects media culture as theme parks, theme cities, shopping malls, and even wars adopt media forms. Fifth, the criteria and frameworks for authenticity, credibility, competence, and acceptability can be widely shared and, indeed, taken for granted as audiences interact in this media context.

More of our daily activities are symbolic, often requiring access to some electronic media or working to comply with "document requirements" that will be processed electronically. As Carey (1989, 123) and others note, the expansion of electronics into everyday life, or what they term the "electrical sublime," did not produce the utopia sought and predicted by many, but it has had consequences for adding machinery, formats, and "logic" for getting things done, for communicating; in our age, one's competence is often judged by communicative performance, but this performance increasingly involves the direct or indirect manipulation of information technology and communication formats.

ACCESS TO MEDIA AND POPULAR CULTURE

Changes in information technology within a capitalistic context have altered mass communications processes, products, and social impacts. (Later chapters note how important Al Jazeera [aljazeera.com] was for a Middle Eastern perspective on the Iraq War. Most of the world relied on CNN for coverage of the earlier "Gulf War I.") Images of the audience and the purpose of the "media communicators" have also been affected. Let's begin with a few points about information technology.

Information technology has increased media access tremendously, particularly in the industrial countries. The availability of inexpensive paper and high-speed printers and other "presses" provide ample supplies of newspapers and magazines, although the economics of the newspaper industry can detract from "massive" circulation to more narrow, targeted consumers. Likewise, technological changes involving transistors and microprocessors have not only lowered costs per volume tremendously but also helped "miniaturize" electronic media (e.g., personal media players, telephones, pagers, and personal computers) so that they can be carried or easily accessed in a vehicle. This makes people more "reachable" and has resulted in a geometric increase in communications activity. Social media, especially Twitter, certainly helped Donald Trump get elected as president of the United States. Not only could he connect with millions of supporters but also he could bypass conventional news media editors and channels and state his views in 140 characters about political opponents, as well as numerous false statements that his followers embraced (e.g., that crime was increasing, and that immigrants accounted for much of the increase).

Changes in information technology had profound effects on how the "audience" was conceived, including what motives and capabilities were attributed to audience members by those who owned, operated, and regulated mass communication. "Broadcasting" has changed, essentially, to "narrowcasting," or more specific marketing. It was the commitment to reach a mass audience, which in turn would produce the highest possible advertising revenue, that led programmers to define their "target audience" to include a heterogeneous audience and especially women between the ages of eighteen and forty-nine. Much of this has changed as social media and the Internet make it possible to market products through individual personalities in specific niches such as Facebook, Twitter, and Snapchat. These social media "influencers"—as they're called in the advertising world—perform, promote, and even wear products that are seen instantaneously by millions of followers. One is Logan Paul, with some thirty million viewers, who is given the freedom to make up promotional messages and activities off the cuff, on the fly:

> Yeah, if someone has an idea, it's like "yeah" we just run with it, you know? When he posted the ad, it was viewed more than seven million times. And Dunkin' Donuts told us this spot had the same reach as a primetime TV ad. For one day's work, Logan Paul was paid almost $200,000. (Whitaker, 2016)

Is it worth it? One advertising professional said, absolutely:

> They're the new rock stars with a bigger audience than old Hollywood ever had a chance to access. When they take a video or a picture and push a button on their phone, [it is] immediately disseminated to millions of people across the planet. That level of access is unprecedented. (Whitaker, 2016)

Technological changes influenced the content and form of mass media, especially television news and entertainment programming. Traditional viewer choices and demographic "loyalties" shifted with the expanding choice of media and "channels." For example, network television news audiences have been declining for several years, with less than half of potential viewers now watching one of the "big 3" nightly newscasts (or CNN). Social media outlets draw on mainstream news sources, but increasingly viewers get more of their news from social media, including Internet sites like Buzzfeed, although some magazines such as the *New Yorker* appear to have more credibility:

> As the internet solidifies its role as a leading news source amid continued declines in print, news organization homepages are losing traction. Magazine stories are increasingly unmoored from the outlets that published them, and from the brands that once all but guaranteed their legitimacy. In the US, more than 60 percent of social media users now access news through platforms like Facebook and Twitter, and news organizations harvest nearly half their traffic from social media. (Funt, Gourarie, & Murtha, 2016)

Taste cultures and media communities accompany broadcasting (i.e., narrowcasting) alternatives. Communication is part of everyday life, personal style, and identity. Products and services are geared for age and consumption identities that crosscut age, gender, social class, and ethnicity. Media logic, as Robert Snow predicted some thirty-five years ago, continues to envelope everyday life and affects interaction and routine social activities; also, constant information feed can be important when news about events and issues are aligned with the entertainment format, including instantaneous, visual, and personal presentations.

> Consider just a few trends in media access. Americans use media, especially social media, more—over 10 hours a day—but TV a little less. The extensive media use does not include texting, which many younger people spend hours each day, although lower income teens with smartphones are communicating nearly twice as much as their wealthier counterparts (6 hours compared to 3 hours) (https://www.commonsensemedia.org/sites/default/files/uploads/pdfs/census_factsheet_teensandsmartphones.pdf).
>
> An estimated 81 percent of American adults use a smartphone regularly, with the number of users growing by more than 20 million in the past year. . . . Of the additional hour in media time that Nielsen has measured this year, smartphone usage accounts for 37 minutes and tablets 12 minutes. Online smartphone use averages an hour and 39 minutes a day—more than double what it was two years ago, Nielsen said. (Bauder, 2016)

However, youth with smartphones are spending more than 4.5 hours a day accessing social media, playing video games, and more (https://www.commonsensemedia.org/sites/default/files/uploads/pdfs/census_factsheet_teensandsmartphones.pdf). With more than half the world's population estimated to be on Facebook, it is perhaps no surprise that people worldwide spend over $265—mostly on digital media, while per capita expenditure on media in the United States in 2014 was $1,160 (https://digitalcontentnext.org/blog/2016/03/11/us-and-global-consumer-spending-on-media-content-and-technology-continues-to-rise/).

Increasingly, media consumptions and use influence how we spend time and regulate daily routines. Normal use of media is also related to identity and how we are known to others. Three things happen in a media age where identities and products are marketed interchangeably and synergistically: (1) we experience them in the same time, place, and manner; (2) the product and process are reflexive (the product is the identity); identity appears explicitly and implicitly in numerous advertisements; and (3) media images "loop" (Manning, 1998) through various media and messages, moving, for example, from initial claim to established fact to background information to standard. Product labels as key membership categories are a triumph for popular culture and mass mediation. And the freedom to purchase and become a member—and participant—reflects the actor's individual freedom and decision making. Social interaction with peers begins to reflect and turn on such familiarity as global popular culture socializes an international audience. A youth from India, who had worked for a bogus call center that would try to extort money from Americans, commented on his desire and readiness to migrate to the United States.

The Fast and the Furious, Vin Diesel and Robert Downey Jr. "I've spent so much time getting to know it, familiarizing myself with its states, talking to its people," Mr. Dubey said. "I feel a bond." (E. Barry, 2017)

An important aspect of the definition of the situation is social identity. The mass media are key to the identity process in the postmodern world (Altheide, 2000; Cerulo, 1997). Media logic that contributes to the definition of situations and identity has been examined in various studies of political reporting and action. Numerous examples of comparative studies of the political relevance of the news process illustrate how context, elite news sources, and communication formats guide news content (Doyle, 2001; D. M. Hunt, 1999; Wasburn, 2002).

The presentation of self has changed drastically. When both actor and audience have at least one foot in popular culture, they hold shared meanings for validating the actor's performance. The mass media promote identity as a resource to satisfy individually oriented needs and interests to "be whomever you want to be." Popular culture's emphasis on entertainment and commodification of the self informs this emphasis. Grossberg, Wartella, and Whitney (1998) agree with numerous researchers who have documented the impact of media logic on everyday life: "Ultimately the media's ability to produce people's social identities, in terms of both a sense of unity and difference, may be their most powerful and important effect" (206).

The impact of mass media on social identity is also evident in the current development of massive electronic communication, or what I term the "E-audience" (Altheide, 2002c). The E-audience refers to those individuals who dwell partially in cyberspace and engage in substantial amounts of electronic interaction and communication (e.g., email, Internet surfing and specific Internet use, pagers, cell phones, and so on). A distinctive feature of this audience is a sense of control and entitlement to communicate whereby the communicative act is demonstrated and displayed to self and others through electronic technology. This audience is constantly interactive but does not exist in relation to a fixed medium (e.g., television). Rather, this audience is very active and reflexive, meaning that it takes into account other communication experiences and renderings of them in other mass media and popular culture. Moreover, the communication process transcends work and play.

Public space is communicative space, but rather than dealing with people in one's immediate surroundings, the existential actor reaches for meaning and involvement as display and communication with those more familiar, even if they are not immediately in one's physical presence. One's personal definition of the situation and of self is what matters, not that shared by others in one's surroundings. So we carry on private conversations out loud on cell phones in public places. Civility gets compromised, manners are called into question, and individual rights are set forth in defense. It is happening all over the world.

Any format that sustains identity will be valued, pursued, and mastered. I suggest that the E-audience, largely because of its visible communicative nature and the implications for identity, increasingly "wear" communicative skill as fashion and as an extension of their technological persona. Of course, all of this has implications for marketing and "commodification" of format:

> Users of leading-edge cell phones know that custom ring tones are out and ring melodies, which signal an incoming phone call by playing short clips of well-known tunes, are in. . . . Like cell phone faceplates, ring melodies are becoming "a fashion item," says Your Mobile CEO Anthony Stonefield. . . . Seamus McAteer, senior analyst at Jupiter Communications, says ring tunes are a way "to customize this very personal device. Everyone wants to be different but still fit in." (www.usatoday.com/life/cyber/tech/net023.htm)

Fitting in can also have deadly consequences if it means succumbing to systematic propaganda to gain one's allegiance for violence. We shall see in more detail in chapter 7 that this has been true of recruits by the Islamic State in Syria (ISIS), who sought to be part of a propaganda-themed glorious past that they could also enjoy in the future, simply by either traveling to Syria and becoming a fighter or becoming a martyr, say, in the United States. This occurred when two brothers planned the Boston Marathon bombing in 2013 and a husband and wife planned the San Bernardino massacre in 2015. Social media, especially texts and personalized tweets, are very inviting, whether they are from a presidential candidate like Donald Trump or an Islamic terrorist recruiter: both employ the same tactics—personal, emotional-rousing messages (and gifts) that support simplified and socially inclusive promises in order to gain trust; and both share similar goals—to alter behavior (e.g., voting, bomb-making, etc.) in order to become a member of something glorious.

Propagandists use praise, promises, and gifts to harvest potential recruits. For example, "Alex" was pursued by ISIS with hundreds of messages, including ideological teachings and books on Twitter, Skype, and email, and letters and packages with the allure with promises of marriage as well as gifts of chocolate and even money. Cautioned by friends and other online detractors to avoid this brand of Islam, "Alex" replied:

> "Can I just ignore them?" Alex asked, "I swear I have, like since last night, cutting off ties is hard and they gave me stuff." On Feb. 13, @KindLadyAdilah advised her to stop accepting their gifts. Alex promised she would tell Faisal to stop sending them. But a few days later another envelope arrived at her cousin's house, containing more chocolate and a Hallmark card decorated with a cutout of a kitten. When she

opened it, two $20 bills fell out. "Please go out and enjoy a Pizza TO-GETHER," it says, signed, "Twitter friends." (Callimachi, 2015)

The important point is that the politics of fear is promoted by media production, use, and routines. Without these new media, Donald Trump would not be president and the contemporary onslaught by ISIS and other terrorist groups would not be as successful. In contemporary society, the logic of media provides the form for shared "normalized" social life. Indeed, Meyrowitz (1985) has argued provocatively that social hierarchies are communication hierarchies and that access to the codes of various media varies inversely with support for social hierarchies. Historically, powerful people used media to define the time, place, and manner of certain activities, including the knowledge to participate in them (Couch, 1984). Thus, Meyrowitz suggests, because television is so widely available and exposes audience members to the same information, it tends to reduce social hierarchies. As the dominant medium in our age, television becomes even more important than print because of the visual nature of the information being transmitted as well as its capacity to transcend temporal locations of experience. Thus, young people can learn at an early age how to be older. The awareness of inequality as well as the promotion of dreams and catastrophic national agendas are enhanced with social media that are instantaneous, personal, and visual.

The present-day dominance of media has been achieved through a process in which the general form and specific formats of media have become adopted throughout society so that cultural content is basically organized and defined in terms of media logic. It is not a case of media dictating terms to the rest of society but rather an interaction between organized institutional behavior and media. In this interaction, the form of media logic has come to be accepted as the perspective through which various institutional problems are interpreted and solved.

MEDIA LOGIC AND SOCIAL INSTITUTIONS

Today, all social institutions are media institutions. A major effect has been on entertainment as content and also as a perspective, orientation, and expectation of audience members. Entertainment and news programming provide "content" that may influence political agendas. There are numerous analyses of mass media content and programming, and only a few points will be made here (Barnouw, 1990). While the major media impact, in my view, goes beyond the mere content of such programs, they are relevant for how many people, especially politicians, make decisions. A key part of the communication order is to give the audience what the message "producers" believe they will accept and find entertaining. According to Snow (1983), one formula that has been used for this is following "ideal norms."

Ideal norms generally refer to those rules and strategies that are regarded as the best possible way to live. Honesty, modesty, fidelity, and hard work are examples of ideals that people will agree to at the public level, even though deviation from those ideals is quite common in everyday life. (Later chapters illustrate how ideal norms are appealed to in propaganda campaigns to promote more social control.) The ideal-norm format resonates through most prime-time offerings, including the news and some daytime programs. Viewers may object to specific acts of violence or scenes and dialogue that emphasize sex, but the ideal of justice and family that forms the heart of the program is rarely challenged. One of the most common "scenarios" to convey these ideal norms is the family or group context. Virtually every popular TV show and Internet streaming program involves symbolic integration—often vicarious participation—and involvement with groups or quasi-families.

Media logic becomes a way of seeing and interpreting social affairs. This involves an implicit trust that we can communicate the events of our daily lives through the various formats of media. People take for granted that information can be transmitted, ideas presented, moods of joy and sadness expressed, major decisions made, and business conducted through media. But at the same time, there is a concern that media can and will distort what they present. This fear of media has been defined by some as a conspiracy in which powerful media moguls willfully set out to determine the character of behavior: how people vote, what they buy, what is learned, and what is believed (Chomsky, National Film Board of Canada, & Necessary Illusions, 1992). No doubt there is intent to shape attitudes and "sell soap," but this is not the most critical factor in understanding mass media.

PUBLIC PERCEPTION AND SOCIAL ISSUES

Mass media materials are organized through an entertainment format that promotes conflict and drama, vicarious and emotional identification, and spontaneity. Mass media and popular culture are relevant in the production of meaning by providing significant symbolic meanings and perspectives that may be drawn on by individuals in specific social situations (Altheide, 2000). One example is the increased use of fear. Research on the use and extent of the word *fear* in news reports indicates a sharp increase during the middle 1990s, suggesting the emergence of a discourse of fear (Altheide, 1997, 2002b; Altheide & Michalowski, 1999). The combination of entertaining news formats with these news sources has forged a fear-generating machine that trades on fostering a common public definition of fear, danger, and dread (Furedi, 1997; Glassner, 1999). Crime and violence have been a staple of entertainment and news programming for decades but have become even more graphic and focused

(Surette, 1998), particularly with numerous daytime talk shows and reality television programs featuring "real cops" and so on (Fishman & Cavender, 1998).

An impressive literature on popular culture in the United States, particularly concerning crime, suggests multiple effects of media messages (Warr, 1980, 1983, 1985, 1987, 1990, 1992), including the rise of "cultural criminology" (Ferrell, Hayward, & Young, 2015; Ferrell & Sanders, 1995) and "perceptual criminology" or the notion that "many of the problems associated with crime, including fear, are independent of actual victimization . . . because it may lead to decreased social integration, out-migration, restriction of activities, added security costs, and avoidance behaviors" (Ferraro, 1995, 3).

Researchers have argued for decades that such concerns are connected to the mass media coverage of news as well as entertainment (MacKuen & Coombs, 1981; Surette, 1998). An abundant body of research and theory suggests that the news media contribute to public agendas, official and political rhetoric, and public perceptions of social problems as well as preferences for certain solutions (Graber, 1984; Shaw & McCombs, 1977). For many people, the mass media in general and the news media in particular are a "window" on the world. How the public views issues and problems is related to mass media, although researchers disagree about the nature of this relationship (Gerbner & Gross, 1976; Gunter, 1987; Hirsch, 1980; Katz, 1987; Schlesinger, Tumber, & Murdock, 1991; Skogan & Maxfield, 1981; R. Sparks, 1992; Zillman, 1987). This is particularly apparent when fear is associated with popular topics like crime, violence, drugs, and gangs, which have become staples of news reports as well as of entertainment media. What audiences perceive as a "crime problem" is a feature of popular culture and an ecology of communication (Bailey & Hale, 1998; Ferrell & Sanders, 1995).

Mass-mediated experiences, events, and issues are particularly salient for audiences lacking direct, personal experience with the problem. Indeed, many observers have wondered how it is possible for a comparatively healthy and safe population to perceive themselves to be so at risk. Research on media violence suggests that violent content can lead viewers to perceive life as scary, dangerous, and fearful (Gerbner & Gross, 1976; Signorielli & Gerbner, 1988; Signorielli, Gerbner, & Morgan, 1995). Linda Heath and Kevin Gilbert note in a review of research on mass media's relevance to crime that "because the media often distort crime by over representing more severe, intentional, and gruesome incidents, the public overestimates its frequency and often misperceives reality" (Heath & Gilbert, 1996, 371). Broader effects of mass media presentations include the ways in which public perceptions of problems and issues (the texts they construct from experience) incorporate definitions, scenarios, and language from news reports (Bennett, 1988; Ericson, 1995; Ferraro, 1995). Indeed, how the mass media report risk suggests that journalists need to be more conscientious and informed in their accounts (Willis & Okunade, 1997).

CHANGING SOCIAL INSTITUTIONS

Virtually all social institutions have been affected by the mass media, popular culture, and changes in information technology. The most general impact has been a move toward an entertainment orientation that is widely shared by "audiences" that participate in institutional activities. The consequences may be described as "media culture" (Altheide, 1995b; Altheide & Snow, 1991). In a broad sense, media culture refers to the character of such institutions as religion, politics, or sports that develops through the use of media. Specifically, when media logic is employed to present and interpret institutional phenomena, the form and content of those institutions are altered. The changes may be minor, as in the case of how political candidates dress and groom themselves, or they may be major, such as the entire process of present-day political campaigning in which political rhetoric says very little but shows much concern. Or the changes may be more significant, as in the way that foreign policy, diplomacy, and "war in prime time" is very much informed by satellite and Internet capability. Religion has adopted a television entertainment perspective to reach the people. In sports, rule changes, styles of play, sports stadiums, and the amount of money earned by players are directly related to the application of a television format.

MEDIA LOGIC AND THE POLITICS OF FEAR

Media politics have entered the framework of all institutions. Serious personal criminal attacks happen rarely, but they are regarded as typical and quite common by American citizens because virtually all mass media reports about crime focus on the most spectacular, dramatic, and violent. With the images of blood, guns, psychopaths, and suffering in front of them and inside their heads, it is quite difficult to offer programmatic criticisms of our current approach to crime and accompanying issues such as prisons and other modes of dispute resolution, including restitution and negotiation.

Highly dramatized school shootings illustrate how formal agents of social control work through the entertainment-oriented problem frame to promote social images of impending doom that in turn fuel public fears and promote more surveillance and social control of social institutions like schools. Notwithstanding the rare nature of school violence, including a "downward trend" since 1992 (and the fact that each American child has one chance in two million of getting killed on school grounds), the exceptional cases that occur have been "linked" as part of an epidem-

ic and trend calling for stringent surveillance and "zero tolerance" of
"weapons" (e.g., pen knives) in school, possibly resulting in expulsion
(Hancock, 2001). The discourse of fear can be illustrated with the impact
of publicity about the shootings on April 20, 1999, at Columbine High
School in Littleton, Colorado. Extrapolating Cerulo's (1997) conceptual
framework, school and fear have been joined through the repetitive news
reports that emphasized narrative sequences as "victims" (twelve dead
classmates) and "performers" (senior students Harris and Klebold) along
with icon-like electronic and magazine visual images of students shot by
students. The joining is so complete that the term *Columbine* implies
school but also fear, social control, and, above all, loss (Altheide, 2009a;
Muschert, 2007; Muschert, 2009). One report argues that students' admission essays to colleges and universities are heavily influenced by Columbine's images and meanings:

> The word "Columbine" is shorthand for a complex set of emotions
> ranging from anxiety to sadness to empathy. . . . "Violence has seeped
> into their daily lives. . . . The once-tranquil school has become a place of
> lockdown drills. Young people are being robbed of what traditionally
> has been the carefree time of adolescence. . . ." The essays show how
> violence in distant schools changed students' habits, and how they
> came to terms with a newfound recognition that safety is not guaran-
> teed. . . . "I think students today heard the word Columbine and they
> are horrified by the image that they have, the negative feelings." ("'Col-
> umbine' Essays Inundating Colleges," *Arizona Republic*, April 20, 2001,
> A13)

So powerful is the discourse of fear, fueled by the massive lobbying of
the National Rifle Association (NRA), that has ravaged the United States
since the 9/11 attacks that most efforts to curtail gun violence have failed.
This includes proposals to restrict assault weapons and to make it more
difficult for mentally unstable persons to acquire firearms. While schools
are one of the safest places for children to be—compared to home and
neighborhoods—there have been some 270 shootings since Columbine.
These include the Virginia Tech slaughter (thirty-three dead) in 2007, and
the especially gripping massacre of twenty first-graders and six teachers
at Newtown, Connecticut (twenty-eight victims), in 2012. But even here,
social media provided outlets for conspiracy theorists suspicious of all
government activity and efforts to regulate firearms. One Internet site
claimed that the Sandy Hook atrocity was a governmental production
using child actors, with the aim of bolstering antigun sentiments (Gorman, 2016).

The interaction and shared meanings of news workers who follow the
entertainment format and audience members who "experience" the
world through these mass media lenses promote sufficient communication to achieve the news organization's goals of grabbing the audience

while also enabling the audience member to be "informed" enough to exchange views with peers. Shared knowledge about the social world in a mass-mediated society tends to be about "bad news."

Public order increasingly is presented as a conversation within media formats, which may be envisioned as a give-and-take, point-counter-point, problem-solution (Ferrarotti, 1988; Furedi, 1997). For example, when mass media depictions stress the breakdown of social order and suggest a failing by agents of social control, we can expect those agents to present dramaturgical accounts of their resolve and success in order to increase citizens' confidence in them. Donald Trump paraded rape victims and survivors of those killed by immigrants in order to heighten voter fears.

The previous examples suggest that formal agents of social control increasingly use the mass media to reach into more areas of the public order. Just as judges use gonzo justice to demonstrate (and promote) their moral character and resolve to audiences who know little about their work routines, other bureaucratic workers, such as politically ambitious county prosecutors, rely on the news media not only to publicize their "achievements" but also to actually work with and through the news formats to "do good work." With an escalating number of interest group concerns, the domain of state control has expanded considerably, and the orientation and tactics of state power have also increased beyond the traditional domains of "public life" to more proactive investigation and surveillance. As Marx (1988) notes,

> Social control has become more specialized and technical, and, in many ways, more penetrating and intrusive. In some ways, we are moving toward a Napoleonic view of the relationship between the individual and the state, where the individual is assumed to be guilty and must prove his or her innocence. That state's power to seek out violations, even without specific grounds for suspicion, has been enhanced. With this comes a cult and a culture of surveillance that goes beyond government to the private sector and the interaction of individuals. (2 ff.)

The exponential growth of the surveillance and undercover options across international, national, state, county, and city jurisdictions has been widely documented (Marx, 1988; Staples, 1997). While much of this work has focused on the increased use of "agents provocateurs," our interest is in the way certain state tactics and orientations can be blended with prevailing mass communication routines and patterns.

The mass media formats that promote visuals packed with dramatic action were certainly consistent with the entire operation. It was regarded as "made for television evidence," even if it may not have been perfect for "courtroom" evidence. As with the "wedding video" that began this chapter, visual reality increasingly is what counts. Several chapters that follow illustrate how visuals of the enemy, such as "the falling towers" from the 9/11 attacks and the videotape of combat in Iraq in both Gulf wars, contributed to the public perception of danger and victory against a strange enemy.

Popular culture entertainment and media logic contribute to the international landscape as well. The politics of fear is apparent in mass media coverage of negative war news. Ironically, much of the news reporting will be propaganda about positive developments rather than fear itself. Major news media do not present bad news, such as casualties, in a prominent place. Deaths of soldiers seldom appear on page 1. When not at war, any American killed abroad—especially if they are affiliated with the government—is quite newsworthy and is featured in major news sections. Not in wartime, however, especially the most recent Iraq War. News organizations have been told to not dwell on negative news, so many newspapers bury reports about American casualties in small-print headlines deep inside the newspaper. The exception to this is when a "local" soldier is killed, in which case the story will be framed as a patriotic one. The young man's or woman's death will be celebrated as an example for all of us to follow. Often we will be told that the person always wanted to join, for example, the Marines and be a soldier, and the article may include a statement that he or she was motivated by the 9/11 attacks and felt that it was his or her duty to join. Seldom will a statement appear like the one in *Newsweek* about Marine Staff Sergeant Russell Stay, who, a short time before he was killed, gave this advice in a letter to his five-year-old son: "Be studious, stay in school and stay away from the military. I mean it" (*Newsweek*, December 6, 2004, 21).

If the politics of fear lasts long enough, the lack of negative coverage about the costs of war or other military adventures will become commonplace. Indeed, the news discourse largely constitutes the politics of fear for mass audiences because this is their main source of information about the state of the political world. Soon, curtailing negative reports about the government, especially foreign policy, becomes the baseline for journalists and editors and, over time, their audiences as well. News media do not like to be cast as unpatriotic or "left" or "liberal." Those terms, especially *liberal*, were popularized during the Reagan administration and have continued to dominate news discourse and commentary about news content.

The politics of fear is apparent not only in news content but also in the basic framework of news. This means that the dominant framing and organization of news material is intended to support the government and the status quo. While there are a few news organizations that are less compliant, their exceptionalism makes them appear to be even more deviant from the way that news reporting is expected to be done. Journalists understand that any critical reports will be interpreted as editorializing against the administration. Yet a few still report negative and controversial materials, but they are heavily documented.

One example is the news reporting about the prisoner abuse in U.S.-controlled prisons in Iraq (Abu Ghraib) and Guantanamo Bay, Cuba. According to reports in the *New Yorker*, *Newsweek*, the MoveOn.org website, and others, the problem began when the Bush administration approved a plan to treat terrorist suspects differently than prisoners of war. The latter are protected (in civilized nations) by the Geneva Convention's guidelines for the treatment of prisoners (Hersh, 2004).

President Bush approved a policy that the Geneva Convention wouldn't apply to suspected al Qaeda and Taliban fighters held in Guantanamo Bay. When the war in Iraq started to go badly, Secretary of Defense Donald Rumsfeld extended these aggressive interrogation policies to Iraqi prisons. According to *Newsweek*,

> It was an approach that they adopted to sidestep the historical safeguards of the Geneva Conventions, which protect the rights of detainees and prisoners of war. In doing so, they overrode the objections of Secretary of State Colin Powell and America's top military lawyers—and they left underlings to sweat the details of what actually happened to prisoners in these lawless places. While no one deliberately authorized outright torture, these techniques entailed a systematic softening up of prisoners through isolation, privations, insults, threats and humiliation—methods that the Red Cross concluded were "tantamount to torture." (Barry & Isikoff, 2004)

Widely regarded as both illegal and inhumane, Guantanamo Bay and torture came under more scrutiny with the election of President Barack Obama in 2008. He immediately called for the end of waterboarding and other methods of torture, and took immediate steps to close the base. However, congressional opposition prevented this throughout his eight years in office, and the best that could be achieved was to reduce the number of illegally incarcerated people from 780 to 60 (https://www.humanrightsfirst.org/sites/default/files/gtmo-by-the-numbers.pdf).

The U.S. Congress approved legislation outlawing waterboarding and other forms of torture. Republican Arizona senator John McCain, who had been tortured as a prisoner in North Vietnam, led much of this effort. Two psychologists under contract with the Central Intelligence Agency (CIA), who oversaw much of the brutal treatment of prisoners, were investigated for illegal and unethical activity.

The treatment of military prisoners was an issue throughout the Middle East wars. Some journalists obtained photographs of prisoners being beaten and sexually humiliated, and other pictures were sent to relatives of guards at the prison in Iraq. The visuals were compelling and raised critical comments by congressional leaders as well as human rights organizations. The reports were heavily documented with many facts and quotations from various government and military officials. Official inquiries were held, and several enlisted men and women were court-martialed while senior-ranking officers were allowed to resign or were exonerated with typical bureaucratic accounts (e.g., other intelligence officials were in charge):

> High-level officials in the Pentagon were sent from Guantanamo Bay to Iraq to implement the more aggressive policies, and it appears that command of the prison was placed in the hands of military intelligence officers. Techniques that had been approved only for suspected al-Qaeda terrorists were suddenly applied to Iraqi prisoners (up to 90% of whom were mistakenly detained, according to the Red Cross).

While many Americans were hopeful that the specter was behind them of U.S. officials and military engaging in torture, the Twitter-inspired candidate for president, Donald Trump, stated in a primary election debate in New Hampshire on February 8, 2016, that he was in favor of torture:

> DONALD TRUMP: Well, I'll tell you what. In the Middle East, we have people chopping the heads off Christians. We have people chopping the heads off many other people. We have things that we have never seen before—as a group, we have never seen before what's happening right now. The medieval times—I mean, we studied medieval times. Not since medieval times have people seen what's going on. I would bring back waterboarding, and I'd bring back a hell of a lot worse than waterboarding. (http://www.truth-out.org/news/item/34748-trump-leads-gop-charge-embracing-torture-i-d-bring-back-worse-than-waterboarding)

This assertion, along with several statements he made demeaning and threatening undocumented immigrants, refugees, and Muslims in the United States, promoted the politics of fear.

CONCLUSION

The politics of fear relies on public perceptions of threats and enemies. These are promoted by repeated news and popular-culture (e.g., movies) images of the "bad guys." The mass media and popular culture contribute to the definition of situations and audience expectations and criteria for self-presentations for themselves and others. A good example was the popular series 24, starring Kiefer Sutherland, who played an agent for the Counter Terrorism Unit, a fictional convergence of the FBI, the CIA, and the less public Homeland Security operations. The key backdrop is the 9/11 attacks, setting the stage for seemingly endless threats from ruthless Middle Eastern terrorists. The series of twenty-four episodes takes the viewer through an entire day of hard-hitting, fast-paced action of a renegade agent against a very well-organized group of terrorists. What is very important for our purposes is that this is the first television program that shows and legitimizes U.S. agents torturing suspects in a "race against time" to get information before the terrorist weapon kills millions of U.S. citizens. This introduction to torture by Americans on American television screens was a preview of photos and accounts of U.S. soldiers and other contract workers—also referred to as mercenaries—torturing Iraqi prisoners in Abu Ghraib prison in Iraq. Similar scenes have been presented on other TV shows such as the *Blacklist*, as well as numerous movies.

The reality of torture is muted by popular-culture depictions that are important for familiarizing and desensitizing audiences to grotesque cruelty. The news media provide sparse coverage of torture and conduct that is reprehensible to most Americans. Like many of the semisecret "black operations" engaged in by the U.S. terrorist forces during the past thirty years, murderous activities are not regarded as part of U.S. foreign policy, but when they do come to light, the brutal tactics are likely to be presented as tough but necessary. We have already seen how the United States handles charges of torture, but what is more astounding is when suspects are turned over to other countries that will apply torture on behalf of the United States. The practice is referred to as "extraordinary rendition" and was practiced against a Canadian citizen who was suspected of being involved in terrorist activities. On September 26, 2002, Maher Arar, a thirty-four-year-old man who had immigrated to Canada from Syria as a teenager, was picked up at Kennedy International Airport. American officials handed Arar over to Syria, a nation condemned by the Bush administration and others as an "outlaw nation" that supports terrorism. Arar was tortured for a year, all the while insisting on his innocence. Of course, he had never been charged with anything, just shipped out of the United States. According to *New York Times* columnist Bob Herbert (2005),

> According to the State Department, torture was most likely to occur at one of the many detention centers run by the Syrian security forces, "particularly while the authorities are trying to extract a confession or information about an alleged crime or alleged accomplices."
>
> Extraordinary rendition is antithetical to everything Americans are supposed to believe in. It violates American law. It violates international law. And it is a profound violation of our own most fundamental moral imperative—that there are limits to the way we treat other human beings, even in a time of war and great fear.

Popular culture legitimizes torture as audiences spend more time with these formats, the logic of advertising, entertainment, and popular culture becomes taken for granted as a "normal form" of communication. As Couch (1995) noted, evocative rather than referential forms of communication now dominate the meaning landscape. The referential forms fall before the electrified rolling formats that change everyday life with the look and swagger of persona, entertainment, and action.

One way power is manifested is by influencing the definition of a situation. Cultural logics inform this process and are therefore powerful, but we are not controlled (and certainly not determined) by them, particularly when one's effective environment contains meanings to challenge the legitimacy, veracity, and relevance of certain procedures. Resistance can follow, but it is likely to be formatted by ecologies of communication. Indeed, the contribution of expanded discourses of control to the narrowing or expansion of resistance modes remains an intriguing area of inquiry.

Some of the most significant cultural logics can be conceptualized within the ecology of communication that is part of the effective environment that competent social actors must take into account as they forge definitions of the situations. Just as "markets" contain a leveling dimension (e.g., anyone with the price of admission can play), so too does the increasingly technical information technology, with its "common key" to a host of activities. And while the price of admission excludes many, so too does the activity built on formats not easily accessible to everyone. It is within these symbolic boundaries that freedom and constraint are routinized and dramaturgically played out through an expanding array of social definitions in the social construction of reality. The next chapter examines how media constructions of crime and danger fuel fears of terrorism and appeals for more social control and drastic action from leaders.

FOUR

Crime and Terrorism

The crime scene, marked off in yellow police tape, doesn't move; no matter when the reporter arrives there's always a picture to shoot, preferably live. No need to spend off-camera time digging, researching, or even thinking. Just get to the crime scene, get the wind blowing through your hair, and the rest will take care of itself.

—Grossman, 1997

Crime continues to hold the attention of vast audiences in the United States and much of the world, but its type and character have somewhat changed with the proliferation of new information technologies and social media formats that render experience more instantaneous, personal, and visual so that more people are filming and recording criminal events—by street criminals as well as police officers—and often their bloody aftermath. This has also changed terrorism events, as would-be terrorists now incorporate media consideration in their planning, staging, and execution, as well as follow-up and even rebuttal of claims and charges by authorities in countries that were attacked.

Objective indicators of risk and danger in American life suggest that most U.S. citizens are healthier and safer and live more predictable lives than at any other time in history, yet numerous surveys indicate these same citizens perceive that their lives are very dangerous (Surette, 2014). The politics of fear requires specific topics or events to promote fear. In the United States, crime policies led the way in promoting crime as a major public issue that citizens should fear and that authorities should control. Crime and fear dominate most U.S. newspapers and television news reports. This chapter examines how crime coverage is linked to entertainment formats that provide the basic underlying logic of commercial television (and newspapers). I draw from two decades of research on the social construction of fear (Altheide, 1997, 2002b, 2014a,

2014b; Altheide & Michalowski, 1999) as well as extensive research on the nature, use, and impact of "moral panic" research that examines how claims makers and elected officials exaggerate threats of certain kinds of criminals and crimes in order to promote broad reforms, usually involving more social control (Altheide, 2009b; Cohen, 1980; Garland, 2008; Victor, 2006). Such efforts hinge on media campaigns to heighten public awareness and fears about the impact of such transgressions on the current and future moral order and safety. One reason crime is so popular is that it is almost always linked to "fear," the most basic feature of entertainment in popular culture. This emphasis has produced a discourse of fear, defined in chapter 1 as the pervasive communication, symbolic awareness, and expectation that danger and risk are a central feature of everyday life. The discourse of fear has important consequences for social policy, public perceptions of social issues, the demise of public space, citizens who are becoming more "armed" and "armored," and the promotion of a new social identity—the victim—that has been exploited by numerous claims makers, including politicians, who promote their own propaganda about national and international politics. These points will be followed by a brief discussion of alternative news formats.

Crime news has been a staple of journalism for decades (Kappeler & Potter, 2005; Surette, 2014). For many years, newspapers emphasized sensational and even erotic aspects of homicides and brutal assaults, sex crimes, and kidnappings (Soothill & Walby, 1991). This emphasis became more "rational" with the emergence of movie "newsreels" as well as television news and the ability to "see" crime scenes, victims, and the accused. Another major change is the rise of a pervasive mass-mediated popular culture that virtually engulfs everyday life. In another age there was the mass media, and there was reality; in our age, there is popular culture—everywhere—and even "reality" is presented to us as entertainment programming. In the United States, for example, dozens of "reality" television programs are about crime and "crime fighting," as caricatures of criminals and police officers (Fishman & Cavender, 1998) are presented back to back with sexually evocative images of people roaming "remote islands" in search of love, treasure, and security.

Running through all this programming is the commercially inspired entertainment format. As suggested by Snow's (1983) analysis of "media culture," the entertainment format emphasizes, first, an absence of the ordinary; second, the openness of an adventure, outside the boundaries of routine behavior; and, third, a suspension of disbelief by the audience member. In addition, while the exact outcome may be in doubt, there is a clear and unambiguous point at which it will be resolved. Packaging such emphases within dramatic formats (visual, brief, and action oriented) produces an exciting and familiar tempo to audiences. Moreover, as audiences spend more time with these formats, the logic of advertising, entertainment, and popular culture becomes taken for granted as a "normal form" of communication.

There are two reasons why crime is so prevalent in American television and, increasingly, throughout the world. First, as noted, crime is connected to fear, a staple of the entertainment format. Second, crime is very easy to cover and therefore fits well with scheduling and personnel constraints of local television. As one vice president of several local TV stations pointed out, "Covering crime is the easiest, fastest, cheapest, most efficient kind of news coverage for TV stations. News directors love crime" (Grossman, 1997). A clear bias of this coverage is that those crimes that occur very rarely, such as homicides and brutal physical assaults, receive the majority of coverage, while those crimes that are more likely to occur, such as theft and burglary, are seldom mentioned. One consequence of this coverage is to give viewers (and readers) the sense that "crime" means "violent crime." There is strong evidence that this perception of the "crime problem" contributes to voter support for "tough crime legislation," including mandatory sentencing, "three strikes and you're out," and capital punishment (Cavender, 2004). Another factor is smartphone cameras that "citizen journalists" use to capture evocative images that are aired by news outlets (Schneider, 2016).

Numerous studies of crime reporting stress how pervasive crime and danger are in American news media, especially television (Budzilowicz, 2002). Crime reports make up 25 to 35 percent of news in some local markets. A study by the *Columbia Journalism Review* noted that nearly 20 percent of all "people" featured in local news are involved with crime reporting (Grossman, 1997):

> Consider this statistic: one has to add up all the educators, school board members, city council members, mayors, state agency officials, state legislators' governors, members of Congress and all other local elected and appointed officials combined just to match the number of criminals and suspects on screen. . . .
>
> Who are the people shown in local TV news stories? After criminals and suspects (who make up 10 percent of all people on screen) the most common group featured is crime victims or their families (9 percent).

Crime is the perennial number-one topic, in large markets and small, but the largest market stations are most likely to pad their crime coverage with tales of mayhem from distant places.

One consequence is that "local" news about the "community" looks like "crime," but numerous other aspects of life are not covered.

1. Forty-two percent of the stories last thirty seconds or less.
2. One in four or five stories is about crime, law, or courts.
3. Less than 1 percent of stories could be called "investigative."
4. Health stories outnumber all other social issues by 32 percent.

There are as many stories about the bizarre (8 percent) as there are about civic institutions.

According to reports by the Project for Excellence in Journalism, crime news is important for the economics of TV news; crime news is apparently institutionalized as a good way to "hook" an audience and "hold" them throughout the newscast. "This approach ['hook and hold'] shows up quite clearly in an examination of the data collected by the Project for Excellence in Journalism during its local TV news study from 1998 to 2002. This trend has largely continued. While 'public safety' news accounted for 36% of stories over all, it constituted nearly two-thirds of the stories that led newscasts (61%) and were given the most time and resources. And public safety news continued to make up the majority of stories until the fifth story in the newscast. (Indeed, 13% of all newscasts began with three crime stories in a row, back to back to back.)" However, as local news stations devoted more time to sports and weather, there is some evidence that crime news declined to 17 percent in 2012, with similar reductions in politics and government—less than 3 percent (Jurkowitz et al., 2013).

And there has been a remarkable increase in the amount of violent crime news presented on network television. Indeed, in recent years, journalism has begun to take a look at the impact of such distorted coverage about crime and fear on American life. Research shows that of the major American TV networks (ABC, CBS, NBC), ABC and NBC increased crime coverage between 2007 and 2012 so that crime news made up 14 percent of ABC news and 11 percent of NBC's content, almost as much coverage as politics (Jurkowitz et al., 2013). Two journalists (Westfeldt, 1998), who were very critical of the news coverage of crime, observed,

> In 1997, even as the prison population was going up and the crime rate was falling the public rated "crime/gangs/justice system" as "the most important problem facing the country today"—and by a large margin.

As they chronicled the preoccupation with crime by local newspapers and television broadcasters in promoting a fear-of-crime agenda, the authors observed the culpability of national and prestigious news outlets in pushing the same views, including television network news:

> The Center for Media and Public Affairs reported in April 1998 that the national murder rate has fallen by 20% since 1990—but the number of murder stories on network newscasts rose in the same years by about 600% . . . not including the many broadcasts of or about the O. J. Simpson trial. (Westfeldt, 1998, 2)

Fear and Crime

In my book *Creating Fear: News and the Construction of Crisis*, I tracked the nature and extent of the use of the word *fear* in major newspapers from 1987 to 1996 and examined ABC news coverage for several years. This project was informed by numerous studies and insights by criminologists and media scholars, particularly the conceptual development of a model—the "problem frame"—of how entertainment inspires news reports about fear (Altheide, 1997). The basic findings were that use of the word *fear* increased substantially—often 100 percent in stories as well as headlines, peaking around 1994. This usage also "traveled" across various topics over time, meaning, for example, that at one point fear would be closely associated with AIDS, while a few years later it was gangs or violence. Two terms closely associated with fear in the 1990s were *children* and *schools*. Numerous news reports about fear pertain to children (Altheide, 2002a). The news media's emphasis of fear with children is consistent with work by Warr (1992) and others on the significance of "third-person" or "altruistic fear"—the concern for those whom you love or are responsible. Specifically, Warr (1992) found that children are the most common object of fear in households. Much of this concern is generated around crime and drugs. Such coverage of crime promotes more communication of fear and control by authorities. One example is the "Amber Alert" program that has been adopted by most states in the United States as well as federal legislation. Named after Amber Hagerman, who was kidnapped and killed in 1997, Amber Alerts are public messages broadcast on radio, television, and freeway signs that a child has been abducted.

Frequent association of terms like *fear* (rather than other descriptors, e.g., *danger* or *risk*) promotes a discourse of fear. Moreover, while the association of certain words (topics) with fear varies, this does not mean that they are no longer connoted as fear. Rather, analysis suggests that words used frequently together in public discourse may become "meaningfully joined" as sign and signifier, as connotation and denotation, so that, over time, it becomes redundant and unnecessary to use *fear* with *violence, crime, gangs,* and *drugs*: the specific word itself implies fear. The rationale for this approach is that the meaning of two words is suggested by their proximity, their association. Indeed, over time, terms merge in public discourse and the actual use and meaning of terms. Consider the example of *violence* and *crime* in the following three sentences:

1. An act of violence that might be regarded as a crime occurred Saturday night.
2. A violent crime occurred Saturday night.
3. A [crime (violence)] occurred Saturday night.

The first sentence treats both *violence* and *crime* as nouns, as separate but perhaps related. In the second sentence, *violence* is an adjective for *crime*, part of its description and meaning. But the third sentence shows what happens when terms are continually used together, often merging. This sentence suggests that *crime* has incorporated *violence* into its meaning and that the word *violent* need not be used. As the audience becomes more familiar with the meaning of the term and the context of its use, it becomes redundant to state *violent crime* since the mass-mediated experience suggests "crime is violent" (despite research to the contrary, such as that most crimes are property crimes). Other work in cultural studies, deconstruction, and semiotics has demonstrated how this happens with numerous social problems and issues (cf. Manning and Cullum-Swan, 1994; Ferrell et al., 2015). Not only is the event distorted by this coupling, but our capacity to deal with it in different ways may be compromised as well. A similar coupling occurs when television reports about crime and violence show individuals of certain racial and ethnic groups. The news reports tend to stress individual causation and responsibility and very seldom place these acts in a societal context that includes poverty (Budzilowicz, 2002). Thus, television visual formats can contribute to social definitions.

SOCIAL CONSEQUENCES OF THE DISCOURSE OF FEAR

The evidence is quite strong that mass media reports about topics inform public opinion on such matters and contribute in no small way to setting social and political agendas (Chermak, 1995; Chiricos, Eschholz, & Gertz, 1997; Chiricos, Padgett, & Gertz, 2000). As Warr (1985) notes, "And like criminal victimization itself, the consequences of fear are real, measurable, and potentially severe, both at an individual and social level" (238). From the standpoint of media content as "cause," researchers ask whether news reports can "cause" or "lead" people to focus on and fear crime, including the extent to which relevant values and perspectives may be "cultivated" (Gerbner, Gross, Jeffries-Fox, Signorielli, & Jackson-Beeck, 1978). From this perspective, the mass media play a large role in shaping public agendas by influencing *what* people think about (Shaw & McCombs, 1977). While there is scant data on "fear" per se among public opinion polls, most measures of fear in recent years are associated with crime. Chiricos and colleagues (2000) note, "With regard to fear, the most consequential of those messages are received from local news, and the volume of crime stories in that medium has achieved proportions that concern many critics" (780). As noted previously, numerous public opinion polls show that fear of crime and personal safety reign above most other concerns. Indeed, many Americans feel that their lives are unsafe and more subject to harm than at previous times (Surette, 1998).

Mapping how fear has become associated with different topics over time can clarify how the mass media and popular culture influence public perceptions of danger and risk. Indeed, Surette's "social ecology of crime" model suggests that the "world of TV entertainment" resembles "citizen-sheep" being protected from "predator wolves—criminals" by "sheep dogs—police" (Surette, 1992, 43).

Several projects have suggested that the media do contribute to political agendas as well as people's perceptions and interests in everyday life (MacKuen & Coombs, 1981). Iyengar & Kinder (1987) employed an experimental design to demonstrate "that television news shapes the relative importance Americans attach to various national problems" (113). Focusing on energy, inflation, and unemployment, they argued that television is most powerful at "priming" or providing accessible bits of information that viewers may draw on to help interpret other events. Making it clear that ultimately it is the viewers' perceptions and everyday life experiences that help interpret social life, nevertheless, television contributes "by priming certain aspects of national life while ignoring others, television news sets the terms by which political judgments are rendered and political choices made" (Iyengar & Kinder, 1987, 4).

In other work, Iyengar (1991) suggests that priming and framing of reports as either episodic, focusing on individual circumstances and responsibility, or thematic, focusing on contextual and societal responsibility, has a bearing on what viewers take from television news reports (Ericson, 1993). For example, Budzilowicz found that most of these reports emphasized individual responsibility rather than the social conditions and context that lead to the acts (Budzilowicz, 2002).

Research has shown that fear and victim are informed by perceived membership (Altheide et al., 2001). Crime and threats to the public order—and therefore to all good citizens—is part of the focus of fear, but, as noted throughout this book, the topics change over time. What they all have in common is pointing to the "other," the outsider, the nonmember, the alien. However, Schwalbe et al. (2000) have shown that "othering" is part of a social process whereby a dominant group defines into existence an inferior group. This requires the establishment and "group sense" of symbolic boundaries of membership. These boundaries occur through institutional processes that are grounded in everyday situations and encounters, including language, discourse, accounts, and conversation. Knowledge and skill at using "what everyone like us knows" involves formal and informal socialization so that members acquire the coinage of cultural capital with which they can purchase acceptance, allegiance, and belonging. Part of this language involves the discourse of fear:

> Discourse is more than talk and writing; it is a way of talking and writing. To regulate discourse is to impose a set of formal or informal rules about what can be said, how it can be said, and who can say what to whom. . . . Inasmuch as language is the principal means by which we express, manage, and conjure emotions, to regulate discourse is to regulation emotion. The ultimate consequence is a regulation of action. . .
>
> When a form of discourse is established as standard practice, it becomes a tool for reproducing inequality, because it can serve not only

to regulate thought and emotion, but also to identify Others and thus to
maintain boundaries as well. (Schwalbe et al., 2000, 433–34)

It is not fear of crime, then, that is most critical. It is what this fear can
expand to, what it can become. Sociologists have noted that we are becoming "armored." Social life changes when more people live behind
walls, hire guards, drive "armored" vehicles (e.g., sport-utility vehicles),
wear "armored" clothing (e.g., big-soled shoes or clothing with the
phrase "No Fear!"), carry mace or handguns, and take martial arts
classes. The problem is that these activities reaffirm and help produce a
sense of disorder that our actions perpetuate. We then rely more on formal agents of social control to "save us" by "policing them," the "others,"
who have challenged our faith.

The major impact of the discourse of fear is to promote a sense of
disorder and a belief that "things are out of control." Ferraro (1995) suggests that fear reproduces itself, or becomes a self-fulfilling prophecy.
Social life can become more hostile when social actors define their situations as "fearful" and engage in speech communities through the discourse of fear. And people come to share an identity as competent "fear
realists" as family members, friends, neighbors, and colleagues socially
construct their effective environments with fear. Behavior becomes con-
strained, community activism may focus more on "block watch" programs and quasi-vigilantism, and we continue to avoid "downtowns"
and many parts of our social world because of "what everyone knows."

Fear is part of our everyday discourse, even though we enjoy unprecedented levels of health, safety, and life expectancy. And now we "play
with it." More of our "play worlds" come from the mass media. News
reports are merging with television "reality programs" and "crime dramas" ripped from the front pages, in turn providing us with templates
for looking at everyday life. The increase in "false reports" is an example.
The expanding interest in fear and victim also contributes to (1) audiences who play with the repetitive reports as dramatic enactments of
"fear and dread in our lives" and (2) individual actors who seek roles that
are accepted as legitimate "attention-getters" in order to accomplish favorable identity vis-à-vis particular audience members.

We also find that the news coverage of the 9/11 attacks brought out a
lingering and pervasive preoccupation with fear that has been exploited
by government officials seeking to expand social control and limit civil
liberties. After all, fear—more than danger or risk—is a pervasive emotional orientation that calls for strong action against those responsible.
The remedy usually involves state authorities taking more control. The 9/
11 terror attacks were presented, essentially, as a "crime story," albeit a
"big crime," and language that was developed over two decades of crime
reporting was applied to terrorism. President Bush said that "it's important for Americans to know that trafficking of drugs finances the world of

terror, sustaining terrorists." The focus on fear provides more revenue for news organizations and related popular-culture outlets (e.g., *America's Most Wanted*) while giving police and law enforcement agencies more credibility and control. Popular culture producers played to audience fear.

> The 9/11 attacks and the ensuing wars in Iraq and Afghanistan spurred a hyper-patriotism and fear of encroaching terrorism. That cultural climate produced TV shows such as the terrorist-themed *Homeland* and hero-driven war movies like *Lone Survivor* and *American Sniper*. But 9/11 also aroused a nationalism that was often intolerant of dissenting views. . . . In the immediate wake of 9/11, special agent Jack Bauer of *24* was aggressive, often using torture to combat one-dimensional terrorists. The show was heavily criticized for its portrayals of Muslims. Years later, *Homeland* was more textured and empathetic, delving deeper into the nuances and motivations of both CIA agents and extremists. (Fleishman & Villarreal, 2016)

Another consequence of the nature and extent of crime reporting is that the discourse of fear becomes taken for granted as a description of reality. What are very rare events are assumed to be common occurrences. For example, audience members not only talk about brutal assaults and even child kidnappings—which are very rare—but they also begin to enact them as hoaxes and to "play with fear" in order to get attention:

> A mother in Mesa, Arizona, claimed that she was sexually assaulted in her child's school restroom when a "man with cigarette breath, dirty fingernails and long, messy hair had placed a sharp object to her neck, knocked her unconscious and assaulted her." Actually, she wounded herself and cut up her clothing in order to get some attention, particularly from her husband. (*The Arizona Republic*, "Mom: 'Rape' Was a Hoax," August 18, 1999, A1)

Stories of assaults and kidnappings blasted across headlines—even when false or greatly distorted—make it difficult for frightened citizens to believe that schools are one of the safest places in American society. It is becoming more common to "play out" scenarios of danger and fear that audiences assume to be quite common with the availability of social media to capture and post images of various performances. Researchers find that many of these hoaxes rely on stereotypes of marginalized groups, such as poor people and racial minorities. The oppositions that become part of the discourse of fear can be illustrated in another way as well. Repetitious news reports that make connections between fear, children, schools, and suspected assailants who fit stereotypes are easy to accept even when they are false. Russell's (1998) study of sixty-seven publicized racially tinged hoaxes between 1987 and 1996 illustrates how storytellers frame their accounts in social identities that are legitimated by numerous reports and stereotypes of marginalized groups, such as racial minorities. For example, in 1990 a George Washington University student reported that another student had been raped by two black men with "particularly bad body odor" in order to "highlight the problems of safety for women."

A schoolteacher in Tucson, Arizona, wrote herself threatening letters before shooting herself. She had claimed that discipline and security were too lax. She implied that a twelve-year-old Hispanic youth sent the letters and then shot her. In the spring of 1999, two Mesa, Arizona, fifth-grade girls, playing a game of Truth or Dare, told a detailed story about a knife-toting transient who grabbed them as they were leaving an elementary school. They fought off the man, whom they said "chewed his nails," and escaped to a neighbor's house. Police and neighbors patrolled the neighborhood questioning various people, only to have the girls admit that it was false. When people "pretend" that they have been assaulted, abducted, or in some way harmed by strangers, they are acting out a morality play that has become part of a discourse of fear, or the notion that fear and danger are pervasive.

Terrorism joins crime as a major source of hoaxes, especially given the constant urging of the public to "see something, say something." Seeing something—or at least seeing a curious email—on December 14, 2015, led New York City and Los Angeles school board members to report they received emails threatening death and mayhem. New York officials proceeded with caution but kept their schools open. Not so with the Los Angeles school district that was shut down for a day.

> The drama began at 10:01 p.m. on Monday, Dec. 14, when school board President Steve Zimmer received the emailed threat. He happened to be on his computer at the time, and he did not know that the threat had also been sent to other past and current board members and to the New York City school system.
>
> "I am emailing you to inform you of the happenings on Tuesday, 12/15/15," the email began. "Something big is going down. Something very big. It will make national headlines. Perhaps, even international ones."
>
> The email then spoke of a desire to avenge bullying suffered for being a Muslim. The sender vowed to detonate pressure-cooker bombs hidden in backpacks, release nerve gas at lunchtime and launch assaults by more than 30 people armed with "Kalashnikov rifles, Glock 18 machine pistols, and multiple handheld grenades." (Blume, 2016)

Unlike a more systematic and organized checking into the threats, the Los Angeles response was more chaotic, resulting in computers crashing, and cafeteria workers, who didn't get the word about the closure, still reporting for work. At least in Los Angeles, the hoax worked.

Pervasive and entertaining messages about fear and dread make rare events appear to be more plausible. Increasingly, audience members participate through hoaxes of fear. The massive number of news reports about terrorism and alleged links to anthrax mailings sparked numerous "hoaxes" in the United States and around the world. The postal service received nearly sixteen thousand anthrax reports, and an additional sixty reports have been investigated in which people claimed to have mailed or received anthrax in a letter. Clayton Lee Waagner, a petty criminal and self-proclaimed "antiabortion warrior," is suspected of sending some 550 letters containing harmless white powder to abortion clinics with the words "Army of God." While this zealot clearly intended to frighten and intimidate recipients, several dozen people around the world sent similar "harmless" letters, intended as a "practical joke," to friends, coworkers, neighborhood foes, and news organizations. At least one postal worker has been indicted for scrawling a note on a package about anthrax in order to take advantage of the public's fear "to settle a score to pull off a prank." Several others claimed that they received anthrax-filled letters. One Missouri woman who initially claimed to have been sent a poisoned letter admitted that she put flour and roach killer in the envelope and then delivered it to police some eighty miles from her home.

These examples suggest that some people may seek attention by being involved in a crime to affirm their identity as a victim. While we discuss victimization more below, it is also significant that the technological changes in media provide ironic examples of how people may approach criminal involvement. It is ironic because new surveillance technologies associated with digital devices such as cameras are used to prevent crime by not only capturing images of perpetrators of criminal behavior but also to deter people from engaging in such activity. However, there is growing evidence that many people engage in what has been termed "performance crime" ("will to representation") by intentionally committing criminal acts on camera, in front of friends filming them, or even in front of surveillance equipment, in order to document their prowess, courage, and activities that can be viewed on social media (Yar, 2012). While mediated performances were previously by and large the domain of celebrities and professional entertainers, access to digital media changed the scope and availability. Now multibillion-dollar industries thrive on social performances. As digital media and popular social media formats (e.g., Facebook, YouTube) promote visual performances to engage friends, attract mates, and make money as personified "brands," so too is a visual space created via smartphones and related devices to enact criminal acts as symbolic proof of authenticity, legitimacy, as well as the elusive "wow factor."

Surette argues:

> Due to enhanced audience participation and involvement in content creation and distribution, crime and justice has changed. This change came about with the emergence of new digital social media and is

reflected in the growth of crime and justice performances. . . . Contemporary performance crime encompasses the spectacle of recording, sharing and uploading crime in order to distribute the performance to new media audiences. . . . With social media, the altered process is that crime involvement and self-promotion are intertwined. In this social reality, social media's encouragement of people to validate themselves has resulted in a plethora of incriminating crime videos being voluntarily posted. (Surette, 2015)

The crime-related performances may include trespassing, robberies, burglaries, assaults (e.g., "Slap Cam"), sexual assaults, as well as murder. For example, it is increasingly common for mass shooters to leave messages on social media, and in some cases, to actually broadcast their upcoming deeds as well as recording their conduct. One of the most gruesome videos was the recording by a former TV station employee of the killing of a reporter and cameraman.

On August 26, 2015, Alison Parker, a TV journalist, and Adam Ward, a cameraman, at station WDBJ in Roanoke, Virginia, were shot to death as they conducted a live interview with Vicki Gardner about tourism, who was seriously wounded. The killer was Bryce Williams (aka Vester Lee Flanagan), a disgruntled former employee, who had been fired from several stations. A former reporter, the killer supplemented his familiarity with social media techniques, formats, and likely audience reactions with his experience as a reporter. He sent a twenty-three-page statement to ABC News about an hour after the shooting, which, among other things, listed some of his grievances—anger at black killings as well as admiration for Virginia Tech shooter Seung-Hui Cho and the Columbine High School killers (Fox News, 2015). While posting video of the shooting on social media, updating his web page, Facebook, and posting tweets that attracted many followers, Williams shot himself in the head when his car was stopped about four hours later.

Williams followed media logic when he assassinated two Virginia journalists with a Glock handgun in one hand and a GoPro camera in the other. Using a gun was nothing new, but using a high-quality hand-held camera to record and publicize the carnage through social media was novel. This mediated murder was a dramatic example of the prevalence of reflexive mediation.

The shooting reflects other coverage of shootings and knowledge of audience and media interests and procedures—the capacity to self-film, report, make a statement, and anticipate how tweets and Facebook posts would be viewed and forwarded by audiences.

Terrorists have adopted this approach in several ways, including suicide bombers making pre-death videos affirming their allegiance and martyrdom, on the one hand, while also recording murderous activities in order to enhance their message and impact. This was done with the Paris terrorist acts in January 2015. And other vicious examples are the executions and beheadings of hostages by ISIS (e.g., Jihadi John) intended to repel enemies as well as recruit followers.

Sophisticated social media and propaganda techniques powered ISIS, and in addition they commandeered untold U.S. military equipment that was left by disbanded Iraqi army units. In addition to committing mass murder of heretics—including Shiites and several varieties of Christians—it also kidnapped and held for ransom many foreign aid workers and journalists. ISIS became a global scourge when it posted graphic beheadings of several of these victims via YouTube and Twitter, along with other videos. The main executioner was profiled as a British citizen, who was soon referred to by his media name "Jihadi John." His family and schoolmates would be interviewed and featured in numerous reports. The theater caught the attention of numerous world leaders, including Middle Eastern heads of state. Indeed, the Jordanian government launched an all-out assault on ISIS when a captured pilot was burned alive—on camera. The symbolic power of this organization touched would-be jihadists worldwide, leading several to avenge profane cartoons of the Prophet Mohammed by killing journalists in Paris at the office of *Charlie Hebdo*.

The importance of social media for changing global conflict was apparent with the attack on the *Charlie Hebdo* offices in Paris on January 7, 2015. Three gunmen stormed the satirical cartoon offices, which had earned the ire of jihadists by publishing cartoon caricatures of the Prophet Mohammed (as well as other satirical representations of other religions, Christianity, Judaism, etc.), and they killed twelve people, including seven journalists. "Hey! We avenged the prophet Muhammad! We killed *Charlie Hebdo*," one of the gunmen could be heard shouting in French in the televised video (Vinograd, Jamieson, Viala, & Smith, 2015).

At another Paris location, a lone gunman, a thirty-two-year-old terrorist, Amedy Coulibaly, who had been in close contact with the *Hebdo* killers, took hostages in a kosher grocery store, killing four. He wore a GoPro camera to record the slaughter that he aimed to upload to news stations in order to complete a scripted program, although he neglected to bring equipment that would work with aid of WiFi (his program was a very old Adobe Flash Player). According to a man pressured to help him in the café, "He needed it for instant replay on jihadi sites." Coulibaly wanted to get online to monitor the news. "What was urgent is that his footage was expected to be uploaded while he was in the store to incite other attacks in Paris." The killer barked, "Connect me to the news desk." Once in touch with newspeople, his less sophisticated French changed to "a more academic French, as if he had been tutored with a formal script." This was a mediated production of terror; carnage was a mere prop to comply with an entertainment format of fear and urgency that guides much public information in our time.

The emphasis on participation as communication has important implications for the construction of social events, even tragic ones. Performances can also be used to lure online crime victims as assailants present themselves as a friend or potential lover during "Internet dating" in order to arrange an embodied interaction that may result in assault or murder. In some cases, then, performances are a matter of deceit, but in other cases there is an intentional display of a criminal and brutal act for symbolic and/or utilitarian benefit. Police agencies recognize the usefulness of surveillance cameras and social media in solving crimes as well as getting citizens involved in "citizen policing," or actively providing tips and information about crime and criminal suspects. Chris Schneider's provocative analysis of the Stanley Cup riots in Vancouver, BC, in June 2011, illustrate how citizens both perform criminal acts in order to gain recognition from their peers, on the one hand, while police and citizen consorts use recorded videos of miscreants' deeds to not only inform police but also to chastise peers for vandalism and criminal conduct, on the other hand.

Recent studies of the role of surveillance on Facebook note how the entertaining social communication format lends itself to social control:

> Citizens not affiliated with law enforcement agencies are increasingly engaging in an emergent form of pseudo-police work (or, what we have termed crowd-sourced policing) on social media sites. We define crowd-sourced policing as communicative interactions that occur on social media websites that collectively purport to act under the support of police work, even while in most such circumstances, forms of "police work" conducted by citizens are actually quite far removed from official police work. Crowd-sourced policing refers to social media user narratives consistent with criminal justice discourse, including, but not limited to: comments that call for the capture and prosecution of any accused persons—often referring to these individuals as "criminals" without any due process, calls to hold individuals "responsible" for their "crimes," criminal labeling or stigmatization of any persons, use of rhetoric that seeks to label individuals in the context of criminal justice. (Schneider & Trottier, 2012)

For example, a young woman, who was arrested after posting a video of herself taking some clothing from a store during the Stanley Cup Riot in Vancouver (June 2011), later stated in a newspaper apology:

> I know a lot of you don't believe me, but the truth is that I take full responsibility for my actions and am sincerely apologetic for what I did. What I did was completely out of character for me, but I did it because I was influenced by mob mentality. I want to shed light onto the thought process that was in my head so that maybe you can all get a little bit of an understanding and sympathize for people like me, who made wrong decisions but have now become victims of this social media form of mob mentality. . . . And still, a lot of people will never find

remorse for me because I had a huge smile on my face. But like I said earlier, it was fun at the time. I thought it was pretty funny because this is the only time that I would ever do something like this. The smile on my face was an "I'm such a badass I can't believe I'm doing this!" kind of look. (Schneider & Trottier, 2012)

Fear also makes us more compliant in seeking help or being "rescued" from formal agents of social control. This is very apparent with the rise of "victimization" as a status to be shared and enjoyed. Fear is a perspective or orientation to the world rather than "fear of something." Fear is one of the few things that Americans share. The discourse of fear is constructed through evocative entertainment formats that promote visual, emotional, and dramatic experience that can be vicariously lived, shared, and identified with by audience members. However, it is not just "fear of crime" or a particular thing but rather a sense or an identity that is held in common by many Americans that we are all actual or potential victims. The "object" of fear (e.g., crime, drugs, AIDS, or fear for children) shifts or "travels" across topics over time. The sense that something has happened to us, could happen to us, or probably will happen to us connects the present moment with resentments and blame about the past as well as anxieties about the future.

The most pervasive aspect of this "victim" perspective is crime. Politicians and state control agencies, working with news media as "news sources," have done much to capitalize on this concern and to promote a sense of insecurity and reliance on formal agents of social control (and related businesses) to provide surveillance, protection, revenge, and punishment to protect us, to save us. Even foreign policy and threats of external enemies support fear:

> The constant articulation of danger through foreign policy is thus not a threat to a state's identity or existence: it is its condition of possibility. While the objects of concern change over time, the techniques and exclusions by which those objects are constituted a danger persist. (Campbell, 1998, 13)

In addition,

> The postwar tests of United States foreign policy certainly located the dangers they identified via references to the Soviet Union. But they always acknowledged that the absence of order, the potential for anarchy, and the fear of totalitarian forces or other negative elements that would exploit or foster conditions—whether internal or external—was their initial concern. (Campbell, 1998, 30)

There can be no fear without actual victims or potential victims. In the postmodern age, victim is a status and a representation and not merely a person or someone who has suffered as a result of some personal, social, or physical calamity. Massive, concerted efforts by moral entrepreneurs to have their causes adopted and legitimated as "core social issues" worthy of attention have led to the wholesale adaptation and refinement of the use of the problem frame to promote victimization. Often couching their "causes" as battles for "justice," moral entrepreneurs seek to promote new social definitions of right and wrong (Johnson, 1995; Spector & Kitsuse, 1977). Victims are entertaining, and that is why they abound. They are evocative, bringing forth tears, joy, and vicarious emotional experience. But a victim is more. "Victim" is now a status, a position that is open to all people who live in a symbolic environment marked by the discourse of fear. We are all potential victims, often vying for official recognition and legitimacy.

Highly publicized mass shootings promote the notion that we are all victims-waiting-to-happen, especially as digital social media have made communications more instantaneous, personal, and visual. Consider a highly publicized "in real time" shooting. On July 12, 2012, a heavily armed, mentally ill gunman opened fire in the Century movie theatre in Aurora, Colorado, during the premier showing of *The Dark Knight Rises*, killing twelve and injuring seventy (Altheide, 2014a, 84–86). James Eagan Holmes was arrested. This was the deadliest mass shooting in Colorado since the Columbine High School shootings on April 20, 1999, discussed earlier in this chapter. The media coverage was intense, including numerous social media messages. Holmes, as with many mass shooters, belonged to online dating services and had posted messages such as "Will you visit me in prison?" (http://nypost.com/2013/10/07/holmes-online-dating-profile-will-you-visit-me-in-prison/)

The social media that blur the lines between private and public behavior provided raw visual materials—the lifeblood of TV—that led initial mass media presentations as "breaking news." Social media visuals dominated the coverage of the event (such as CNN's), but also by hundreds of smartphone tweets and videos that were often sent simultaneously to friends, families, and the Internet, including YouTube.

This shooting was very different than the first reporting of the Columbine massacre thirteen years prior, which relied mainly on interviews with eyewitnesses. Numerous smartphone recordings enabled CNN and other TV networks to use split-screen presentations to display several at once. Though context-free, the coverage of the shootings was captivating, featuring nearly live coverage of suffering and the death of young people—indeed, children—the ultimate innocent victims. Driven simultaneously by new technologies and old scripts about fear and evil, the complex explanations, meanings, significance, and implications of more gunshot deaths remained elusive.

Politicians' performances against evil make a good sound bite that can be tweeted. The official reaction to this tragedy came from actual-potential-virtual-leaders: President Barack Obama and presidential candidate Mitt Romney offered concise statements about family, prayer, and love: Obama talked of how "My daughters go to the movies . . . "; Mitt

Romney's four-minute statement emphasized his faith, love, and our great country—"hearts break for victims and families." He quoted the Apostle Paul: "Our prayer is that the comforter . . . brings peace to their souls."

Politicians are not the only actors adept in this script of fear and evil. The film industry helps to socialize audience members, who reproduce the standard roles by imitating the reporters that their use of social media has engendered. Consider CNN's eight-minute interview with witness Chris Ramos, which included the following:

> "Like the true message in *Batman*, standing up against evil, against death . . . that is basically the message the Batman movies give out, standing up for something that's right . . . and the darkness is always darker before the dawn. The second movie, that's what it says. . . . It is exactly like this." The reporter concludes: "That's as powerful as it gets. I'll leave it right there and let viewers soak it in." (CNN, July 20, 2012) (http://www.cnn.com/2012/07/20/us/colorado-theater-scene/)

While crime has been a staple of the discourse of fear that pervades mass media entertainment formats, things do change over time. Social scientists had argued for decades, to no avail, that the United States had overreacted to crime, often engaging in moral panics about drugs and violence and had unwisely engaged in a massive mandatory sentencing movement that expanded the number of people incarcerated—mostly minority groups. Moreover, it had been pointed out for decades that the crime rate in the United States had been dropping precipitously since the 1990s, but still the popular culture depictions of threat and danger propelled the elected officials to adopt the position of "Tough on Crime" as a way to appeal to voters and appease the growing power of massive lobbies representing police and correctional officers unions, as well as a rapidly expanding "prison industrial complex" that advocated for longer sentencing and more prisons. This basically lasted until the election of President Barack Obama in 2008 when there was renewed focus on the number of African Americans incarcerated, as well as the skyrocketing costs of imprisoning over two million people, more than the combined population of six million of the United States! Of course, the economic condition also mattered, especially the recession of 2008 caused by corrupt lending practices of Wall Street banks. There was simply less money for prisons, and gradually the politicians as well as big-city police chiefs began to acknowledge that many of the inmates were serving sentences for drug-related offenses. Moreover, many of the minority inmates had not received proper legal representation, and in many cases they had been railroaded into confessing to crimes in order to avoid costly trials, even when the evidence was quite slim. In many cases, they were in fact innocent of the charges against them.

This changed the rhetoric from "Tough on Crime" to "Smart on Crime," which essentially meant that scarce public resources and money should be spent on violent offenders and that less threatening inmates, such as those sentenced for drug offenses, should not be incarcerated for as long, or at all (Altheide & Coyle, 2006). Indeed, there were movements across the United States, and particularly California, for alternatives to incarceration, such as more closely supervised parole. Further, the discussion about drug offenses dovetailed with a several-decades-old discussion about the fallacy of drug laws. Numerous states began to consider what amounted to the decriminalization of drugs such as marijuana, and began putting more emphasis on education, prevention, and treatment.

CONCLUSION

The politics of fear is fed by popular culture and entertaining crime news. Crime news and fear influence national and international affairs, including the election of Donald Trump as president of the United States in 2016. As noted above, Mr. Trump capitalized on fear and corresponding hatred of the alleged sources of fear: immigrants, refugees, Muslims, China, and politicians—like Hillary Clinton—who were accused of supporting "trade deals" that eliminated or threatened factory jobs while being indifferent to working-class suffering. His crude language and general discourse of hate made it seem respectable to state in public what many might have felt privately. I repeat here a quote from Trump used in an earlier chapter. On June 16, 2015, he cast Mexican immigrants as criminals:

> When Mexico sends its people, they're not sending their best. They're not sending you. They're not sending you. They're sending people that have lots of problems, and they're bringing those problems with us. They're bringing drugs. They're bringing crime. They're rapists. And some, I assume, are good people. (Hee, 2015)

Nearly sixty-three million voters agreed with him. Similar to the successful anti-immigrant appeals by British advocates of "Brexit," or the United Kingdom (UK) pulling out of the European Union in 2016, Mr. Trump mobilized fears buttressed by social media and fake news sites that the United States was failing to control rampant violence and crime at home while neglecting to protect citizens from "radical Islamic Terrorism."

And the major news media followed the entertainment format of media logic that has governed news coverage for several decades (Altheide, 1976) by emphasizing negative reporting rather than promoting discussion of key issues. A postelection study confirmed the power of this format:

> On topics related to the candidates' fitness for office—their policy positions, personal qualities, leadership abilities, ethical standards—Hillary Clinton's coverage was identical to Trump's—87% negative to 13% positive. From the end of the party conventions through Election Day, our research team at the Shorenstein Center studied the campaign coverage on five television networks and in five major newspapers. What we found is that the news media had a strong bias toward negative coverage and didn't make a concerted effort to explain the relative magnitude of the allegations leveled at the two candidates. . . . Journalists couldn't get enough of the various controversies that bedeviled Clinton—her private server, Benghazi and the like. There was no week in which they accounted for less than 7% of her coverage and, in the campaign's final week, they constituted more than a third of her coverage. . . . Journalists defend themselves by saying they bash both sides. True enough. But indiscriminate criticism has the effect of false equivalencies. (Patterson, 2016)

It all played out on an inferno of fear that has smoldered in U.S. culture for decades but was rekindled after the 9/11 attacks, celebrated through domestic surveillance and reduced tolerance during the sixteen years, respectively, of the Bush and Obama administrations, and stoked with Donald Trump's inflammatory propaganda of hate and racism.

A month after Donald Trump's election victory some of his supporters were not at all fazed by intelligence community reports that Russia had hacked computers to give him an advantage:

> "The way it is nowadays, unless I see positive proof, it's all a lie," Mr. Ameling said in a telephone interview on Wednesday. He added he was more concerned that government officials might have leaked the material to the news media. "I don't know if it was classified, but if it was, whoever leaked it needs to go to jail," he said. "We need law and order back in this country." . . . Many were hazy on specific policy details about how, say, House Republicans were seeking to replace Medicare with a voucher system. These voters feared an outbreak of European-style terrorist attacks by Muslims in the United States, maybe in their own communities. And overwhelmingly, Trump supporters did not want their hard-earned money redistributed to people they regarded as undeserving. (Gabriel, 2017)

Fear is a key component of the entertainment format that has shaped news reports for several decades. This usage has intensified in the United States around certain topics such as crime and terrorism. I suggest that the U.S. militant policy against Afghanistan and Iraq was fueled by decades of crime reports and harsh efforts in pursuing the drug war. Citizens became accustomed to giving up civil liberties to surveillance and enforcement efforts by formal agents of social control. Numerous

"crises" and fears involving crime, violence, and uncertainty were important for public definitions of the situation after 9/11. Government officials
used the foundation of fear to build even more fear in the United States
and to enact draconian legislation that has negated civil liberties. The
drug war and ongoing concerns with crime led to the expansion of fear
with terrorism. News reports and advertisements joined drug use with
terrorism and helped shift "drugs" from criminal activity to unpatriotic
action. A $10 million ad campaign that included a 2002 Super Bowl com-
mercial stated that buying and using drugs supports terrorism, or, as
President Bush put it, "If you quit drugs, you join the fight against terror
in America." Criminals and terrorists are now joined in popular-culture
narratives of evil, control, and conquest. The war on drugs increased our
prison population 600 percent since 1970 and destroyed numerous minority communities in the United States. The war on terrorism brought
death and destruction to untold thousands of Iraqis. And still we receive
messages promoting fear, asking for more security and promising more
surveillance. Crime news has gone global. The American public and their
legislators apparently accepted the Bush administration's trumpeting
about the necessity of the various Patriot acts despite an unprecedented
violation of civil liberties at the expense of more surveillance and less law
enforcement accountability. Even Bush's successor, Barack Obama,
stressed the dangers of terrorism and, along with approving of hundreds
of drone strikes in numerous countries that killed hundreds of civilians,
he also supported massive deportations and confinement of undocumented people, mostly from Mexico. Donald Trump capitalized on the
cascading fear of hyperinflated threats by promising to "Make America
Great Again," a slogan that resonated with a disproportionate number of
less educated, older white men.

As I concluded in *Creating Fear*,

> Fear accumulates and is deposited over a wide social terrain. Like
> agates that were formed some 40 million years in the interstices of
> cooling magma and have been transported by rivers to oceans and then
> beaches ever since, fear retains its essential elements. . . . The origin of a
> specific fear can also be uncovered in specific instances, but most peo-
> ple do not care about where it began; one fear merely gets compiled
> with others on the beaches of our experiences and social encounters.
> (Altheide, 2002b, 195)

FIVE

Consuming Terrorism

When a whole nation is roaring Patriotism at the top of its voice, I am fain to explore the cleanliness of its hands and purity of its heart.

—Ralph Waldo Emerson

Keep America Rolling.

—General Motors

There were people over in New Jersey that were watching it, a heavy Arab population, that were cheering as the buildings came down. Not good.

—Donald Trump

Since 2001 the war on terrorism in the United States reflects the power of the politics of fear while also reinforcing policies and social changes that invigorate public fears, culminating in the election of Donald Trump as president in 2016. President Obama's administration (2008–2016) expanded U.S. military action against terrorist countries, primarily through the use of drones and "Special Ops," while tamping down the rhetoric about global war against Islam, despite several "homegrown" terrorist attacks in the United States as well as in France. Obama insisted that terror groups did not represent the majority of Muslim citizens in the United States, while Trump's campaigning for the presidency painted a much different picture, even claiming—without any evidence whatsoever—that the 9/11 attacks were cheered by thousands of "Arabs" in New Jersey.

I watched when the World Trade Center came tumbling down. . . . And I watched in Jersey City, N.J., where thousands and thousands of people were cheering as that building was coming down. Thousands of people were cheering. (Carroll, 2015)

103

Like 70 percent of Trump's statements, this was completely false, but it did not matter since many of his supporters believed it, partly because of corroborating "fake news" sites (http://www.politifact.com/truth-o-meter/lists/people/comparing-hillary-clinton-donald-trump-truth-o-met/). Most importantly, such statements fueled the politics of fear that would carry him to the White House. This chapter examines some of the subtle and not-so-subtle ways that the "new threat" in 2001 was blended with previous threats, and subsequently seemed to be credible for the Trump campaign years later. The longer-term effects on public discourse and perspectives about the future will be examined in the next chapter.

Donald Trump's campaign built on fourteen years of fear and propaganda that began with the Bush administration. Trump attacked President Bush for a harsh military response to the perpetrators—al Qaeda—and sympathizers—Iraq—of the 9/11 attacks, and he also pilloried President Obama for fulfilling an agreement with the Bush administration and Iraq to withdraw U.S. troops, on the one hand, while strongly criticizing Obama and Trump's opponent—former Secretary of State Clinton—for not using stronger military force against ISIS in Syria. On the other hand, these relationships require a review of the aftermath of the U.S. response to 9/11.

The terrorist attacks on September 11, 2001, awakened the American spirit of giving and spending. The tragic loss of lives and property fueled patriotic slogans, thousands of commercial advertisements, public contributions of more than $2 billion, major domestic and foreign policy changes, and the largest increase in the military budget in thirty-five years. Stores sold out of flags, businesses linked advertising to patriotic slogans (e.g., General Motors' "Keep America Rolling"), baseball fans sang "God Bless America" instead of "Take Me Out to the Ball Game," and children helped raise money for the Afghani kids who were "starving" (and being bombed). Analysis of news reports and advertisements suggests that popular-culture and mass media depictions of fear, patriotism, consumption, and victimization contributed to the emergence of a "national identity" and collective action that was fostered by elite decision makers' propaganda. Initial declarations about recovery and retaliation to promote patriotism became a "war on terrorism" with no end in sight.

Patriotic giving and spending to help victims and combat terrorism were linked to an expanded military posture. As suggested by Vidich (1991), any adequate social theory must consider the central trends and tendencies in our bureaucratic order, including the following:

1. the penetration of bureaucracy as a form of organization in all institutional orders
2. the development of mass communications and mass media and their pervasive global penetration

3. the consequences of industrial capitalism and the machine process of traditional sodalities, communal relations, universities, economics, political totalism, religion, and war

The communication order is a critical foundation for constituting social and political changes and that the logic of this order underlies how power is communicated. The following analysis is informed by research on commensuration, communalism, the politics of fear, and institutional logics.

The subsequent military and terror attacks—at home and abroad—contributed a rich trove of rhetoric and documents for analysis. Pervasive propaganda soon becomes taken-for-granted and hardly scrutinized critically. Through repetition the various claims soon become uncontestable and facts-in-their-own-right, especially when various social media reinforce them, and in some cases, challenge anyone's patriotism who does not agree. Thus, reality gets constructed in a very targeted way. A good example is the widespread false claim that veterans returning from the Vietnam War were spat upon and treated very badly (Lembcke, 1998). Lembcke could not find one documented case of that happening, although numerous antiwar protesters were spat upon:

> I suggest that we must understand the creation and consequences of the image of the spat-upon veteran as part of a cultural myth, a story that symbolizes societal values, which during the Gulf War period was employed to serve political interests. (Lembcke, 1998, 3)

And,

> The fact that so many Vietnam veterans came forward during the Gulf War with accounts of having been spat upon suggests that their memories of their own coming-home experiences have been altered by the prevalence of the spat-upon image. (Lembcke, 1998, 7)

Several presidents, including George H. W. Bush, used this claim to promote support for the first Gulf War in 1991, directing people to support the troops, even if they did not support the invasion of Iraq. I suggest that Hillary Clinton became the "spat upon" image during the 2016 presidential campaign as she was repeatedly cast as corrupt and undesirable.

As media, especially social media, have become more instantaneous, visual, and personal, the propaganda, advertisements, and public reactions reveal emergent cultural scripts about individual and national character and identity, on the one hand, and provided numerous examples of heroism and fear. Examining Espeland's (2002) analysis of commensuration as "the expression or measurement of characteristics normally represented by different units according to a common metric" conceptually joins individually oriented consumption and communally oriented giving to patriotism and national unity. Immediately after the 9/11 attacks elites and advertisers promoted cash donations and expenditures as commensurate with personal caring and national identity within the context of popular culture. While "camo" color and fashion became very popular, so too did automatic weapons. Popular culture continued to respond to the 9/11 attacks with heroic accounts. In 2014, more a decade later after the Obama administration successfully killed 9/11 promoter Osama bin Laden, there was a flurry of movies and documentaries about the national and international campaigns to defeat terrorism, including the very popular saga of Chris Kyle, *American Sniper*, that will be discussed in chapter 9.

Unlike reactions to previous "external attacks" (e.g., Pearl Harbor) that stressed conservation, personal sacrifice, and commitment, a prevailing theme of consumption as character and financial contributions as commitment and support pervaded mass media messages surrounding the 9/11 attacks. These messages made giving and buying commensurate (Espeland, 2002) with patriotism and national unity. The key metaphor was investment for victims and against "evil" victimizers. More specifically, the argument is that the widely seen (and repetitious replaying) visuals of the Twin Towers destruction became an icon of membership in a common victimization and, ultimately, that "all" who viewed/cared/opposed destruction could fight back by giving and spending. Citizens were asked to not only give blood and money but also grant elites and formal agents of social control all authority to take whatever measures deemed necessary to protect citizens, take revenge, and prevent such a deed from reoccurring. This would take a lot of investment and "giving up" certain conveniences for the sake of protection. The metaphor of "investment" covered a context of meaning that joined contributing to "victims" of 9/11, buying products to "Keep America Rolling," and supporting military action and budget increases. These messages promoted a national identity (Shapiro, 1992; Thiele, 1993) based on the politics of fear that was later used by President Bush to pursue a "first-strike" policy against U.S. enemies, and by his successor, President Obama, to justify numerous drone strikes in various countries.

It is the context and promotion of spending that is especially relevant to the politics of fear: (1) fear supported consumption as a meaningful way for audiences to sustain an identity of substance and character; (2) consumption and giving were joined symbolically as government and business propaganda emphasized common themes of spending/buying to "help the country get back on track" (and related euphemisms); (3) the absence of a clear target for reprisals contributed to the construction of broad symbolic enemies and goals; and (4) consumption as investing promoted a massive increase in military spending.

PROPAGANDA AND THE MILITARY-MEDIA COMPLEX

It is helpful to distinguish the loss of life and property associated with 9/11 from its meaning. How would this situation be interpreted, defined, and accepted? While the terrorists were implicated in the technology of explosives and strategic deceptions to hijack four aircraft that were used as missiles of death, the meaning was provided essentially by the United States. This involved propaganda.

Chapter 1 stressed that propaganda of any event is tied to the historical and social context as well as basic structural arrangements. It is worth reviewing some of those key points. Propaganda thus reveals certain symbolic foundations for meaning and identity in social life. Crisis provides opportunities for heads of state to present themselves as leaders and to dramatically define the situation as tragic but hopeful and to bring out the "resolve" of national character. Symbolic interaction theory suggests that identity and meaning are socially constructed by applying familiar experiences and routines to specific situations (Altheide, 2000; Cerulo, 1997; Cerulo, Ruane, & Chayko, 1992; Holstein & Gubrium, 2000; Perinbanayagam, 1974). Thus, continuity and novelty are linked in meaningful ways. The theorist Hans Gerth (1992), who was familiar with the brilliant Nazi propaganda efforts in World War II, discussed the context of national conflicts and propaganda during the Cold War in the 1950s:

> Loyalty to a national state is implemented by means of public educational systems. . . . Since the territory dominated by the nation is typically larger than that dominated by, say, the blood or religion, modern nationalism has had to rely more on mass education and propaganda. (338)

In noting that leadership is challenged and demonstrated by joining the power of large organizations with occupational, professional, religious, and club associations, Gerth stressed that "in order to avoid unexpected and unwanted results, social and political administrations require a deep and extensive understanding of the total equilibrium of the given social structure" (342). In the final analysis, Gerth emphasized that "propaganda, however, can be fully understood only if we recognize its most significant purpose, namely, to define the level of reality on which people think, discuss, and act" (347).

Like many analyses of propaganda, Gerth's experience with World War II was tied to propaganda as representation, as media content that was distinctive from nonpropaganda and other realms of everyday life. But communication formats that link experience with meaning are part of everyday life. As McDonald (1994) provocatively notes,

> Formats are complex and multidimensional. They include a constellation of people, activities, and the implements important to them, as well as the kinds of discourses and relations that result. . . . The formats

of technology and power are intimately connected because formats structure social fields of behavior—the possibilities for human perception and relationships. These techno-formats blur and redefine the boundaries between public and private self in the learning process. (538)

The reality of a social order grounded in media logic (Altheide, 1995a; Altheide & Snow, 1979) is constituted by shared understanding of communication formats and symbolic meanings conveyed increasingly by visual media that blur the lines between fantasy, news, and reality:

> [It] is a battle of imitation and representation, in which the relationship of who we are and who they are is played out along a wide spectrum of familiarity and friendliness, indifference and tolerance, estrangement and hostility. It can result in appreciation or denigration, accommodation or separation, assimilation or extermination. It draws physical boundaries between peoples, as well as metaphysical boundaries between life and the most radical other of life, death. It separates human from god. It builds the fence that makes good neighbors; it builds the wall that confines a whole people. And it sanctions just about every kind of violence. (Der Derian, 2002)

This would become more prominent as the United States launched hundreds of drone strikes during President Obama's eight years in office.

The importance of media formats in the communication process is apparent in the rise of the military-media complex that followed the decline of the Soviet Union and played a major role in the emergence of nationalism (Altheide, 1999). It was not until the 1960s that television surpassed print media as a cultural force. The military-media complex is a feature of programming in an entertainment era dominated by popular culture and communication forms that share sophisticated information technology promoting visual media and evocative content. Social media became more important during subsequent years. Der Derian (2002) noted that "the first and most likely the last battles of the counter/terror war are going to be waged on global networks that reach much more widely and deeply into our everyday lives," but this development turned on shared media logic between nightly newscasts and military planners. With an expanding revenue base, the emergence of the concept as well as actual "target audiences," and sophisticated marketing techniques, the mass media, and especially television, flexed its technology and discovered that visuals not only sold products but also conveyed powerful messages about social issues, such as civil rights, that could sell products. A flood of information technology—from CDs to cable to VCRs to the Internet to video games—produced a popular culture inspired by entertainment forms and the visual image. These technological and organizational changes influenced the renewed convergence of military and the mass media.

The symbolic boundaries drawn by decades of war coverage with "Middle Eastern" (Adams 1981, 1982) foes were reconfigured as the crashing towers of the World Trade Center. The background work had been done by the military-media complex that produced the Gulf War (Altheide, 1994; Gattone, 1996; Kellner, 1992). Coalition formation, "surgical strikes," and bomb-site videos were seen in briefings, news reports, movies, and commercials. The level of reality for action against an uncertain enemy with no clear state identity involved the use of mass media and information technology to connect patriotism and membership with consumption and giving. This approach was related to emergent redefinitions by President Bush and others of the terrorists (from "those folks" to "evil ones") and the hijackings (from "terrorist attack" to "act of war"). Anger at loss of life and property would prompt revenge and vengeance, which it surely did. However, Americans and our "leaders" did not just drop words and bombs in anger; citizens also bought, gave, and participated in an identity ritual of membership even before the bombs fell. Such communalism, Cerulo (2002, 163) notes, emerges when

> social actors become connected via a specific task, event, or characteristic. . . . Similarities are stressed over differences; common knowledge is stressed over specialized knowledge. The good of the citizenry takes precedence over any subgroup or individual.

The communal reaction involved drawing on national experiences of fear, consumption, and the role of national leadership in molding a response that would also constitute and justify future actions and relationships between nations, state control, and citizens. As Shapiro (2002) noted,

> The Euro American approach to war and peace sees sovereignty as an expansive, cooperative venture. Cooperation is no longer constituted as merely an alliance against a common threat; it is enacted as a continuing preparation for engagement with what are regarded as disruptive modes of violence (threats to "peace") within sovereign territories. The new venture requires, in the words of one analyst, whose observation fits the current attack on Afghanistan, "a coalition of war and humanitarianism," where politics is deployed in the form of humanitarian war.

While the military-media complex familiarized audiences with coalitions against evil, the collective response to the terror attacks was framed as a communal patriotic experience that provided opportunities to "come together" and be "united." Numerous messages also appealed to a nostalgic past about U.S. moral and military dominance, authentic lifestyles, traditional values (e.g., family and respect), and institutions of social control (e.g., police, fire departments, and the military). Buying and selling was commensurate with communal goodwill in a context of fear and uncertainty.

Qualitative Media Analysis of news reports and advertising materials following the 9/11 attacks revealed various ways that fear and consumption were related (Altheide, 1987a, 1996).

1. *Fear supports consumption as a meaningful way for audiences to sustain an identity of substance and character.* The meaning of the attacks was constructed from the context of previous domestic and international events and, especially, well-established cultural narratives surrounding fear, justifying both it and the place of fear in the lives of many citizens. Gerth's (1992) mastery of character and social structure was applied to making sense of the Cold War, but the logic holds in contemporary times as well:

> The advent of war, no matter how long it has been anticipated, inevitably comes as a shocking surprise. Its outbreak is experienced as a great crisis full of stress and uncertainty. This sense of insecurity is not nourished solely by the particular event which sets it off, such as a surprise attack by an enemy, but also upon whatever factors may give rise to personal insecurity in industrial society: competitive pressures in markets, achievement competition, gaps between personal aspirations for success and frustration endeavors, etc. The intensity and volume of insecurity at the outbreak of war focuses and polarizes all otherwise dispersed and segmented feelings of insecurity. . . . The lasting virtue of representative government is that it integrates the whole people and all vital currents in society. (341)

Terrorism from the sky inspired political terrorism in the mass media. One definition of terrorism certainly describes the thrust of news media reports after 9/11: "The purposeful act or threat of violence to create fear and or compliant behavior in a victim and or audience of the act or threat" (Lopez & Stohl, 1984, 4). By this definition, the U.S. citizenry was being terrorized by strategic news sources providing entertaining news to a compliant audience willing to support all efforts to save them. A history of numerous "crises" and fears involving crime, violence, and uncertainty was important for public definitions of the situation after 9/11. A major source of insecurity was a pervasive fear that was promoted in news reports, popular culture, and politicians' mantras about the "cure" for what ails America (Shapiro, 1992).

Americans answer to the 9/11 attacks by giving and spending was informed by a long tradition of dealing with fear, especially fear of crime. Fear is related to cultural values and social structure (Glassner, 1999). Ironically, Americans rely on fear to save them; it is fear in general as well as a specific "fear of X" (often crime) that is responsible for shortcomings in a market-dominated culture. This uncertainty and concern is expressed in numerous narratives of fear. While life in the United States for most citizens is quite safe, public perceptions are that everyday life is filled with risks, and thereby people are quite fearful.

Other analysis of the contributions of narratives of fear suggests that fear plays a part in identity statements about what is lacking in an otherwise (nearly) perfect world (Altheide, 2002b). The dominant popular culture promotes identities, vision, and futures that reflect social affluence in a market economy. Technical, chemical, and psychological information is combined to produce a commodified social order that is valued for its symbolic meanings as well as the utility of the products. If we can solve the problems and sources of fear, the argument goes, then we could find salvation in a secular age that is very affluent, mobile, yet disconnected from community, or a shared sense of identity, purpose, and concern. Specific objects and targets of fear (e.g., crime, drugs, and immigrants) reflect an underlying cultural value for fear. Fear has been transformed from natural events, catastrophes, and "uncontrollable phenomena" that characterized life in the Middle Ages to social life. The big trouble for the United States since 9/11 is terrorism.

Fear is used to deal with what social life lacks. It can be a substitute or catch-all explanation for numerous troubles and disjuncture between what is and what ought to be. Fear provides a rationale for the management and control of social order. Fear provides explanations and solutions that often involve formal agents of social control, involving police, control, and surveillance:

> It is nothing as sharp as panic. . . . It is low-level fear. A kind of background radiation saturating existence. . . . It may be expressed as "panic" or "hysteria" or "phobia" or "anxiety." (Massumi, 1993, 24)

The terror attacks were unsettling, but the subsequent campaign to integrate fear into everyday life routines was consequential.

2. *Consumption and giving were joined symbolically as government and business propaganda emphasized common themes of spending/buying to "help the country get back on track" (and related euphemisms).* Consumption messages that dominated popular culture after the attacks reflect elite management of a nation-state held together by mass-mediated markets, desires, and expectations (Ewen, 1976). A nation's grief was directed to giving and spending dollars. Cultural scripts of generosity and sympathy were processed through organizational entertainment formats emphasizing market participation and consumption (Ewen, 1976). "The imagery employed to inspire the consuming impulse can be transparently revealing of both social values and neuroses" (Kingston, 2002).

Business became a key symbol of fighting terrorism. The World Trade Center towers were powerful symbols to the terrorists and Americans. Advertising and the market economy joined with giving and "selfless" assistance to others. Americans gave millions to charities to help the victims of 9/11. Indeed, businesses and corporate America offered rebates and contributions to charities from individual purchases. The slumping U.S. economy was in a recession prior to 9/11 and plummeted thereafter. Fear of air travel topped public perceptions that more attacks might follow and that it might be best to stay close to home. Purchases of "big-ticket" items like automobiles and appliances dropped rapidly.

The U.S. advertising industry sprang into action. For example, the Ad Council (Advertising Research Foundation) adopted a strong coalition stand against terrorism, noting in one communication that "it was originally founded as the War Advertising Council during World War II in the aftermath of the bombings of Pearl Harbor." Following an "all advertising industry meeting," a strategy was adopted on September 18, 2001, to "inform, involve and inspire Americans to participate in activities that will help win the war on terrorism." Advertising "creatives" (Jackall & Hirota, 2000) developed the theme of "Freedom," and several public service announcements were created to stress, "I am an American," "Laura Bush (President Bush's wife): Comfort Your Children," and "Mental Health Awareness" (Advertising Research Foundation, 2001).

Showing support meant travel. Bush implored Americans to "fly, and enjoy America's great destination spots. Take your families and enjoy life, the way we want it to be enjoyed. Greatness is found when American character and American courage can overcome American challenges, and we will." United Airlines and other carriers presented messages of caring employees who were part of "United's family" (but also the entire country) as "we're United." Arizona congressman John Kyl authored a bill to give $600 tax deductions for family vacations. As one of my irreverent colleagues, who is also a decorated Vietnam War veteran, stated in a postcard from Disney World, "We came here so the terrorists wouldn't win!"

The travel industry was not alone in commercial empathy. Numerous ads appeared for products and services that would benefit individuals yet serve the country (e.g., American flags, teeth whiteners, the Ithaca Gun Company's "Homeland Security" pump-action shotguns, anthrax antibiotics, cars, and vacation "deals").

American news media promoted the reopening of the American Stock Exchange as a major symbolic victory, quoting President Bush, "We'll show the world" that we can get American economic life back to normal. One writer commented,

> We were being asked to bounce back in the name of commerce. Somehow running out and buying stuff or suffering through TV's increasingly excessive commercials would serve as a rebuke to Osama bin Laden and all those who had helped perpetrate the atrocities. It didn't quite scan, but as part of the new patriotism, we complied. The new patriotism itself became an industry, as entrepreneurs cranked out American flags in various sizes and shapes, CDs of patriotic songs, tokens and totems meant to commemorate the catastrophe and supposedly honor the dead and injured. . . . What's sacred to broadcasters and cablecasters is not the programming but the commercials. Rarely if ever, then, do networks continue their crawls across space that has

been bought and paid for—although if there's a way to do that for added profit, it might some day become common. Perhaps General Motors could buy only a part of the screen and Ford Motor Co. another part. The TV picture is turning into a collection of animated billboards, with viewers challenged to ferret out actual information as it vies for space with ads and promos and visual junk. We're not just back to business-as-usual. We've gone on to business-with-a-vengeance. (Shales, 2001)

The gun industry and the National Rifle Association (NRA) urged fearful Americans to buy their slogans and products. Many Americans responded to the 9/11 attacks by arming themselves. As one reporter noted, "People may say: 'Let Tom Ridge watch out for our shores. I'll watch out for my doors'" (Baker, 2001). Gun sales were up nationwide 9 to 22 percent despite the concern of police officials: "We are always concerned with the overall numbers of guns that are available and out on the street making things unmanageable for law enforcement," said William B. Berger, the police chief of North Miami Beach, Florida, who is president of the International Association of Chiefs of Police, the nation's oldest and largest group of law enforcement executives with nineteen thousand members worldwide (Baker, 2001). The gun industry accommodated the public concerns with creative advertising such as "Ithaca Gun Company is selling its Homeland Security model for 'our current time of national need.'" Its advertising pitch states, "In our current time of national need Ithaca Gun is ready to meet the challenge. . . . In every respect, these new Homeland Security Model shotguns are up to the demanding tasks which lay [sic] before us as a nation." The Beretta gun company has its "United We Stand," a 9-millimeter pistol bearing a laser-etched American flag. The company sold 2,000 of them to wholesalers in one day in October (Baker, 2001). The company lists the New York Police Department and the Survivors Fund of the National Capital Region as the charities to which they would donate. As noted in previous chapters, gun sales soared with the election of President Obama, as well as during the presidential campaign of Hillary Clinton.

Similar to the fear generated by a decade of "drug war" and "rampant crime" reports, the 9/11 attacks implied that all Americans were vulnerable. Investing in a gun made sense to a lot of people. The California Rifle Association (an NRA affiliate) placed a billboard that read, "Society is safer when criminals don't know who's armed." Such marketing led Congressmen Waxman and McCarthy to join the Washington-based Alliance for Justice at a news conference to draw attention to gun makers' marketing efforts (AP, 2001). Gun sales continued to climb. According to one report,

Guns are being bought with the feeling that they will make the buyer safer. Scott Abraham, a Long Island investment broker in his 30's, said he never dreamed of buying a gun until Sept. 11. Last month he bought a Mossberg shotgun because "I don't want to be caught shorthanded," and made a spot to hide it in his house. Thomas M. Iasso, 53, a former police officer who stopped carrying a gun two years ago, bought a .40-caliber Glock after the terrorist attacks—and he carries it.

"You can't sit there and tell me you can protect me anymore, because you can't," Mr. Iasso said, explaining his purchase. (Baker, 2001)

Notwithstanding Gun Industry Watch's caution that "there's nothing patriotic about flooding our streets with lethal weapons," their research found that gun manufacturers are also using the events of September 11 to sell weapons:

At the Firing Line, a South Philadelphia gun shop and pistol range where gun sales have increased 20 percent since Sept. 11, the owner, Gregory J. Isabella, said economic fears have not stopped sales. He said he sold 58 guns in the first 20 days after the attacks, an increase of 20 percent or more over the same period last year, and sold 18,000 rounds of ammunition in the same period, an increase of more than 30 percent. Sales at his shop have steadied, but are still ahead of last year's pace. He said women were buying their own guns, or ammunition for their husbands as a Christmas stocking stuffer. Other customers, he said, come by just to shoot at the Osama bin Laden targets.

"I got him!" Mr. Isabella said he could hear shooters saying, or, "I got even with him!" He said: "It's a way to blow off steam and, perhaps, practice for some nebulous future event." (Baker, 2001)

Efforts by others to add context and perspective made little difference.

The Red Cross efforts reflect the widespread communalism spirit, although some money was donated in anger, as a type of "vengeful philanthropy"—giving not out of sympathy but out of anger—against the terrorists (Strom, 2002). The country had become "unified" through various giving campaigns, but there remained doubt, skepticism, and opportunism about the process, amount, and appropriateness of the settlements. Numerous appeals were made for citizens to donate blood and money. Heeding the voices of politicians and pop-culture celebrities, Americans contributed more than $2 billion to a host of charities. They also gave thousands of pints of blood that were destroyed when not used. The donations were part of a symbolic healing (and vengeful) act that fused individuals with a national identity that was sustained by seeing and hearing television commentators, coworkers, and family members discuss how generous Americans were, how they always pulled together in times of crisis, and how a new resolve was being constructed. The most important point of the communal narrative was what Americans held in common rather than what separated them. Such outpouring was unprecedented in the history of U.S. generosity:

Much of the frustration has arisen because many charities, from the Sept. 11 Fund to the city firefighter union's Widows' and Children's Fund, have yet to distribute a total of roughly a billion dollars in aid. The Robin Hood Relief Fund, administered by the Robin Hood Foundation in Manhattan, has $23 million left; the World Trade Center Relief Fund, administered by New York State, still has $29 million of the $65 million it has raised; the Uniformed Firefighters Association is locked in a fight with families about its plan to allocate only a portion of its $60 million. (Strom, 2002)

But all was not well with the giving and especially with the distributing of the funds:

The massive giving foretold an impending crisis in trust and social justice as the rules for dispersing the fortunes smacked of social inequality and privilege. This was the first time that those unfortunate to be "in the line of fire" were officially entitled to compensation. While later congressional action and lobbying would include individuals killed in previous attacks on U.S. embassies, the entitlement status was new.

Sept. 11, they say, challenged the basic principles of many charities and the assumptions underlying them as never before. In many respects it obliterated the question of need, which has traditionally defined aid distribution. For instance, many people, including financially well-off victims, were given hundreds of thousands of dollars and stand to receive perhaps millions more from the federal government. (Strom, 2002)

Indeed, the larger organizations like the American Red Cross had more money than was necessary for the current need, so another fund (Liberty Fund) was established to help prepare for future terrorist attacks and emergencies. Bernadine Healy, head of the American Red Cross, was fired for allegedly withholding more than $250 million donated to families of people who were killed in the attacks. The Red Cross came under increasing pressure to spend all the funds for the deserving, and this led to an expanded category of what victimization was and who would deserve it.

The Red Cross expanded its program to include a wide range of "victims" in order to satisfy those monitoring the dispersal of funds. Applicants for Red Cross help included drivers of luxury sedans whose big-spending clientele was reduced by the attacks. Even though the two thousand to three thousand drivers were still working and earning around $1,000 a week, they could pick up disaster relief funds of $5,000 to $10,000 if they could prove that their company had accounts near the World Trade Center (*Newsweek*, February 11, 2002, 40).

The Red Cross funds were in addition to the billions of dollars of the federal Victim Compensation Fund set up to reduce lawsuits against airlines and other businesses. Special master of the fund, Kenneth Feinberg, estimated that his "economic scale" of compensation that took into account occupation, age, and other assets would provide an average payment of nearly $3 million in government and charitable contributions for each person who died in the attacks, with firefighters and police officers receiving an additional $1 million (Chen, 2004). However, there were grave problems associated with dispersing these millions. Family members of those killed in the attacks were reluctant to accept the government's Victim Compensation Fund.

Nearly six months after the federal government opened its checkbook to the relatives of the 3,200 people killed or seriously injured on September 11, fewer than ten families had filed completed applications, illustrating the complex nature of the process, the anguish or wariness some families still have about settling a victim's financial affairs, and lingering concerns about the government fund's fairness.

About five hundred families filed partial claims with the government's Victim Compensation Fund. But even that figure has been smaller than expected, disappointing some supporters of the fund and surprising detractors, too (Chen, 2002b). The problems grew as, on the one hand, family members battled over "inheritance rights" and several dozen "dueling claims" (Chen, 2002a) and, on the other, compensation to foreigners got bogged down in cultural differences regarding taxation, and inheritance rights (e.g., polygamous marriages) (Chen, 2002c). One example is a young man who had been sending money he earned to his parents in Peru:

> Mr. Carpio, a black belt in martial arts who aspired to be a lawyer, was his family's primary breadwinner, sending about $400 home to Lince, Peru, each month. But according to the Internal Revenue Service, non-Americans like Ms. Bautista and her husband do not count as dependents. As a result, Ms. Bautista would receive about 30 percent less than what an American family would.
>
> "It seems to me that they are being treated like second-class victims based on just the aberration of geography," Ms. Steinberg said. "And I think that would be unfair." (Chen, 2002c)

The compensation for survivors of those killed on 9/11 was potentially extended in 2016 when Congress overrode President Barack Obama's veto of a bill that permitted filing suit against Saudi Arabia, a sovereign nation suspected of aiding the 9/11 attackers. As noted in an earlier chapter, this nearly unanimous congressional approval was largely self-serving to encourage voter approval of them during the 2016 election.

3. *The absence of a clear target for reprisals contributed to the construction of broad symbolic enemies and goals referred to as "terrorism."* Patriotism was connected with an expansive fear of terrorism and enemies of the United States. The term *terrorism* was used to encompass an idea as well as a tactic or method. (Terrorism would also be viewed as a condition that

would only respond to force.) The waging of the "war on terrorism" focused on the "idea" and "the method," depending on the context of discussion and justification. The very broad definition of terrorism served the central authorities' purposes while also justifying action of others (e.g., Israel) in their own conflicts. Fear reflected the military-media complex:

> But how men and women interpret and respond to their fear—these are more than unconscious, personal reactions to imagined or even real dangers. They are also choices made under the influence of belief and ideology, in the shadow of elites and powerful institutions. Since September 11, the politics of fear has followed two distinct tracks: First, state officials and media pundits have defined and interpreted the objects of Americans' fears—Islamic fundamentalism and terrorism—in anti-political or non-political terms, which has raised the level of popular nervousness; and, second, these same elites have generated a fear of speaking out not only against the war and US foreign policy but also against a whole range of established institutions. (Robin, 2002)

Virtually all the major news media bolstered this view of terrorism, as network anchors cried on camera, evoked an angry tone, wore flags in lapels, and draped their sets and visual signatures (e.g., backgrounds) in patriotic slogans. Dan Rather, CBS anchorman, acknowledged the pressure to comply with propaganda and that many of the tough questions were not being asked. Rather told a British journalist,

> "It is an obscene comparison . . . but you know there was a time in South Africa that people would put flaming tyres around people's necks if they dissented. And in some ways the fear is that you will be necklaced here, you will have a flaming tyre of lack of patriotism put around your neck," he said. "Now it is that fear that keeps journalists from asking the toughest of the tough questions." . . ."It starts with a feeling of patriotism within oneself. It carries through with a certain knowledge that the country as a whole—and for all the right reasons—felt and continues to feel this surge of patriotism within themselves. And one finds oneself saying: 'I know the right question, but you know what? This is not exactly the right time to ask it.'" . . ."Limiting access, limiting information to cover the backsides of those who are in charge of the war, is extremely dangerous and cannot and should not be accepted. And I am sorry to say that, up to and including the moment of this interview, that overwhelmingly it has been accepted by the American people. And the current administration revels in that, they relish that, and they take refuge in that." (Engel, 2002)

These were extraordinary times requiring extraordinary measures. Patriotism and American resolve were central parts of the U.S. response, and numerous government and business messages of support ruled the day. There were few specific targets as "nation-states," so the focus was on a key individual, Osama bin Laden, and his "terrorist network" of camps that were located in Afghanistan, although the official message was emphasized that the United States was not at war with Afghanistan or Muslims but rather with terrorism and those who harbor them. Thus, even though Afghanistan was attacked, the official target was global terrorism whether it was connected to bin Laden or not (e.g., South America). One consequence of this was to promote more fear from potential terrorists and enemies of the United States.

The atmosphere of alarm and fear was heightened as federal law enforcement officials warned that more attacks were likely. On October 12, 2001, the House of Representatives advanced "antiterrorist" legislation to grant broad surveillance and detention powers to the federal government. The USA Patriot Act passed by a vote of 337 to 79 with little debate despite pleas from civil liberties advocates that the legislation could be a dangerous infringement on rights. Senator Russ Feingold (Wisconsin) was the only member of the Senate to oppose this draconian act that unleashed a multibillion-dollar surveillance industry that would undermine the civil liberties of U.S. citizens throughout the next decade. Some members of Congress acknowledged that they had not read the legislation. This act removed restraints that had been placed on the FBI and CIA because of their numerous civil rights violations (e.g., those associated with COINTELPRO) (Churchill & Vander Wall, 1990). One of the major changes was to permit warrantless email and Internet searches. One of the dissenters, John Conyers Jr. (D-Mich.), stated, "But we must remember that just as this horrendous act could destroy us from without, it could also destroy us from within" (*New York Times*, October 13, 2001, B6). Representative Conyers was concerned with the provisions to relax civil rights and expand state power. The ease with which these extraordinary measures were passed foreshadowed an expanding circle of "terrorism control" to other areas of American life.

Leaders in the United States added to communalism and promoting a like mind among U.S. citizens by insisting that terrorists could be anywhere and ratcheted up various Homeland Security measures. Americans were implored to seek not only retribution but also salvation from fear by supporting a series of draconian measures. The common identity flowing from popular culture post-9/11 echoed support of leadership as identity. As Campbell (1998) argued, U.S. foreign policy actions and definitions are oriented to establishing its identity to citizens and others. Dangerousness, or the "evangelism of fear," with death as its impetus and salvation as its goal, required concern not only with external issues but with the self as well.

Elite propaganda efforts promoted joining the self with the state. This was operationalized as security. Security was expanded at airports, borders, and public events, particularly major popular-culture performances (e.g., the World Series, the Super Bowl, and the Winter Olympics). The general message to the public was that security was being provided by the state. This included federal regulation of airport security. Security rituals reminded thousands of Americans at airports and millions of television audience members that it was essential to take off one's shoes, endure invasive "pat downs," and even frisk "little old ladies in wheelchairs" in front of guards armed with automatic weapons. It was barely mentioned that nine of the eleven hijackers who took over the deadly jets had been stopped and checked by the security system in place on that tragic day (Eggen, 2002). Clearly, the problem was not primarily with airport security.

The situation was not unlike the paranoia about spies during World War II and especially the Red Scare during the Cold War (Barson & Heller, 2001; Jenkins, 1999). How would terrorists be distinguished from law-abiding followers of the Muslim faith? After all, the terrorists had been in the country for months before striking; they had been "sleepers," infiltrating American life and institutions, even receiving flight training from private flying schools. What could be done to prevent those "sleeping" from engaging in further attacks? Such questions were answered with more surveillance. More state control and regulation was accepted as a collective view of the struggle against terrorism. Rallying around the flag in fear of our survival was the key theme, and it was rekindled during Donald Trump's campaign for president in 2016.

Chapter 2 discussed how popular-culture programs help defuse concerns about civil liberty violations, including torture. There was little criticism and dissent about administration incursions into civil liberties and violations of due process. Authorities called for relaxing civil rights and detention protections as several thousand immigrants and some citizens were questioned and more than 1,200 were detained without due process. The social definition of impending attacks by terrorists among us was unchallenged in public discourse, with the exception of some Internet traffic. The major news media presented virtually no detractors from this view. Major political leaders were all but silent in opposing such action. Indeed, major news magazines like *Newsweek* offered a columnist who promoted more secret police at home with a "domestic" CIA:

> There's only one way to get security and liberty at the same time. Authorize the FBI to engage in domestic intelligence with clearly demarcated powers; put the agency under much stronger "civilian" oversight, including from Congress, and let it know specifically what it can and cannot do. "Without a national reorganization, every agency in government will get into domestic intelligence furtively, and that will be much worse for civil liberties," says Zelikow. "As last week's frenzy makes clear, no one will want to be blamed for missing a lead after the next terrorist attack." (Zakaria, 2002)

Civil libertarian Alan Dershowitz argued that judges should issue "torture warrants" when terrorist suspects were jailed (Walker, 2002), and ABC's *Nightline* discussed using torture. As a producer for Ted Koppel's show stated in an email to prospective audience members,

> One of the questions that Ted is going to ask tonight, and probably the first one, is about torture. Now I think it's fair to say that six months ago, before the attacks, no one would have thought that there was any question about a total ban on torture. We, as a country, don't believe in that. *We take people's rights very seriously.* We criticize those countries that don't.
>
> But as we all know, *things have changed.* Now no one is really advocating that anyone in the U.S. resort to torture, but let me lay out the question as Ted has laid it out to us. Say that you knew that a bomb was going off somewhere in your city in the next 12 hours. Say that you had captured one of the terrorists, and you knew he knew where the bomb was. In order to save innocent lives, would you still be willing to say no to the idea of torture, if nothing else was working? How far are we willing to go in this war against terrorism? Especially when we're talking about trying to save lives? Hopefully, no one will ever be in this situation, but it does raise some interesting questions. (*Nightline*, March 8, 2002; emphasis added)

The discussion of how we should treat the enemy also included prisoners. The writ of habeas corpus was greatly compromised. According to a report by Amnesty International,

> It states that a "disturbing level of secrecy" continues to surround the detentions and suggests "that a significant number of detainees continue to be deprived of certain basic rights guaranteed under international law." . . .
>
> "These are really issues that cut to the heart of our American understanding of justice, to say nothing of international standards," said William F. Schulz, executive director of Amnesty International USA. (*Washington Post*, March 13, 2002, A13)

Subsequent abuses of U.S. and international standards of justice and human rights would be well documented over the next decade, including the brutal photographs of mistreatment at Abu Ghraib prison in Iraq and the kidnapping, detention, and torture of more than 150 individuals at CIA "black" (viz., secret) sites in at least six countries: Afghanistan, Lithuania, Morocco, Poland, Romania, and Thailand.

> The Bush Administration referred to these methods as "enhanced interrogation techniques." "Enhanced interrogation techniques" included "walling" (quickly pulling the detainee forward and then thrusting him against a flexible false wall), "water dousing," "waterboarding," "stress positions" (forcing the detainee to remain in body positions designed to induce physical discomfort), "wall standing" (forcing the detainee to remain standing with his arms outstretched in front of him so that his fingers touch a wall four to five feet away and support his entire body weight), "cramped confinement" in a box, "insult slaps"

(slapping the detainee on the face with fingers spread), "facial hold" (holding a detainee's head temporarily immobile during interrogation with palms on either side of the face), "attention grasp" (grasping the detainee with both hands, one hand on each side of the collar opening, and quickly drawing him toward the interrogator), forced nudity, sleep deprivation while being vertically shackled, and dietary manipulation. (Horowitz & Cammarano, 2013)

The United States engaged in extensive torture of prisoners during the Bush administration. In particular, the use of waterboarding, or inducing the experience of drowning, was widespread, having been used on a prominent Al Qaeda leader, Khalid Sheikh Mohammed, 183 times after his capture in March 2003 (http://waterboarding.org/). The Senate Committee's Report on the Use of Torture (the declassified version released on December 3, 2014) detailed some of the excesses. President Obama signed Executive Order 1349 in January 2009 to prohibit the CIA and other agencies from torture and to limit interrogation techniques to those approved by the Army Field Manual and international law (http://www.nytimes.com/interactive/2014/12/09/world/cia-torture-report-document.html). Particularly outspoken against torture was Arizona senator John McCain, who had been tortured after being captured during the Vietnam War. During a speech in 2014, the senator stated:

"I know from personal experience that the abuse of prisoners will produce more bad than good intelligence. I know that victims of torture will offer intentionally misleading information if they think their captors will believe it. I know they will say whatever they think their torturers want them to say if they believe it will stop their suffering."

McCain added (emphatically) that "the use of torture compromises that which most distinguishes us from our enemies, our belief that all people, even captured enemies, possess basic human rights." (http://www.theatlantic.com/politics/archive/2014/12/John-Mccain-Speech-Senate-Republican-CIA-Torture-Report/383589/)

With such clear-cut statements, along with President Obama's previous assertion that U.S. forces would not engage in torture, the matter appeared to be settled and the United States would return to its own legal standards of pre 9/11 as well as those of the international community. But then Donald Trump campaigned for president, and as he sought to distance himself from more than a dozen challengers he brazenly declared, as noted in a previous chapter, that, as president, he would reinstitute waterboarding—and more—even stating that he would authorize the killing of terrorists' families. In a follow-up interview, he said:

"Did somebody tell ISIS, 'Look, we're going to treat your guys well. Will you please do us a favor and treat our guys well?' They don't do that. We're not playing by—we are playing by rules, but they have no rules. It's very hard to win when that's the case," Trump said, adding that the United States' ban on waterboarding is a sign of weakness. (http://www.cnn.com/2016/03/06/politics/donald-trump-torture/)

Trump was very critical of Bush's decisions to invade Afghanistan and Iraq, and he insisted—incorrectly—that he had always opposed those wars. But his sharp tone about torture of terrorists, as well as claims that he had surefire plans to defeat ISIS, inadvertently turned him back toward the Bush policies. Indeed, he was endorsed by several former members of the Bush administration.

Following Bush's decision to invade Iraq, there was some dissension, but with a few exceptions, most of the criticism was against the detractors. Criticism was limited as Bush gained 90 percent approval in opinion polls. The "younger generation" was implored to meet the new challenge; this was, after all, their war, and the mass media carried youthful testimonies of newfound loyalty and awakening that would have made a tent-meeting evangelist proud. For example, *Newsweek* published two statements by young people, one "confessing" her naïveté about the "real world" and another by a former university student who criticized "antimilitary culture" with a call to arms:

> "Before the attack, all I could think of was how to write a good rap. Now I'm putting together a packet on our foreign policy toward the Middle East. . . . "In an ideal world, pacifism is the only answer. I am not eager to say this, but we do not live in an ideal world. . . .
>
> "Americans may want peace, but terrorists want bloodshed. I've come to accept the idea of a focused war on terrorists as the best way to ensure our country's safety. In the words of Mother Jones, what we need to do now is 'pray for the dead and fight like hell for the living.'" (R. Newman, 2001)

Nearly three weeks later, university campuses were chastised in a "My Turn" column from a Marine Corps officer:

> As anyone who has attended a top college in the past three decades knows, patriotism in the eyes of many professors is synonymous with a lack of sophistication at best, racism at worst. Yet, it is clear to me that the antimilitary culture that exists on many campuses is remarkably out of step with the views of the vast majority of Americans. . . . Now is the time for America's brightest young adults to enlist in this good fight against global terrorism—to join organizations like the military's Special Forces, the FBI and the CIA, whose members risk their lives on the front lines of this battle. It is also time for America's universities to support and encourage—not undermine—this call to service. (D. Sullivan, 2001)

Such pronouncements would be used by elites in the weeks after the attacks not only to claim a national consensus for a massive infusion of social control and military intervention but also to push for the reinstatement of the ROTC at Harvard and other campuses.

Academics and traditional critics were all but silent, and *Sacramento Bee* president and publisher Janis Besler Heaphy was booed off the stage during a commencement address at California State University, Sacramento, after she suggested that the national response to terrorism could erode press freedoms and individual liberties. One professor in attendance stated, "For the first time in my life, I can see how something like the Japanese internment camps could happen in our country" (*New York Times*, December 21, 2001, B1). (Fifteen years later associates of president-elect Donald Trump would propose a registry for Muslims and possibly internment camps [Bromwich, 2016]). Attorney General John Ashcroft made it clear that anyone concerned with the civil rights of the suspicious was also suspect. Ashcroft told members of a Senate committee that critics "aid terrorists" and undermine national unity:

> "To those who pit Americans against immigrants and citizens against noncitizens, to those who scare peace-loving people with phantoms of lost liberty, my message is this: Your tactics aid terrorists, for they erode our national unity and diminish our resolve," he said. "They give ammunition to America's enemies, and pause to America's friends." (Minneapolis-St. Paul *Star Tribune*, December 9, 2001, 30A)

Ironically, this was exactly what presidential candidate Trump did during the 2016 campaign when he proposed more surveillance of Muslim citizens.

Academics and other critics were targeted for their critical comments, even though they were not well publicized. One nonprofit group, the American Council of Trustees and Alumni (one founding member is Lynn Cheney, wife of Vice President Cheney), posted a web page accusing dozens of scholars, students, and a university president of unpatriotic behavior, accusing them of being "the weak link in America's response to the attack" and for invoking "tolerance and diversity as antidotes to evil" (*Arizona Republic*, November 24, 2001, A11). (This association also issued a report, "Defending Civilization: How Our Universities Are Failing America and What Can Be Done about It.")

Students of propaganda know that the mass media are central propaganda instruments, not only in content but also in the format and overall presentation and "look" (Altheide & Johnson, 1980; Doob, 1966; Ellenius & European Science Foundation, 1998; Jackall, 1994; Powell, 1999; Speier, 1969). With network and local nightly newscasts draped in flag colors, lapel flags, and patriotic slogans reporting events primarily through the viewpoint of the United States (e.g., "us" and "we"), news organizations presented content and form that was interpreted by the publisher of *Harper's Magazine* as sending

> signals to the viewers to some extent that the media are acting as an arm of the government, as opposed to an independent, objective pur-

veyor of information, which is what we're supposed to be. (Rutenberg & Carter, 2001)

Such unanimity added pressure to say and do the right thing and above all to avoid saying the wrong thing. The formal and informal pressure on dissent was enormous:

> "We've never seen a rollback of free speech like this," says Will Doherty of the Electronic Frontier Foundation, a San Francisco–based organization that advocates for freedom of expression in new technology. "Dissent exists," insists Anthony Romero, executive director of the American Civil Liberties Union, sounding like a man trying to convince himself. "But it's not heard as loudly as it should be."

A number of factors virtually silenced America's culture of dissent. One central element is a tidal wave of public opinion, forged by both anger and fear, supporting the broad goals of defeating terrorists and protecting against terrorism. The Bush administration has used that mandate to convey a message that dissent is, if not downright un-American, at least dangerous. But there is more to it than that.

Institutions that would typically offer opposition—the Democratic Party, college campuses, and the political left—were all reeling from September 11, too traumatized, polarized, and disorganized to produce much more than a peep of protest. And the powerful forces that control society's megaphones—the news media and entertainment industry—are too wary, too corporate, and too concerned about audience share to give voice to anything other than mainstream views (*Boston Globe*, January 27, 2002, 10).

The drug war and ongoing concerns with crime contributed to the expansion of fear with terrorism. News reports and advertisements joined drug use with terrorism and helped shift "drugs" from criminal activity to unpatriotic action. As the destructive acts were defined as "war" rather than "attacks," it became apparent that the propaganda about one war would replicate the other war. By this I refer to the demonization of drugs/terrorists, the call for harsh measures against both, and the unanimity—especially among news media—that force was the best weapon. Messages demonizing Osama bin Laden, his Taliban supporters, and "Islamic extremists" linked these suspects with the destructive clout of illegal drugs and especially drug lords. One implication, then, was to extend the war against terrorism to those countries producing drugs:

> "Twelve of the 25 groups designated as terrorist organizations by the State Department have ties to drug traffickers," administration officials say.
>
> "Drug traffickers benefit from the terrorists' military skills, weapons supply and access to clandestine organizations," the State Department's ambassador at large for counterterrorism, Francis X. Taylor,

told the Senate subcommittee. "Terrorists gain a source of revenue and expertise in illicit transfer and laundering of proceeds from illicit transactions."

The head of the Drug Enforcement Administration, Asa Hutchinson, urged Congress to free up $18 million to permit the agency to resume drug interdiction efforts in Afghanistan. "We have to understand that by reducing demand for drugs, we will also reduce the financial structure that supports terrorist groups," Hutchinson told the senators. "There is multisource information that Osama bin Laden himself has been involved in the financing and facilitation of heroin trafficking activities." . . . "It seems to me that we have an opportunity today to really change the farm processes in Afghanistan," she said. "If we can't do it today, when our people are there, we are never going to be able to do it." Hutchinson and the State Department's assistant secretary for international narcotics suggested there might be significant impediments that keep the United States from destroying the upcoming crop. (*Dallas Morning News*, March 14, 2002, KO487, reprinted in *Arizona Republic*, March 14, 2002, A8)

The politics of fear extended beyond the U.S. borders as policymakers at home and abroad defined their "problem" as a terrorist threat that also needed strong government action. The extraordinary rendition mentioned above was aided by no fewer than fifty-four countries, including those that granted air space to secret CIA aircraft. The broad use of terrorism as an idea and as a method that required (and justified) extensive retaliation was seized by other countries to define and legitimize control and military policies. Numerous "internal" conflicts and revolutionary movements were classified as "terrorism," and any government that opposed them would, presumably, be joining the United States in its fight against global terrorism. Within a matter of days, several countries vowed to join the United States in its fight against terrorism, including Colombia, Peru, and Israel. President Bush's call for an end to global terrorism and his vow to do whatever it takes to win the struggle was quickly seized on by Israeli prime minister Ariel Sharon to justify and intensify the conflict with the Palestinians and Palestine Liberation Organization leader Yasser Arafat:

"Arafat chose a strategy of terrorism and established a coalition of terrorism," Mr. Sharon told the Parliament today. "Terrorist actions against Israeli citizens are no different from bin Laden's terrorism against American citizens." (Bennet, 2001)

Placing virtually all "opposition" forces in the terrorist camp was consistent with the military-media script of pervasive fear and opposition. This would set the tone for Israel's brutal bombardment of the Gaza Strip in the years to follow. The serious opposition that disappeared with the end of the Cold War was reconstituted worldwide as "global terrorism." More marketing and investing would be required.

4. *Consumption as investing promoted a massive increase in military spending.* The military support was part of a larger effort to market security for homes, families, and businesses. These efforts were sustained by weekly reports about terror alerts, asking Americans to be more vigilant and report suspicious activities. Truck drivers were enlisted as another line of defense against terrorism. Of course, the public confidence in the American military to protect us was related partly to a heightened respect for key institutions and their leaders. For example, the *Washington Post* reported that a National Opinion Research Center survey found that more than three-fourths of respondents had a "great deal" of confidence in the military, nearly double from a year ago (*Arizona Republic*, no date). Certainly all public employees—and especially the military, police, and fire department workers—benefited from this outpouring of support that underscored a major message that varies with social issues over time: that "they" are "us" and are working on our behalf. Reports and images resonated communal themes of support for our "heroes." The participatory rhetoric was aimed even at children who were asked to send a dollar to Afghani youngsters.

One of the largest increases in military spending since World War II quickly followed September 11. By mid-2005, the war in Iraq was costing the United States $1 billion per week. The Department of Defense and the reborn military-industrial complex heeded President Bush's pledge to combat terrorism with "whatever it takes, whatever it costs." Fueled by the burning message that the United States was ill prepared to wage war against terrorism abroad and still protect its mainland, a proposed 20 percent increase in the military budget was hardly debated, although the exact benefits to homeland security were far from clear. The general message was less about shoring up military coffers than it was about investing in the nation's future to protect the country against terrorism in "far-flung" Afghanistan—at a cost of $1 billion per month—but also at home (Westphal, 2001). Vice President Cheney noted in an interview that such investment was essential for the security of the United States:

> "I don't see . . . how anybody can argue that we cannot afford to defend America," he said. "And we're going to have to defend it against conventional threats. We're going to have to defend it against ballistic missile threats. We're going to have to defend it against the threat of terrorism." (Westphal, 2001)

A military and defense budget was proposed that was commensurate with the communal "fear of terrorism." A military budget that dwarfed other nations got even bigger over the next few weeks (Knickerbocker, 2002). The call to arms strengthened the "iron triangle"—Congress, the Pentagon, and the defense industries—that had been subdued during the "peaceful 90s," as a projected defense budget of nearly $400 billion was emerging from reconstructed domestic and global responsibilities. Business and industry were called on to help: "Within weeks of the terrorist attacks, the Defense Department issued a 'Broad Agency Announcement' in which military contractors were asked for 'help in combating terrorism.' Thousands of proposals have been submitted since then" (Knickerbocker, 2002). British journalists noted,

> The attacks and the subsequent war in Afghanistan—not to mention two sharp annual rises in US military budgets by President George W. Bush—have persuaded investors to pay attention to defence stocks after years of neglect. (Burt & Nichol, 2002)

Another analyst noted that investment was good for business and the military and also for former administration officials (e.g., Frank Carlucci, former Secretary of Defense, and James Baker, former Secretary of State):

> The "military-industrial complex" that General Eisenhower warned of presents potential political landmines for any administration. For example, many former Republican officials and political associates of those now in the Bush administration are associated with the Carlyle Group, an equity investment firm with billions of dollars in military and aerospace assets. (Knickerbocker, 2002)

The House of Representatives passed a $383 billion defense budget on May 9, 2002. The Senate passed (71 to 22) a $31.5 billion counterterrorism bill on June 6, 2002. This was $2 billion more than the measure approved in May by the House. This legislation reflected the mood of leaders who sought to be decisive and appear strong to their constituents, who were receiving virtually no contextual or historical information about underlying issues that may have contributed to the attacks.

The widespread support for military expenditures and the public's tacit approval of civil liberty restrictions—including profiling of Arab Americans—reflected fear-induced communalism surrounding terrorism. The politics of fear was becoming more visible in numerous social policies. The military expenditures were commensurate with a socially constructed morality play of the enemy and its horrendous acts. News reports reflected the mass media's use of routine "elite" news sources to "get the story" of attacks and promote entertaining reports about "America Strikes Back." The public support quickly became a resource to use in "striking back" when the Bush administration proposed a "first strike" — not against Afghanistan or al Qaeda networks but against sovereign nations that either support terrorist activities or engage in threatening acts. Iraq and several other nations were part of the "axis of evil" that was targeted by President Bush for possible first strikes by the United States. President Bush implored Pakistan and India to resolve their ongoing dispute peacefully. But just a few days after posing at World War II cemeteries for a "photo op," the blustering Bush threatened international law and order when he told West Point cadets that the only strategy for defeating America's new enemies was to strike first.

> "If we wait for threats to fully materialize, we will have waited too long," the president said, speaking at the commencement of the 204th graduating class of West Point, the nation's oldest military academy. "We must take the battle to the enemy, disrupt his plans and confront the worst threats before they emerge."
>
> In a toughly worded speech that seemed aimed at preparing Americans for a potential war with Iraq, Mr. Bush added, "The only path to safety is action. And this nation will act." He did not mention Iraq by name, but warned that "even weak states and closed groups could attain a catastrophic power to strike great nations. . . ."
>
> Looking directly at the graduates, he added: "I am proud of the men and women who have fought on my orders. The nation respects and trusts our military, and we are confident of your victories to come." (Busmiller, 2002)

The commercial consumption of terrorism continued to escalate over the next decade. This was done indirectly in various ways. Most notably, perhaps, was the growing militarization of American culture, particularly through the adoption of military parlance and slang—partly derived from dozens of movies—but also clothing—camouflage fashion. One of the most blatant, you may recall, was when baseball's traditional seventh-inning-stretch song "Take Me Out to the Ballgame" was superseded by "God Bless America," and gradually the militarization of sports, ranging from putting American flags on uniforms, to having military celebrations at more and more events. This includes the "pay for patriotism" deals in which the military paid fifty teams—especially the National Football League—across all the major professional sports nearly $7 million for showing patriotic themes and celebrations to help with recruiting.

> "Those of us go to sporting events and see them honoring the heroes," U.S. Sen. Jeff Flake (R-Ariz.) said. "You get a good feeling in your heart. Then to find out they're doing it because they're compensated for it, it leaves you underwhelmed. It seems a little unseemly." (Gantt, 2015)

The report revealed that 72 of 122 professional sports contracts involved paid patriotism.

> They included on-field color guard ceremonies, performances of the national anthem, and ceremonial first pitches and puck drops. . . . "Americans deserve the ability to assume that tributes for our men and women in military uniform are genuine displays of national pride, which many are, rather than taxpayer-funded DOD marketing gimmicks," the report said. . . . "Even if we accept the DOD's assurances that the young men and women watching these games may be sufficiently inspired to military service by a half-time reenlistment ceremo-

ny, some of the displays funded in these contracts defy explanation as a legitimate recruiting purpose and may be little more than a taxpayer-funded boondoggle." (Baron-Lopez & Waldron, 2015)

But that wasn't enough. More professional, college, and even high school teams have militarized their uniforms. Arizona State University got special approval from the NCAA to honor former football player Pat Tillman (see chapter 9) by having ASU players wear a special quasi-military uniform, complete with "special op" cleats, a version of combat boots, in a game against Oregon in 2015.

CONCLUSION

The politics of fear benefited from terrorism. The 9/11 attacks were defined in the news media and popular culture as an assault on American culture. As later chapters show, by 2015 terrorism was viewed as a condition that would require extreme measures of surveillance, stealth drone attacks, and a combative discourse during the 2016 presidential election to ride a politics of fear into the White House. News media and popular-culture depictions of the U.S. reaction to terror attacks reflects a culture and collective identities steeped in marketing, popular culture, consumerism, and fear. Elite news management and propaganda by the military-media complex produced terrorism scenarios that reflected in national agendas and everyday life.

Communalism and commensurability were joined through consumption as social participation. On the one hand, mass media symbolic constructions of victims and terrorism contributed to a "national experience" oriented to communal values and reaffirmation of cultural narratives. Citizens were asked to give, buy, and support. On the other hand, these powerful symbolic definitions supported open-ended commensurate increases in military and police authority while expanding governmental surveillance and diminishing civil liberties. Opinion polls indicated that American citizens accepted reduced civil liberties because the "world has changed." It is as though "pre-9/11" civil liberties were there to protect citizens but "post-9/11" civil liberties could endanger citizens. Indeed, political bluster about engaging in "first strikes" against sovereign countries suggests that "risk policing" will be proactive (Ericson & Haggerty, 1997).

News reports stressing communal suffering as well as opportunities to participate in helping survivors and defeating terrorism promoted the collective identity of terrorist attacks. More traditional and culturally resonant narratives about crime, drugs, and evil were, essentially, transformed into the "terror story." Sorrow, suffering, empathy, and pain were merged with fear and vengeance. National character was played out in scenarios of heroics, sacrifice, suffering, marketing, and spending.

Patriotic responses to the attacks were joined with commercialism and pleas for donations as well as support for an ill-defined and nebulous "war on terrorism" that referred to an idea as well as a tactic or method. Building on a foundation of fear, citizens who saw the repetitive visuals of the World Trade Center attacks generously followed governmental directives to donate blood, supplies, and money to the immediate victims of the attacks. They were also urged to travel, purchase items, and engage in numerous patriotic rituals, while civil liberties were compromised and critics were warned by the attorney general to not "give ammunition to America's enemies."

A new foreign policy, born nine months after the attacks of 9/11, was skillfully implanted in a fertile womb of fear and victimization. Avowed social unanimity of agreement was a strategic tool for expanding commensurate reaction to the attacks. Patriotic rituals continued months after zero-percent financing of cars disappeared. News reports reminded audiences of the "long struggle" ahead, and the repeated "accidental bombing" of civilians in Afghanistan was cast as part of the struggle against terrorism and the ongoing stand against evil. The circle was completed when advertising and public service announcements connected evil drug use with the support of terrorism. Consistent with symbolic commensuration, attacking one was attacking the other. And we could do it together. The impact of U.S. reactions to terrorism at home and abroad, including the "blowback" of a failed foreign policy that greased the rails of massive military intervention in the Middle East, are examined in the remaining chapters.

SIX

Terrorism and the Politics of Fear

Al Qaeda is to terror what the Mafia is to crime.

—George W. Bush

We did not finish the job against al Qaeda in Afghanistan. . . . Instead, we got a color-coded politics of fear. . . . A deliberate strategy to misrepresent 9/11 to sell a war against a country that had nothing to do with 9/11.

—Barack Obama, 2007, campaigning for president

They're bringing drugs, they're bringing crime, and they're rapists.

—Donald Trump, 2016, campaigning for president

Fear expanded after 9/11. The media changed terrorism and terrorism changed the media, which became more instantaneous, personal, and visual. The politics of fear promoted the sense of risk. This became evident with the accelerating rise of digital media during Barack Obama's presidency, and it culminated with Donald Trump's campaign propaganda that relied heavily on his personal daily tweets about terrorists, immigrants, and other threats to American life. His comments were often false and incorrect, but it did not matter in an era that cared less about authenticated facts than about mere opinions that supported one's prejudices (Altheide, 2014a).

The journalistic stature of terrorism has changed since the initial panic after 9/11. Terrorism has joined crime as a master narrative of fear that contains many accounts (e.g., justifications) and disclaimers for all kinds of behavior. This means that terrorism and its numerous artfully constructed meanings and nuances are an important context of experience in its own right, essentially blocking out other considerations. Thus, terrorism has become a social definition that encompasses a self-referential discourse and justification, on the one hand, while also serving as a rationale for revenge and counterattacks, on the other hand. Carefully orchestrating, restricting, and controlling images can manage terrorism and news sources that get to make claims about social reality. Essentially, the terrorism narrative holds that terrorism (and terrorists) does not follow civilized rules of warfare and that since terrorism is not justified insofar as "innocent" civilians are targeted, then the moves against them can also be outside acceptable limits—torture, kidnapping, and widespread killing of civilians in the pursuit of terrorists. This chapter examines how the constant bombardment of media messages about fear has contributed to more surveillance, resistance, cynicism, and ultimately, less trust and good faith. A cursory examination follows of how terrorism was linked to the politics of fear through specific events over a relatively short time period.

Previous chapters have set forth the concept of the politics of fear and provided explanations and examples of its logic and how it is connected to the mass media and popular culture. The context of crime reporting by an increasingly entertainment-oriented mass media contributed to the expansion of media logic throughout social life. Increasingly it seems that what people experience as audiences of popular culture is reflected in their experiences with social institutions, especially agents of social control. The preceding chapter argued that the war on terrorism was enmeshed in this same politics of fear but greatly extended it by drawing analogies with crime and the drug war and even suggesting that dissent at home was aiding the enemy. A number of examples were given about how social life changed to accommodate this newest politics of fear, particularly the intrusiveness of social control and surveillance into more of our lives. This chapter examines another aspect of the politics of fear: language. The argument is that changing the meanings and definitions of words and symbols of everyday life to reflect fear and social control is a very powerful way to connect social changes with social consciousness.

Fear as a topic was presented in news reports about terrorism and victimization. The news media's use of these terms is tied to a longstanding linkage of fear and victimization with crime that has been fueled by government and police officials who serve as dominant news sources and therefore are significant actors in defining problems and setting political agendas (Chiricos et al., 2000; Kappeler et al., 1999; Surette, 1998). As noted several times in previous chapters, propaganda research shows that decision makers who serve as key news sources can shape perceptions of mass audiences and promote acquiescence to state control measures (Ellenius & European Science Foundation, 1998; Gerth, 1992; Jackall, 1994). An expansive use of the word *fear* in news reports has been documented (Altheide, 2002b; Altheide & Michalowski, 1999; Furedi, 1997; Glassner, 1999). Indeed, the extensive use of fear to highlight crime news has produced a discourse of fear that may be defined as the pervasive communication, symbolic awareness, and expectation that danger and risk are a central feature of the effective environment, or the physical and symbolic environment as people define and experience it in everyday life. Journalistic accounts about terrorism reflect news organizations' reliance on official news sources to provide entertaining reports compatible with long-established symbols of fear, crime, and victimization about threats to individuals and the United States in the "fight against terrorism." I argue that tying terrorism coverage to an expansive discourse of fear has contributed to the emergence of the politics of fear, or decision makers' promotion and use of audience beliefs and assumptions about danger, risk, and fear in order to achieve certain goals. News reports about terrorism in five nationally prominent newspapers reflect the terms and discourse associated with the politics of fear. The terms *crime, victim,* and *fear* are joined with news reports about terrorism to construct public discourse that reflects symbolic relationships about order, danger, and threat that may be exploited by political decision makers.

An overview of the discourse of fear will be followed by an elaboration of the politics of fear and a discussion of the materials and content analysis of news reports. Data about the emerging politics of fear and how it is manifested in news coverage involving fear, victimization, terrorism, and crime will then be presented.

NEWS AND THE DISCOURSE OF FEAR

As noted previously, the common thread for most scholarly and popular analysis of fear in American society is crime and victimization. Social constructionist approaches to the study of social problems and emergent social movements stress how mass-media accounts of crime, violence, and victimization are simplistic and often decontextualize rather complex events in order to reflect narratives that demonize and offer simplistic explanations (Best, 1999; Best, 1995; Ericson, Baranek, & Chan, 1991; Fishman & Cavender, 1998; Johnson, 1995) that often involve state intervention while adding to the growing list of victims.

To reiterate a previous point, the discourse of fear has been constructed through news and popular-culture accounts. The main focus of the discourse of fear in the United States for the past thirty years or so has been crime. News reports about crime and fear have contributed to the approach taken by many social scientists in studying how crime is linked with fear. Numerous researchers link crime, the mass media, and fear (Chiricos et al., 1997; Ericson, 1995; Ferraro, 1995; C. A. Garland, 1997; Pearson, 1983; Shirlow & Pain, 2003b). There is also an impressive literature on crime, victimization, and fear (Baer & Chambliss, 1997; Chiricos et al., 1997; Ferraro, 1995; Warr, 1987, 1990, 1992). Other researchers have examined the nature and consequences of fear in connection with crime but also in relationship to political symbols and theories of social control

(Altheide, 2002b; Ferrell et al., 2015; Furedi, 1997; C. A. Garland, 1997; Glassner, 1999; Massumi, 1993; Moehle & Levitt, 1991; Naphy & Roberts, 1997; Russell, 1998).

Crime and terrorism discourses are artfully produced. The most pervasive aspect of this "victim" perspective is crime. Criminal victimization, including numerous crime myths (e.g., predators, stranger-danger, and random violence) (Best, 1999), contributed to the cultural foundation of the politics of fear, particularly the belief that we were all actual or potential victims and needed to be protected from the source of fear—criminals or terrorists (D. Garland, 2001). Politicians and state control agencies, working with news media as "news sources," have done much to capitalize on this concern and to promote a sense of insecurity and reliance on formal agents of social control—and related businesses—to provide surveillance, protection, revenge, and punishment to protect us, to save us (Chiricos et al., 1997; Ericson et al., 1991; Surette, 1992).

The mass media and popular culture are best conceived of as key elements of our symbolic environment rather than as independent causes and effects. News does not merely set agendas (Iyengar & Kinder, 1987; Shaw & McCombs, 1977); rather, consistent with symbolic interaction theory, news that relies on certain symbols and promotes particular relationships among words, deeds, and issues also guides the perspectives, frameworks, language, and discourse that we use in relating to certain problems as well as related issues. My focus in this chapter is on news that guides discourse.

Social meanings are constructed through news reports by associating words with certain problems and issues. Repeated use of certain terms is linked to public discourse (Altheide & Michalowski, 1999; Beckett, 1996; Ekecrantz, 1998; Fowler, 1991; Gamson, Croteau, Hoynes, & Sasson, 1992; Potter & Wetherell, 1987; van Dijk, 1988; Zhondang & Kosicki, 1993). Tracking the emergence of new "connections" over a period of time is one way to assess the process of the social construction of reality. Research documents how fear and crime have been joined. Crime and threats to the public order—and therefore all good citizens—are part of the focus of fear, but the topics change over time. As noted in chapter 4, what they all have in common is pointing to the "other," the outsider, the nonmember, the alien.

Fear, crime, terrorism, and victimization are experienced and known vicariously through the mass media and social media by audience members. Information technology, entertainment programming, and perspectives are incorporated into a media logic that is part of the everyday life of audience members. News formats, or the way of selecting, organizing, and presenting information, shape audience assumptions and preferences for certain kinds of information. The mass media are important in shaping public agendas by influencing what people think about and how events and issues are packaged and presented. Certain news forms have been developed as packages or "frames" for transforming some experience into reports that will be recognized and accepted by the audience as "news." Previous research has shown how the "problem frame" was encouraged by communication formats and in turn has promoted the use of "fear" throughout American society (Altheide, 1997). Other work has demonstrated that the linkage of crime with fear has promoted a discourse of fear, or the pervasive communication, symbolic awareness, and expectation that danger and risk are a central feature of everyday life (Altheide, 1997, 2002a; Altheide & Michalowski, 1999; Ericson & Haggerty, 1997).

NEWS SOURCES AND THE POLITICS OF FEAR

A politics of fear rests on the discourse of fear. The politics of fear serves as a conceptual linkage for power, propaganda, news and popular culture, and an array of intimidating symbols and experiences such as crime and terrorism. The politics of fear resides not in an immediate threat from an individual leader (e.g., Senator Joseph McCarthy [Griffith 1987]), but rather in the public discourse that characterizes social life as dangerous, fearful, and filled with actual or potential victims. This symbolic order invites protection, policing, and intervention to prevent further victimization. A public discourse of fear invites the politics of fear. It is not fear per se that is important in social life but rather how fear is defined and realized in everyday social interaction. The role of the news media is very important in carrying selective news sources' messages. News sources are claims makers, and studies of crime news show that government and police officials dominate how crime is framed (Ericson, Baranek, & Chan, 1987; Ericson et al., 1989; Surette, 1992). Likewise, government and military officials also dominated news reports about terrorism and fear:

> But how men and women interpret and respond to their fear—these are more than unconscious, personal reactions to imagined or even real dangers. They are also choices made under the influence of belief and ideology, in the shadow of elites and powerful institutions. There is, then, a politics of fear. Since September 11, that politics has followed two distinct tracks: First, state officials and media pundits have defined and interpreted the objects of Americans' fears—Islamic fundamentalism and terrorism—in anti-political or non-political terms, which has raised the level of popular nervousness; and, second, these same elites have generated a fear of speaking out not only against the war and US foreign policy but also against a whole range of established institutions. (Robin, 2002)

Newspapers as well as television network news relied heavily on administration sources that directed the focus and language of news coverage. This was particularly apparent with those persons interviewed. A study by the *Columbia Journalism Review* documented this trend:

> It exacerbates our tendency to rely on official sources, which is the easiest, quickest way to get both the "he said" and the "she said," and, thus, "balance." According to numbers from the media analyst Andrew Tyndall, of the 414 stories on Iraq broadcast on NBC, ABC, and CBS from last September to February, all but thirty-four originated at the White House, Pentagon, and State Department. So we end up with too much of the "official" truth. (Cunningham, 2003)

Even newsmagazines like *Newsweek* concurred that the news was being managed:

> News management is at the heart of the administration's shake-up of Iraq policy. The National Security Council recently created four new committees to handle the situation in Iraq. One is devoted entirely to media coordination—stopping the bad news from overwhelming the good. (*Newsweek*, October 27, 2003)

Very dramatically, journalists cried on camera, wore flag pins on their lapels, and often referred to those involved in planning and fighting the Afghanistan and Iraq wars as "we." Moreover, they invoked routinely the claim that the "world is different," that security and safety can no longer be taken for granted, and that many sacrifices would have to be made.

While the Bush administration manipulated much of the U.S. national news media, the situation would change dramatically some eight years later when Donald Trump campaigned for president. His style was to make bombastic statements without any foundation in fact, and the major news outlets would often make those points. Indeed, his campaign was marked by journalists altering their traditional reportorial approach of simply quoting a candidate to one where they would add corrective statements, including stating that the candidate's statement was not true (http://mediamatters.org/blog/2016/10/09/journalists-are-calling-out-trumps-lies-second-debate/213668).

News reports promoted the collective identity of victims of terrorist attacks, stressing communal suffering as well as opportunities to participate in helping survivors and in defeating terrorism. More traditional and culturally resonant narratives about crime, drugs, and evil were transformed into the "terror story." Sorrow, suffering, empathy, and pain were merged with fear and vengeance. National character was played out in scenarios of heroics, sacrifice, suffering, marketing, and spending. This was the context for constructing the politics of fear.

The following materials illustrate how words of fear have become incorporated into news reports. A graduate seminar undertook the challenge to build on research about the discourse of fear by examining the relationship and changing connections among fear, crime, and victims.

That work focused on the various meanings of *victim* in news reports from several countries (Altheide et al., 2001). We wanted to understand whether and to what extent terrorism would "challenge" crime for "ownership" of fear and victim. The next project took place within days of the 9/11 attacks. The general focus was to investigate news themes about victims, patriotism, and consumption. This project was inspired by the extraordinary amount of coverage given to terrorism after the 9/11 attacks.

In one of our studies we compared coverage of terrorism with crime and victim and note how these may be related to use of the word *fear* (Altheide, 2009c). Accordingly, the research design called for comparing newspaper coverage of fear, crime, terrorism, and victim (in headlines and reports) at two eighteen-month time periods: time 1 was from March 1, 2000, to September 10, 2001; and time 2 was from September 12, 2001, to April 1, 2003. The first newspaper examined was the *Los Angeles Times*. Subsequently, students in a seminar project obtained data from the *New York Times*, the *Washington Post*, the *San Francisco Chronicle*, and *USA Today*. News reports were selected using Lexis/Nexis materials. News reports were selected according to the following search criteria:

1. reports with *fear* in headlines and *victim* in report
2. reports with *fear* in headlines and *crime* in report
3. reports with *fear* in headlines and *terrorism* in report
4. reports with *fear* in headlines and *crime* and *terrorism* in report
5. reports with *victim* and *fear* in headlines
6. reports with *crime, terrorism,* and *fear* in headlines
7. reports about *victim* within two words of *fear*
8. reports about *crime* within two words of *fear*
9. reports about *terrorism* within two words of *fear*
10. reports dealing with *crime, terrorism,* and *victim*

A qualitative content analysis study of news coverage sought to examine the politics of fear and terrorism. This emphasis in this chapter is on the changing pattern of fear, terrorism, and victimization in news reports. The politics-of-fear thesis can be demonstrated by examining the nature and extent of news coverage of fear, crime, terrorism, and victim before and after the attacks of 9/11. The discourse of fear is considered to be expanded to incorporate the politics of fear if terrorism and victimization appear closely associated with fear in a substantial number of news reports after 9/11 (time 2). Following the steps outlined in previous work (Altheide, 1996), additional qualitative data were collected with a protocol to check from a theoretical sample of reports. While some qualitative materials will be presented, the emphasis is on the changes in the extent of coverage in news reports linking fear with terrorism and victimization that occurred after 9/11.

NEWS AND THE POLITICS OF FEAR

A central argument of previous research (Altheide, 2002b) is that fear is cumulatively integrated into topics over time and, indeed, becomes so strongly associated with certain topics that, on repetition, it is joined with that term—as with an invisible hyphen—and eventually the term *fear* is no longer stated but is simply implied. Examples from previous work include *gangs, drugs,* and, in some cases, even *crime,* although *crime* continues to be heavily associated with *fear* (Altheide, 2002b). My aim here is to show the continuity between major events—the attacks of 9/11—and a history of crime reporting emphasizing fear and social control. Victim and victimization are common to each.

The key questions for this project concerned the comparisons between time 1 and time 2. The changes in coverage were considerable although varied. Building on previous work, the focus was on whether fear and terrorism were strongly associated with articles featuring *fear* in headlines. Of course, they were but to varying degrees. Tracking changes in the use of *fear, crime, terrorism,* and *victim* in several newspapers eighteen months before and after 9/11 reveals the following changes:

1. There was a dramatic increase in linking terrorism to fear.
2. Coverage of crime and fear persisted but at a very low rate.
3. There was a large increase in linking terrorism to victim.

First, the materials show that the five newspapers that provided data for this project varied considerably in the increases of *fear* in headlines and *crime* in report. The *Los Angeles Times,* which already had a strong "base" in crime reporting at time 1, showed the least increase during time 2 (32 percent), while *USA Today* (73 percent), the *New York Times* (85 percent), and the *Washington Post* (116 percent) all trailed the most massive increase in crime reporting by the *San Francisco Chronicle,* from fifteen to forty-five reports, for an increase of 181 percent, although about a third of these reports also dealt with terrorism. (It should be noted that the *San Francisco Chronicle* had the smallest number of reports with *fear* in the headline and *crime* in the report at time 1.) The relevance of terrorism and sensitivity to crime can be illustrated by an editorial in the *San Francisco Chronicle* on October 15, 2002, about the "Tarot Card" serial killer, who was shooting people, seemingly at random. In this and subsequent reports by other news media, shooting people is linked to terrorism, and the shooters are labeled as terrorists:

> This inexplicable string of murders has triggered yet another disappointing overreaction from the media. But this is different from the Chandra Levy or O. J. Simpson overreactions. We are a different country from the one that weathered those stories. We feel more vulnerable to terrorism, and no matter how you cut it, this killer is a terrorist. His

purpose, or at least one of them, is to spread terror. And the media playing right into his hands, as if Sept. 11 never happened.

"We may be entering a time when what has been ghetto-ized in Israel and the Middle East breaks its boundaries," says UC Berkeley dean of journalism Orville Schell, referring to suicide bombers and other acts of terrorism. "The unspoken thought is, 'What if this guy is a Muslim?' The media is feeding this most paranoid fear of all but without acknowledging it. . . ."

"The national climate of fear, energized by this psycho sniper, demands that the media examine its decisions more critically than ever. What kind of coverage serves the public interest? What information helps, and more important what harms?" (Ryan, 2002, 23)

Our study also found that the increase in reports associated fear with terrorism. Fear in headlines and terrorism in news reports greatly exceeded the increases in fear and crime. Each of the newspapers increased the linkage of fear with terrorism by more than 1,000 percent, with the *San Francisco Chronicle* exceeding 4,500 percent (having published only two reports of this nature before 9/11) at time 1. Clearly, terrorism was a relatively new and bold connection for fear. This included a few articles that were critical of the government's use of fear to exact more social control, but the overwhelming majority demonstrated that terrorism was bonded to the discourse of fear.

A context of crime reporting proved to be consequential for the seemingly easy public acceptance of governmental proposals to expand surveillance and social control. The resulting measures reflected a foundational politics of fear that promoted a new public discourse and justification for altering everyday life and social interaction. While the following discussion is informed by insights of others about social context and change (Shapiro, 1992; Thiele, 1993) and various studies about fear and the media (Furedi, 1997; Glassner, 1999) and especially fear and crime (Chiricos et al., 1997; Ferraro, 1995), the focus is on political action that utilizes widespread audience perceptions about fear as a feature of crime, violence, deviance, terrorism, and other dimensions of social disorder.

The politics of fear is buffered by news and popular culture stressing fear and threat as features of entertainment that increasingly are shaping public and private life as mass-mediated experience has become a standard frame of reference for audiences, claims makers, and individual actors (Best, 1995). Similar to propaganda, messages about fear are repetitious and stereotypical of outside "threats" and especially suspect and "evil others." These messages also imply moral panics, with the implication that action must be taken to not only defeat a specific enemy but also save civilization (Altheide, 2009b; Garland, 2008; Victor, 2006). Since so much is at stake, it follows that drastic measures must be taken—that compromises with individual liberty and even perspectives about "rights," the limits of law, and ethics must be "qualified" and held in abeyance in view of the threat.

In addition to propaganda effects, the constant use of fear pervades crises and normal times; it becomes part of the taken-for-granted world of "how things are," and one consequence is that it begins to influence how we perceive and talk about everyday life, including mundane as well as significant events. Tracking this discourse shows that fear pervades our popular culture and is influencing how we view events and experience. This is particularly relevant for the use of victims and victimization, particularly in the context of 9/11.

Still another consequence of the emphasis on *fear* that foretells the emerging politics of fear is the rise of victimization. Entertaining news emphasizes *fear* and institutionalizes *victim* as an acceptable identity. Other work has shown that *fear* and *victim* are informed by perceived membership (Altheide et al., 2001).

The world of popular culture and news stressing crime and victimization promotes the pervasive awareness of "victimage" that is easily cultivated by officials who respond to terrorist acts. Victims abound in American life. Victims are but the personal side of crisis; a crisis is where victims reside. A personal crisis may affect "one victim," but more generally "crisis" refers to "social crisis," involving numerous people. All take place in a time of fear. All of this requires that citizens have information and constant reminders of the pitfalls and hazards of life, whether potential or realized (Ericson & Haggerty, 1997). News reports, talk shows, newsmagazine shows, and a host of police and reality crime dramas seem to proclaim that everybody is a victim of something even though they may not know it. The notion that "life is hard" and that things don't always work out the way we'd like seems to be lost on popular-culture audiences who clamor for "justice," "revenge," and, of course, redemption, often in the form of monetary rewards. And it is not just in the United States:

> It is in the USA that victimhood is most developed as an institution in its own right. . . . Victimhood is one of the central categories of the culture of abuse. . . . Celebrities vie with one another to confess in graphic detail the painful abuse they suffered as children. The highly acclaimed BBC interview with Princess Diana symbolized this era of the victim. (Furedi, 1997, 95)

Just as our culture has become obsessed with fear, it has also become accepting of victim and victimization. My analysis of news and popular culture indicates that these two terms are linked. We even use the term *victim* when we don't have a victim, as in "victimless crime," although reports are far more likely to stress the "victim" status. And certain domestic violence "presumptive arrest" policies define people as "crime victims" even though they do not perceive themselves as such and refuse to press charges. We even have "indirect victim."

Patriotism was connected with an expansive fear of terrorism and enemies of the United States. The term *terrorism* was used to encompass an idea as well as a tactic or method. The waging of the "war on terrorism" focused on the "idea" and the "method," depending on the context of discussion and justification. The very broad definition of terrorism served the central authorities' purposes while also justifying the actions of others (e.g., Israel) in their own conflicts.

A brief recap of this project provides another important piece to the conceptual argument about the politics of fear. These data show that each of the newspapers substantially increased the number of reports with *fear* within two words of *terrorism* after 9/11: *Los Angeles Times*: 1,467 percent; *New York Times*: 986 percent; *Washington Post*: 1,100 percent; *San Francisco Chronicle*: 1,620 percent; and *USA Today*: 2,950 percent. Clearly, terrorism was strongly linked to the discourse of fear.

Claims makers' accounts of the attacks of 9/11 contributed to an expanding use of *fear* with *victim* and *victimization* that increased much faster than an already established tradition of reports linking *fear* and *crime*. *Victim* and *terrorism* did not replace *crime* but simply expanded the *fear* and *victim* connection that has long been associated with *crime*. And it is this expansion that is consistent with the politics of fear. The upshot is that *terrorism* and *victim* have been more closely joined with *fear* at time 2, while time 1 reporting was more likely to associate *fear* and *victim* with *crime*. *Victim* continued to "grow" from *crime* at time 2, but it was engorged by *fear*. While *crime* and *terrorism* do coexist and can expand together, *terrorism* became more strongly associated with *victim*.

The discourse of fear now includes terrorism as well as victimization and crime. Terrorism and fear have been joined through victimization. Crime established a solid baseline in its association with fear, and it continues to grow, but it is terrorism that now occupies the most news space. The primary reason for this is that government officials dominate the sources relied on by journalists. When journalists rely heavily on government and military officials not only to discuss an immediate war or military campaign but also for information about the security of the country, rationale for more surveillance of citizens, and comments about related domestic and international issues, then the body politic is symbolically cultivated to plant more reports and symbols about the politics of fear. This is particularly true during periods of war, such as the ongoing war with Iraq. Messages that the war on terrorism and the importance of homeland security, including periodic elevated "terror alerts," will not end soon lead journalists to turn to administration news sources for information about the most recent casualties, operations, and reactions to counterattacks as well as the omnipresent reports about soldiers who have perished and those who are still in peril. In this sense, news updates from authoritative sources quickly merge with orchestrated propaganda efforts.

Terrorism plays well with audiences accustomed to the discourse of fear as well as political leadership oriented to social policy geared to protecting those audiences from crime. I am proposing, then, that the discourse of fear is a key element of social fears involving crime and other dreaded outcomes in the postmodern world. The pervasive threat of terrorism is given credibility by events that are interpreted as part of an unfolding and very uncertain schema for the future:

> Terrorism discourse singles out and removes from the larger historical and political context a psychological trait (terror), an organizational structure (the terrorist network), and a category (terrorism) in order to invent an autonomous and aberrant realm of gratuitous evil that defies any understanding. The ironic dimension of terrorism discourse derives from its furthering the very thing it abominates. (Zulaika & Douglass, 1996, 22)

Terrorism is more than a narrative, but its essence is the definition of the situation, one that extends beyond the present into a distal future, gray but known. The forebodingness of events (e.g., the 9/11 attacks is cast as a terrible trend inevitably, but the power comes from the uncertainty of "when" and "where"). Like the prospective victims of crime in the future, citizens will be made terrorist victims in the future.

Terrorism—and especially the attacks of 9/11—enabled political actors to expand the definition of the situation to all Americans as victims. Moreover, all those fighting to protect actual and potential victims should be permitted to do their work, unimpeded by any concerns about civil liberties or adding context and complexity to the simple analysis that was offered: evil people were attacking good people, and evil had to be destroyed.

> Victimhood has also been expanded through the concept of the indirect victim. For example, people who witness a crime or who are simply aware that something untoward has happened to someone they know are potential indirect victims. . . . With the concept of the indirect victim, the numbers become tremendously augmented. Anyone who has witnessed something unpleasant or who has heard of such an experience becomes a suitable candidate for the status of indirect victim. (Furedi, 1997, 97)

Victims are a by-product of fear and the discourse of fear. Fear and victim are linked through social power, responsibility, and identity. The linkage involves concerns about safety and perceptions of risk. Thus, President Bush was relying on more than skilled speechwriters in connecting the mafia and terrorism; he was also relying on audience's acceptance of mythical mafia dons and godfathers depicted in entertainment to grease the conceptual slide of terrorism as a similar threat. What audiences were presumed to share, then, was the sense that terrorism, like crime (especially mafia crime), was a monstrous black hand that was invisible, omnipresent, and all powerful and that could be stopped only by a stronger force if ordinary Americans were to survive. I refer specifically to the "role and identity of victim," as held by numerous audiences who expect victims to perform certain activities, speak a certain language, and in general follow a cultural script of "dependence," "lacking," and "powerlessness" while relying on state-sponsored social institutions to save and support them (Garland, 2001). Clearly, the terrorists, like their criminal predecessors, had put us all at risk:

> The precondition for the emergence of the victim identity was the consolidation of the consciousness of risk. In the UK and the USA, the growing fear of crime and the growing perception of risks have contributed to the sentiment that everyone is a potential victim. However, crime and the fear of crime are only the most striking manifestations of the kind of insecurity that strengthens the belief that everyone is at risk. (Furedi, 1997, 100)

Several years later the Tea Party appealed to American victims of Washington, and politicians like Donald Trump championed the cause of the victims to defend them against the onslaught of terrorists, immigrants, and refugees, who, Trump claimed, had been supported by former Secretary of State Hillary Clinton and her boss, Barack Obama.

Recall that the politics of fear refers to decision makers' promotion and use of audience beliefs and assumptions about danger, risk, and fear in order to achieve certain goals. The politics of fear promotes attacking a target (e.g., crime or terrorism), anticipates further victimization, curtails civil liberties, and stifles dissent as being unresponsive to citizen needs or even unpatriotic. The Homeland Security Office advised the American people to buy duct tape and plastic sheeting as a barrier to terrorism. This advisory had little to do with "chemical protection" and much to do with the politics of fear. As one observer noted,

> Since September 11, that politics has followed two distinct tracks: First, state officials and media pundits have defined and interpreted the objects of Americans' fears—Islamic fundamentalism and terrorism—in anti-political or non-political terms, which has raised the level of popular nervousness; and, second, these same elites have generated a fear of speaking out not only against the war and US foreign policy but also against a whole range of established institutions. (Robin, 2002)

This argument has no counterproposal because of the symbolic links that are made between an event, a threat, and the avowed character and purpose of the terrorists, who, like criminals, are construed as lacking any reason, moral foundation, or purpose except to kill and terrify. Not likely to be ravaged by childhood diseases or workplace injuries, postindustrial citizens are prime potential victims, viewing mass-mediated scenarios of crime, mayhem, and destruction; they have no option but to believe and wait:

> The most typical mode of terrorism discourse in the United States has been, indeed, one of Waiting for Terror. . . . That which captivates every mind is something so meaningless that it may never happen, yet we are forced to compulsively talk about it while awaiting its arrival. In the theater of the absurd, "no significance" becomes the only significance. . . . When something does happen, after decades during which the absent horror has been omnipresent through the theater of waiting, the vent becomes anecdotal evidence to corroborate what has intuited all along—the by-now permanent catastrophe of autonomous Terror consisting of the waiting for terror. (Zulaika & Douglass, 1996, 26)

As suggested previously with the examples of hoaxes, victims are entertaining, and that is why they abound. They are evocative, bringing forth tears, joy, and vicarious emotional experience. But victim is more. Victim is now a status, a position that is open to all people who live in a symbolic environment marked by the discourse of fear. We are all potential victims, often vying for official recognition and legitimacy. This sense of victimization was exploited by government officials seeking to contain future threats.

The constant news bombardment about terrorist threats did raise American shackles against anyone appearing to be "Middle Eastern" or "Arab." Not only were people physically attacked but also mosques were struck by graffiti and vandalism. Numerous Internet sites appeared attacking Muslims at home and abroad and challenging their character and true loyalty. Fake news stories circulated about Muslim practices and their intentions of establishing a radical Sharia law in the United States. Social media carried the hateful messages, including one of the most prominent hate-filled videos that had international repercussions.

Anti-Muslim Video

Perhaps nothing matches the impact of social media as a video of a blasphemous attack on the Prophet Mohammed. On September 12, 2012, a homemade video disparaging the Prophet Mohammad was placed on YouTube. "Innocence of Muslims," described as a very amateurish and poorly edited—and acted—production, was made by Nakoula Basseley Nakoula (aka Mark Basseley Youssef; aka Sam Bacile), who was subsequently sentenced to one year in prison for fraud and for violating his parole. The video was viewed by millions of people worldwide and had immediate repercussions, including leading to protests in two dozen countries where nineteen people were killed, as well as being linked to outrage that may have contributed to the attack on a U.S. embassy in Benghazi, Libya, that led to the deaths of Ambassador Stevens and three others. International displeasure was loud, even demanding retribution

(Barnes, 2012). The upheaval garnered a statement from President Obama about the individual's right to produce such things in a free society, even though the president did not agree with the statements (August 25, 2013).

I was a visiting Fulbright Specialist at the time (2012) in Germany, and I was asked to comment on the action as it pertained to international diplomacy as well as social media. The general question was: What was the role of the media in the reporting about the video play concerning the riots in the Arab world?

In order to grasp the impact of reports about the video in the diverse Arab world, we appreciate the power of the Internet and more basically the role of new social media in our lives. Very significant for this situation is how the situation has changed: previously global world communications were sort of synonymous with official positions because of restricted access to media, because accesses to communications media were quite restricted. If a message was viewed internationally, it was supposedly sanctioned by world leaders. Several years ago an individual regular citizen's voice would have hardly mattered, except maybe to a few friends. Social media has changed this: an individual voice—or hastily produced video—can have world leaders concerned, and may be given credit for sparking riots and mass destruction.

The hateful anti-Arab video demonstrates the power of the media and new communication formats. The maelstrom that followed the hateful video indicates that world diplomacy has not really adjusted to the new reality of the wave of digital media and the changing ecology of communication. The current situation is sociologically like a natural experiment: it demonstrates how one person could upset thousands of people—including diplomats—worldwide, and even how that person can receive unofficial death threats from other countries' representatives. Now the problem is that much of the world has not adjusted its expectations, its diplomatic channels, and the timing and rhythm by which it expects certain things to occur.

Accordingly, it would not be surprising if these sorts of messages are going to become quite commonplace in the world. Governments—their leaders and advisory staff—need to become educated in the nature of these media and the ecology of communication to which all these things are going to be connected. Furthermore, it is important to reiterate the point, like it or not, that such hateful and uninformed messages are the views of perhaps only one person, and as crazy as they are, as insulting as they are to an educated citizenry, we can't simply ban them or censor all the hateful and ignorant messages because, in the United States at least, we also support freedom of speech, within certain limits. We have to contend with these, but we can be prepared for incendiary comments that are intended to spark anger and violence.

The media coverage of some of the outbursts was a bit sensational. In keeping with the entertainment format promoting conflict, selected media outlets' use of crowd visuals suggested that the reactions were more uniform than they were, often neglecting to point out that most of the people in the Muslim world did not agree with the action of some of these people that are taking to the streets. Most followers of any religious faith these days who are aware and have some education regardless of their beliefs do not support violence. It is a mistake to say that this is the Arab world reacting as a whole to this video. These are typically factions within a country and within a political system that are using this for their own advantage.

Paradoxically, media logic guided much of the coverage: just as the hateful video portrayed an inaccurate view of the "Arab world," much of the Western media's emphasis on entertainment, fear, and violence supported such sensationalist narratives as "the West vs. the Muslim world" that promotes the discourse of fear and reinforces many negative stereotypes that, unfortunately, have for too long guided news coverage of the Middle East (Adams, 1981, 1982; Adams & Schreibman, 1978; Altheide, 1981; Voice of America News, 2014). The initial message/video was one thing, but more important was the reaction and the construction of various media interpretations and meanings by various countries, political factions, and organizations. The mass media have historically done this kind of media framing along very simple story lines that involves using visuals promoting certain kinds of accounts that are entertaining, depicting violence. Care must be taken to put such events in a context; for example, discussing and showing what other people think, what other things are going on, and how there may be four or five other sides of the story. In other words, put the events in more of a context, taking pains to avoid merely sensationalized "episodes" that can be thematically presented as conforming to stereotypes (Iyengar & Kinder, 1987) that tend to resonate with the discourse of fear.

Politicians like to play to the discourse of fear, the sense of danger and threat of everywhere, and they like to use it for their own political purposes. It becomes really easy for audiences who are watching these reports to believe it, unless they are given some context to get an opinion about the other side and how they operate. It is common for the media to send the wrong message to the world and suggest that there is a battle between the East and the West. This is especially true when social media and numerous blogging sites compete for the attention of the fragmented audience seeking more validation for stereotypical views of an event rather than promoting critical thinking. And that of course serves political interest within certain countries. But again, it is very astounding that one person can play into the hands of a very select audience, who will take this as an occasion to claim: We are all under attack.

The politics of fear expanded and was further justified by terror attacks in the United States. Even before attacks that happened during President Obama's administration (e.g., the Boston Marathon bombing, shootings in Orlando, Florida, and San Bernardino, California, etc.), as well as highly publicized attacks in Paris, surveillance had been drastically increased, largely supported by the Patriot Act that seemed to give carte blanche for government agencies to take extraordinary steps to prevent such attacks and reduce victimization. These steps included illegal massive electronic surveillance of American citizens and "sting" operations primarily against Muslim Americans.

The immense National Security Agency (NSA) grew tremendously after 9/11, and spawned a massive surveillance industry. Policing and social control at home and abroad have dominated public perceptions and contributed to the expansion of national defense rhetoric and surveillance and control throughout social life. The U.S. government splurged on war machinery and expanded surveillance organizations and technology after 9/11. Journalists who have attempted to track this largely secret infestation into American life have been astonished.

The top-secret world the government created in response to the September 11 attacks is so large, so unwieldy, and so secretive that no one knows how much money it costs, how many people it employs, how many programs exist or how many agencies do the same work.

> After nine years of unprecedented spending and growth, the result is that the system put in place to keep the United States safe is so massive that its effectiveness is impossible to determine.

The investigation's other findings:

- Some 1,271 government organizations and 1,931 private companies work on programs related to counterterrorism, homeland security, and intelligence in some ten thousand U.S. locations.
- An estimated 854,000 people hold top-secret security clearances.
- In the Washington, D.C., area, thirty-three building complexes for top-secret intelligence work are under construction or have been built since September 2001.
- Many agencies do the same work, creating redundancy and waste. For example, fifty-one federal organizations and military commands, operating in fifteen U.S. cities, track the flow of money to and from terrorist networks.
- Analysts who make sense of documents and conversations obtained by foreign and domestic spying share their judgment by publishing fifty thousand reports each year; many are routinely ignored. (Priest & Arkin, 2010)

The quest for more data, including revelations about the massive data mining of American's telephone calls and computer communications in search of patterns, is misdirected, even though organizations and techno-logical/communication industries have much to gain from this unfortu-nate metaphor mistake. Two statements illustrate part of the problem. Officials claimed that PRISM provided the "haystack" in which terrorist needles may be found. According to the director of the FBI:

> "What concerns me is you never know which dot is going to be key," he said. "What you want is as many dots as you can. If you close down a program like this, you are removing dots from the playing field." . . . "Now, you know, it may make that decision that it's not worth it. But let there be no mistake about it. There will be fewer dots out there to connect" in trying to prevent the next terrorist attack. (Robert S. Muell-er, director of FBI, *New York Times*, June 19, 2013)

Some analysts challenge this claim, which underlies the questionable epistemology of the NSA that justified trying to get "total information." Good intelligence is more than having several tons of data; the critical thing is having knowledge of the codes, syntax, and overall narrative that forms a whole or the "plan."

> Rather than thinking of intelligence as a simple connect-the-dots pic-ture, think of it as a million unnumbered pictures superimposed on top of each other. Or a random-dot stereogram. Is it a sailboat, a puppy, two guys with pressure-cooker bombs or just an unintelligible mess of dots? You try to figure it out. (Schneier, 2013)

Indeed, many of the FBI interdictions involved sting operations (see below) in which informants worked with undercover agents posing as fellow "jihadists" to assist "jihadist wannabes" in their efforts until a dramatic resolution could be filmed and presented on the evening news as evidence of the continuing terrorist threat (Aaronson, 2013). The key issue for Americans is the collection and central repository of data that can—and will be—used for other surveillance purposes beyond terror-ism. A feature of information technology and the ecology of communica-tion—and demonstrated by Edward Snowden's revelations about PRISM, and more— is that if electronic communication data can be col-lected, it will be collected. And there will be compelling justifications to use it, if it is available. For all practical purposes, such information is not completely destroyed, and it can be useful for marketing for corpora-tions, social media, and Internet providers.

> Self-confessed leaker Edward Snowden's disclosures about domestic spying by the NSA have sparked a broad debate about whether the government is using sophisticated surveillance and data-mining tech-niques on its own citizens without sufficient oversight.
>
> But information gathered and exploited by Internet giants such as Google, Amazon and Facebook—and traded by lesser-known data bro-kers such as Datalogix and Acxiom—can be more revealing than what the NSA can legally collect on most Americans. Few consumers under-

stand what data are being shared, with whom, or how the information is being used.

"We normally think of the NSA as being far ahead of corporate America, but I'm not so sure they are that far ahead anymore," said Mark Herschberg, chief technology officer at Madison Logic, a New York–based company that provides data for advertisers.

"There are thousands of companies out there collecting information on customers, and together they are really aggregating quite a bit of data," he added. "Google is reading through your email. Amazon is looking at not just what you buy, but what you shop for." (Dilianin, 2013)

A vice-president of an information technology company explained how industry and government surveillance were quite compatible:

Mobile carriers, including Verizon Wireless, have begun selling aggregate location data. Verizon, on its website, promises advertisers "detailed demographics; location analysis to determine where your target consumer   segment lives and works; and foot-and-mobile traffic habits," though not names or phone numbers.

"These companies have been practicing what I call privacy arbitrage for the last 10 years or so, mining all of our personal information," said a former U.S. intelligence official who now works for a data company. He asked for anonymity so he could be more candid. "I don't know to what degree the common person understands how much data is being collected about them by these Silicon Valley companies that are saving the world." (Dilianin, 2013)

Paradoxically, the widespread availability of personal data to corporate interests has been used as a legal basis for permitting the NSA and other governmental surveillance of telephone communications. U.S. District Judge William A. Pauley stated his disagreement with a previous ruling that NSA eavesdropping violated the Fourth Amendment (right to privacy) of the U.S. Constitution in ruling that the U.S. government could continue to collect personal communications:

Pauley disagreed. Americans' relationship with their mobile telephones may have changed, he wrote, but customers' "relationship with their telecommunications providers has not changed and is just as frustrating."

"Every day, people voluntarily surrender personal and seemingly private information to transnational corporations, which exploit that data for profit," Pauley said. "Few think twice about it, even though it is far more intrusive than bulk telephony metadata collection." (Phelps, 2013)

The massive electronic surveillance also involves future uses of the data such as interventions in viral epidemics, tracking down suspected serial killers and child abductors, (and other criminal matters), and background checks for employees "as warranted." After all, when an urgent situation arises, who can deny the necessity of using allavailable information?

Another significant disclosure by Edward Snowden is the complicity of not only the major telecommunications and Internet providers but also the eager lucrative cooperation of numerous "high tech"—the chief security officer for Facebook went to work for the NSA—and other governmental agencies avowedly interested in curtailing terrorism and other national security threats. This creates a complex reality:

> Silicon Valley has what the spy agency wants: vast amounts of private data and the most sophisticated software available to analyze it. The agency in turn is one of Silicon Valley's largest customers for what is known as data analytics, one of the valley's fastest-growing markets. To get their hands on the latest software technology to manipulate and take advantage of large volumes of data, United States intelligence agencies invest in Silicon Valley start-ups, award classified contracts and recruit technology experts like Mr. Kelly.
>
> "We are all in these Big Data business models," said Ray Wang, a technology analyst and chief executive of Constellation Research, based in San Francisco. "There are a lot of connections now because the data scientists and the folks who are building these systems have a lot of common interests." (Risen & Wingfield, 2013)

Much of this work was, after all, authorized by the broad interpretation of the Patriot Act. The only senator who voted against the Patriot Act, Russ Feingold, was particularly concerned about information seeking. He stated his opposition:

> One provision that troubles me a great deal is a provision that permits the government under FISA to compel the production of records from any business regarding any person, if that information is sought in connection with an investigation of terrorism or espionage. (Terkel, 2013)

Extensive governmental surveillance was revealed in 2004 by a whistleblower, Thomas Tamm, a former attorney in the U.S. Department of Justice, who became aware of a secret electronic surveillance program of U.S. citizens code-named "Stellar Wind" while working for the Office of Intelligence Policy and Review (OIPR). Telecommunications companies cooperated with the government in allowing access, and later were granted immunity from suites brought by U.S. citizens. Tamm informed journalists of this then-illegal activity, who kept it under wraps for a year. They then won a Pulitzer Prize for their book, although they, like Tamm, were charged with violating national security. Tamm lived in legal limbo for nearly three years when the charges were dropped because the government did not want to discuss the secret surveillance. Tamm explained his reasoning: "If somebody were to say, who am I to do that? I would say, 'I had taken an oath to uphold the Constitution.' It's stunning that somebody higher up the chain of command didn't speak up." (Isikoff, 2008)

When the *New York Times* published the report, Congress and future presidential candidate Barack Obama were outraged. Then-senator Obama "denounced the Bush administration for violating the FISA law and demanded hearings" (Isikoff, 2008, 42). Congress passed legislation requiring that surveillance should be conducted in a way that is consistent with civil liberties. Nevertheless, there remained strong support for surveillance efforts, even if civil rights were compromised. This would become even more pronounced during Donald Trump's 2016 presidential campaign when he advocated keeping a close eye on Muslim Americans as well as curtailing immigration of Muslims into the United States. However, many Americans apparently were less concerned about the civil liberties problem since Trump went on to win the election. Perhaps part of the nonchalant view of these harsh comments is that Americans had become accustomed to numerous press reports about how effective FBI sting operations had been against homegrown terrorists. The FBI expanded sting operations against Muslim Americans after 9/11.

FBI Stings and the Politics of Fear

FBI terrorist sting operations suggest that Superman's adaptable archenemy Lex Luthor had it right when he said, "The more fear you make, the more loot you take." The audience's fear of terrorism is cultivated with entertaining popular culture and mass media reports about terrorism threats. Pew opinion surveys show that terrorism continues to be one of the United States' top three priorities—much higher than reducing crime, providing health insurance, or protecting the environment. Sting operations help with the programming. Stings have become popular in the United States over the last forty-five years or so as the FBI became more oriented to popular culture and media logic. Improved and smaller audio and video recording technology has helped provide "evidence" for legal proceedings as well as news and other entertainment shows. One of the first FBI stings was "Abscam" (short for Arab Scam) in 1980, a scheme to grease the immigration bureaucracy for Middle Eastern high rollers. Video clips of government officials accepting bribes were shown on news reports four months after the initial trial. The courts, for the most art, condoned stings. Many local police departments followed the feds' lead, including one in Arizona ("Azscam") in May 1991, which involved video recordings of legislators being bribed by a stooge hired by the Maricopa County attorney general and the Phoenix Police Department (Altheide, 1993). These tapes were the talk of the town when broadcast one day after the indictments. Expanded surveillance is now part of everyday life and entertainment.

Audiences nurtured with decades of fear of crime and now, terrorism, are also familiar with the sting genre of reality TV shows such as *To Catch a Predator*. The FBI has become skilled at recording the planning, carrying out, and prevention of would-be terrorist acts. The general approach is to assist people who make verbal threats to actually do something more "operational" (their word). According to a report by the Center for Human Rights and Global Justice at New York University (NYU), Muslim "homegrown terrorists" would be good recruits for dramatic presentations of fear and threat:

> Since September 11, 2001, the U.S. government has targeted Muslims in the United States by sending paid, untrained informants into mosques and Muslim Communities. This practice has led to the prosecution of more than 200 individuals in terrorism-related cases. The government has touted these cases as successes in the so-called war against terrorism. . . . "The government played a significant role in instigating and devising the three plots featured in this Report—plots the government then 'foiled' and charged the defendants with," according to the study. "The defendants in these cases were all convicted and are facing prison sentences of 25 years to life." (Center for Human Rights and Global Justice, 2011, 2)

The NYU study focused on three cases, summarized by a journalist:

> The first of three cases is the so-called Newburgh Four, residents of the impoverished city in Orange County, N.Y., ensnared for plotting to blow up synagogues and shoot down military airplanes. They say an FBI informant picked the targets, provided mock weapons and promised them $250,000, along with other material and afterlife rewards. The men . . . failed to convince the jury that they were entrapped and were convicted in October.
>
> A federal judge dismissed their appeals, despite finding there was "some truth" to their position that the "Government 'created the criminal and manufactured the crime.'"
>
> The second case that the report profiles involves the New Jersey residents known to their supporters as the Fort Dix Five, who came under FBI surveillance after a Circuit City clerk noticed a video in which a man with a rifle shouted "Allahu Akbar."
>
> Three brothers Eljvir, Drikan and Shain Duka say it was footage of a hunting trip in the Poconos. The video also captured them riding horses, skiing and playing paintball, according to the report.
>
> But the home movie prompted an investigation involving two informants who they say goaded them into making statements and collecting literature that would connect them with a plot to attack the Fort Dix military base.
>
> Unlike the Newburgh Four, however, the Duka brothers did not use an entrapment defense. They said the informant never even told them about the conspiracy, the report states.

The jury did not believe them and returned guilty verdicts on Dec. 22, 2008. According to the final case of the report, an New York Police Department informant made more than 575 visits to mosques before meeting would-be Herald Square bomber Shahawar Matin Siraj.

Before ensnaring Siraj, the informant failed to interest his imam in radicalism, but he tried to interest Siraj in jihad for months by showing him photos of Abu Ghraib and Guantanamo prisoners, the report states.

Siraj "finally crumbled" after seeing pictures of young Iraqi girls being threatened and raped, and he agreed to be a lookout for the bombing of an unoccupied subway station provided there was "no killing," according to the report.

Siraj's entrapment defense failed, and he is currently serving a 30-year sentence. (Klasfeld, 2011)

Officials strongly disagreed with the report's conclusions and recommendations:

Deputy Commissioner of the New York City Police Department Paul J. Browne dismissed the report's "biased polemics" in an emailed statement.

"The accusations are false and the product of sloppy and biased polemics that don't merit the term 'research' or association with NYU or any other university worthy of the name." (Klasfeld, 2011)

While police officials seldom approve of social science findings regarding entrapment and undermining claims about crime prevention through police intervention, few would disagree that active solicitation of the occasional Jihadist "wanna-be" has increased since 9/11. Even the hapless Antonio Martinez, who was busted with a fake bomb in Baltimore, wondered if he was being set up as he prepared to drive a van provided by the FBI to a military recruiting station. Some six months later, two men in Seattle—one of whom was diagnosed as mentally ill— discussed their plans with a would-be accomplice, who was part of a police/FBI sting, to shoot people at a military recruiting station. The other conspirator posted more than a dozen YouTube videos urging Muslims to stand up to the United States. The paid informant, who had a long police record, provided inoperable weapons and ammunition just before the wannabe jihadists actually tried to act on their plans. Tape-recorded conversations played well in news reports. The agent in charge stated,

"Just with the number of cases we've had in the past six months, I'm going to be asking for a 10 to 20 percent increase in our current (budget) numbers." (Bernton, Carter, & Miletich, 2011)

The FBI asked for far more than a budget increase. They requested that the approximately fourteen thousand agents be given more authority and latitude to conduct surveillance and use of informants without prior judicial approval. Some of the new procedures have been in effect since

2008, and despite the concerns raised by the American Civil Liberties Union and other "privacy advocates," the procedures will be codified in the new edition of the manual *The Domestic Investigation and Operations Guide.*

> The new rules will also relax a restriction on administering lie-detector tests and searching people's trash. Under current rules, agents cannot use such techniques until they open a "preliminary investigation," which—unlike an assessment—requires a factual basis for suspecting someone of wrongdoing. But soon agents will be allowed to use those techniques for one kind of assessment, too: when they are evaluating a target as a potential informant. . . . The revisions also clarify what constitutes "undisclosed participation" in an organization by an FBI agent or informant, which is subject to special rules—most of which have not been made public. The new manual says an agent or an informant may surreptitiously attend up to five meetings of a group before those rules would apply—unless the goal is to join the group, in which case the rules apply immediately. (C. Savage, 2011)

The FBI's role and that of supporting actors in numerous police departments, as well as the seventy-two "fusion centers" that monitor, gather, and synthesize surveillance information, has changed.

> Located in states and major urban areas throughout the country, fusion centers are uniquely situated to empower front-line law enforcement, public safety, fire service, emergency response, public health, critical infrastructure protection, and private sector security personnel to understand local implications of national intelligence, thus enabling local officials to better protect their communities. Fusion centers provide interdisciplinary expertise and situational awareness to inform decision-making at all levels of government. They conduct analysis and facilitate information sharing while assisting law enforcement and homeland security partners in preventing, protecting against, and responding to crime and terrorism.
>
> Fusion centers are owned and operated by state and local entities with support from federal partners in the form of deployed personnel, training, technical assistance, exercise support, security clearances, connectivity to federal systems, technology, and grant funding. (http://www.dhs.gov/state-and-major-urban-area-fusion-centers)

The emphasis is more on terrorism and less on traditional crimes. Capturing homegrown terrorists is becoming more prevalent in news reports. A *Philadelphia Inquirer* report about FBI activities is an example:

> In Philadelphia, counterterrorism agents have scored three high-profile successes since 9/11: the busts of the homegrown terrorist known as "Jihad Jane," the five men convicted of plotting an attack on Fort Dix, and the 26 men charged in a Hezbollah gun-running and Stinger missile case. (Shiffman, 2011)

And, a prominent politician, who heads the Department of Homeland Security subcommittee on counterterrorism and security, added:

> "What you're seeing is a transformation of the FBI, from how it's oper-
> ated for the last century," said U.S. Rep. Patrick L. Meehan, the senior
> federal prosecutor in Philadelphia from 2001 to 2008 and now chair of
> the House Homeland Security subcommittee on counterterrorism and
> intelligence. "The FBI is engaged in a new challenge—identifying a
> potential act before it's committed and preventing it from happening."
> (Shiffman, 2011)

Of course, not all agents agree that "chasing ghosts" is the best use of scarce resources that were previously committed to criminal investigations of "corrupt politicians, bank robbers, drug dealers, and financial scammers." One agent told a reporter:

> "Look, obviously terrorism is important, but it's not why I joined the
> FBI and you have to wonder what we're missing—people are getting
> away with things we would have been all over 10 years ago," said a
> veteran agent. (Shiffman, 2011)

There are other cases that could be cited to illustrate the pandemic of proactive net widening to capture would-be terrorists. One example is a Texas man, Barry Bujol Jr., accused of plotting to help al Qaeda. After being fingered by an informant, the Prairie View A&M student has been in a Houston jail on a terror charge for more than a year, although he claims that the feds are really after the wrong man. Others agree that perhaps the organizational concern with terrorist attacks can cloud judgment:

> And if it were not for the government coercing and harassing him,
> including enlisting a confidential informant posing as an al-Qaida
> member, events leading to his arrest never would have happened, he
> contends. He's not alone with such concerns. An FBI agent who retired
> in 2006 said he worries that the U.S. government has used rogue infor-
> mants in various parts of the country to bust people in exchange for
> cash. In former agent Jim Wedick's perspective: "9/11 happens, we see
> those buildings come down, and all of sudden we are not only paying
> informants hundreds of thousands of dollars but we have these guys
> with criminal records going around, suggesting this and that. I am
> worried that people get caught up in these schemes." (Schiller, 2011)

The language of terrorism has become more prominent in the crime-fighting agenda as well. Pittsburgh police Chief Nate Harper referred to the arrests of several "Original Gangster" (OG) members as "home-grown terrorists."

> "They terrorized the neighborhoods with gunfire, with the homicides
> that were committed in the Manchester area and the North Side area,"

he said. "There are still remnants out there, but this is a takedown of the most violent OG members." (Lord, 2011)

It remains uncertain how the discourse of fear associated with home-grown terrorism inspired by FBI programming will inform the actions of real terrorists in the future.

Research shows that the significance of media formats for the politics of fear can also be illustrated with the widespread adoption of social media and smartphones (Altheide, 2014a). Fear was further expanded in 2014 with the rise of the Islamic State in Iraq and Syria (ISIS), an out-growth of the failed U.S. policies in Iraq and throughout the Middle East. Many of the leaders, especially the military strategists, were experienced soldiers who had been loyal to the Sunni faction of Islam—and the Baath-ist Party of Saddam Hussein in Iraq—which lost power after the United States aided the overthrow of the government. Their exclusion was an opportunity for a rising Shiite leader, Ibrahim Al-Badri, in search of mili-tary leaders and soldiers, to establish a new Islamic state, a caliphate, in Syria and Iraq. Part of their aggressive strategy was to terrorize the peo-ple in the physical territories they invaded, as well as through social media to recruit new followers. They also showed executions as a kind of performance crime that would be broadcast over several media formats, including Facebook. These images were terrifying and further heightened domestic fear in the United States that Muslim Americans—and other immigrants, for that matter—were potential ISIS agents.

> Undercover operations, once seen as a last resort, are now used in about two of every three prosecutions involving people suspected of supporting the Islamic State, a sharp rise in the span of just two years, according to a *New York Times* analysis. Charges have been brought against nearly 90 Americans believed to be linked to the group. . . . The F.B.I. has about 1,000 open investigations into "homegrown violent extremists," which it defines as Americans motivated by a foreign ter-rorist group, including the Islamic State, to conduct attacks at home, officials said. They said that a "significant number" of cases—hundreds in all—had entailed undercover operations against people suspected of being Islamic extremists. (Lichtblau, 2016)

CONCLUSION

The war on terrorism fuels the politics of fear that reside in entertaining communication mass media and social media formats that are increasing-ly instantaneous, personal, and visual. The politics of fear is a dominant motif for news and popular culture. Moreover, within this framework, news reporting about crime and terrorism are linked with "victimiza-tion" narratives that make crime, danger, and fear very relevant to every-day life experiences. The social construction of social problems, as Best

(1999) noted, is an ongoing process, building from previous experience. However, the politics of fear as public discourse represents an emergent feature of the symbolic environment: moral entrepreneurs' claims making is easier to market to audiences anchored in fear and victimization as features of crime and terrorism. The politics of fear can be theoretically useful in understanding the relevance of mass-mediated fear in contemporary popular culture and political life. This concept is useful for clarifying the closer ties between entertainment-oriented news and popular culture on the one hand and media-savvy state officials on the other. The politics of fear is consistent with entertainment-oriented news and mass media, particularly its resonance with "victim" and victimization. On the other hand, the politics of fear helps political decision makers as news sources and as political actors define social life as dangerous and requiring formal social control and state intervention.

The politics of fear joined crime with victimization through the "drug war," interdiction and surveillance policies, and grand narratives that reflected numerous cultural myths about moral and social "disorder." We are in the midst of an emerging politics of fear that discourages criticism and promotes caution and reliance on careful procedures to "not be hasty," to "cover oneself," to "not be misunderstood." The politics of fear promotes extensive use of disclaimers, those linguistic devices that excuse a comment to follow by providing an explanation to not "take it the wrong way," usually taking the form of "I am not unpatriotic, but . . ." or "I support our troops as much as anyone, but . . ." Very few politicians will stand up to the politics of fear because it is the defining bulwark of legitimacy.

Skillful propaganda and the cooperation of the most powerful news media enabled simple lies to explain complex events. Like entertaining crime reporting, anticipation of wars, attacks, and the constant vigilance to be on guard is gratifying for most citizens who are seeking protection within the symbolic order of the politics of fear. The skillful use of heightened "terrorist alerts"—such as "see something, say something"—to demand attention to the task at hand is critical in avoiding any detractor. And that is the key point: an otherwise sensible or cautionary remark that signals that one is aware, rational, and weighing alternatives marks one as a detractor, someone who is "against the United States."

The rituals of control are easier to accept as they become more pervasive and institutionalized. Fear is perceived as crime and terrorism, while police and military forces are symbolically joined as protectors. The politics of fear with a national or international justification is more symbolically compelling than "mere crime in the streets." Accompanying heightened terror alerts are routine frisks, intrusive surveillance, and the pervasive voyeuristic camera, scanning the environment for all suspicious activity. The next chapter discusses how the politics of fear has been extended to control surveillance on the Internet.

SEVEN

Mediated Interaction and the Control Narrative of the Internet

> The FBI must draw proactively on all lawful sources of information to identify terrorist threats.
>
> —John Ashcroft, U.S. attorney general (2001–2005)

> Honestly, people are definitely dumber. They just keep passing stuff around. Nobody fact-checks anything anymore—I mean, that's how Trump got elected.
>
> —Fake News Writer

The politics of fear as a form of social control in modern societies has changed as media have become more instantaneous, visual, and personal. The surveillance and control policies put in place after the 9/11 attacks have expanded during the last decade or so, and have been usurped in some cases by the widespread institutional and personal use of web pages and social media for nefarious, even deadly, purposes. I noted in chapter 1 that the politics of fear results in policies and procedures affecting many aspects of our lives. Chapter 6 argued that regulating words and meanings in public discourse begins to affect how we talk and discuss things and ultimately how we see the world. This chapter is about the expansion of control and surveillance on the Internet and social media. There are three contexts that reappear throughout this chapter: first, the concern with crime, particularly sexual predators preying on young children, as well as the growing concern about identity theft on the Internet; second, threats to national security by terrorists and others who might obtain information via the Internet but also use this "electronic superhighway" to communicate with co-conspirators in planning future attacks; and third, the disbelief in facts that has accompanied the decline of news authority and legitimacy as social media have enabled everyone to become producers of information, while also promoting the reliance on self-serving sources that are often "fake news" sites. But there is much more to it than merely trying to dupe people into voting for a political candidate:

> In fact, the dangers posed by fake news are just a symptom of a deeper truth now dawning on the world: With billions of people glued to Facebook, WhatsApp, WeChat, Instagram, Twitter, Weibo and other popular services, social media has become an increasingly powerful cultural and political force, to the point that its effects are now beginning to alter the course of global events.
>
> The election of Donald J. Trump is perhaps the starkest illustration yet that across the planet, social networks are helping to fundamentally rewire human society. They have subsumed and gutted mainstream media. They have undone traditional political advantages like fundraising and access to advertising. And they are destabilizing and replacing old-line institutions and established ways of doing things, including political parties, transnational organizations and longstanding, unspoken social prohibitions against blatant expressions of racism and xenophobia. (Manjoo, 2016b)

Social media make it possible to have multiple narratives or general story scenarios about an event or even social reality, and it can be of your own choosing. This is beyond the adage that "people believe the damndest things"; now, people can cite "evidence" to support their views, even though it may lack important context, or in many instances, is simply false.

The Internet opens up possibilities for people, including escaping certain bounds of social control (e.g., the ease with which pornography can be viewed, contraband merchandise purchased, and so on). The aim of social control is to have people regulate themselves by avoiding activities that could get them into trouble with authorities. The Internet and social media have made it possible for like-minded people sharing the same biases, prejudices, and gross misinformation to regulate and reinforce each other. Ironically, people are seeking to validate their take on events and problems, and they are being largely successful.

> Documentary proof seems to have lost its power. If the Kennedy conspiracies were rooted in an absence of documentary evidence, the 9/11 theories benefited from a surfeit of it. So many pictures from 9/11 flooded the internet, often without much context about what was being shown, that conspiracy theorists could pick and choose among them to show off exactly the narrative they preferred. There is also the looming specter of Photoshop: Now, because any digital image can be doctored, people can freely dismiss any bit of inconvenient documentary evidence as having been somehow altered. (Manjoo, 2016a)

The Internet is the latest arena for surveillance and massive misinformation.

We celebrate the increased freedom and opportunities that accompany computers and the Internet while demanding more control, protection, and surveillance of our use. I will address the increase in computer and Internet surveillance, monitoring, and control by the users, the state, and business as features of mediated interaction. The visual communication of the Internet exemplifies surveillance culture and that a control narrative is becoming the story of the Internet. The control narrative refers to the relevance for the communication process of actors' awareness and expectation that symbolic meanings may be monitored and used by diverse audiences for various purposes. Control is implicated in rules, prescriptions, and proscriptions involving access, presentation, and use of the Internet. Nuances and intentions can be monitored and objectified by traces or the record of use (Beniger, 1986; Castells & Himanen, 2002). Born of the risk society (Beck, 1992), the control narrative reflects the sanctioning process of mediated communication, including perceived and actual preparation, precautions, and consequences (e.g., being warned or fired about communicative behavior). The technology of the Internet can track and profile at the same time, and the communication format of the Internet—the logic of its operation and use—permits users to search and allows others to control. A supporter of Attorney General John Ashcroft's call for more Internet authority stated, "In the 1970s, maintaining a clip file on someone was a big deal. Now, Google does it for you," referring to the popular Internet search engine (Savage, 2002a). Formal agents of social control do act as "Big Brother" on the Internet, but the control narrative operates apart from Big Brother's actions. The control narrative is consistent with Staples's (2000) notion of "meticulous rituals of power" partly because "cyberspace is deeply mired in consumerism surveillance and voyeurism" (Staples, 2000, 130). Particular features that mediate interaction on the Internet inform the control narrative, including the format features of the Internet, visual character, private/public audiences, the societal context of fear, and control. I will illustrate the control narrative with an overview of Internet security and the paradox of privacy and violation.

The control narrative is made up of the communication format of the Internet, described by Surratt (2001) as "net logic" that must be considered in trying to understand the place of the Internet in the lives of those who use it and the social relationships that are informed by it:

> The Internet is unique not because "it conquers space and time," but because it is the first strategy that operates according to a many-to-many and (one-to-one) communications pattern or logic. (Surratt, 2001, 42)

The visual character of the Internet and the ease with which communication can be seen suggests that on the one hand Internet users are exhibitionists—in the sense that they communicate to be seen—while on the other they are voyeurs, aiming to see others' communications (Denzin, 1995). "Surfing the Net" is a surveillance activity.

Computer technology in general and the use of the Internet in particular is one of many forms of mediating communication and interaction between people. These new forms of communication have arisen during a period of heightened expectations of freedom and opportunity within a massive campaign to promote fear of the "other" and especially crime. Indeed, the expansion of surveillance throughout the social order (Marx, 1988, 2016) involves much more than crime; rather, the tools and perspectives of "policing" against crime have been extended as a format of control to "policing" society more generally. Ironically, it is the knowledge we have that is now being used as a foundation for more control, regulation, and surveillance. The preoccupation with protecting us from what is a potential threat has been referred to as "policing the risk society" by Ericson and Haggerty (1997) and others who contend that postindustrial society is marked by an expanding body of knowledge about risks:

> Risk communication systems are entwined with privacy and trust. The more that foreboding and fear lead people to withdraw from public involvement, the more they value privacy and withdraw into privatized lifestyles. The greater the privacy, the greater the need for surveillance mechanisms to produce the knowledge necessary to trust people in otherwise anonymous institutional transactions. Paradoxically, these mechanisms intrude on privacy and are a constant reminder of the uncertainties of trust. Yet it is only in a framework of trust that patterns of risk can be adequately institutionalized and forms the basis of decisions. Privacy, trust, surveillance, and risk management go hand in hand in policing the probabilities and possibilities of action. (Ericson & Haggerty, 1997, 6)

The possibility of quick and easily accessible communication with others is paradoxically linked to the fear and control of others to us and our children (Altheide, 2002b). As Lyon (2001) notes,

> Surveillance today is a means of sorting and classifying populations and not just of invading personal space or violating the privacy of individuals. In post modernizing contexts surveillance is an increasingly powerful means of reinforcing social divisions, as the superpanoptic sort relentlessly screens, monitors and [is] classified to determine eligibility and access, to include and to exclude. . . . Surveillance has become an indirect but potent means of affecting life chances and social destinies. (151)

As Staples (2000) suggested, Internet surveillance by formal authorities and by everyday users is a microtechnology of surveillance performed millions of times each day as users perform surveillance ceremonies as they surf the Internet and thereby enact meticulous rituals of power.

The challenge is to identify how mediation and control operate in cyberspace. I will focus mainly on the expansion of Internet surveillance and particularly the use of "Internet stings" by formal agents of social control. Surveillance and control are expanding in everyday communication on the Internet, and it is becoming more acceptable to compromise privacy. The nature of privacy is changing because of this surveillance. The awareness of monitoring and surveillance informs all Internet communication. Moreover, other social effects, not addressed in this chapter, are likely to follow as users engage in deceptive practices (e.g., using false names, multiple email addresses, and so on) to protect their privacy.

A THEORETICAL RATIONALE FOR MEDIATED INTERACTION

The politics of fear rides on social meanings and taken-for-granted assumptions about threats to social order and ways of avoiding such threats. Symbolic communication and the processes that produce it mediate all interaction. An entire theoretical orientation to the study of social life, symbolic interaction, along with multiple versions of other "social psychologies" incorporate (albeit in different ways) the "communication process." So basic are many of these precepts to any understanding of social life—including all its "macro" forms—that David Maines (2001) finds an increasing trend toward the widespread use by general sociology of standard concepts and propositions once held almost solely by pragmatists and interactionists. I will touch on only a few components of this process in order to move on to a discussion of mediated interaction and the Internet.

The elements of the process involve the definition of the situation and identity and what Schutz (1967) termed typification, or typical course of action. Each of these, along with information technologies, mediates interaction. The communication process involves an actor taking into account an audience by "taking the role of the other" outlined by Mead and Morris (1962) and articulated by Blumer (1962). As Surratt (2001, 218) observes, the key to this process is the actor's identity, or that part of the self by which he is known to others: "Defining the self and the generalized other in a meaningful way becomes of the key problems of social order in the highly modern world."

These in turn reflexively join the communicative act with the definition of the situation that is also influenced by a broader context of meaning, memories, and history. For example, work on the changing nature and conceptions of identity suggests that broader social changes, including information technology and popular culture, can affect the emerging conceptions of self within an altered communications order (Altheide, 2000; Cerulo, 1997). Most of these elements that are involved in comput-

er-mediated communication were not present throughout most of human
history:

> The information/communications revolution creates a vast and myster-
> ious electronic landscape of new relationships, roles, identities, net-
> works, and communities, while it undermines that cherished luxury of
> the modern self-privacy. (Anderson, 1997, quoted from Surratt [2001]).

Each element that influences social interaction can be regarded as a potential contributor or mediator to interaction. For example, the visual and
temporal nature of computer interfaces mediates the communicative act.
Actors must develop sophisticated understandings, skills, styles, and
even rhythm for operation of these "interfaces" in order to run a computer as well as "operate" online (Altheide, 1985). Moreover, the equipment,
skills, and social capital essential for online participations are differential-
ly accessible because of social and economic considerations. (Pew Charitable Trusts, 2002)

A unique feature that the Internet shares with cell phone use is that
communication is visible (Altheide, 2002c, 2014a). The increasing visual
nature of the Internet is consistent with a trend in all media:

> "There is so much media around," said Mr. Wenner, who retains the
> title of editor. "Back when *Rolling Stone* was publishing these 7,000-
> word stories, there was no CNN, no Internet. And now you can travel
> instantaneously around the globe, and you don't need these long sto-
> ries to get up to speed." "All the great media adventures of the 20th
> century have been visual," said Mr. Needham, 37, who grew up in
> Cambridge, England. "Television, movies, the Internet, they're all visu-
> al mediums, and I don't think people have time to sit down and read.
> The gaps in people's time keep getting smaller and smaller, and the
> competition is getting more intense. It's one of the facts of media life."
> (Carr, 2002)

The public and visual nature of one-to-one communication on the
Internet invites surveillance and control. As media become more visual,
they are more visible, less private, and more susceptible to deception by
users who may use multiple identities for different purposes and websites. Deceptive communication breaches trust and legitimacy and contributes to an expansion of social control and surveillance. Efforts to monitor and regulate social behavior have reached the Internet (Lyon, 2001;
Staples, 1997). Part of Internet logic includes awareness and anticipation
by many that there may be unintended consequences of their actions
because of surveillance and control by agents seeking to take advantage
of their activity. These external controls, monitors, and surveillance can
mediate interaction insofar as an actor takes them into account in defining a situation. For example, surveys indicate that 17 percent of Internet
users know someone who has lost a job because of computer infractions
(Pew Charitable Trusts, 2002):

The AMA's [American Management Association] survey of major U.S. firms found that 77.7% now record and review some sort of employee communications and activities on the job. For example, Internet connections were monitored by 63% of the more than 1,600 companies responding to the survey. Telephone use was tracked by 43%. Computer use such as time logged on or keystroke counts was monitored by 19%. Video surveillance for security purposes was used by 38%. (*USA Today*, 2001)

Some fifteen years later there were more businesses offering the surveillance service. But people and organizations are often less vigilant in protecting computer information. An example was hacking by North Koreans into Sony's website in December 2014, and Russian hackers' attempts to interfere with the 2016 U.S. presidential election by divulging personal and organization communications from Hillary Clinton and the Democratic National Committee, respectively. Nevertheless, the American people appear to be more accepting of commercial and governmental surveillance (http://www.veriato.com/ppc/veriato-360/internet-monitoring?utm_source=GOOGLE&utm_medium=PPC&refer=92013&cid=70170000001PXyU&keywo).

Internet security and surveillance are now linked to provide privacy as well as protection and control:

Similarly, Americans are just as likely to approve of FBI or law enforcement surveillance of criminal suspects' phone calls and postal mail as they are to approve of surveillance of suspects' email. Fully 56% of all Americans approve of the FBI or law enforcement agencies intercepting telephone calls to and from people suspected of criminal activities; 55% of all Americans approve of the FBI or law enforcement agencies intercepting letters and packages sent by mail to and from people suspected of criminal activities; 54% of all Americans approve of the FBI or law enforcement agencies intercepting email over the Internet sent to and from people suspected of criminal activities. (Pew Charitable Trusts, 2002)

Increasingly, the very act of communicating—keystrokes, emojis, URL addresses—feeds both current and planned algorithms for mining information that can be used to anticipate individuals' needs as a category of consumers and voters. This "datafication" has important implications:

This is because data operate as a medium of identification and communication, they encompass testimonies of spatially bound actions and attitudes which are transported to a virtual interface, where profiles and archives are then established, codified and acted on. (G. J. Smith & D. Smith, 2016, 113)

Consumer transactions and protection from "hackers" require monitoring and surveillance to achieve various goals. Numerous computer and security publications report that thousands of attempts to breach computer "security" by domestic and international hackers. The latter has implications for national security, but the biggest concern is commerce. As a spokesperson for one computer security company put it,

> You need security, privacy and trust to get to the real electronic wallet," said Christiansen. You need a high degree of confidence, not that you won't be ripped off, but that someone isn't tracking your interactions—that it will be a trusted connection with the party you intended.

Adult Internet users are about split between those who are more or less trusting of Internet interaction. Survey data suggest that they take various measures to "protect" themselves, including engaging in deception:

> 63.1 percent of generalized trusters say that they use their real names on the web, compared to 55.7 percent of mistrusters. . . . We see similar effects for whomever used a fake ID on the web and replied to an e-mail from strangers—and slightly larger ones for using a credit card on the phone, and receiving an offensive e-mail from strangers. (Uslaner, 2000)

Children tend to be more trusting of Internet communications than adults and are more likely to provide personal and identifying information (Electronic Privacy Information Center, 2002).

The context of use and format of computer and Internet mediation produces the conundrum that surveillance and privacy violations are justified in order for users to have confidence in the privacy of communication and transactions. It is the context and the power to define situations of use as "legitimate" or not that produces the contradiction. It is as though whoever controls a server and/or rules of use controls intrusion and surveillance rights. Thus, we have seen that employers essentially have been sanctioned to intrude on employees, while businesses can now monitor critics with "snoop tools":

> Beware the public relations person with a modem. Now corporate spinmeisters, too, can go online to track customers—especially the disgruntled ones who vent their spleen in cyberspace. . . . To me, there's something very troubling about cyberspinning. Good public-relations personnel can quell panic and remind people of their company's side of the story in the heat of a crisis. But personalized spin campaigns? The potential for abuse seems too high, and the idea sounds ominous to those who cherish free speech without risk of punishment. (Stepanek, 2000)

INTERNET SURVEILLANCE AND THE LAW

While U.S. citizens are aware that social control of the Internet can influence constitutional rights to free speech, perceived threats to safety of oneself, children, and, more recently, national security have promoted various efforts to regulate and monitor Internet use. The knowledge and use of Internet surveillance is inconsistent, with huge gaps separating legality from what is done in practice. Formal agents of social control have long sought more regulation of information technology such as the Internet, although the courts have not supported such efforts. For example, regulating "private use" of computers was dealt a blow when the Supreme Court opposed a law in 1997 that made putting "indecent" material on the Internet a crime, and in 2002 the Court ruled against rules aimed at keeping minors away from commercial pornography on the World Wide Web (D. G. Savage, 2002b). The U.S. Court of Appeals for the Third Circuit sustained public use of Internet technology when it ruled that legislation is unconstitutional that requires libraries to screen Internet communications:

> The judges, who heard eight days of testimony, concluded that software programs designed to filter out such material are flawed and ineffective. Although the law sought to block access to "visual depictions" of sex, the software scanned for words, not images. Students researching breast cancer or sexual orientations were blocked, while some pornography slipped through. The law "requires [librarians] to violate the 1st Amendment rights of their patrons," said Chief Judge Edward R. Becker of the U.S. 3rd Circuit Court of Appeals. "The filtering programs bar access to a substantial amount of speech on the Internet that is clearly constitutionally protected for adults and minors." (D. G. Savage, 2002b)

Justices' concerns about Internet surveillance were dramatized in May 2001, when federal judges in the U.S. Court of Appeals for the Ninth Circuit disabled software that had been set up by the Administrative Offices of the Court to detect downloading of streaming video, music, and pornography (Lewis, 2001). Notwithstanding the American Management Association's finding that 63 percent of companies monitored employees' communications, the Ninth Circuit workers—and their judicial bosses—were not impressed and disconnected the surveillance equipment. Chief Judge Mary Schroeder wrote that the rationale to monitor the court was objectionable because it was not based on concerns about overloading the system but rather "content detection":

> Many employees had been disciplined, she noted, because the software turned up evidence of such things as viewing pornography, although they had not been given any clear notice of the court's computer use policy. Moreover, she wrote, the judiciary may have violated the law. "We are concerned about the propriety and even the legality of monitoring Internet usage," she wrote. Her memorandum said that the judiciary could be liable to lawsuits and damages because the software might have violated the Electronic Communications Privacy Act of

1986, which imposes civil and criminal liability on any person who intentionally intercepts "any wire, oral or electronic communication."

She noted that the Ninth Circuit had ruled just this year that the law was violated when an employer accessed an employee Web site. In fact, the issues of what is permissible by employers have produced a patchwork of legal rulings and the matter has never been addressed directly by the Supreme Court. (Lewis, 2001)

The 9/11 attacks boosted the momentum of authorities to expand surveillance of the Internet even though it would reduce civil liberties and give the FBI more unbridled surveillance of citizens and potential terrorists. Despite cautions raised by civil rights advocates, the "war on terror" resurrected the spectacle of FBI domestic spying and surveillance:

> In tandem with the perception of the Net as a technology that is difficult to control is a pessimistic view of humanity that assumes the worst about people's intentions. The darkest elements of humanity are seen as finding a home on the Net to pursue their anti-social and destructive ends. Combined with the panic of the potential damage a borderless medium can do to the authority of the State, the Net is seen by Western governments as a potential source of destabilisation.
>
> The anxieties expressed by Western elites about their direction and purpose have attached themselves to the Net—a new medium that represents the unknown. It used to be that the unknown was viewed as a potential opportunity to be explored and exploited to aid social and material progress. Now the unknown, regardless of its real potential is viewed as a risk that has to be contained and managed so it inflicts as little disruption and harm as possible. (Amis, 2002)

The USA Patriot Act (USAPA) was passed on October 26, 2001. This Act expanded governmental authority to engage in surveillance and challenge limits to civil liberties.

> The civil liberties of ordinary Americans have taken a tremendous blow with this law, especially the right to privacy in our online communications and activities. Yet there is no evidence that our previous civil liberties posed a barrier to the effective tracking or prosecution of terrorists. In fact, in asking for these broad new powers, the government made no showing that the previous powers of law enforcement and intelligence agencies to spy on US citizens were insufficient to allow them to investigate and prosecute acts of terrorism. These changes opened a floodgate for subpoenas to investigate numerous groups and activities:
>
> "The amount of subpoenas that carriers receive today is roughly doubling every month—we're talking about hundreds of thousands of subpoenas for customer records—stuff that used to require a judge's approval," said Albert Gidari, a Seattle-based expert in privacy and security law who represents numerous technology companies. (Benson, 2002)

As noted, several major changes were contained in the USA Patriot Act, but other changes were forthcoming as well:

> President Bush and Attorney General John Ashcroft said the changes are needed to boost the FBI's arsenal against terrorism. But civil libertarians and others complained that the FBI is being rewarded for its investigative lapses before the Sept. 11 terrorist attacks.
>
> "We intend to honor the Constitution and respect the freedoms that we hold so dear," Bush assured. Added Ashcroft: "Our objective today is not to sift through the rubble after another terrorist attack."
>
> The changes will enable FBI agents to do such things as monitor mosques, churches and synagogues, listen in on Internet chat rooms, watch library or supermarket card use, or even photograph or make lists of people attending political or other public gatherings without first providing any evidence of criminal activity.
>
> "As we have heard recently, FBI men and women in the field are frustrated because many of our own internal restrictions have hampered our ability to fight terrorism," Ashcroft said at a news conference. (House, 2002)
>
> Ashcroft's announcement Thursday changed the government's guidelines to encourage agents to gather more information, even when they have no evidence of a crime in progress. "The FBI must draw proactively on all lawful sources of information to identify terrorist threats," Ashcroft said. (D. G. Savage, 2002a)

A related issue that has been raised is the career of information, or what happens to the massive amount of material being collected. Government agencies have not been particularly successful at protecting the information for one specific purpose and are less likely to do so now that interagency cooperation essentially has been mandated:

> Prosecutors, acting under the authority of grand jury investigations, may issue subpoenas without prior approval of a judge. Critics complain that the Patriot Act makes it possible for CIA agents working with law enforcement officers to jointly draw up subpoenas, obtain information, and never have to appear in court to explain how the information was used. (Benson, 2002)

Part of the context of this new information access and use is that most Americans are unaware that the FBI and CIA, for example, have not openly shared information in recent years in order to protect civil rights and to prevent the kind of witch hunts that occurred previously in American history, particularly the civil rights era. As one observer stated,

> In the '60s and '70s, the FBI ran a massive program called COINTEL-PRO that included secret investigations, surveillance, infiltration and disruption of political activist groups that were not engaged in illegal conduct, including the civil rights movement, anti-war protesters and feminists. . . .

> "Consumers should know that the information they give to America Online or Microsoft may very well wind up at the IRS or the FBI," said Jeffrey A. Eisenach, president of the Progress & Freedom Foundation, a think tank that studies technology and public policy. "Security is not costless." (Benson, 2002)

Today the information access and monitoring of the Internet as well as cell phone messages is more insidious because it is about control and making money. Business and formal agents of social control not only have interests in security and surveillance but also are often partners in a complex dance of communication and control.

Consider the development of two computer snooping programs, Carnivore and Magic Lantern. Essentially, both are designed to monitor computer keystrokes and messages (MSNBC, 2001). The first one was Carnivore. After news organizations broke the story about this software that could "snoop" on one's email and Internet use, the FBI addressed their work on the project:

> Two weeks ago, the *Wall Street Journal* published an article entitled "FBI's system to covertly search E-mail raises privacy, legal issues." This story was immediately followed by a number of similar reports in the press and other media depicting our Carnivore system as something ominous and raising concerns about the possibility of its potential to snoop, without a court order, into the private E-mails of American citizens. . . . In response to a critical need for tools to implement complex court orders, the FBI developed a number of capabilities including the software program called "Carnivore." Carnivore is a very specialized network analyzer or "sniffer" which runs as an application program on a normal personal computer under the Microsoft Windows operating system. It works by "sniffing" the proper portions of network packets and copying and storing only those packets which match a finely defined filter set programmed in conformity with the court order. This filter set can be extremely complex, and this provides the FBI with an ability to collect transmissions which comply with pen register court orders, trap & trace court orders, Title III interception orders, etc. (Kerr, 2000)

American citizens were about evenly divided on whether this software would be used appropriately by the FBI (Pew Charitable Trusts, 2002). Carnivore requires access to a user's computer in order to be installed, but Magic Lantern does not. This is a virus that can be sent to individual computers to monitor keystrokes and send the information to the FBI (or earlier versions sent information to hackers). Magic Lantern, which would be an extension of the Carnivore Internet surveillance program, takes the idea one step further by enabling agents to place a Trojan on a target's computer without having to gain physical access (Leyden, 2001).

However, the virus detection programs available on most computer systems can detect them if the software is programmed to find them. Ironically, the confidence and trust of software manufacturers could be compromised if word got out that they had cooperated with the FBI in installing a virus:

> Prior to the FBI's official disclosure, several major antivirus companies told news sources earlier this week that they would not aid the FBI in allowing its viruses any special advantage over other viruses and worms, saying that selective virus interception would diminish public confidence in the effectiveness of their security products (Weisman, 2001). "If it was under the control of the FBI, with appropriate technical safeguards in place to prevent possible misuse, and nobody else used it—we wouldn't detect it," said Chien. "However we would detect modified versions that might be used by hackers."
>
> Graham Cluley, senior technology consultant at Sophos, disagrees. He says it wrong to deliberately refrain from detecting the virus, because its customers outside the US would expect protection against the Trojan. Such a move also creates an awkward precedent. (Leyden, 2001)

The politics of fear contributed to the massive increase in surveillance by the National Security Agency (NSA), which was revealed by Edward Snowden. Several governments have expanded surveillance efforts to combat real and imagined terrorist threats as well as keep up with allies' espionage of each other. This came to a head in 2013 when whistleblower Edward Snowden released documents showing that the United States' NSA had eavesdropped on allies' telephone messages, including the cell phone of Germany's Angela Merkel. By then surveillance became business as usual. As stated by Democratic Majority Leader Harry Reid:

> Right now I think everyone should just calm down and understand that this isn't anything that is brand new, it's been going on for some seven years, and we have tried often to try to make it better and work and we will continue to do that. (CBS Evening News, June 12, 2013)

Subsequent investigation revealed that both U.S. and British agents routinely mine citizens' cell communications:

> In their globe-spanning surveillance for terrorism suspects and other targets, the National Security Agency and its British counterpart have been trying to exploit a basic byproduct of modern telecommunications: With each new generation of mobile phone technology, ever greater amounts of personal data pour onto networks where spies can pick it up. . . . The N.S.A. and Britain's Government Communications Headquarters were working together on how to collect and store data from dozens of smartphone apps by 2007, according to the documents, provided by Edward J. Snowden, the former N.S.A. contractor. Since then, the agencies have traded recipes for grabbing location and planning data when a target uses Google Maps, and for vacuuming up

address books, buddy lists, telephone logs and the geographic data embedded in photographs when someone sends a post to the mobile versions of Facebook, Flickr, LinkedIn, Twitter and other internet services. (Glanz, Larson, & Lehren, 2014)

The pervasiveness of the politics of fear is partly due to the acceptance of certain programs by people throughout social life, especially certain key organizations and industries. For example, if the military and law enforcement organizations enact certain policies, this can have widespread consequences. By the same token, when computer and Internet companies accept the principle that computers should be made to comply with government surveillance, that is also consequential. When this occurs, the government oversight is no longer just the government's; it is societal wide. In fact, this has happened with the computer industry. The Associated Press reported that the FBI was no longer going to use Carnivore but instead would rely on surveillance by Internet providers (*Arizona Republic*, January 19, 2005, A3). Instead, the FBI said it has switched to unspecified commercial software to eavesdrop on computer traffic during such investigations and has increasingly asked Internet providers to conduct wiretaps on targeted customers on the government's behalf, reimbursing companies for their costs. This means that the use and logic of communication using the computer also is based on a format of control that permits surveillance. To communicate is to be observed. The politics of fear is essentially an integral feature of computer hardware and software. But this is only half of the story.

The other half of the story is that the CIA and FBI are in conflict about surveillance and control. While the FBI's interest has been in developing Magic Lantern to monitor computer use, the CIA has developed software to avoid this surveillance. The CIA has had a hand in developing more software that will override Carnivore and Magic Lantern. A CIA-backed software company, Safe Web, created Triangle Boy, which enables people in "tyrannical" countries (e.g., China) to get access to blocked Internet sites:

> Yet, as the FBI struggles to introduce its new system to monitor the Internet, the CIA is working to develop a software program that thwarts government monitoring. The CIA is a major sponsor of Safe Web, a company that distributes a free program called Triangle Boy. Triangle Boy allows users to surf the Web anonymously. Citizens inside dictatorships are using the program to avoid monitoring by the oppressive regimes.
>
> Triangle Boy operates much like a mail forwarding service. Each user request to view a Web page is scrambled and randomly sent to another machine, which actually performs the request, returning the data to the original user. Triangle Boy is very popular inside China, and the Chinese government is working hard on ways to counter secure access to the Internet. (C. R. Smith, 2001)

A potential problem is that terrorists could use Triangle Boy to avoid detection by the FBI's Magic Lantern (although officials deny that this is likely). Ironically, many inside the computer security field declined to describe ways to stop Triangle Boy—not for technical reasons but for political reasons:

> Software experts are usually anxious to publish flaws inside Microsoft operating systems or other major software packages. Yet this is not the case for Triangle Boy. "Normally, I'm all for publishing flaws in software, but on this one I have to vote against," stated one computer security expert located in the Netherlands.
>
> "The Chinese finally have access to the Internet. The flaws could be used by the Chinese government to block the Internet once again." (C. R. Smith, 2001)

It is important to stress what the foregoing has implied: it is now official that anyone who uses the Internet is now legally subject to surveillance and monitoring by formal agents of social control. As one observer cautioned,

> The bottom line here is that companies and individuals will be responsible for protecting themselves from both cyberterrorism and the government's response to it. (Weisman, 2001)

Resistance, WikiLeaks, and Snowden

WikiLeaks is another example of officials using extreme punitive efforts to punish those involved in sending disapproved messages. In this case, Julian Assange, a renowned hacker, who headed an organization dedicated to exposing governmental and organizational secrets—WikiLeaks—was held to be responsible for publicizing thousands of classified governmental documents from the United States and other diplomatic exchanges related to some countries, as well as U.S. military operations, which included videos of U.S. soldiers/pilots killing civilians. He, along with a young military intelligence worker (Bradley Manning, aka Chelsea), who copied the materials, were charged with divulging classified information, and more, and some people wanted them—especially Bradley Manning—charged with treason. In addition to the U.S. government's drastic actions of blocking WikiLeak's bank funds and prohibiting future contributions via the Internet—thereby crippling the organization—Julian Assange was also a suspect in Sweden for forced sexual relations with two Swedish women. Sweden wanted him extradited, but he remained in Ecuador's embassy in London. Bradley Manning (who became Chelsea Manning), on the other hand, was in custody since May 2010, before he was sentenced to thirty-five years in prison. Assange stated in August 2012:

"Bradley Manning must be released. If Bradley Manning did as he is accused, he is a hero, an example to all of us and one of the world's foremost political prisoners," he said. The US must also "renounce its witch-hunt against WikiLeaks," Assange demanded from the Ecuadorian embassy. (http://www.guardian.co.uk/media/2012/aug/19/assange-witch-hunt-release-manning)

After serving about seven years, Manning's sentence was commuted by outgoing President Barack Obama on January 17, 2017, just three days before his term of office expired.

Many world leaders supported WikiLeaks actions, even inviting Assange to address the United Nations within a few days of President Obama's repeated call for tolerance of free speech regarding the Muslim video (http://www.democracynow.org/2012/9/27/in_un_address_wikileaks_julian_assange).

Notwithstanding wide support for Assange's—and WikiLeaks'—right to publish information even though it may be embarrassing to U.S. policies, President Obama expressed his "concern" about the leaking of classified information, and virtually all officials acknowledged that their acts were illegal, could not be tolerated, and that strong measures must be taken to prevent the leaking of classified information.

The use of surveillance and the Internet by WikiLeaks took a strange twist during the 2016 presidential campaign. Assange, who was wanted on a criminal charge by the United States for releasing classified documents provided by Chelsea Manning, was also sought by Sweden on a charge of sexual molestation. He was granted political asylum in the Ecuadorian embassy in London in 2010, where he continued to release documents to the press. His well-known dislike of Hillary Clinton, a candidate for president in 2016, came to the fore. U.S. security agencies concurred that Russian computer hackers captured thousands of documents from the Democratic National Committee, the Republican National Committee (RNC), as well as former Secretary of State Hillary Clinton and her campaign manager John Podesta. It appeared that this information was provided to WikiLeaks, which strategically released embarrassing information from the DNC and about Hillary Clinton, in particular, during the final months of her campaign. Virtually no information was released about Mr. Trump and the RNC. It was widely believed that these reports, which were enthusiastically broadcast by the entertainment-oriented mass media and numerous social media sites, harmed her election chances. Moreover, Mr. Trump, who had conveyed positive sentiments about Russia and President Vladimir Putin, invited Russia to release information about Hillary Clinton, who had been accused of deleting emails that had been on her personal computer server while she had been Secretary of State. During a press conference on July 26, 2016, Trump stated:

"I will tell you this, Russia: If you're listening, I hope you're able to find the 30,000 emails that are missing," the Republican nominee said at a news conference in Florida. "I think you will probably be rewarded mightily by our press." (Crowley & Pager, 2016)

WikiLeaks, essentially serving as Russia's agent, did release many of the emails, excerpts from private speeches, as well as internal documents about the DNC campaign as well as several congressional elections. In a bizarre twist, Donald Trump rejected intelligence committees' conclusions that Russian-related hackers were involved.

The Internet and the politics of fear invite control—to either promote one's views and/or to restrict the persuasive and propaganda efforts of others. This is especially a problem if the offending messages suggest or give a hint about some cracks in the authenticity or complete truthfulness of other views. One example is ISIS.

ISIS AND DIGITAL BOOTY

A cataclysmic blowback of U.S. failed foreign policy in the aftermath of the wars with Afghanistan and Iraq contributed to the emergence of the so-called Islamic State of Iraq and Syria (ISIS) in June 2014. This hodge-podge fighting force, staffed by many former military commanders of Saddam Hussein with the goal of establishing a caliphate to rule Muslims globally, cut ties with the better-known terrorist organization al Qaeda and struck out on its own crusade of murder and pillage that was felt in Syria, Iraq, Lebanon, Yemen, and parts of Africa.

The ISIS propaganda program is a good example of reflexive mediation. It was powered by sophisticated social media and propaganda techniques, in addition to commandeering untold U.S. military equipment that was left by disbanded Iraqi army units. In addition to committing mass murder of heretics—including Shiites and several varieties of Christians—it also kidnapped and held for ransom many foreign aid workers and journalists. ISIS became a global scourge when it posted graphic beheadings of several of these victims via YouTube and Twitter, along with other videos.

Despite murdering people in order to achieve a mythical past, ISIS is part of contemporary media culture and understands how the world increasingly operates with media logic. ISIS not only used YouTube to publicize executions, it also sent emails to the slain journalists' families demanding ransom. A camcorder and videotape captured the grisly beheading of journalist Daniel Pearl in 2002; James Foley's murder was uploaded to YouTube by ISIS propagandists. The main executioner was profiled as a British citizen, who was soon referred to by his media name "Jihadi John" (Mohammed Emwazi). His family and schoolmates would be interviewed and featured in numerous reports. The theater caught the attention of numerous world leaders, including Middle Eastern heads of state. Indeed, the Jordanian government launched an all-out assault on ISIS when a captured pilot was burned alive—on camera. The symbolic power of this organization touched would-be jihadists worldwide, leading several to avenge profane cartoons of the Prophet Mohammed by killing journalists in Paris at the office of *Charlie Hebdo.*

The instantaneous, personal, and visual statements presented challenges to news organizations that did not want to actually show the beheadings but would show the dramatic moments just prior. These executions were deadly theatrical stunts orchestrated to generate social media action and political reaction. Terrorists, politicians, and even marketers are using this new communication environment. Notwithstanding the relatively frequent beheadings in the Middle East against enemies, such as rebels fighting pro-Assad forces, U.S. audiences are most familiar with the deaths of Americans. The sudden emotional reaction to imminent danger seems real when we actually see horrific acts on familiar social media that we share with family, friends, and political leaders. Citizens and officials receive information and comments at virtually the same time. Reactions with little reflection and planning fly off into previous discourses of fear framed by events and issues of the day, including ongoing terrorist threats, immigration, and fragmented foreign policy decisions.

Opinion polls suggest that Americans are once again succumbing to fear of terrorism, aided in part by sensational media reports about the growing menace, but also by politicians, who trumpet potential threat in press conferences and off-the-cuff statements that will be carried over social media. Tens of thousands of viewers would view the images online. ISIS's skilled use of digital media and recruitment of hundreds of converts worldwide posed a counterpropaganda challenge for various countries. So skilled were they with the global outreach that they were able to hack military databases and post a list of names and addresses of "wanted" U.S. military personnel, much like the United States had done after the 9/11 attacks. The postings urged jihadists worldwide to kill these people. Clearly, the media genie was out of the bottle; the major industrial powers were no longer the sole propaganda agents. The U.S. media acted in conventional ways, sharing the horror, denouncing the brutality, and occasionally carrying interviews with officials, who urged stronger military action. Very few comments, save an occasional comment online, discussed how the ecology of communication had produced this horrific situation.

ISIS hate, fear, and recruiting successes are due to "digital booty," which refers to the theft or appropriation of digital technology—such as social media—and accompanying formats for goal achievement and profit. ISIS communications rely on Western innovations (e.g., YouTube, Facebook, Twitter, etc.) to stage and deliver their messages. ISIS replays many popular culture themes by copying Western traditions and relying on them to carry global messages. Ironically, media-logic-driven entertainment genres, programs, and formats that the West—especially the United States—developed and transformed to attract audiences and profits with tantalizing self-enhancing products, fear-generating scenarios (especially crime shows and TV newscasts), and emotionally inspiring narratives of conquest in contrived fictional worlds (including video games) have been appropriated by ISIS to dramatically present real-life deadly theater of individual and mass executions. Even here, they are playing off popular culture.

ISIS has simply adopted well-established formats for a version of horrific murder. A basic production model of ISIS is to borrow entertainment programming and movie scripts, such as demanding outrageous ransoms of tens of millions of dollars from kidnapped victims' families. Reminiscent of Batman's nemesis, the Joker, or Superman's arch-enemy, Lex Luthor, ISIS plagiarizes fiction with their own versions of clock-ticking-until-death. As Lex Luthor observed, "The more fear you make, the more loot you take." Even the horror of executions has been dulled for American audiences accustomed to seeing "good guys" combating evil, such as Jack Bauer (24) and Ray Reddington (*The Blacklist*) routinely erasing despicable characters without benefit of law.

It is clear, then, that the Internet mediates interaction in several ways. On the one hand, certain monitoring is not new to Internet users, most of whom simply take it for granted that various businesses, organizations, and universities collect information from them and sell parts of their "social identity" for marketing and cash. On the other hand, the mediation of Internet interaction goes well beyond "buyer beware": it extends to the communicative foundations of trust that may be utilized to "trick" and deceive actors.

INTERNET STINGS

Surveillance takes on a different meaning with new technology. Virtually everyone who uses a "search engine" is gathering information that is available in public, so formal agents of social control reason that anyone should be able to do so. A law professor who did not regard the new FBI Internet surveillance as unconstitutional added, "Still, if sleazy credit card companies can look up our supermarket or other purchases, then I see nothing wrong at first blush with letting the FBI agents do the same thing" (House, 2002). Many Americans share this sentiment, particularly when it comes to preventing crime and protecting their children from pornography.

The concern with sleazy surveillance extends beyond credit card companies and FBI agents to the monitoring and deception by law enforcement officials in setting up "Internet stings." Internet stings have been conducted by formal agents of social control on topics ranging from prostitution and escort services, gay chat rooms, drugs (including Viagra), computer software, stolen goods, stolen credit cards, fraudulent IDs, satellite dish cards, animal videos, stock Internet scams, and child pornography.

Stings are commonly used in order to protect children from online predators and pedophiles. These stings tend to focus on (1) participants in chat rooms and web pages where sex tours or traveling (across town or around the world) to meet children for sex or pornographic purposes and (2) websites where information and materials are exchanged about child pornography as well as child or adult prostitution. Like all stings, the intent is to create a false scenario and opportunity for a crime to be committed, such as undercover police officers acting as prostitutes. Internet stings involve providing information about any regulated "bait," which may be merchandise, activities, or opportunities, such as stolen goods, credit cards, cell phone numbers, pirated video cards for cable reception, drugs, escort services and prostitution, pornography, drugs, child pornography, and pedophilia. Typically, police officers (but also citizen vigilantes) using a deceptive and false identity will broadcast via the Internet that they have certain goods or services. This is done very aggressively, using role-playing, typical scenarios, presentations of self, and relevant discourse and terminology in order to draw the interest of potential customers/buyers who will be treated as offenders. Many Internet stings bait a "suspect" to buy something (e.g., drugs) or "meet" someone for some deviant/illegal purpose. The provider of the service, who is usually a police officer, will show up to sell a product or meet the suspect, who will typically be arrested after money is exchanged—or some other incriminating information is provided to represent intent.

Undercover sting operations appear to have increased dramatically over the past forty years (Marx, 1988) and particularly since the mid-1990s. Virtually every major city in the United States—and several smaller ones—have used the Internet for sting operations. Sting operations are easy to sell to audiences consuming popular culture and the discourse of fear—the pervasive communication, symbolic awareness, and expectation that danger and risk are a central feature of everyday life (Altheide, 2002b). Particularly popular are stings that target corrupters of children such as "child pornographers" and pedophiles.

> Americans are deeply worried about criminal activity on the Internet, and their revulsion at child pornography is by far their biggest fear. Some 92 percent of Americans say they are concerned about child pornography on the Internet, and 50 percent of Americans cite child porn as the single most heinous crime that takes place online (Pew Charitable Trusts, 2002). As one federal prosecutor put it, "There are only two

ways to do these cases. . . . A sting operation or wait till a kid gets hurt." (Stern, 2002)

The concern with protecting children is a feature of the discourse of fear that calls for more control (Altheide, 2002a). While officials estimate that a very small fraction of sexual abuse victims began their relationships on the Internet (five of four thousand in Chicago [Miller, 1999]), public perception is that it is rampant. Moral entrepreneurs promoting sensational news reports have prompted officials to spring into action and get involved. Operating under various names (e.g., Operation Landslide and Innocent Images), federal and state police increasingly are in the sting business. Even before the terrorist attacks cemented the perception that everyday life is dangerous and that "evil" predators are lurking everywhere, formal agents of social control were given substantial support to "crack down" on child molesters and perverts. Innocent Images, for example, is an annual $10 million FBI operation that sprang from the 1995 Innocent Images National Initiative. Its purposes are the following:

- to identify, investigate, and prosecute sexual predators who use the Internet and online services to sexually exploit children
- to establish a law enforcement presence on the Internet as a deterrent to subjects that use it to exploit children
- to identify and rescue witting and unwitting child victims (https:// archives.fbi.gov/archives/news/stories/2006/february/innocent_ images022406)

One of the first FBI operations under Innocent Images was Operation Candyland, which was named after an e-group web page oriented to posting messages and images about children. "In the 10 years since we officially launched the program and established the Innocent Images Unit, we and our law enforcement partners—many of whom we've trained—have opened more than 15,500 cases; charged more than 4,700 criminals; and arrested more than 6,100 subjects" (https://archives.fbi. gov/archives/news/stories/2006/february/innocent_images022406).

Like the undercover police officers studied by Marx (1988) who were often spying on other undercover police officers, Internet police are often "talking to themselves":

> Agents posing as teens almost certainly outnumber actual teens in many of the Internet's seedier chat rooms these days. And though would-be sexual predators are surely aware of this ploy, the number of them stepping into these digital traps continues to soar. . . . "It's probably overkill," said Shari Steele, director of legal services for the Electronic Frontier Foundation. "At least half the 13-year-old girls in chat rooms are probably policemen." (Miller, 1999)

There have been other Internet stings where the focus is on belonging to an illegal web page. Supported by the FBI's Innocent Images cyberpatrol, New Jersey police closed down a pornographic website and arrested its operations. Formal agents of social control restarted it within two months using the same domain and explained to "surfers" that the site had been down but was now open for business. They invited prospective subscribers to join for a $19.99 membership fee and to share their materials of prepubescent males. Law enforcement officials throughout the world seized computers in sixteen nations and twenty-nine states. The suspects included a teacher, a principal, a police officer, and a firefighter (Wire Services, 2002).

Another web page sting trapped journalist Larry Matthews, who had published several reports on pedophiles and was conducting research on pedophilia. Matthews joined a website and frequented chat rooms that traded child pornography because he felt that it was a better method of doing quality journalism:

> He told prosecutors that conventional research methods for his latest project, like posing questions as a journalist in open chat rooms, were unsuccessful and that to delve deeper, he needed to assume the persona of a trader in child pornographic images. (Janofsky, 1999)

In a bizarre twist of events, Matthews himself was arrested as a result of the FBI's Innocent Images program in Baltimore, Maryland, where agents had adopted a similar strategy of frequenting anonymous chat rooms to catch adults who solicit minors and exchange child porn (Burton, 2002). He was not permitted to use a conventional journalistic defense of First Amendment rights and was convicted and sentenced to eighteen months.

The surveillance is very real in Internet stings, although the characters are just that: usually caricatures of stereotypes of "child molesters" and pedophiles. While laws were established to protect "real persons" from those intending to harm them, the mediated nature of the Internet warrants presentation of identity as one thing when, in fact, it may be something else—it may be a middle-aged formal agent of social control rather than a thirteen-year-old girl or boy.

This point was made in a case in Wisconsin when the accused's attorney argued that no crime could have occurred since the intended victim was "virtual" and not real, although he did travel to a hotel room where he believed that an encounter would follow. The defense attorney argued that one might have also had a change of heart because of guilt, shame, remorse, or fear of getting caught. Attorneys claimed that the law should be overturned:

> Department of Justice spokesman Randy Romanski said that if the law is overturned, it will shake up the way the agency's Internet Crimes Against Children Task Force does business. "It would be unfortunate if it was decided that those investigators could not continue operating the way they are," Romanski said, noting that since 1999 the task force has

arrested 72 people—including 57 men who traveled to meet "children" who were actually undercover agents. (Chaptman, 2002)

Regardless, the prosecution claimed that what matters before the law is clear intent, and that is where most cases seem to reside. As the prosecution wrote,

> Sound public policy . . . supports identifying those who would inflict such harm on children and preventing them from doing so, rather than waiting for real children to be victimized. (Chaptman, 2002)

The massive news reports about threats to children have spurred some citizens to set up their own Internet sites and pose as available victims. Julie Posey, a Colorado grandmother, regularly signs on to various Internet sites as Kendra, a fourteen-year-old girl who is looking for a good time. When strangers bite, she entices them, sets up a meeting, and alerts police, who move in for the bust. She has done this nearly two dozen times and joins forces with other individuals and groups around the United States, such as Predator-Hunter, Soc-Um, and Cyberarmy Pedophilia Fighters. One of the largest groups is Cyber-Angels. This spin-off of Guardian-Angels boasts nearly ten thousand members. As the reach of the Internet grows, Posey counts herself among a handful of private citizens who have assumed the role of online crime fighters, hoping to smoke out sexual predators and traders in kiddie porn. They say they fill the gap that many local police departments leave because of meager resources (Leonard & Morin, 2002).

Police officers may decry such cybervigilantism, but they enlist the help of the public routinely. Posey offers seminars to teach officers about computer enticements. Described as a "bulldog" by a child abuse investigator whose office provided her with an award, Posey pursues her cyber-sleuthing calling with gusto without leaving her house:

> It's there that Posey spends about 40 hours a week trolling the Net. When the chat rooms are silent, she turns to her Web site, http://www.pedowatch.org, a one-woman watchdog operation that has passed hundreds of tips to police. She finances her detective work through banner ads on the site, which have brought in as much as $1,000 a month. (Leonard & Morin, 2002)

CONCLUSION

This chapter addressed some issues about mediated interaction and the relevance of communication processes on the Internet for surveillance practices by formal agents of social control and others. Examples are of domestic upsets, including a presidential election upset, along with international surveillance and propaganda efforts. I suggested that a control narrative is implicated in numerous attempts and logics to monitor and regulate Internet use. The control narrative refers to actors' awareness and expectation that symbolic meanings may be monitored and used by diverse audiences for various purposes. Far more is involved than efforts to restrict access and use of information technology as fear and control are reflexively joined to virtual communication.

In a risk society, governance is privatized and dispersed across myriad fragmented institutions. The onus is placed on organizations and individuals to be more self-sufficient, to look after their own risk management needs. This emphasis on self-governance is underpinned by the interconnected discourses of morality, rights, responsibility, and accountability (Ericson & Haggerty, 1997).

Internet users are voyeurs and exhibitionists; we watch others, are seen watching others, and want to be seen. Ours is a society that relies on "dataveillence," or the widespread mining and sharing of consumer information (Staples, 2000). Even as I write this, my "computer jar" fills with "cookies" sent by technological voyeurs to monitor and track. What will we "get back" from a message sent, who will see it and for what purpose, and will there be consequences?

Internet technology, formats, and the push to police risks in a societal context grounded in fear mediate interaction on the Internet (and elsewhere). While the existence of the Internet may be unimaginable without extensive security, it is security that has produced some paradoxes. Ultimately, people are helping to normalize communicative control. Crises of the day (e.g., terrorist attacks and the control of children) are treated with an Internet twist. Similar to the "concern about television" in an earlier time, parents are instructed to "watch their children" and use "Internet filters" to keep them away from inappropriate sites, and formal agents of social control want to monitor the Internet, control its use, and engage in the surveillance of everyone.

Numerous research questions accompany the casting of Internet communications as part of an ecology of communication and control. Applying a mediated interaction perspective to Internet use suggests questions such as the following: How do Internet users perceive and account for surveillance and control by friends, businesses, and formal agents of social control? What are organizational consequences of such surveillance and control? How does such control inform actors' efforts to manipulate their own and others' identities? Over what aspects of Internet and electronic communication is this control—and adjustments to it—manifested? How do users resist and even subvert the control narrative and logic? How is other communication influenced by actors' awareness and use of the control narrative? And we should ask, in view of Russia's hacking attempts to influence the U.S. 2016 presidential election, how is Internet surveillance tied to other aspects of social, economic, and political action and policy? These and many other questions should be addressed using a variety of research methods, including field and case studies, if social scientists hope to understand the social relevance of the Internet. The next chapter examines how the Internet provided some contrary information to the propaganda onslaught to sell the Iraq War to the American people.

EIGHT

Propaganda of Fear, the Iraq War, and the Islamic State

The success of "Bush's PR War" . . . was largely dependent on a compliant press that uncritically repeated almost every fraudulent administration claim about the threat posed to America by Saddam Hussein.

—MacArthur, 2003, 62

And he [John McCain] will keep us on offense against terrorism at home and abroad. For 4 days in Denver and for the past 18 months Democrats have been afraid to use the words "Islamic Terrorism." During their convention, the Democrats rarely mentioned *the attacks of September 11.*

—Giuliani's speech at the Republican National Convention, September 3, 2008 (my emphasis)

On this day, we gather because we have chosen hope over fear, unity of purpose over conflict and discord.

—President Obama's inauguration speech, January 20, 2009

We will reinforce old alliances and form new ones—and unite the civilized world against radical Islamic terrorism, which we will eradicate completely from the face of the Earth.

—Donald Trump's inauguration speech, January 20, 2017

Politicians sold the Iraq War to the American people with a massive propaganda campaign. They underestimated the political, economic, social, and human costs of the war that became the longest conflict in our history. Their actions set the tone for subsequent wars, as well as an expansive view of terrorism that quickly grew out of control and had immense domestic and international impacts on domestic and global politics. This chapter focuses mainly on the foundation of these efforts in planning and selling the Iraq War, but some context will be provided for

185

what transpired after George W. Bush left office and the terrorism car-
ryover into domestic or homegrown terror, on the one hand, and the
expansive surveillance of American citizens.

Propaganda dominates the politics of fear. This is most apparent in
time of war. This chapter examines how propaganda and fear were combined in selling a war against terrorism. The Iraq War was presented to
U.S. and international audiences as a war program, although foreign audiences interpreted the visuals and official narratives much differently
since they did not share the ideologically embedded accounts of previously broadcast U.S. wars. This chapter documents how the Project for a
New American Century (PNAC), the Iraq propaganda campaign, and a
compliant news media developed, sold, enacted, and justified a war with
Iraq that has resulted at this writing (January 2017) in more than ten
thousand dead or wounded American soldiers, plus numerous contract
workers and mercenaries hired by the U.S. government, as well as an
estimated one hundred thousand Iraqi civilians (Cooney, 2004) and ten
thousand Iraqi soldiers who defended their country.

This chapter has three major objectives. The first is to show how the
PNAC shaped the most massive propaganda campaign since World War
II and engaged in a public conspiracy that laid the groundwork for the
United States to invade Iraq on March 20, 2003. By public conspiracy, we
mean that available but not widely publicized documents show that a
well-organized group of individuals reshaped defense and foreign policy
and then became active political officials. The second objective is to describe and clarify why the PNAC's plans for Iraq and for an imperialist
foreign policy received very little news media coverage. In general, we
argue that this plan was not publicized by the major news media because
it fell outside the focus of the Bush administration's propaganda campaign to demonize Iraq and its leader Saddam Hussein.

The third objective of this chapter is to set forth a theoretical argument
for analyzing modern propaganda campaigns as a feature of mass-mediated discourse crafted by media logic, defined as a form of communication, and the process through which media transmit and communicate
information (Altheide & Johnson, 1980). Elements of this form include the
distinctive features of each medium and the formats used by these media
for the organization, the style in which it is presented, the focus or emphasis on particular characteristics of behavior, and the grammar of media communication (Altheide & Snow, 1979; Hepp, 2013; Hjarvard, 2013;
Livingstone, 2009; Meyen, Thieroff, & Strenger, 2014; Snow, 1983). Another feature of media logic is that audience experiences through media
accumulate and blend with certain symbols and images; stereotypes are
reinforced, and simplistic divisions between friends and foes become reified. On the one hand, this logic will be examined while testing a model
of war programming that was developed through previous analysis of
war planning and coverage (Altheide, 1995a), while on the other hand,

recent events called for a revision of this model for terrorism programming (Altheide, 2009c).

Students of propaganda and American journalism have long noted that the press capitulates to the government during times of war (Der Derian, 2002; Ellenius & European Science Foundation, 1998; Gerth, 1992; Herman & Chomsky, 2002; Jackall, 1994; Jackall & Hirota, 1999; Kellner, 1992, 2003; Shapiro, 1992). Typically scholars, journalists, and others reflect on the "poor coverage" after a conflict (see step 4 later in this chapter). My intent is different. While I will discuss the lax news coverage that was part of the propaganda drive to conduct the Iraq War, this critique is included within a model of media logic and war programming (Altheide, 1995a). This means that with most wars no critiques are given until after the propaganda preparation, the war, and the attendant slaughter. I continue with an overview of war programming.

WAR PROGRAMMING

Sociological theory suggests that social actors' definitions of situations are informed by previous experiences and meanings (Altheide, 1987b; Blumer, 1962, 1969; Couch, Saxton, & Katovich, 1986; Denzin, 2003; Hall, 2003; Hewitt & Shulman, 1991; Nash & Calonico, 2003; Perinbanayagam, 1986; Stone & Farberman, 1970). This process holds true for audiences, politicians, and journalists (Shapiro, 1997). The irony, of course, is that each new "war situation" is presented by producers as something unique and novel, while the informational and emotional context for relating to it is historically embedded in previous wars, often experienced mainly through mass media. Analysis of news media coverage of previous wars indicates that each "current" war is greatly informed by the images, symbols, language, and experience associated with "previous" wars, including the demonization of the enemy, the virtues and necessity of waging war, and the social and political benefits of doing so. Thus, we draw on war programming, an ordered sequence of activities:

1. Reportage and visual reports of the most recent war (or two)
2. Anticipation, planning, and preparing the audiences for the impending war, including "demonizing" certain individual leaders (e.g., Noriega or Hussein)
3. Coverage of the subsegments of the current war, using the best visuals available to capture the basic scenes and themes involving the battle lines, the home front, the media coverage, the international reaction, and anticipation of the war's aftermath
4. Following the war, journalists' reaction and reflection on various governmental restrictions and suggestions for the future (which are seldom implemented)

5. Journalists' and academics' diaries, biographies, exposés, critiques, and studies about the war and increasingly the media coverage
6. Media reports about such studies, which are often cast negatively and often lead to the widespread conclusion that perhaps the war was unnecessary, other options were available, and that the price was too high (all of this will be useful for the coverage of the next war)
7. For the next war, return to step 1.

Each of these phases has been verified empirically with other U.S. wars and will not be repeated here (Altheide, 1995a; Skoll, 2010; Werning, 2009). The aim is to apply this model to the Iraq War and make conceptual adjustments in order to enhance our theoretical capacity to explain modern propaganda.

As war programming indicates, a gamelike structure has emerged for joining action and critique sequentially. The challenge of the Iraq War is that while it officially ended on May 2, 2003, with Bush's dramatic photo-op landing on an aircraft carrier—"major combat operations in Iraq have ended"—the war continued fourteen years later. Nevertheless, critiques (steps 4 and 5) are forthcoming. (Indeed, this chapter itself falls within step 5.) This model is different than conventional propaganda analyses because war programming builds in critique as part of the narrative and script of promotion.

The current structure of policy and critique is now institutionalized and, essentially, connects criticism and "challenge" within the action as a war program. The scope of the action is so immense that it precludes and preempts its critique. I contend that a new approach is needed to offer critique before the event. This can be accomplished by theorizing as praxis or stating by drawing on previous experiences how an action's planning, execution, successes, and failures will produce social consequences. That this has already been anticipated is apparent from certain websites that forewarned journalists to avoid making mistakes and promoting propaganda. For example, in an open letter to an "editor, publisher, producer, reporter" dated March 4, 2003, two weeks before Baghdad was bombed, a list of academics, journalists, politicians, and celebrities besieged "media people" to avoid common mistakes:

> We are writing to convey a level of heightened expectation in your forthcoming coverage of the U.S.-Iraq situation. . . . Access to truly independent sources of information is essential, given the government's control of knowledge, data, pictures and other information during this period. The media's display of all significant points of view is especially important because of the tendency of our top officials to equate patriotism with uncritical support of official policy. Precisely for this reason, the public expects its media to meet this challenge by main-

taining its independence for the good of the country. It is your professional duty and your obligation to our democratic ideals.

Unfortunately, objectivity and critical questioning of official sources, which is a measure of your separation from officialdom, have not been true in war-time reporting during Gulf War I and during proposals for Gulf War II. (https://blog.nader.org/2005/03/04/journalists-criticize-iraqwar-media-coverage/)

The signees then listed common propaganda errors, such as the horse race theme, simplifying problems and the "evidence" to justify war, overlooking the importance of oil, disregarding how American firms had actually contributed to Hussein's stock of biological weapons, and so on. All indications are that these warnings—indeed, pleadings—had little if any impact on media reports that followed. The problem, then, is not simply lack of "knowledge" and information on the part of the press. The argument is that an alternative format to the current sequence of action-then-research/critique of social policy, particularly war making, is essential.

PREPARING FOR WAR

The propaganda campaign in the Iraq War consisted of what was omitted from presentation to the public as well as what was selected for coverage and the way in which information was managed. The United States was well on its way to justifying the attack on Iraq in 1992 when Secretary of Defense Dick Cheney and others, who would occupy positions in the Bush administration eight years later, drafted the Defense Planning Guidance document. The thrust of the message was to act unilaterally and to use military force freely, with preemptive strikes if necessary. Making a pitch for a threatened military budget in 1992, Chairman of the Joint Chiefs of Staff Colin Powell told the House Armed Services Committee that the United States required "sufficient power" to "deter any challenger from ever dreaming of challenging us on the world stage." To emphasize the point, he cast the United States in the role of street thug. "I want to be the bully on the block," he said, implanting in the mind of potential opponents that "there is no future in trying to challenge the armed forces of the United States" (Armstrong, 2002, 78). The plan was carried forth by the PNAC. The plan, with revisions, was promoted repeatedly during the next decade, even though some members were out of office for eight years, and was in full swing one month before the 9/11 attacks.

This message was not widely publicized to the American people. Indeed, we located eighteen reports (discussed later in this chapter) about this endeavor by public officials and a conservative think tank to alter fundamentally U.S. foreign policy and attack sovereign nations before missiles hit Baghdad. The major television networks were practically silent about the commitment to attack Iraq even though many members and "signees" of the PNAC were in control of the Bush administration's foreign policy and a revealing magazine article (Armstrong, 2002) was read into the *Congressional Record* on October 8, 2002, as part of the Spratt-Moran resolution to support UN guidelines some six months before the "official" bombing began. Not a single regular evening network newscast mentioned this public conspiracy prior to the start of the war. We offer an account of the role that the news media played in the construction of the Iraq War and some of its consequences.

MASS MEDIA WAR

Administration news sources provided a compliant news media with ample material and conjecture about both of the claims that linked Iraq and Hussein with the terrorist attacks of 9/11. Prior to the invasion (as well as after the president triumphantly declared from the deck of an aircraft carrier that victory had been won), the Bush administration insisted that Hussein had supported the terrorists and had weapons of mass destruction that he planned to use. Even though no one in the administration directly stated that Iraq was involved, the innuendo, tone, and slant of numerous reports stressed this relationship before, during, and after the invasion of Iraq. Indeed, it was not until October 2003 that President Bush acknowledged that Hussein and Iraq were not involved in the 9/11 attacks, but even then Vice President Cheney was reported to still believe that Hussein was implicated:

> The propaganda campaign to "sell the Iraq War" emphasized Iraq's connections with Al-Qaeda and development of "weapons of mass destruction" (WMD), including chemical, biological, and nuclear weapons.
>
> As the Associated Press put it: "The implication from Bush on down was that Saddam supported Osama bin Laden's network. Iraq and the Sept. 11 attacks frequently were mentioned in the same sentence, even though officials have no good evidence of such a link." Not only was there no good evidence: according to *The New York Times*, captured leaders of Al Qaeda explicitly told the C.I.A. that they had not been working with Saddam. (Krugman, 2003, 29)

This propaganda error would haunt the 2016 election. Just weeks before Americans went to the polls, the Intelligence Community Assessments (ICA) stated that Russia was behind the leak of hacked computer information about Hillary Clinton and the Democratic National Committee that appears to have influenced the close election outcome. Donald Trump disputed the report claiming that the same agencies had miscalculated Saddam Hussein's capability to launch an attack with weapons of mass destruction (WMD). Actually, the CIA did not support the Bush administration's interpretation of questionable information about WMDs, but candidate Trump never mentioned this.

The politics of fear were at a fever pitch before the United States attacked Iraq in 2003. Public opinion surveys provide one way to assess how public support could be influenced by information about Iraq. Several opinion polls tracked public perceptions of administration claims, especially after the invasion of Iraq. The results make it clear that when the public has more information about critical issues, they are less supportive and, moreover, actually prefer, when asked, more information from the administration. In April 2003, 58 percent of those polled were "somewhat or very concerned that U.S. troops have not yet found any weapons of mass destruction." Two months later (June), the Harris Poll reported that while the majority of Americans continued to believe that Iraq had weapons of mass destruction, 40 percent also believed that the "U.S. government deliberately exaggerated the reports of weapons of mass destruction in Iraq in order to increase support for war."

The doubts about the Bush administration's justification for the war with Iraq have gradually increased over time, as more press information has been forthcoming about the elusive weapons of mass destruction as well as much stronger evidence that Hussein was not directly involved with those who flew planes into the buildings on 9/11. The strongest data for the chipping away of credibility are provided by a *Newsweek* report in October 2003 on the gradual but consistent erosion of support by a public that is better informed about the information management of the war. Citizens were asked the following question:

> Before the Iraq War, the Bush administration said it had intelligence reports indicating that Iraq was hiding banned chemical or biological weapons from United Nations weapons inspectors. So far, however, no such banned weapons have been found in Iraq. Do you think the Bush administration misinterpreted or misanalyzed the intelligence reports they said indicated Iraq had banned weapons?

> Purposely misled the public about evidence that Iraq had banned weapons in order to build support for war?

These data show that the credibility of the "evidence for the war" gradually declined, as 42 percent of the public indicated that the administration had "purposely misled the public," while another 8 percent (50 percent total) was more charitable, accepting the wording that the administration had "misinterpreted or misanalyzed the intelligence reports they said indicated Iraq had banned weapons."

The documents and plans to topple Iraq were known about but were not widely covered by the major news media for the decade preceding the Iraq invasion, nor were they covered by network television in the months preceding the Iraq War. Publicizing these materials for the

Table 8.1.

Date	Yes	No	Don't Know
October 23-24, 2003	50%	39%	11%
October 9-10, 2003	49%	39%	12%
August 21-22, 2003	44%	47%	9%
July 24-25, 2003	41%	49%	10%
July 10-11, 2003	45%	41%	14%
May 29-30, 2003	36%	54%	10%

American people may have made a difference in public support for the Iraq War and an emerging foreign policy that included "preemptive strikes" and bypassing the United Nations and international agreements about aggression. However, previous conflicts and wars provided experiences and a context that prepared audiences for what would follow. We turn briefly to this context.

THE POLITICAL CONTEXT FOR PROPAGANDA

Ideas about world domination existed in popular-culture accounts of outlaw nations and rulers such as Nazi Germany and imperial Japan and even back as far as Genghis Khan. Not the United States. Only conspiracy theorists and a few ardent Marxists would claim, until recently, that the United States had imperialist intentions. This all changed during the Reagan administration and was exacerbated several years later when a conservative "think tank" gained the ear of key national staff members and indeed recruited them among its ranks. This is the PNAC, a major lobbying and influential cadre of ideologists dedicated to the proposition that the world had changed after the fall of the Soviet Union and that the United States was now not only a "superpower" but also a hegemon that needed to lead and dominate. Its members have been active in conservative politics—including serving under presidents Reagan, George H. W. Bush, and George W. Bush—and publishing magazines and newspaper editorials and serving as television commentators for two decades. All of this was done under the guise of a "new defense policy" for the United States. Indeed, Robert McGovern, a veteran CIA analyst of twenty-seven years who represented a group of former intelligence officers (Veteran Intelligence Officers for Sanity) noted that Hitler's hegemonic horrors were set forth in his book *Mein Kampf*. McGovern told CNN's Jonathan Mann that the PNAC provided Bush's imperialistic game plan (Mann, 2003):

Table 8.2.

Date	Yes	No	Don't Know
October 23-24, 2003	42%	49%	9%
October 9-10, 2003	45%	45%	10%
August 21-22, 2003	43%	51%	6%
July 24-25, 2003	39%	56%	5%
July 10-11. 2003	38%	53%	9%

> Well, all you need do is look at "Mein Kampf." The U.S. "Mein
> Kampf." You probably remember that "Mein Kampf" laid down the
> framework for Hitler's campaigns and for his strategy. Well, there's a
> "Mein Kampf" for the U.S. scene, and it's called the "Project for a New
> American Century." Download it from its Web site and you'll see the
> documents going back to 1992, which outline everything that is in-
> tended by this crew that's running Iraqi policy.

Indeed, two prominent members of the Bush administration, Paul H.
O'Neill and Richard A. Clarke, claimed that war with Iraq was a foregone
conclusion. The Bush administration's willingness to carry out the PNAC
commitment to attack Iraq without further provocation was made clear
several months after the war began. O'Neill, longtime Republican stal-
wart and President Bush's former treasury secretary, stated in an interview on CBS's *60 Minutes*, "From the very beginning, there was a conviction that Saddam Hussein was a bad person and that he needed to go"
(*New York Times*, January 12, 2004, A11). Regarding the claim that war
would uncover and destroy the threat of weapons of mass destruction,
O'Neill told *Time* magazine,

> In the 23 months I was there, I never saw anything that I would charac-
> terize as evidence of weapons of mass destruction. I never saw any-
> thing in the intelligence that I would characterize as real evidence.

O'Neill was joined in his criticism of the rush to war with Iraq by
former White House counterterrorism chief Richard A. Clarke, who, in a
book and subsequent press interviews, stated that there was pressure to
find an immediate link between Al Qaeda, Iran, and the 9/11 attacks that
was not warranted by evidence from the intelligence community. Clarke
claimed that

> while neither president [Clinton and Bush] did enough to prevent the
> attacks of Sept. 11, 2001, the Bush administration has undermined
> American national security by using the 9/11 attacks for political ad-
> vantage and ignoring the threat of Al Qaeda in order to invade Iraq.
> (*New York Times*, March 22, 2004, A18)

There was an important context for defining this situation as war worthy and consistent with war programming.

DEFINING THE SITUATION

The general public derives most of its understanding of international affairs and foreign policy from news and particularly television news (Adams, 1981, 1982; Alali & Byrd, 1994; Aldridge & Hewitt, 1994; Altheide, 1997, 2003; Barson & Heller, 2001; Bennett, 1988; Best, 1999; Chiricos et al., 2000; Comstock & Scharrer, 1999; Douglas, 1970; Doyle, 2001; Edelman, 1985; Graber, 1984; Hall, 1988; Hertog & Fan, 1995; D. M. Hunt, 1999; Jackall, 1994; Margolis, 1996; Shaw & McCombs, 1977; Wasburn, 2002). In 2003 the American public's major window on the world of foreign affairs is framed by what is presented on the nightly newscasts of ABC, NBC, CBS, and CNN. This does not mean that the only source of foreign affairs news was television but that it was the most consistent and widely used source of information for the American public. Television was less important with the rise of social media around 2008, which became particularly critical in the presidential campaign of Donald Trump in 2015 to 2016. However, in 2003 the public understanding of issues, particularly those involving non-Western cultures, was filtered through the daily information and visual images. Moreover, public perceptions are greatly informed by the repetition of certain themes, slogans, and symbolic representations of problems and issues:

> War stories are told with the flourish of explicit moral discourse. Trade stories are told with the patient repetition of words suggesting, but not directly stating, that the rival nation is unreasonable and unfair. (Wasburn, 2002, 125)

The American news media, and especially network television news organizations, chose not to present important contextual and background information about the Middle East and especially Iraq because it was not consistent with other news themes, nor was it as entertaining. The dominant "story" since the attacks of 9/11 was the "war on terrorism." This broad story included U.S. retaliation, the hunt for al Qaeda leaders (e.g., Osama bin Laden), and plans to attack countries and "outlaw regimes" that supported or harbored terrorists. Implementing these programs involved invading Afghanistan and expanding the U.S. military presence throughout the world. Other adjustments were made in foreign policy, military budgets, domestic surveillance, and attacks on civil liberties. Threats to invade other countries (the "axis of evil") that included Iraq were part of an effort to "defend" the United States from future attacks. It is hard to believe that the American people would not have been interested in carefully presented reports about systematic efforts to undermine international treaties, destroy the United Nations, expand the military, and engage in more military attacks, including preemptive first strikes.

THE NEWS MEDIA CONTEXT FOR PROPAGANDA

The PNAC was critical in managing information for a compliant U.S. press in order to sell its "claims" about Iraq without making it widely known that a small but very influential number of officials had been working to change foreign policy in general and attack Iraq in particular for about a decade. The neglect of these issues reflects major organizational shifts in the production and presentation of news. Nowhere is this more apparent than with network television news. The infotainment urge to "pander" to the audience in order to gain viewers would soon become the networks' established way of doing business.

Other analyses have documented how the climate and organization of network news changed over the past two decades. Changes in technology and marketing approaches helped "normalize" infotainment, particularly the expansion of the entertainment for network television news. Former *CBS Evening News* anchor Dan Rather's reluctance to embrace infotainment was gradually eroded by increased competition with traditional rivals as well as CNN and Fox. Research on network trends shows that between 1977 and 1997, "hard news" declined from 67.3 to 41.3 percent, while celebrity news tripled, from 2 percent in 1977 to 7 percent in 1997, and that "soft" lifestyle news doubled during the same time period, from 13.5 percent to nearly 25 percent, or one-fourth of all network news offerings. Network news time was increasingly devoted to celebrity news, and the "morning news" shows emphasized more commercial and product advertising to promote the conglomerates that owned them.

In June 2001, network morning news programs had become, in significant part, a way of selling things, often lifestyle products, books, movies, television shows, cookbooks, products for the home, and the like. Excluding commercials and inserts for local news, 33 percent of the news time on these programs was devoted to selling some product.

THE PROPAGANDA SAGA

The PNAC received very little news media coverage prior to the invasion of Iraq even though it was part of the "public record" in government documents and had been briefly mentioned in several newspaper and radio reports in the late 1990s (see table 8.1). The most detailed coverage of the history of the PNAC and its role in shaping U.S. foreign policy was David Armstrong's essay in *Harper's Magazine* in October 2002:

> The plan is for the United States to rule the world. The overt theme is
> unilateralism, but it is ultimately a story of domination. It calls for the
> United States to maintain its overwhelming military superiority and
> prevent new rivals from rising up to challenge it on the world stage. It
> calls for dominion over friends and enemies alike. It says not that the
> United States must be more powerful, or most powerful, but that it
> must be absolutely powerful. (Armstrong, 2002, 76)

Only a few newspaper articles dealt with PNAC six months before the
United States attacked Iraq on March 20. No reports appeared on the
major television networks' regular evening newscasts during this time,
although *Nightline* did examine the "conspiracy claims" and interview
William Kristol, chairman of the PNAC, on March 5. Reporter Ted Koppel dismissed the conspiratorial charges by several foreign newspapers.
He framed it in terms of what could be called "it depends on how you
look at it":

> They did what former government officials and politicians frequently
> do when they're out of power, they began formulating a strategy, in
> this case, a foreign policy strategy, that might bring influence to bear on
> the Administration then in power, headed by President Clinton. Or
> failing that, on a new Administration that might someday come to
> power. They were pushing for the elimination of Saddam Hussein.
> And proposing the establishment of a strong US military presence in
> the Persian Gulf, linked to a willingness to use force to protect vital
> American interests in the Gulf. (ABC News, 2003)

When reporter Jackie Judd asked Gary Schmitt, a long-time PNAC
architect, if they were fanatics or conspirators, he, and fellow interviewee,
William Kristol, denied it:

> [William Kristol]: Of course I'll feel some sense of responsibility. The
> only point I would also make, though, is one also has to take respon-
> sibility, would also have to take responsibility if one advocated doing
> nothing and then if something terrible happens. And, and I worry. I
> worry, not because I'm going to look bad, I worry because people could
> die and will die in this war. (Wu, 2000)

News organizations explicitly and implicitly editorialize through their
use of news sources for certain issues. The major news agencies in the
United States and particularly the television networks limited their coverage of the role the PNAC played in shaping the Iraq War. These propaganda efforts occurred as the various PNAC members served as routine
news sources, primarily in television network news accounts oriented to
infotainment.

Our analysis of Iraq War coverage by the *New York Times* and other
news organizations revealed that several individuals were closely associated with PNAC over the past decade: Thomas Donnelly, William Kristol, Richard Perle, Marc Gerecht, Gary Schmitt, and Robert Kagan. Other

individuals, such as Paul Wolfowitz, Secretary of Defense Donald Rumsfeld, and Dick Cheney, were heavily involved with supporting PNAC, but they and other PNAC supporters who were in the Bush administration were not included in this analysis. We compared the coverage they received in the *New York Times* as news sources six months before and after 9/11. We did the same with four individuals that our review of news reports identified as critics of the PNAC proposal and plans to invade Iraq.

The results are clear. The pro-PNAC sources were used seventy-two times before 9/11 and 133 times within six months after 9/11, an increase of 85 percent. Only five references appear for the anti-PNAC sources (four refer to Joseph Nye), and eight appear after 9/11 (seven refer to Nye).

The meaning of these large differences is more complex. First, it is important to note that the the *New York Times* used PNAC sources quite often prior to 9/11. This is particularly noteworthy for William Kristol (*N* = 42), former chief of staff for Vice President Dan Quayle and publisher and editor of the conservative *The Weekly Standard*, and Richard Perle (*N* = 21), former assistant secretary of defense and member of the Defense Policy Board, which advised Donald Rumsfeld. These were prominent Washington sources that were called on to discuss a range of foreign and domestic policy issues. The circulation of Kristol's publication was small, but the media play from his numerous references extended his influence:

> The circulation of *The Weekly Standard,* which was founded by the News Corporation in 1995, is only 55,000. *The Nation,* a liberal beacon, has 127,000. The *New Republic* has 85,000, and *National Review,* long a maypole for conservatives, counts 154,000 readers. But the numbers are misleading in a digital age in which thought and opinion are frequently untethered from print and reiterated thousands of times on Web sites, list servers and e-mail in-boxes . . .
>
> "Look, these guys made up their own minds," he (Kristol) said. "I would hope that we have induced some of them to think about these things in a new way. We have a lot of writers who have independently articulated a version of how we deal with this new world we live in that has been read by Dick Cheney, Condi Rice and Donald Rumsfeld. Hopefully it had some effect." (Carr, 2003, 1)

In sum, this plan was not publicized by the major news media because it fell outside the focus of the Bush administration's propaganda campaign. The evidence suggests that mainstream media failed to bring important ideological shifts and the people behind them to the attention of the general public. Prior to the U.S. war against Iraq, the American news media neglected to publicize the PNAC's agenda, which illustrates that aggression against Iraq had been planned long before the 9/11 attacks. It also neglected to bring to the forefront crucial information regarding similar policy recommendations from PNAC that were in existence prior to

9/11. The evidence indicates that the media are indirectly responsible for encouraging the public's support of the war against Iraq through its acts of omission and/or compliance.

Organizational Reasons for Propaganda

The lack of reporting about the PNAC's success at planning the Iraq War illustrates embedded propaganda as a feature of institutionalized news sources and media formats. While there were detractors in editorial pages, the Internet, and the foreign news media, the major television networks were tightly aligned with the war scenario. It is important to stress the critical contribution of news formats and the emerging common definition of the situation—that the nation had to act, that audiences supported action against enemies, and that simplistic emotionally tinged messages would carry the day. Key to the Bush administration's success was journalists' penchant to get on the "war" bandwagon not only for patriotic purposes but also because that was what "people were interested in" and that's "where the story was." Network television played to the administration.

Most of the Gulf War coverage originated from the White House and the federal government. Journalists now acknowledged that they did not cover many aspects of the impending war with Iraq. A veteran producer for a major network television news program indicated that the story was about the preparation for war. In his words, things were set in motion for over a year, and the "rock was rolling downhill." That's where the story was (interview notes).

That other network news producers must have surely agreed with this position is suggested by a dearth of network television news coverage of virtually any congressional opposition to the impending war, including Senator Robert Byrd's impassioned speech on the floor of the Senate on February 12, 2003, just weeks before Baghdad was bombed, in which he referred to the drastic changes in foreign policy. The U.S. Senate approved the Iraq War Resolution on October 12, 2002, by a vote of 77–23. Democratic senator Hillary Clinton's "yes" vote would haunt her presidential campaigns in 2012 and 2016, when her opponents—Obama in 2012, Trump in 2016—reminded voters that she supported the propaganda-inspired war.

While there was some discussion in newspaper editorial pages, Senator Byrd noted that there had been little in the Senate:

> We stand passively mute in the United States Senate, paralyzed by our own uncertainty, seemingly stunned by the sheer turmoil of events. . . . This nation is about to embark upon the first test of a revolutionary doctrine applied in an extraordinary way at an unfortunate time. The doctrine of preemption—the idea that the United States or any other nation can legitimately attack a nation that is not imminently threaten-

ing but may be threatening in the future—is a radical new twist on the traditional idea of self-defense. It appears to be in contravention of international law and the UN Charter. (*Pittsburgh Post-Gazette*, February 23, 2003, E2)

Network news shows were quite consistent with guests who supported the war. An analysis by Fairness and Accuracy in Reporting (FAIR) of network news interviewees one week before and one week after Secretary of State Powell addressed the United Nations about Iraq's alleged possession of weapons of mass destruction found that two-thirds of the guests were from the United States, with 75 percent of these being current or former government or military officials, while only one—Senator Edward Kennedy—expressed skepticism or opposition to the impending war with Iraq (FAIR, 2003).

Journalists did not present this very important story for various reasons. Studies of news rules and news values support Snow's (1983) observations that the news media, like much of popular culture, tend to support and reflect "ideal norms," or preferred ways of living, feeling, and behaving. Likewise, research on "news decision making" suggests that commercial news organizations tend to select items and events for news reporting that can be told in narratives that express ethnocentrism, altruistic democracy, responsible capitalism, small-town pastoralism, individualism, modernism, social order, and national leadership (Gans, 1979; Wasburn, 2002). In other words, reports are favored that sustain the worldviews of news audiences about social order and legitimacy. This includes the conduct of their leaders. Thus, reports will be less favorable or "sensible" to audiences if they suggest that the institution of government has failed, that the process of selecting leaders is corrupt, and that decisions about life and death, such as declaring war, are made with the national interest in mind and with the well-being of citizens as a priority. Network television news relied on the administration for news and, in the spirit of objectivity, seldom challenged statements from such high sources. This approach to journalism produced untruths and major distortions:

> It exacerbates our tendency to rely on official sources, which is the easiest, quickest way to get both the "he said" and the "she said," and, thus, "balance." According to numbers from the media analyst Andrew Tyndall, of the 414 stories on Iraq broadcast on NBC, ABC, and CBS from last September to February, all but thirty-four originated at the White House, Pentagon, and State Department. So we end up with too much of the "official" truth. (Cunningham, 2003, 24)

Still another factor was that challenging sources would not be popular with administration officials and the ever-dominant PNAC news sources, which were closely tied to the Bush administration. This was not American journalism's finest hour. Bush administration officials had

their way with the major television networks, offering their interpretations, plans, and rationales for domestic and international policies that
would follow. Major network television journalists, wearing American
flag pins on their lapels, occasionally crying on camera, and offering
constant moral support to an expanding network audience, offered very
little perspective and understanding of the 9/11 events, seldom asking the
most basic questions of administration officials who were pushing draconian legislation to limit civil rights through Congress while military ap-
propriations were increasing drastically in pursuit of an emerging ambig-
uous war plan to attack Iraq. Clearly the pressure was on journalists to
conform and not rock the boat, to not challenge those who were protecting us against evil and terror. This involved the "snubbing" of veteran
United Press International correspondent Helen Thomas, whose critical
reports resulted in President Bush breaking decades of tradition and not
permitting her to ask the first—or any—question during a news conference. A few months prior, Ms. Thomas remarked that Mr. Bush "is the
worst president in all of American history." (Mike Allen of the *Washington Post* was also excluded from questioning at the same press conference.) (Curl, 2003)

The coverage of the war was clearly influenced by such pressure,
along with the availability of "visuals" that permitted "live" shots of
advancing tanks, Marines, gunfire, and explosions. Other journalists covering the Iraq War reported censorship and intimidation. The management of the Coalition Media Center at the Sayliyah military base in Doha,
Qatar, which "handled" the press requests and assigned the more than
five hundred "embedded journalists" who rotated through various units,
kept a tight grip on information and questioning decorum by journalists.
Massing (2003) suggests that veterans of this campaign likened the information control to the infamous "Five O'Clock Follies" of the Vietnam
War, a briefing scenario that became a ludicrous joke by all respected
journalists covering that war.

REFLECTIONS ON PROPAGANDA

News coverage of the Iraq War—and particularly the PNAC—reflects
how the nature and timing of journalistic critique and alternative interpretations of official directives lags behind critical events but eventually
appears as though it is part of a narrative script for war programming.
The organizational and format limitations of war programming misdirected journalists from major topics. Moreover, as our model suggests,
news organizations began to reflect on "what went wrong" in their coverage of Iraq, including missing the PNAC influence.

Consistent with war programming, other journalists joined in reflecting on the news coverage of the Iraq War:

In the rush to war, how many Americans even heard about some of these possibilities [problems such as the forming of an Iraqi interim government and the recovery of health and water resources]? Of the 574 stories about Iraq that aired on NBC, ABC, and CBS evening news broadcasts between September 12 (when Bush addressed the UN) and March 7 (a week and a half before the war began), only twelve dealt primarily with the potential aftermath. (Cunningham, 2003, 24)

These wars essentially failed to achieve stated goals, but they did further destabilize the tenuous religious-cultural and political relations that defined the Middle East. Those problems would be passed along to the new president, Barack Obama, who would become immersed in yet another chapter of combating terrorism with the politics of fear.

From War Programming to Terrorism Programming

When President Obama took office in January 2009 he inherited a terrorism mess to go along with an imploding economy. He pledged during his successful campaign to end the wars in Iraq and Afghanistan. He, along with many members of Congress, became ever more distrustful of the previous administration's incorrect information about weapons of mass destruction in Iraq—this was all false. They had also become impatient with leaked information by various whistleblowers about the massive illegal domestic surveillance that was discussed in previous chapters. The Bush supporters, particularly the increasingly aggressive right-wing media, attacked the doubters as ignorant, unpatriotic, and even supportive of terrorism. Political discourse in the mass media became hateful and accusatory, well beyond mere "negative" campaigning. The right-wing media, especially "talk radio," had been given license by 9/11 and the war on terror to be incredibly hateful of their political opposition. More than just doubting an opponent's qualifications, there was an avalanche of scurrilous name calling and attacks, including questioning patriotism and Americanism. The harsh rhetoric, although very mild compared to the cascading vitriol that Donald Trump would rain on Hillary Clinton in 2016, was a preview of things to come. Massing's (2009) investigation revealed the depth of the hate-filled permissiveness:

> Any inventory of the right's media bombast must begin with talk radio. In reach and rancor, it had no equal. Leading the way was Rush Limbaugh. An estimated fourteen to twenty million people tune in to his show every week, and he treated them to nonstop character assassination, calling the Democratic candidate the Messiah, a revolutionary socialist, a liar, "Osama Obama" [a reference to terrorist Osama bin Laden], a man with a "perverted mind" who wants to destroy America and the middle class, a frontman for terrorists who wants to turn the country into a version of Castro's Cuba or Mugabe's Zimbabwe. . . . As documented in a recent report by the group Media Matters, these hosts

harped on the notion that Obama is a Muslim whose true loyalties lay outside the United States. . . . Cincinnati's Bill Cunningham stated that Obama wants to "gas the Jews." (Massing, 2009, 14)

During the 2008 campaign for president, the Republican vice presidential nominee, Sarah Palin, sprinkled her campaign banter with claims that Obama had "been palling around with terrorists." Audiences listening to the candidates and the hateful TV and radio broadcasts were clearly affected. At one point Republican candidate John McCain, who had been attacking Obama's character, finally objected when his audience referred to Obama as a traitor and an Arab:

> When a woman referred to Obama yesterday as "an Arab," McCain cut her off and seized the microphone from her hands. "No, ma'am," he interjected. "He is a decent family man with whom I happen to have some disagreements." In fact, the most rousing applause of the afternoon came not for McCain, but for one of several questioners who appealed to the candidate to "fight" in next Wednesday's final debate. . . . There was a rumble of disapproval from the crowd when McCain defended his Democratic rival. "I have to tell you he is a decent person and a person that you do not have to be scared of as president of the United States," McCain said. (Issenberg, 2008)

This civil curtailment of excessive irrational zeal about one's opponent is in marked contrast to the hateful vindictive of Donald Trump's 2016 campaign as he led the crowd chanting "Lock her up," a refrain joined in by his future (now former) National Security Advisor, Michael Flynn, who had urged the closing of mosques:

> "The enemy camp in this case is Hillary Rodham Clinton. . . . This is a person who does not know the difference between a lie and the truth. . . . She is somebody who will leave Americans behind on the battlefield."
>
> He went further at the Republican convention in Cleveland, saying the US didn't need a "reckless president who believes she is above the law" and clapping as the crowd began to chant, "Lock her up!" Flynn made it clear that he felt much the same way. "You're damn right!" he said. (Dreazen, 2016)

President Obama took office in a very hostile context. Almost immediately he tried to reach a political solution in Iraq and was reluctant to commit more troops, although it was clear that al Qaeda was far from defeated. His efforts to ramp down the war in Iraq led to his receiving the 2009 Nobel Peace Prize, although it was clear in his remarks at the award ceremony that he was aware of the continuing risk and that, somewhat to the chagrin of some of his supporters, he would continue the fight:

> "We must begin by acknowledging the hard truth: we will not eradicate violent conflicts in our lifetimes," Mr. Obama said, addressing the paradox of receiving an award for peace as commander in chief of a

nation that is escalating the war in Afghanistan as it continues to fight in Iraq. "There will be times when nations—acting individually or in concert—will find the use of force not only necessary but morally justified." (http://www.nytimes.com/2009/12/11/world/europe/11prexy.html)

This statement could be viewed as a watershed moment and partial vindication of the Bush thesis that the United States would be fighting to stop terrorism, notwithstanding the initial invasions of Iraq and Afghanistan. This was a clear movement beyond the stages of war programming to terrorism programming.

Terrorism Programming and the Terrorism Narrative

A new narrative accompanied the U.S. approach to terrorism. Terrorism was coming to be viewed as an ongoing condition rather than as a tactic used by a definable enemy in a specific country. Thus, even after the United States withdrew from Iraq and declared "victory," fighting terrorism continues. In this sense, the war will never be won, and therefore the final steps in the war programming conceptual scheme will be elongated. *Essentially, the terrorism narrative holds that terrorism (and terrorists) do not follow civilized rules of warfare and that since terrorism is not justified insofar as "innocent" civilians are targeted, then the moves against them can also be outside acceptable limits; that is, torture, kidnapping, and widespread killing of civilians in the pursuit of terrorists.* Indeed, this is exactly what happened when the vast majority of troops were withdrawn from Iraq in 2011 in keeping with an agreement between former president Bush and Iraqi prime minister Nouri al-Maliki in 2008. President Obama would also take the fight to terrorists, and indeed, would drastically expand it into other countries, even those that officially did not welcome the antiterrorism fight. This means that terrorism and its numerous artfully constructed meanings and nuances are an important context of experience in its own right, essentially blocking out other contexts and considerations. Thus, terrorism has become a social definition that encompasses a self-referential discourse and justification, on the one hand, while also serving as a rationale for revenge and counterattacks, on the other hand. Carefully orchestrating, restricting, and controlling images can manage terrorism and news sources that get to make claims about social reality. Ironically, President Obama did not want to include torture in this view of terrorism, but his successor, Donald Trump, did, making it clear that he would waterboard terrorists and do even worse.

The terrorism narrative made risk pervasive and timeless. An attack could happen anytime, anywhere. And terrorism would have to be combatted regardless of borders. As noted previously, President Obama—essentially a "peace candidate" when he ran for office—authorized far more drone attacks than did his predecessor, killing more civilians in the prosecution of his global war. On May 2, 2011, a Navy SEAL team killed Osama bin Laden in Pakistan. Numerous Special Operations similar to this had been carried out in various countries. These quick, targeted, and deadly strikes generated fear abroad, while at home there were a series of homegrown terrorist attacks that escalated fear and strengthened the appeal of the politics of fear. Some of the more horrendous attacks:

November 5, 2009: Major Nidal Hasan goes on a shooting rampage at a military processing center at Fort Hood, Texas, killing thirteen and wounding thirty-two.

December 25, 2009:   A Nigerian man on a flight from Amsterdam to Detroit attempted to ignite an explosive device hidden in his underwear.

April 15, 2013:   Twin bomb blasts explode near the finish line of the Boston Marathon, killing three and wounding at least 264.

December 2, 2015:   Married couple Syed Rizwan Farook and Tashfeen Malik open fire on a holiday party taking place at Inland Regional Center in San Bernardino, California, killing fourteen people.

June 12, 2016:   A mass shooting at an Orlando nightclub in the early hours of a Sunday morning, leaves fifty people dead, including the gunman, and more than fifty injured.

There have been other horrendous attacks in Europe, including the gruesome murder of journalists at *Charlie Hebdo* publishers in Paris, along with murders in a delicatessen, and then the horrific November 13, 2015, terror attacks in Paris that killed 130 people and wounded hundreds.

Another major change occurred prior to some of the mass killings: the emergence of the Islamic State in Syria (ISIS) that grew out of the remnants of the Iraq and Afghanistan wars, and particularly the availability of former Sunni Iraqi military personnel. As described in previous chapters, ISIS was very effective in wreaking terror across several countries, and had even recruited fighters from Europe and the United States, although most of their efforts in the United States were to motivate and train homegrown terrorists to kill and injure through convenient means, including driving vehicles into crowds. These actions received a different emphasis than the numerous, but more deadly, nonterrorist homicides and mass shootings in the United States, which were often masked, if not shielded, as unfortunate alignments of mentally ill and disturbed people, who had access to semiautomatic weapons (Altheide, 2013). After all, it is a constitutional right, according to gun lobbyists and many elected officials, for essentially anyone to obtain a firearm.

We are reminded that what matters in social life are the meanings given to certain acts and to the perpetrators (e.g., demented, criminals, troubled, terrorists). The much larger deaths at the hands of mass shooters in the United States are invariably accompanied by reports and pleas to try to understand "why," why would someone kill a large number of people, who are often unknown to them? But with suspected terrorists it is different; there are no individual explanations accepted beyond their religious orientation—therefore, it was their religion that is to blame. Thus, when well-publicized events like the Orlando shooting mentioned above took place, the fear of terrorism spikes, leading Americans to be even more concerned and fearful of future attacks. All these horrific deaths—by "radical Islamic terrorists"—were viewed by many Americans as evil as the result of "Islamic radicalism," and President Obama and his heir-apparent, Hillary Clinton, were accused by future president Donald Trump and others in 2016 with neglecting to see—and state—the obvious. At one point Trump stated, "I think Islam hates us," and then on October 9, 2016, at the second presidential debate with Hillary Clinton, he said:

> "These are radical Islamic terrorists and she won't even mention the word, and nor will President Obama. He won't use the term 'radical Islamic terrorism,' Trump said during the Oct. 9 debate at Washington University in St. Louis. "Now, to solve a problem, you have to be able to state what the problem is or at least say the name. She won't say the name and President Obama won't say the name. But the name is there. It's radical Islamic terror." (http://www.politifact.com/truth-o-meter/statements/2016/oct/09/donald-trump/trump-clinton-wont-use-term-radical-islamist-terro/)

CONCLUSION

The planning and selling of the war with Iraq is one of the most egregious propaganda campaigns in history. The aftermath of this horrendous political decision is still being felt globally as ISIS has overpowered Bush's nemesis al Qaeda. The aim of the campaign was to get public support; in the short term it worked, but the longer term—at this writing fifteen years later—remains an open question. And we haven't seen the end of propaganda and the politics of fear, especially as media have become more instantaneous, personal, and visual, and actually more subject to manipulation through emotional appeals as well as fake news. This works well in a culture ensconced in media logic, the entertainment format that promotes drama, conflict, and essentially strives to follow the consumer model of advertising, that tells you what you already believe, appealing in such a way that since it agrees with a previous point of view no critical thinking or fact checking is required. During the Nuremberg trials, Prosecutor Robert Jackson's closing speech, widely regarded as one of the most compelling statements about the planning of World War II by Hitler and his followers, stated,

> The dominant fact which stands out from all the thousands of pages of the record of this Trial is that the central crime of the whole group of

Nazi crimes, the attack on the peace of the world was clearly and deliberately planned. The beginning of these wars of aggression was not an
unprepared and spontaneous springing to arms by a population excit-
ed by some current indignation. A week before the invasion of Poland
Hitler told his military commanders: "I shall give a propagandist cause
for starting war never mind whether it be plausible or not. The victor
shall not be asked later on whether we told the truth or not. In starting
and making a war, it is not the right that matters, but victory." (Jackson, 1946)

What would Robert Jackson say about the vicious attacks on political
opponents through tweet limitations of 140 characters as President
Trump did? No weapons of mass destruction were found, and this was
predicted by weapons inspectors as well as "intelligence reports" that
were known to the Bush administration even before the 9/11 attacks. Yet
President Bush insisted repeatedly that everyone thought Hussein had
weapons, even his critics and opponents, including Democratic senator
John Kerry. In fact, that was not correct. There were clear statements to
the contrary, and President Bush and his advisors were well aware of this
information because in some instances it came from their own staff members. Before 9/11 and prior to the U.S. invasion of Iraq, there were reports
by governmental agencies that denied or cast serious doubt on Iraq's
possession of weapons of mass destruction (Editorial Staff, 2004). While
some reports indicated that Iraq might be motivated to develop such
weapons, there was no evidence of their existence. These sources included the IAEA, the CIA, the Department of Energy, the defense intelligence, the State Department, the Air Force, and key White House cabinet
members and advisors. In a press conference on February 4, 2001, Secretary of State Powell stated that Saddam Hussein "has not developed any
significant capability with respect to weapons of mass destruction" (Editorial Staff, 2004). National Security Advisor Condoleezza Rice stated in a
CNN interview on July 29, 2001, "Let's remember that [Saddam's] country is divided, in effect. He does not control the northern part of this
country. We are able to keep arms from him. His military forces have not
been rebuilt" (CNN, 2001).

The PNAC was the underlying force propelling the malleable President Bush to take decisive action and attack Iraq. But the American people were not aware of the story behind this push. The war story was told,
but the PNAC story was not told. The dominant discourse and thematic
emphasis was that Hussein was evil, that he was involved in the 9/11
attacks, that he supported terrorism, and that he planned to use weapons
of mass destruction or give them to terrorists. Thus, there was a clear
sense of urgency to intervene. The major news media presented virtually
no strong disclaimers to this scenario; notwithstanding an occasional
voice asking for patience and more information (e.g., Senators Byrd and

Kennedy), all meaningful opposition to these claims was buried within the discursive framework of the war program.

Analysis of the coverage of the Iraq War and the specific construction of the PNAC is consistent with the conceptual framework of war programming. The news media did not present much information about the PNAC for several reasons. Organization and planning were important factors. News agencies, like the military and other large organizations, must plan ahead. News media plan future coverage with broadly defined themes or story lines in order to anticipate staffing and logistical needs. Even though satellite technology makes global coverage more manageable, there are nevertheless complex logistics involved in covering a war halfway around the world. There is always a game plan for future news coverage, although certain events, such as natural catastrophes, may alter the plan. Moreover, the planning of news organizations often follows that of the relevant organization that will be involved in upcoming and anticipated events. Military planning is key for the conduct of war, but so too is media planning to cover that war. It is hardly surprising, then, that the news media tend to follow the military's lead in planning.

Research and sociological theory suggests that war programming/terrorism programming will continue unless we break format, or revise our methods and media for defining, selecting, organizing, and presenting information. This can occur, but not easily. First, we must revise our understanding of propaganda and the role communication plays in setting the stage for conflict, carrying out the conflict, and making that conflict meaningful. Second, it must be recognized that the way in which modern wars have been covered is predictable and now is part of the planning for the conduct of war. The PNAC's claims makers knew that reframing policy could be easily connected with the tragedy of 9/11 and that messages and meanings could be easily shaped with exhaustive media support, particularly television visuals. Third, social scientists must work with journalists to provide theoretical understandings about how news practices are reflexive of power, war programming, and now terrorism programming. It was because of the success of this discourse that journalism failed to provide the important context and particularly clear statements about the think tank that pushed for war so strongly, altered U.S. foreign policy, and challenged basic civil liberties. These were not relevant until later, after the war, and then they would be taken up, on schedule, as part of war programming and the terrorism narrative. The next chapter examines how heroes are socially constructed to support the logic of war programming.

NINE

Constructing Heroes: Pat Tillman and Chris Kyle

I want my son to be like Pat. . . . Pat's the man I want to be.
— Sports talk show host Jim Rome at Pat Tillman's memorial service

President Obama has not one word to say for American hero Chris Kyle? Nothing? Unsurprising but that does not make it less egregious.
— Email, February 11, 2013

The military let him [Pat Tillman] down. The administration let him down. It was a sign of disrespect. The fact that he was the ultimate team player and he watched his own men kill him is absolutely heartbreaking and tragic. The fact that they lied about it afterward is disgusting.

— Pat Tillman's mother, Mary

Ours is an age of mediated heroes. Who we choose as heroes says a lot about us and the media we use to promote or denigrate heroics. And fear invites many heroic acts to keep us safe. The power of the politics of fear is that it pervades social institutions and influences social routines and social interaction. Previous chapters noted how politicians who rely on the politics of fear can promote it through controlling news sources that journalists rely on as well as other forms of propaganda to promote a view that the world is dangerous, that our lives are threatened by numerous sources of fear, and that we should be willing to sacrifice civil liberties and other freedoms in order to be secure. Sport is a great propaganda vehicle, and sports personalities are surefire sources of fan identification. But so is military service, especially those who sacrifice themselves for comrades. Propagandists, such as government officials, seek to link athletes and celebrities with values, causes, and even justifications for a war. The positive link can be forged through "heroism," as the dead individual(s) are deemed "heroes." Joining individuals to collective definitions of patriotism involves social constructions that rely on symbolic meanings of words and images (van Dijk, 1988).

This chapter tells the story of how the deaths of two soldiers were used to promote patriotism and the politics of fear. The major portion will focus on Pat Tillman, a professional football player, who volunteered to serve in the Special Forces and was accidentally killed by his comrades in 2004. Tillman's heroic transformation will be briefly contrasted with that of former Navy SEAL Chris Kyle, discharged in 2009 as a highly decorated sniper and gun enthusiast, who was killed—along with a fellow former Marine—at a shooting range in 2013 by a troubled soldier they were trying to help.

Pat Tillman was a promising twenty-seven-year-old professional football player who walked away from a multi-million-dollar contract with the Arizona Cardinals to join the U.S. Army and serve as a Ranger in Afghanistan, where he was killed by fellow Rangers on April 22, 2004. On the one hand, he was honored, given medals, and celebrated in several football arenas, and his collegiate jersey number (42) was retired and his professional jersey sold widely. A high school football stadium was named after him, and Arizona State University (ASU) started the Tillman Foundation, which sponsored an annual charitable Pat's Run that raised funds for veterans. There was much more: a bridge across the Colorado River between Nevada and Arizona was named for him; a bronze statue was erected outside the University of Phoenix Stadium where the Arizona Cardinals play their games; the Arizona Cardinals wear a patch on their uniforms stating PT-42 (his number); and his father's alma mater, the Lincoln Law School of San Jose, California, established a Tillman scholarship. On the other hand, the meaning of his death was given different interpretations and sparked rancor and reprisals against those who "misused" his symbolic meaning.

Like all lives lost in war, Tillman's death was tragic, but he was given special significance for making such sacrifice. The social construction of Tillman is informed by sociological theory and particularly symbolic interaction concepts and perspectives about the mass media and popular culture. News media reports, informal interviews, and a colleague's participant observation at one memorial service in Tempe, Arizona, guide this analysis. Chris Kyle's materials are taken from Internet files, news media accounts, and one movie.

Chris Kyle's story is different from Tillman's in several important ways. First, while Tillman's death occurred near the beginning of the Iraq/Afghanistan wars, Kyle, although discharged in 2009, was killed about the time that the United States was withdrawing most of its forces from the Middle East. Second, Kyle gained fame before his death as America's deadliest sniper, with 160 "confirmed kills," although other estimates by him and others put the number closer to 250. Third, he was not killed in combat but was shot, along with a colleague, during a kind of therapy shooting session with a Marine suffering from post-traumatic stress disorder (PTSD). Fourth, at the time of his death, he was pursuing commercial ventures to capitalize on the sniper reputation he had gained during four tours of duty, including a well-received book (*American Sniper: The Autobiography of the Most Lethal Sniper in U.S. Military History*), and a movie, *American Sniper*, that was in production when he was killed. Fifth, and perhaps most importantly, Chris Kyle did not get the public and official governmental recognition that Pat Tillman did. One reason was that Tillman had been portrayed as being patriotic and unselfish — turning down a multi-million-dollar NFL contract to become a Ranger — while Kyle was best known for shooting people. Certainly another important factor was that Tillman was one of the early deaths of the war and quickly became "the face" of that war, a face that the Bush administration desperately needed as part of a major propaganda effort to maintain the support of the American people. Moreover, by 2013 many U.S. soldiers had been killed in the war, and the public was accustomed to news reports about heroic deeds being celebrated with medal of honor awards and related somber rituals, as well as self-serving soldiers attempting to capitalize through books and movies about battle exploits, such as the members of SEAL Team 6 who participated in the killing of Osama bin Laden in May 2011. But Kyle's legacy would be cemented with a very popular war movie, *American Sniper*, grossing $500 million as the top-grossing film in the United States in 2014.

Both deaths were shrouded in patriotism and the politics of fear, but to varying degrees. The symbolic significance and narrative of Kyle's death was more consistently positive than Pat Tillman's, who was killed by his own men in a botched military exercise in Afghanistan that was systematically covered up by military and political officials. Tillman's fellow Rangers were ordered to burn his uniform and body armor, as well as his notebook. Tillman wrote critical comments about the war in diaries that he shared with his wife, Marie. For example, Tillman wrote the following while in training at Fort Lewis, Washington, just seventeen days after Colin Powell addressed the United Nations on February 5, 2003, as a prelude to the Iraq invasion:

> It may be very soon that Nub [his brother Kevin] & I will be called upon to take part in something I see no clear purpose for . . . I believe we have little or no justification other than our imperial whim. Of course Nub & I have . . . willingly allowed ourselves to be pawns in this game and will do our duty whether we agree with it or not. All we ask is that it is duly noted that we harbor no illusions of virtue. (Krakauer, 2010, 193)

But Tillman was duty-bound, several times making it clear that he and his brother would do their job, such as providing support for what would become a staged rescue of fellow soldier Jessica Lynch from an Iraq hospital on April 2, 2003, where military reports claimed that she was not being well treated, despite being shot and stabbed during a battle. Apparently, she was being treated well and was not even under an armed guard when the staged rescue occurred. Tillman saw this and wrote in his diary on March 30, 2003, days before the fictitious rescue would occur:

> This mission will be a POW rescue, a woman named Jessica Lynch. I do believe this to be a big public relations stunt. Do not mistake me, I wish everyone in trouble to be rescued but sending this many folks in for a single low-ranking soldier screams of media blitz in any case, I'm glad to be able to do my part and I hope we bring her home safe. (Krakauer, 2010, 243)

The notion of a public relations stunt would appear again, months after his death, when his brother, Kevin, testified before the U.S. House Committee on Oversight and Government Reform:

> The deception surrounding this [Tillman] case was an insult to the family: but more importantly, its primary purpose was to deceive a whole nation. We say these things with disappointment and sadness for our country. Once again, we have been used as props in a Pentagon public relations exercise. (http://edition.cnn.com/2007/US/03/27/family.tillman/)

This insight should not be too surprising since Tillman was a marketing major at Arizona State University. He was aware of promotional efforts to put the best foot forward, and he knew that reality could be distorted. Prophetically, he expressed concern that if he were killed the military might try to capitalize on his death. He did not like it a bit. He confided to a fellow Ranger: "I don't want them to parade me through the streets."

It is not too far-fetched to imagine how his perspective might have darkened during the next year, and what his diaries might have included, but these were burned as part of the cover-up of his killing. Perhaps those statements would not have been overly nationalistic.

Things were much different with Chris Kyle. After leaving the U.S. Navy he became a bit of an entrepreneur, cowriting books with professional writers, clearly designed to be the best sellers they were. He also made several videos about his patriotism, support of the war, and had entered the political fray about gun control by online video statements linking it to constitutional rights and core American values. One blemish on Chris Kyle's story was that he incorrectly claimed one more medal than he was awarded, even though he was cautioned about this during a review of the book manuscript. "After an exhaustive investigation lasting more than two years, it has been determined that Mr. Kyle did in fact embellish his medal count," said the official. "The charge of stolen valor will go forward." (Another concern involves his wife and attorneys more than Chris himself. This is to what extent his wish that the proceeds from the book and movie go to the families of two of his fellow Navy SEAL comrades who were killed. That remains in dispute.)

As suggested above, the contexts of the two deaths were different: the deaths were nearly a decade apart, and occurred during the terms of two very different presidents. Ironically, the Bush administration touted the more reflective Tillman's sacrifice and patriotism as a way to validate the wars in Afghanistan and Iraq. As noted below, Tillman's parents were very critical of the propaganda campaign that used their son as a "poster boy." (Indeed, Tillman's perceived opposition to the wars led some critics, including his own mother, to suggest that his killing may have not been "accidental" [Yan et al., 2016].) As we saw in previous chapters, the selling of the war, especially the importance of the military involvement, was quite successful, particularly when Bush's successor, President Obama, was overseeing a reduction in forces in the Middle East in opposition to a Republican congressional majority and a hostile segment of right-wing media, led by Fox News, that campaigned against a variety of social reforms as well, including the controversial Affordable Care Act (that came to be known as "Obamacare").

Chris Kyle would have been a better fit with President Bush than with the Obama presidency. President Obama campaigned on the promise to extricate the United States from these wars, which he essentially did, although he would also be criticized for withdrawing too many troops too soon and for not sending more troops into the emerging Syrian quagmire. It was different with Kyle, whose pro-gun statements and book about American guns in U.S. history certainly did not promote President Obama's efforts to make gun use safer and more controlled through background checks (Velencia, 2016). This opposition was celebrated through social media by audiences, especially advocates, and was very significant in 2013 in carrying more specific messages about the importance of Chris Kyle's love of country, interest in guns, and political messages about defending the United States from officials who would compromise individual rights involving gun ownership, access, and use.

MEDIATED HEROIC DISCOURSE IN A TIME OF FEAR

Previous chapters focused on the importance of language in established public discourse that resonate fear and control. Examining the language used in describing Tillman helps add some perspective and context for not only his death but also for the point of view of those who commented and their support of the values making up the sporting and military activities that defined him. Mills (1940) and other students of symbolic meanings (Hewitt & Stokes, 1975; Scott & Lyman, 1968) argue that the language we use—and particularly the motives we attribute to others—reflects understandings and socially acceptable views about moral meanings and social order. Descriptions or adjectives of some act (e.g., "that was a patriotic act") ascribe motives to the actor. It is not important whether such characterizations are valid for the individual; what does matter is that audiences accept these meanings as an adequate explanation or answer to the question, Why did he or she do that? Not surprisingly, then, certain motives (e.g., bravery) are associated with deeds that we value (e.g., fighting for one's country), while those acts that are less valued (e.g., assaulting a neighbor) are described in very negative terms. Thus, we would like to believe that a soldier died in order to protect his country and his compatriots because he or she was brave and resourceful rather than scared to death or accidentally fell on a grenade while attempting to flee the danger. And regarding Chris Kyle's book and movie deals, part of the narrative is that a true hero does not try to capitalize on the use of deadly force to make money, so his intent must have been to just tell the story of sacrifices by the military personnel and their families, especially their wives. This is what he told an editor for *Time* about why he wrote a book:

> I wanted to get it out, not just about the military sacrifices, but the sacrifices that their families have to go through, about single mothers raising their children, doing all the day-to-day house chores, but then also stories about my guys who deserve to be out there, they didn't get the medal of honor so you don't know about them, but they died heroes and people should know about them. (Klein, 2016)

Pat Tillman and Chris Kyle fit the hero character well that is promoted by popular culture: handsome, strong men, and in Tillman's case, an accomplished professional athlete, serving in the military. The audience is the key target of the ascription of motives and other linguistic accounts. Successful leaders must use language and narratives that resonate with audiences. From this perspective, leaders are those persons who are most capable of speaking and acting in ways that media formats promote and that audiences prefer. Thus, President Reagan's popularity and his moniker "The Great Communicator" were due, in part, to his acting skill in portraying emotions valued by the audience. The same could be said of other politicians elected to high national office, including actor and California governor Arnold Schwarzenegger, professional wrestler and Minnesota governor Jesse Ventura, comedian and Minnesota senator Al Franken, and reality TV actor and president Donald Trump.

We saw above that Tillman was suspicious of how military public relations people might capitalize on his death. However, it was the entertainment format employed by skilled promoters that produced the "Pat Tillman Story" as a patriotic narrative. Tillman was constructed through news reports to reflect dominant values about cultural symbols (e.g., patriotism and "God Bless America"), masculinity (e.g., sports), and the war with Iraq. Positive vocabularies of motive were attributed to Tillman by major sports organizations (e.g., the NFL) and publications (e.g., *Sports Illustrated*) and institutions (e.g., the military, the university, and government), including nationally prominent politicians (e.g., Arizona senator John McCain). In addition, numerous audience members affirmed such constructions to associate their own identities with the values, legitimacy, and support of audiences while also linking their own identities and biographies to the communal celebration of higher values. However, not all comments about Tillman represented the dominant values and support for patriotism, God, and war. But most of these were published only in Internet chat and blog communications.

Many of the accounts about Tillman informed an emerging narrative about who he was, his individual character, and the principles for which he stood. Within hours after his death was reported, I was told by an ASU vice president that this "puts a face" to this war for us. Part of what the administrator meant is that this was the first ASU student killed in the conflict, but there was also a wider meaning. His was a preferred face and story. This would be established years before Chris Kyle's unfortunate killing would boost his movie celebrity persona to a higher level. The celebration of Tillman's death around the United States and much of the world also reflected a strong urge for many Americans, especially supporters of the war on terrorism, to find an example of outstanding character and valor to help elevate the legitimacy of the war. After all, volunteers and National Guard troops who, with exceptions, were drawn from the underclass and poor of American life were carrying out most of the fighting in the war. Young men from minority groups dominated the portraits of the Americans killed in Iraq who were presented on *Nightline*. Morale was reported to be horrible, especially among troops whose tour of duty was extended in Iraq as well as among National Guard troops, whose job, historically, has been to protect American soil and aid in national emergence, including natural disasters. That scenario was countered by the narratives of Tillman and Kyle, who were portrayed as making selfless sacrifice for the good of others, especially comrades. After all, Tillman had stepped away from the National Football League and millions of dollars, while Chris Kyle had four tours of duty in Iraq, reportedly compelled to return to kill the enemy that threatened fellow soldiers. And the atrocities that accompany wars need to be carefully balanced in order to maintain propagandized scenarios. Indeed, the headlines in many newspapers reporting Tillman's death shared the front page with reports about the sexual abuse and torture of Iraqi prisoners by U.S. troops.

Tillman's face was a timely makeover for the war. Another Arizonan, Lori Piestewa, a Hopi mother of two, who was actually killed by enemy troops in combat in Iraq in March 2003, was the pervious "face" of the war for Arizona. Piestewa was "missing" on the same day (March 23, 2003) as Jessica Lynch, who would later be rescued and featured on numerous television shows for her heroism. One scholar believes that the "silence" that befalls dead heroes helps cement others' accounts and beliefs about them:

> "Because (Pfc. Jessica Lynch, Piestewa's roommate who was rescued last week by special forces) is still alive, she can be flawed and can't be sanctified," De Pauw said. "Whereas, Piestewa is dead. She is never again going to say a wrong word. . . ." "It's hard to say," Laderman said. "But her ethnic-religious status as a marker of identity likely makes this something that will not just disappear. I imagine her name on mountains, streets and other kinds or forms of memorializations that will keep her in mind." (House & Shaffer, 2003)

Partly because she was believed to be the first Native American women killed in a foreign war, Lori was heralded as a hero, her family was feted, and highways and a mountain were named for her in Arizona. Very little was written about why a young, single mother with two children would join the army. One account stressed her uniqueness:

> Piestewa, 23, already has been the focus of spots on programs as varied as *Hardball with Chris Matthews* and *Good Morning America*. Dozens of other programs, from *Inside Edition* to the *Oprah Winfrey Show*, are pursuing interviews with family members. German- and Spanish-language television stations also want to tell her story. . . .
>
> She came from the same environs that produced the famed Navajo Code Talkers of World War II, who have enjoyed a recent renaissance in the public spotlight because of last year's movie *Windtalkers*. And, with the number of U.S. war dead in Iraq at just over 100, the media focus on the victims has been concentrated and intense, especially on those with unusual backgrounds like that of Piestewa. (House & Shaffer, 2003)

Others saw her service, like that of many poor Americans, as an opportunity to obtain some income, escape the grinding poverty of reservation life, and have an opportunity for her children. But it had been more some time since Piestawa was killed, and until her death, she was unknown outside her community.

Tillman was different; he was male, white, successful, and a rich professional athlete who had a clear local reputation and a bit of a national identity as a professional football player. There were few like him in this war or any U.S. war of the past thirty years. He was a prime icon, and there was an essential story line waiting for him: a courageous, patriotic, strong, successful, wealthy professional athlete who put it all aside to defend his country while bravely defending his comrades. Most of these points stuck, except for the disquieting discovery that he was killed by his own men.

TELLING STORIES

Sociologists refer to how Tillman's and Kyle's stories were put together as a retrospective interpretation, which refers to how past events get reinterpreted in view of a more recent action. Tillman's story is a retrospective interpretation of many discrete events (Cicourel, 1974; Garfinkel, 1967; Schutz, 1967) framed as an athlete-warrior with proper morals, values, and character as distinct from other selfish athletes who care about fame and fortune and put themselves above the welfare of others. This is an important contrast with Chris Kyle, who was not a sports hero. Even though Kyle's name and image may be more recognizable to a younger generation of moviegoers, the presentation of his passing and contributions to the patriotic narrative are qualitatively different. The accounts about Tillman also reflect the special organizational treatment he received, who, like many high-profile college and professional athletes, was popularly regarded as exceptional. He was an intelligent, aggressive, outstanding football player at ASU. He was also white. Apparently, no one at ASU knew—or at least it was not mentioned—that he served thirty days in detention for a brutal beating he delivered outside a pizza parlor before coming to campus. He played football for four years at ASU, where he received numerous recognitions for his aggressive defense play and relentless perseverance. These traits contributed to the Arizona Cardinals' decision to draft him, where he competed well for four years despite being "undersized" and slower than most NFL defenders. (Indeed, a bona fide NFL starter was ridiculed when he opined that Tillman was not really top NFL material but that he could play for the Cardinals.) Rule violations that may have been treated as unacceptably deviant by another athlete—and certainly another student—apparently did not hinder Tillman's success at ASU. In addition to the violent beating he administered shortly before hitting campus, he was also given to climbing the light towers at ASU's Sun Devil Stadium to "meditate" and reflect on things. Indeed, a photo of Tillman in a light tower accompanied several media reports about his death. The caption in a *Sports Illustrated* report read, "Solitude: When in need of his own space in college, Tillman climbed to the top of Sun Devil Stadium" (G. Smith, 2004, 46). Nothing was said about this being a rule violation.

Tillman was said to be unlike other athletes, never really seeking the limelight, interested in ideas, and stating that life was just too easy. Following the hijackings and attacks on several buildings on 9/11, Tillman and his brother, Kevin, were reported to have been very upset. They joined the army six months later, aiming for the Rangers, and Pat and Kevin Tillman gave up, respectively, a $3.6 million contract with the Arizona Cardinals and a minor league baseball career. This action was interpreted as turning away from fame and fortune in favor of patriotism and duty to country. The Tillman brothers received the Arthur Ashe

Courage Award at the ESPY Awards ceremony after their enlistment. While it was reported that Tillman also left his new bride of a few months to join the Rangers, the departure was told from his vantage point—listening to an "inner voice"—that she may or may not have shared. Thus, the sense of selflessness—forsaking fame and fortune and living with his wife—were part of the character and commitment statement that would be told about Tillman after his death. Several Internet writers would later comment that while they, too, had joined the military, they did not leave such a contract. As Tillman told an interviewer, playing football seemed "unimportant compared to everything that's taken place" (G. Smith, 2004, 42). Senator John McCain proclaimed before an audience at a memorial service and on television,

> There is in Pat Tillman's example, in his unexpected choice of duty to his country over the riches and other comforts of celebrity, and in his humility, such an inspiration to all of us to reclaim the essential public-spiritedness of Americans that many of us, in low moments, had worried was no longer our common distinguishing trait. (G. Smith, 2004, 46)

The drive and character that led to his athletic successes included his intelligence and work as a student. Graduating in three-and-a-half years with a 3.8 grade-point average in marketing, Tillman stood heads and shoulders above most ASU and major college football players, who seldom take academics seriously and fail to graduate. He was regarded as an iconoclast, a nonconformist who wore his hair long when it was popular to wear it short. He was regarded as rebel who "listens to his inner voice."

Tillman was described in the most laudatory terms of hero, heroic, patriot, courageous, inspiring, selfless, and role model. A book was quickly published (Rand, 2004), a song was distributed over the Internet, but it was in the laudatory statements by politicians, fans, and many Americans who widely commented that the dramatic presentation of character is perhaps most evident. Thousands of comments echo terms such as *patriot, athlete, hero, honor, character, true American, role model*, and so on. Former ASU athletic director Kevin White stated,

> Larger than life, one writer described him as an intense boy governed by a personal code of honor, a machismo that he defined and no one else, a Hemingway character out of the 1920s in Spain transplanted seven decades later to California soil that produced surfers and cyber-boomers and seekers of the next trend. . . (G. Smith, 2004, 43).
>
> Pat Tillman is without question the biggest hero of my lifetime. (G. Smith, 2004, 46)

His stature as a professional football player was blended with his choice of the elite Rangers. Sports talk show host Jim Rome (master of ceremonies at Tillman's memorial service) stated, "Athletes today are referred to as heroes or warriors when in reality they are neither" (Rand, 2004, 20). Tillman became a warrior. As New England Patriots owner Robert Kraft commented while the 2004 NFL draft was in progress,

> When you consider all the qualities that make a football team great—courage, toughness, perseverance, hard work, and an almost noble sense of purpose—this guy embodied them all. In the end, he was the ultimate team player. I've been thinking about him all weekend, even in the draft room, because I don't think that we as a league can forget this guy. He was the kind of guy I'd want on my team—in any business. (G. Smith, 2004, 24)

The military, like all organizations, promote themselves by providing dramatic performances of their members. In the movie *American Sniper*, Kyle's skill in killing a lot of people was glamourized like many popular culture depictions of snipers, but the cold-bloodedness was softened by an emphasis on making difficult decisions and his commitment to protect comrades, and—after the book and movie—his attempt to help soldiers suffering from PTSD became more important. The absurdity of his death at the hand of a former soldier he was trying to help was contextualized as consistent with selfless acts of compassion.

Tillman's death was cast in glorified but false terms. The initial report was that Tillman and his Ranger patrol were ambushed and that Tillman showed initiative that saved the lives of several comrades. According to the army report,

> Tillman's platoon was split into two sections for what officials called a ground assault convoy. Tillman led the lead group. The trailing group took fire, and because of the cavernous terrain the group had no room to maneuver out of the "kill zone."
>
> Tillman's group was already safely out of the area, but when the trailing group came under fire he ordered his men to get out of their vehicles and move up a hill toward the enemy.
>
> As Tillman crested the hill he returned fire with his lightweight machine gun. "Through the firing Tillman's voice was heard issuing fire commands to take the fight to the enemy on the dominating high ground," the award announcement said. "Only after his team engaged the well-armed enemy did it appear their fire diminished."
>
> "As a result of his leadership and his team's efforts, the platoon trail section was able to maneuver through the ambush to positions of safety without a single casualty," the announcement said. (Rand, 2004, 10)

Numerous publications, including the quickly published book (Rand, 2004), carried the army's account of Tillman's death. One version from the *Arizona Republic* stated,

> As Tillman and other soldiers neared the hill's crest, the Army reported, Tillman directed his team into firing positions and was shot

and killed as he sprayed enemy positions with fire from his automatic weapon. (House, 2004, 1)

A *Sports Illustrated* account provided graphic details of his death:

> Dusk fell . . . the shadows twitched with treachery . . . the Rangers scrambled out of their vehicles as they came under ambush and charged the militants on foot. Suddenly Pat was down, Pat was dying. Two other US soldiers were wounded, and a coalition Afghan fighter was killed in a firefight that lasted 15 or 20 minutes before the jihadists melted away. (G. Smith, 2004, 42 & 46)

For this action, Tillman was awarded a Silver Star and a Purple Heart and was posthumously promoted to corporal. This account would later be called into question.

This was all different for Chris Kyle. There was little embellishment of his death, and certainly nothing heroic: he and a colleague were shot dead at a shooting range by a Marine with PTSD whom they were trying to help. This from the *New York Times*:

> But on Saturday, far from a war zone, Mr. Routh turned on Mr. Kyle, 38, and a second man, Chad Littlefield, 35, shortly after they arrived at an exclusive shooting range near Glen Rose, Tex., about 50 miles south-west of Fort Worth, law enforcement authorities said Sunday. The officials said that for reasons that were still unclear, Mr. Routh shot and killed both men with a semiautomatic handgun before fleeing in a pickup truck belonging to Mr. Kyle.
>
> "Chad and Chris had taken a veteran out to shoot to try to help him," said Travis Cox, a friend of Mr. Kyle's. "And they were killed."
>
> Mr. Routh was captured a few hours later near his home in Lancaster, a southern Dallas suburb, following a brief pursuit. He will be charged with two counts of capital murder, law enforcement officials said.
>
> Friends of Mr. Kyle's said he had been well acquainted with the difficulties soldiers face returning to civilian life, and had devoted much of his time since retiring in 2009 to helping fellow soldiers overcome the traumas of war.
>
> "He served this country with extreme honor, but came home and was a servant leader in helping his brothers and sisters dealing with post-traumatic stress disorder," said Mr. Cox, also a former military sniper. "Everyone has their own inner struggles, but he was very proactive about the things he was dealing with." (Klinkner, 2016)

The politics of fear needs heroes to hold up to audiences members as role models who not only do heroic things but, more important, support the political order without question, including dying for it. Heroes are propaganda products and reflect the mass media construction process. This includes media logic and entertainment formats: numerous public statements, Tillman's two memorial services, local television specials about Tillman, and the ESPY Awards, including the tribute from Tom

Cruise the year after the Tillman brothers received the Ashe Award. Amid an athletic-celebrity celebration of fame and entertainment, Cruise's statement about Tillman was described on ESPN's web page:

> Actor Tom Cruise—who stars with Jamie Foxx in the upcoming film *Collateral*—presented a tribute to the late Pat Tillman, recipient of the 2003 Arthur Ashe Courage Award. The Phoenix Cardinals standout left his NFL career following the events of September 11, 2001 to join the Army Rangers, and was killed in action in Afghanistan in April. "Pat Tillman surrendered a life of fame and security to set an example," Cruise said. "An example of something that we deeply value but so often take for granted—our freedom in this nation to choose our own destinies." (http://espn.go.com/espy2004/s/04attendees.html)

Clearly, Tillman provided a terrific opportunity for this. In addition to his media character and persona, there was a lot of file film and compelling visuals of his football prowess. These were continually replayed. Indeed, several Sun Devil football games were rebroadcast in his honor. There were also the accolades from former teammates who, as professional football players, commanded even more attention.

THE MILITARY PERFORMANCE: THE BIG LIE

The military construction of Tillman's death became, for all practical purposes, the official one that was restated at memorial services, that appeared in a book and in songs, and that was the most consistent with the notion of a hero. The important point here is that looking up to heroes carries with it veneration for their cause and their principles. The adjectives used to describe Tillman and the values and cause for which he stood clearly reflected military propaganda and the major themes pushed by the military in instructing soldiers how to communicate with loved ones as well as the press. The military, like most organizations, seeks to control information about its activities and members (Altheide & Johnson, 1980; Gerth, 1992; Jackall, 1994).

There were other more creative and innovative constructions of Tillman. Numerous eulogies and testimonials of Tillman blended his athletic prowess with a false account of his death. Virtually every athlete who was asked about Tillman gave fairly stock answers. For example, Bob Feller, renowned Major League Baseball Hall of Fame pitcher who was decorated with eight battle stars for his service in World War II, told a crowd at the Georgia Sports Hall of Fame,

> I'm no hero, I'm a survivor. There are two different types of soldiers: those who survive and the heroes. The survivors come here. The heroes don't. (Associated Press, *Arizona Republic*, May 17, 2004, C5)

But not every detail supported an idealized version of Tillman. On the one hand, over three thousand people, including celebrities, athletes, and politicians, attended a memorial service, with ESPN's Jim Rome acting as master of ceremonies, on May 3 in San Jose, California, Tillman's home. Among the celebrities was Maria Shriver, President John F. Kennedy's niece and wife of absent California governor Arnold Schwarzenegger. Shriver quoted both of these men, ending with an application of one of her uncle's famous statements: "Ask not what your country can do for you, ask what you can do for your country." "Pat," she said, "has lived those words" (*Almaden Times*, May 6, 2004,http://espn.go.com/espy2004/s/04attendees.html).

On the other hand, Tillman's brother and several others openly drank Guinness as a statement of Pat's style. His younger brother, Rich, toasted with beer, commented that his brother didn't have a religious bone in his body, and proclaimed, "He's dead" (Bickley, 2004, C1), "spicing up his brief comments with several obscenities of the kind Tillman himself was known to let fly with abandon" (Flannery, 2004, A1). Local television stations carrying the event live quickly cut off broadcast. A station vice president stated,

> We never imagined at a service like this, with Senator [John] McCain in attendance, Maria Shriver in attendance and other guests, that that kind of language would be used. . . . It just came to a point where we thought that our viewers should not be hearing that type of language on the air. (Goodykoontz, 2004, A10)

A few days later, on May 8, some eight hundred people attended a service at Sun Devil Stadium. Attendees included fellow pro athletes, students, coaches, Governor Janet Napolitano, and ASU president Michael Crow, who, along with former coach Larry Marmie, quoted stories of Pericles about warfare and heroes. Marmie added that Tillman was "all about truth," and an elementary school teacher was reported to have said that second- and third-grade students have been writing narratives about Tillman (Collom, 2004). Pat Tillman Sr. commented on the outpouring of support for his son in a letter to the *Arizona Republic*. He also commented on the reaction to statements made by another son, Richard:

> I understand that Richard, our youngest, stung a few ears during Pat's memorial with his heart-felt rendition of "A World without Pat." Tough; get over it, and don't go to any more funerals. To all others, he too sends his best regards. (Tillman, 2004, B6)

Several weeks after the memorial services, a different story appeared. The facts that later emerged challenged the heroic tale of his death. The problem was that most of the account was not true. Tillman and his Rangers were not ambushed; rather, a mine exploded, and in the confusion he, like numerous comrades in the last two U.S. wars, was shot by his own men. For some journalists, this was troubling.

> That everyone from George W. Bush to NFL commissioner Paul Tagliabue to we in the media—the player's likeness graced the cover of *Sports Illustrated* the week after his death—rushed to confer immortality after Tillman made the ultimate sacrifice is understandable. As a nation we were eager to believe the army's official version of Tillman's tragic demise, which turns out to have been a fanciful illusion—sort of like Weapons of Mass Destruction. . . .
>
> Only six weeks later—after Tillman had been posthumously awarded the silver star and purple heart, been promoted to corporal, been lauded by Congress and had a plaza at the Cardinals' new stadium named in his honour—did the truth begin to emerge. Tillman wasn't killed by "enemy" fire, because there wasn't any enemy present. He was shot by his fellow soldiers . . . killed by what the army chooses to oxymoronically describe as "friendly fire." (Kimball, 2004, 24)

Tillman's death had already been defined as heroic not only for the way he died but mainly, as suggested previously, for his sacrifice volunteering to serve his country. While most media accounts stressed that death by friendly fire should not diminish his heroism, having one of the nation's prime heroes killed by his own troops did tarnish the polish a bit, although not without controversy.

Many comments were made in the minor media, mainly the Internet by the e-audience, those who communicate electronically throughout daily life via the Internet, cell phones, and even pagers. Like the more polished media performers, the e-audience's statements resonate identity competence and performance; they could relate to Tillman, often through values but also through unique biographical circumstances. Unlike the performative media logic that guided most of the presentations on television and at memorial services by featured speakers, the e-audience does not rehearse or write drafts of statements before speaking them; rather, they tend to make curt replies that blend routine communicative format and content with the "news of the day," in this case Tillman's death and its meaning. Most comments we've seen tend to be very supportive of Tillman's choices, resonating the applause and sentiments of the celebrities and others noted previously. A few critical comments appeared in the press, but they were less about Tillman and the construction process and more about context and the war. Interestingly, in the same *Sports Illustrated* issue that Smith's (2004) dramatic—and largely incorrect—account of Tillman's death appeared, renowned writer Rick Reilly contrasted Tillman's interest in obscurity and being like everyone else with the death of another soldier, Todd Bates, an impoverished black athlete who wanted recognition but was able to join only the Ohio Army National Guard:

Pat Tillman and Todd Bates were athletes and soldiers. Tillman wanted to be anonymous and became the face of this war. Bates wanted to be somebody and died faceless to most of the nation.

Both did their duty for their country, but I wonder if their country did its duty for them. Tillman died in Afghanistan, a war with no end in sight and not enough troops to finish the job. Bates died in Iraq, a war that began with no just cause and continues with no just reason. Be proud that sports produce men like this.

But I, for one, am furious that these wars keep taking them. (Reilly, 2004, 80)

The mainstream press offered little reflection and context. The Internet was a different story. There were also many exceptions, gadflies perhaps, who raised other points, including such views as Tillman was killed by the CIA and so on. Identity connections and emotions were found in a number of statements. Some writers commented on the waste of war:

I feel bad that so many are being sent to kill and die, yet some are considered better than others for doing so. it falls into the "life isn't fair" category and it's a shame. i suppose i did mean a some denigration, which was rude mean and thoughtless of me, and for that, i apologise. It is better directed at the liars, thieves and cheats who convinced him to go, then lionised him in death. Another American dead Hero. the loss of Brother Tillman and all of the American and Coalition members civilian and military and Iraqi men women and children is a terrible waste of life, talent and spirituality. it brings us all down as members of the human race. (Internet notes; spelling as in the original)

ANOTHER VOICE FROM THE TILLMAN POSTER

The politics of fear is a discourse that can be loaded, aimed, and fired. It is the meaning of the attacks that is crucial. The politics of fear renders all attacks defensive. The target is justified in defense of a protected domain, but it is the overall narrative that gives the attack its appeal. The meaning and ownership of Tillman is illustrated by the defense of a counterclaim. Tillman was sacrificed to the God of War. His was a self-sacrifice; after all, he did join up on his own accord. The problem was how to make his life meaningful to us all, the audience. His family and fiancée certainly did not need that; they knew he was an exceptional individual, unique and free-spirited. They did not need our support of them; they had each other, and like any family grieving for a soldier slain in war, they would have to sort out the raw emotions of pride that he volunteered to serve and defend the country while missing him sorely. After all the analysis of news reports and claims about what Tillman stood for, represented, and beckoned us all to do, who is he really? Clearly, he had become a face for the war in Iraq, a face that would serve war proponents well, a face that would enable social control agents in the mass media to proclaim his significance as a model or, perhaps more to the point, a command performance by which we should all be measured. The idea, of course, is that anyone who did not do what he did would not measure up. But the charge to the mass media audience was not to actually enlist and become a Ranger (most would not be wanted by the military anyway) but rather to avow symbolic support for the selflessness, the sacrifice, and the courage to, if not actually serve the country by going off to war, at least support the country. The United States of America looked like Tillman, and we were told that just as we were proud of him, he would be proud of us. The problem is that his parents and family members and friends did not control his meaning and his identity; this was taken up by the mass media for their entertainment purposes. Politicians and organizational leaders also took over Tillman and made him their own, to use for their purposes. They owned the image and the identity of Tillman, and they were jealous of their control. Their perspective on Tillman can be illustrated with a conflict that occurred over the meaning of Tillman.

John Leanos, a young Chicano studies art professor at ASU, constructed his own meaning of Tillman and invited audiences to examine the heroic discourse about him. He created a poster with Tillman's image in his military uniform, with the words, "Remember me? I was killed by my own Army Ranger platoon in Afghanistan on April 22nd, 2004. I am a hero to many of you. My death was tragic, my glory was short lived. Flawed perceptions of myself, my country and the war on terror resulted in the disastrous end to my life." He put the posters up around campus and on several buildings in Phoenix. "The idea was to open up a dialogue about Tillman's story—about Tillman's heroic nature," Leanos said. He said he designed the first-person message in the tradition of the Day of the Dead, a Latin American holiday that happened to be on election day, November 2, 2004. "We celebrate and remember our dead every year," Leanos said (James, 2004).

The cultural significance of the Day of the Dead apparently was lost on many who commented on the poster. That meaning is contextualized and often contested was not an official option with Tillman. Many people objected to the poster, challenging his right to use the image (Saidi, 2004). Responses included more than three hundred negative emails, and letters were sent to the campus newspaper, to the head of the Arizona Board of Regents, to the president of ASU, and to many other officials. Most, from what we can tell, were negative, some being very critical, even calling for the firing of the young professor.

Critics seemed to imply that the poster was a misuse of Tillman and that it was using him for a purpose and a message that he would not have supported. Leanos's art challenged certain claims and uses of Tillman by the university and others.

"The University is using Tillman as a brand for marketing," Leanos said. "My whole issue is that Tillman is being used by the University and the right wing as a hero. He's being used as a hero figure to propose a pro-war, nationalistic stance." (Saidi, 2004)

The president of the Board of Regents and ASU's president wrote letters criticizing the artist, decrying the effort at degrading and using our hero and even adding that apologies would be sent to Tillman's family. A letter from the president of the Board of Regents stated that an "administrative review" was underway to "explore whether anyone else at ASU was involved in what appears to be a blatant attempt to trade on the celebrity and patriotism of one of ASU's most honored and respected graduates" (Saidi, 2004), and a letter from ASU president Michael Crow stated that the words on the poster were "offensive and insensitive to the Tillman family" (Saidi, 2004).

Tillman became an object of study on campus. Students conducted various projects on the controversy, investigating the legal write to verify—and learn—how symbolic claims and statements are protected free speech. Many students expressed opinions that this was just wrong. On the one hand, the subtext was that we knew what Tillman stood for, what he believed in, and what he would have supported, while on the other, there was a claim that the image should not be used by the artist as though it was actually owned and operated by someone else. Indeed, it may have been copyrighted, but it was not. The constructed reality of Tillman was reified.

People were very interested in protecting an image that had been constructed of Pat Tillman, but so was his father, who expressed disgust at the role the military played in providing its self-serving scenario of heroics in order to cover up its blunders. When it became apparent the military covered up how Tillman died, Arizona senator John McCain ordered an investigation. Over the next eighteen months more details emerged about how his Ranger unit, split into two parts, suffered miscommunication, ultimately mistaking Tillman for an enemy and fired repeatedly without verifying the target.

The soldiers in Afghanistan knew immediately that they had killed Tillman on April 22, 2004, and quickly began the cover up, including burning his uniform and body armor. Army officials insisted that they did not know the truth, but later investigations revealed that a general was informed of this within the next ten days. Tillman's nationally televised memorial service on May 3, 2004, benefited the army and other participants in the military-media complex. Tillman's parents did not learn how he died until weeks later, and even then many details were not disclosed (Staff, 2005). Patrick Tillman Sr., an attorney, decried the "botched homicide investigation," adding:

"After it happened, all the people in positions of authority went out of their way to script this," Patrick Tillman said. "They purposely interfered with the investigation, they covered it up. I think they thought they could control it, and they realized that their recruiting efforts were going to go to hell in a handbasket if the truth about his death got out. They blew up their poster boy." (Staff, 2005)

The politics of fear shrouded Tillman as a subject and an object. The flesh and blood of Tillman was not relevant to the construction process. He was used for various purposes, and this use was constituted through mass media coverage, publicity, and the entertainment format. He belonged to media worlds, very much of this world but certainly not a private, personal world. He became an agent of the politics of fear, a guardian of claims about the legitimacy of war, and certainly a defender against those who might question the legitimacy of war.

KYLE TRIBUTES

Like Pat Tillman, Chris Kyle was lauded as a hero. His funeral at the Dallas Cowboys' stadium was attended by an estimated seven thousand people that included sports heroes such as former professional football star Troy Aikman and country singer Randy Travis, and others.

> ARLINGTON—Former Navy SEAL Chris Kyle's autobiography introduced the public to the "most lethal sniper" in U.S. military history. But his public memorial service Monday at Cowboys Stadium reveled in the contrasts of the man called softhearted by family and the Devil of Ramadi by enemies in Iraq.
>
> Kyle was a warrior who choked out countless friends as a gag, something they described as his hug. But one friend also spoke about how "that proud cowboy cried his eyes out" when one of his closest friends died.
>
> Speaker after speaker—from family to military—described Kyle as a father who loved cuddling with his children, a passionate husband, the most devoted friend possible and a prankster with a "cackling" laugh. He was given the nickname The Legend by friends as a joke but eventually earned it with more than 150 confirmed kills, the most of any U.S. military sniper. . . . "Chris always said, 'The body will do whatever the mind tells it to,' she said. 'I'm counting on that now. I stand before you a broken woman, but I am now and always will be the wife of a man who was a warrior both on and off the battlefield.'" (W. Williams, 2016)

And like Pat Tillman's remembrances, there were numerous YouTube testimonials posted on the Internet as well as explicit political statements about gun control, President Obama, and the wars in Iraq and Afghanistan. Unlike Pat Tillman, there were several reports about Kyle's hubris and personal embellishments that were discredited as gross exaggerations. These included his claims that he: (1) killed two men who had attempted to steal his truck; (2) punched out former Minnesota governor Jesse Ventura—for which Ventura was awarded more than a $1 million settlement; (3) shot thirty rioters during Hurricane Katrina. There was no evidence for any of these claims.

CONCLUSION

The politics of fear were reinforced by numerous symbolic acts in the days following the 9/11 attacks. Leaders celebrated the resurrection by posing with firefighters and police officers wearing various insignia and markers, including T-shirts emblazoned with "FDNY." They became our homeland heroes, and the transition to the military forces was assisted with handing off flags from the Twin Towers to be displayed on military vessels or to fly over military outposts as well as writing revenge-laden messages on missiles and bombs destined for Afghanistan and Iraq. This realization, along with the public discourse about being under attack, avenging the fallen uniformed forces, and making supreme sacrifices, would be appealing within the politics of fear, whereby individuals can join forces to defeat the latest threats to moral and symbolic order. Pat Tillman and Chris Kyle were constructed to stand for all of this.

The construction of Pat Tillman and Chris Kyle as heroes invites some reflection on the changing meanings and criteria of the heroic, including such questions as whether heroism is a feature of an individual act or of general courage or its aftermath. Their living accomplishments were recast to promote their reputations in death, and in general, to maintain a propaganda narrative about sacrifice to keep us safe.

Numerous scholars have explored the changing meanings of heroism throughout history, including how exceptional deeds were interpreted in view of political context, the legitimacy and utility of the act for the survival of the group or state, and the courage, suffering, and character of the individual (Klapp, 1962). And it should be no surprise that propagandists have sought to manipulate the criteria and meaning of *heroic* throughout history (P. Cohen, 2016). Indeed, the Nixon administration— during the Vietnam War—and the Bush administration—during the start of the Persian Gulf War—promoted the false claim that Vietnam veterans had been spat upon by war protesters. Not only was this theme heavily promoted by various war movies (e.g., *Coming Home* and *Tracks*), but the Bush administration pushed it so that a divided citizenry would support the troops in "Operation Desert Storm" during the first Iraq War in 1991. The project aided by social media continues nearly three decades later.

TEN

Conclusion:
Beyond the Politics of Fear

No one can terrorize a whole nation, unless we are all his accomplices.
—Edward R. Murrow

And if a person can't prove that they're from an area . . . they're not coming into this country. And I would stop the Syrian migration and a Syrian from coming into this country in two seconds.
—Donald Trump

Power is communicated. Powerful people assert their will in the modern world through the politics of fear by being part of the communication process that defines social issues and social problems. This usually involves the mass media, but it increasingly involves social media and even fake news. The opening pages in chapter 1 told the story of Paula Zasadny, the mother of the young girl killed in Iraq, who thought that she and her daughter were being patriotic and serving their country because they were sacrificing in order to attack the object of fear: "terrorists" in Iraq. They were serving their country, but the foreign policy decisions that led to the death of her daughter, Holly McGeogh, were not based on solid military planning, coherent global trends, or a cogent analysis of U.S. interests; those policies were grounded in fear and sold to the American people through the mass media. A few years later in December 2008, another mother in Gaza mourned the death of eleven family members, including five four-year olds, who were torched by an Israeli missile in a decades-long war with Palestine. President Bush blamed Hamas for the war. The mother was fixing her baby something to eat when he was blown up, so that's why "he died hungry." The baby's father said, "My son has been turned into pieces." Children die from routine military planning against terrorism. This is justified by the terrorism narrative. In

229

2016 Donald Trump added social media (Twitter) to his propaganda arsenal in promoting the politics of fear. It is a deadly game, usually paid for in blood and sacrifice by the weakest members of society.

The banality of evil, or the normal and ordinariness of horrific acts (Arendt, 1963), has been recast as the terrorism narrative, which holds that since terrorism (and terrorists) do not follow civilized rules of warfare and target civilians, then fighting against them can also be outside acceptable limits—torture, kidnapping, and widespread killing of civilians in the pursuit of terrorists. President Bush adopted this view, so did President Obama, and based on his campaign promises to use torture, ban Muslims from the United States, and deport undocumented people, and so does president-elect Donald Trump. There was no intent to harm others, just the terrorists themselves, but if the others get in the way, well, that is just too bad. Indeed, the United States has helped normalize killing civilians since the 9/11 attacks. President Obama, who, during his campaign promised to revisit the drone program but increased the drone strikes tenfold (in Pakistan, Yemen, and Africa) of that of his predecessor George W. Bush, said that killing civilians and children was not the intent but just "heartbreaking tragedies." Nevertheless, he went to great lengths to "institutionalize and normalize" the strikes (P. Zenko, 2016). The president defended his drone policy in remarks to the National Defense University on May 22, 2013:

> But as commander-in-chief, I must weigh these heartbreaking tragedies against the alternatives. To do nothing in the face of terrorist networks would invite far more civilian casualties—not just in our cities at home and facilities abroad, but also in the very places—like Sana'a and Kabul and Mogadishu—where terrorists seek a foothold. Let us remember that the terrorists we are after target civilians, and the death toll from their acts of terrorism against Muslims dwarfs any estimate of civilian casualties from drone strikes. (https://www.whitehouse.gov/the-press-office/2013/05/23/remarks-president-national-defense-university)

In the ensuing years the Obama administration went to great lengths to "institutionalize and normalize" the practice (P. Zenko, 2016), which does not include the fifty thousand missiles and bombs on Iraq and Syria—a bomb nearly every twenty minutes for two years—since late 2014 (Asher-Schapiro, 2016).

Previous chapters have stressed that terrorism has joined crime as a master narrative of fear that contains many justifications and disclaimers for all kinds of behavior. The basic idea is that you do what is necessary against this horrific threat, and if civilian deaths occur, so be it. As discussed in previous chapters, we have moved from war programming to terrorism programming, which promotes the terrorism narrative that the war against terror is never ending against actual and suspected global terrorists. And whatever is done in the name of terrorism is not evil since it is combatting a major source of fear. Going after targets that may include civilians and children is standard procedure and okay. It is not personal or political. It is banal. Syrian dictator Bashar al-Assad said essentially the same thing as his army and Russian proxies used artillery, barrel bombs, and chemical weapons to destroy the city of Aleppo—2.3 million at the start of the war—and killed more than four hundred thousand people (Silva, 2016).

> So, this story, and this narrative, is a mendacious narrative, to be frank with you. Of course, unfortunately, every war is a bad war, in every war you have innocent victims, whether children, women, elderly, any other civilian, any other innocent who is not part of this war, he could pay the price, this is unfortunate. That's why we have to fight terrorism. (al-Assad, 2016)

We make up narratives and myths to provide coherent meaning across the details (Kappeler & Potter, 2005). Narratives are very powerful, and propagandists work hard to establish a narrative, which basically becomes an explanatory justification for whatever is done and said; any unfortunate details that arise are less important, and, indeed, can be disregarded. This has happened through repetition of common themes, repeated day in and day out; with social media they can be repeated and retweeted dozens of times throughout a single day. Establishing the narrative is the hard part, but once it is set, things can run smoothly. Thus, under President Obama, the avowed peace president, drones attacked enemies-in-the-midst-of-civilians. The public fear and anger increased when attacks occurred in the United States, thus providing more legitimacy for attacking targets defined as terrorists. And Donald Trump promised more attacks on not just terrorists, but those with the name of Islamic terrorists, adding the religious descriptor of some two billion people to potential targets. This illogic demonstrates how narratives go astray when they are reified as actual descriptions of the object of fear. Contingencies get in the way in pursuing the narrative, and children are killed, innocent people are ridiculed, attacked by racist white nationalists in the United States after Donald Trump's election, and decades of public symbolic tolerance of group differences essentially are destroyed. And this has all been achieved through a communication order that held such promise for integration, tolerance, and critical thinking and inquiry.

The politics of fear is paradoxical. The complexities are illustrated in various crime control efforts (Ferrell et al., 2015) as well as military interventions discussed in this book. On the one hand, the policies, programs, and changes that occur are perceived as beneficial in the short run because they keep us safe, solve problems, and prosecute—and kill—those who threaten us. On the other hand, public perceptions change over time as more people come to regard such policies as reckless, destructive, and serving the interest of the manipulators. Recall that excesses and egregious civil rights violations by the FBI and the CIA were made public; these agencies were reined in by congressional action. However, the collective memory seems to last about as long as the next crisis, when entertainment-oriented news media fan the flames of "emergency" and shut out the soothing language of context and perspective. The problem, then, is that we are all increasingly implicated as being manipulators. More of us enjoy the alleged safety and security that is credited to the formal agents of social control with whom we have entrusted more of our lives. Part of the challenge, then, is to recognize how publics are cultivated through the mass media to accept the *ethic of control*: problems can and should be solved by more invasive control. After a brief overview of how citizens become involved in reducing their own citizenship rights, I will suggest some ways to offset, if not overcome, the pervasive politics of fear.

As stressed in the previous chapters, social change and expansion of social control occur through acts of power. When social control changes are institutionalized, they become part of the fabric of social life. To the extent that formal social control efforts expand, we can see the growth in the politics of fear. To repeat, the politics of fear refers to decision makers' promotion and use of audience beliefs and assumptions about danger, risk, and fear in order to achieve certain goals. The politics of fear should correspond well with the amount of formal social control in any society. The source of fear may be an authority, God, or an internal or external enemy. Tracking the expanded control efforts over time can illustrate how the politics of fear has evolved in any social order. Moreover, behind most efforts to enact more control will be a series of events and accounts about "what should be done." Changes in public language and in the discourse of fear will also accompany social control changes. And things do change. Recall the discussion in chapter 8 about the important role played by William Kristol in formulating the "attack Iraq narrative" that was part of the PNAC. He supported the invasion, spewed the politics of fear, and despite the gross failure of the war in Iraq and false information (about WMDs), he continued to blame others for the mishap, including President Obama. Yet he strongly disapproved of President Donald Trump's hints at a nontraditional "conservative" foreign policy:

> "He is discrediting conservatism. He needs to be separated and severed from conservatism," Kristol said. "And every Republican and conservative who cares about the future of the Republican party and conservatism needs to say now, I really do believe this, needs to say now, 'I'm not with Trump.'" (Warren, 2016)

Once such changes are enacted, they symbolically enshrine the politics of fear even when public perceptions about the specific source of that fear process may diminish. A troublesome example is how the discourse of fear about terrorists has led to a change in the unofficial "no first strike" nuclear policy of the United States. The incredible threat to not vow a first strike is a direct result of the war on terrorism and the routine use of drones and special op forces to go into other countries. The American people have been fed the discourse of fear so much that first strikes are now cast as "really defensive" and serving American interests. Playing with nuclear weapons policy is an outgrowth of this extended military conflict. According to a *New York Times* report:

> Former Defense Secretary William J. Perry said in a recent interview, "It's the right time," noting that the pledge would formalize what has been America's unspoken policy for decades.
>
> But in the end, Mr. Obama seems to have sided with his current advisers, who warned in meetings culminating this summer that a no-first-use declaration would rattle allies like Japan and South Korea. Those nations are concerned about discussion of an American pullback from Asia prompted by comments made by the Republican presidential nominee, Donald J. Trump. (Sanger & Broad, 2016)

Chapter 2 stressed that force requires fear to be effective socially and politically. One aim of this book is to clarify the narrative of the politics of fear so that it may be read more clearly. Part of the story is that there is a temporal and cyclical nature to it. The capacity of human beings to adjust, normalize horrendous conditions, and eventually resist social control is the ultimate challenge to politicians of fear: the longer fear is promoted, the less effective it is. There is a temporal dimension of fear that must be regarded by the politics of fear: it cannot endure indefinitely; for it to be effective there must be respites but not a predictable rhythm. This means that leaders cannot sustain a claim that they will forever be against fear or a source of fear—such as terrorism—by continually battling it in order to eradicate it. Paradoxically, the claim that the war will go on forever until the enemy is "eradicated" also serves to diminish its support and ultimately will reduce support and effectively stop the most current war:

> This shift towards eradication politics is futile. An ongoing war against the causes of fear creates a condition of chronic fear. Unlike acute fear, which is expressed intensely and is over as quickly as the intense threat it responds to, chronic fear is a response to an enduring and persistent or growing threat to the subject. It encourages gnawing reflective worries to creep in, grinding away at the fearful one's integrity. Thus, the ongoing general condition of fearfulness produced by long-term war against the causes of fear eventually wears down the fear-ridden society, a process which is exacerbated by the fact that, while it endures, the fear-ridden society provides a fertile location for terrorist activity. (C. Sparks, 2003, 204)

Of course, this does not mean that the politics of fear disappears; it is merely taken off the stage, so to speak, and awaits another opportunity

for media-inspired propaganda efforts to promote the next crisis, drawing on the context and nuances of the previous episodes of fear, including
the policies and practices that have been institutionalized in everyday
life, such as uniforms and surveillance. The rise of Donald Trump illustrates how the fear shifted slightly to embrace not only terrorists but also
immigrants, mainly from Mexico, but also Muslims, who were cast as
potentially too dangerous to trust with admittance to the United States.

This process of the politics of fear is also consistent with the expansion
of war programming into terrorism programming discussed in chapter 8.
Even criticism of war making is included within the overall narrative of
war; it has a place, but the script of caution and opposition is a feature of
the entertaining news formats and popular culture. In this sense, criticism
is itself scripted and is part of the narrative of war programming that has
emerged over the past thirty years or so. It is the context of meaning and
experience that lends credibility to the most recent threat and crisis. Images and scenarios are drawn on and recycled as part of the continuing
battle against threats to morality, civilization, and "our way of life." An
example of a pushback against the politics of fear promulgated by Donald Trump's campaign was journalists challenging many lies that were
being told, such as Trump's claim that President Obama started ISIS. A
number of journalistic organizations opposed President Trump's efforts
to disparage minority groups and to bully the press—which he regularly
attacked at campaign events, and in general to speak power to truth.
Rather than doing the usual of getting another point of view, so egregious were many of the campaign statements that journalists would include statements, to the effect, that it just was not true.

> Whereas national newspapers and TV outlets attempt to delineate be-
> tween their supposedly neutral coverage and media activism, momen-
> tum is building among many digital upstarts and magazines behind
> the idea that Trump's presidency should be framed as a broader threat
> to American political norms.
>
> During the campaign, The Huffington Post, BuzzFeed, Vox and
> other growing players explicitly referred to Trump as "racist," among
> other descriptors, while the outpouring of anti-Trump editorials from
> newspapers largely followed the argument that Trump was a unique
> threat to American democracy as we know it. (Uberti, 2016)

Any response to the politics of fear must first recognize that it is a
social construction that is linked to cultural meanings produced by the
mass media. I have stressed that individual politicians are not to blame
and should not be given credit for a country like the United States to
wage war. There are numerous checks and balances in the U.S. system,
and Congress, journalists, and the mass media, as well as public opinion,
can—and ultimately will—stop reigns of terror that emerge from the politics of fear. It was not a "power grab" per se that enables conspirators

like the members of the Project for a New American Century (chapter 8) to gain control of the reins of government and dominate foreign and domestic policy. This took a lot of work, a lot of cooperation from many people of goodwill who, ironically, were just trying to do the right thing, to protect their families and country from harm. As I have tried to show in this book and in other work, it is what these social actors take into account about their past, how they draw on manipulated media images to understand their situation, and in turn what meanings they project into the future.

Fear promotes fear. Fear limits our intellectual and moral capacities, it turns us against others, it changes our behavior and perspective, and it makes us vulnerable to those who would control us in order to promote their own agendas. The politics of fear, as argued repeatedly in these pages, simply translates these concerns into preventive action; claims are made that the bad situation can be fixed through more control. This is true regardless of whether the hot issue is crime, illegal drugs, immigration, or international conflict. In most cases, the control is focused on regulating individuals rather than on broader social issues (e.g., poverty and oppressive foreign relations) that have contributed to the problem. More recently, however, the work linking fear to the politics of fear has become far more sophisticated; the recent war on terrorism, for example, rests on important changes that have occurred in our culture and social institutions and owes less to cunning individuals who simply ride these cultural changes.

A truism in social science is that all social products reflect the process that made them. Fear is a product, and the politics of fear is part of the process. It is a process that includes both social and mass media because in the modern world we know very little beyond our immediate experience that is not mass mediated. I have argued in this book that the mass media, popular culture, and the process of media logic are the key to our strengths and weaknesses. We are an entertainment-oriented society and virtually everything that is meaningful to us and taken for granted is part of a "program" that repeats, resonates, and reproduces our lives. Today, propaganda abounds; we just call it by different names. Hitler's propagandist, Joseph Goebbels, created unique blends of glamorized falsehoods, refining the delivery of emotional symbols and slogans across radio, movies, and newspapers and building on a historical context of "Germany against the world." In our day, things are different; all major mass media are governed by propaganda, often in the guise of advertising and marketing, which rely on simplification, distortion, and emotional appeals to increase the "bottom line," the cultural culmination of profitability and success (Ewen, 1976, 1999; Jackall, 1994; Jackall & Hirota, 1999). Anything that brings in the market—that is, the people and their dollars—is permissible. The current generation—the age of my students—is the most marketed generation in history. Every aspect of their lives is fair game to commercial manipulators. This is critical because the most effective form of social control is when it is taken for granted as part of the normal course of things and is not even recognized as "control" but just as "what everyone knows."

Most of my students were born into the politics of fear and know nothing else. The pervasive surveillance that regulates more of our lives is part of their taken-for-granted baseline of experience (Marx, 1988, 2016; Staples, 2000). To some extent, this is true of each generation, but this one is different. For example, my generation (born in the mid-1940s) was taught about the dreaded superpower that challenged us: the Soviet Union, Russia, the communists, or the commies. And the Russian students learned the same thing about us. We learned that there were many aspects of our lives that had to be regulated in order to protect us, including foreign travel. And as the opening quote to this chapter from Edward R. Murrow indicates, there was a lot of concern about internal enemies and infiltration by the commies. Senator Joseph McCarthy, eventually brought down by independent journalists like Murrow and others who dared to face him, raised havoc among American legislators, cultural creators, intellectuals, and activists. The Cold War chilled the culture. But unlike the present politics of fear, the technology of control did not penetrate our bodies. That is different today. Many of my students have had urinalysis and other drug screenings. They were born at a time of pervasive control, and for the most part they have normalized it; most see nothing wrong with being asked "to pee in a cup if you've got nothing to hide." They do not see the control. This is part of the politics of fear. Social routines and activities change to reflect the ethic of control: problems can and should be solved by more invasive control. This is especially the case when control is justified to contain threats to personal safety and national security. Few of my students are aware of a prior time when individual rights as citizens would not permit such bodily transgressions, where there were clear limits to how far surveillance could go.

Previous chapters addressed how crime and war are two sides of the politics of fear that have drastically changed our culture and paved the way to widespread acceptance of the latest justification known as the "war on terrorism." The politics of fear becomes part of culture, and it changes through the cultural process. One way to understand how this works is to monitor popular culture and the mass media (Surette, 2014). While the politics of fear operates alongside cultural products, the cultural products demonstrate the results. We can examine some of these changes about crime, punishment, and the shifting focus from protecting the individual to protecting the state and the interests of the mass audience (Ferrell et al., 2015). This has important implications for citizenship.

Consider television programs about crime. Numerous scholars have noted how mass media scenarios, narratives, and rhetoric have shifted since the 1960s from more concern with rights of the accused to the rights of the prosecution (Cavender, 2004; Ericson, 1995; Garland, 2001; Surette, 1998). Typically, popular-culture rhetoric does not celebrate both simultaneously. Moreover, the nature of rhetoric and cultural narratives entails treating individuals and the state in opposition; both cannot be promoted at the same time. Rather, when one is promoted, the other is often disparaged and delegitimized or treated as morally contemptible. Many readers will recognize this in portrayals of the "rights of the accused" that are often presented in crime dramas. Also referred to as the Miranda rights (named after a famous legal case *Miranda v. Arizona*), these are commonly depicted when an arresting officer informs an arrested person that they "have the right to remain silent . . . have the right to an attorney," and so on. Typically, the arresting officer will make a derogatory comment about the suspect, such as "you've heard it before . . . you probably know it better than we do." The message, as Surette (2014) argues, is that the courts and legal protections like the Bill of Rights are hampering law enforcement and are helping criminals, terrorists, and other merchants of fear.

Television crime shows shifted their emphasis between 1960 and 2000, from defense attorneys to the prosecution and from the deviant/outlaw to the law enforcer. Notwithstanding the seemingly constant fascination with the bravado of the Old West marshal, who outdueled desperadoes in taming the West, movies and television programs in the 1960s encouraged audiences to identify with the outlaw heroes (e.g., *Bonnie and Clyde*). Cavender (2004) observes that widespread deviance from standard expectations of social control changed in the 1970s with a shift in crime policy. Popular-culture heroes emerged from their strong actions against violent fiends, and they are hardly likable:

> Story lines began to change in the 1970s with films like *The French Connection* (1971) and *Dirty Harry* (1971). The Robin Hood–like crimes of Bonnie and Clyde or Butch and Sundance are replaced by serial murder, rape and the heroin trade. The depiction of the criminals who commit these crimes changes, too. They are psychopaths, rapist, terrorists and heroin traffickers, not the likable rogues of the 1960s films. These shifting depictions begin the process of "othering" the criminal. The films suggest that there is an evil side of human nature, and the villains personify it. There are not people with whom the audience might identify. (Cavender, 2004, 344)

These studies, along with this book, represent an attempt to track some of the changes in symbolic representations of social order. The emphasis is on documenting changes that led to more acceptance of control, including the use of more membership criteria (us/them), more symbols and language of insiders/outsiders, as well as resistance that may be generated against this foundation, particularly by young people.

Efforts to reduce some risks heightens fear and shields the importance of other potential challenges (Altheide, 2013b). We become accustomed to more control, and it is gradually taken for granted. It becomes part of our cognitive and emotional baseline of experience, even how we structure our living conditions (Ellin, 1997). It seems normal when it is expressed and somewhat different when it is challenged. The language of social control agencies pervades cultural experience. Each new step is a feature of the politics of fear and the cultural context of our age. And propaganda plays a large part in these efforts.

The politics of fear is a feature of the ecology of communication, which refers to the structure, organization, and accessibility of information technology, various forums, media, and channels of information (Altheide, 1995a, 2016). It provides a conceptualization and perspective that joins information technology and communication (media) formats with the time and place of activities. Routine activities and perspectives about everyday life reflect political decisions that have been made to increase social control activities that were justified to combat sources of fear. Political decisions have cumulative effects on social life as they "backwash," or flow over time, from their originating event and debates to seep into other aspects of everyday life. Crime control policies of the 1970s, for example, still inform everyday routines by police agencies and other social institutions. Numerous efforts to prevent crime that are taken for granted include "stop and frisk," "no-knock searches," "preventive detention," "presumptive arrest," and "police DUI checkpoints." Many citizens supported the "stop and frisk" policies of the New York Police Department that mainly affected seven hundred thousand minority youth. The judge that helped stop the practice stated:

> They didn't seem to understand the impact of these policies on real people and real neighborhoods and real communities and the detrimental impact it was having, even on policing. And that's the point. They didn't seem to get it. It was all about fear—New York would blow up. (Weiser, 2016)

Technological changes promote the politics of fear as well. Fundamentally, the face of fear is expanded surveillance; it is ubiquitous and penetrating, ranging from satellite cameras to monitoring weather, troop movements, and terror suspects to invasive drug testing (e.g., urinalysis) and increasingly DNA surveillance to detect health risks. Surveillance is more pervasive because of technology that is less obtrusive and that can do more things for lower costs. More miniaturization of microchips, improved optics, and better wireless communication contribute to more communication devices like computers, cameras (including closed-circuit television), smartphones, and more, but all of these promote surveillance. Surveillance is virtually everywhere: work, home, school, stores and malls, sports stadiums, highways, airports, and even restrooms (Marx,

1988; Staples, 2000). For example, most cell phones come with a GPS locator that enables anyone with appropriate communication gear to find where you are at any time. Cameras abound in public, and they are becoming less expensive.

Controlling our borders is also about controlling us. I refer not just to the occasional capture of the bad guy but rather to how our expectations about everyday life become muted to numerous transgressions of basic civil rights as citizens. Recall that virtually no control movement put into effect is justified explicitly as "we want to control and regulate all citizens so that we can have more power over them." Rather, the case tends to be put in very apologetic if not painful terms, such as "unfortunately, we have to give up a few rights for our own protection" or, as more broadly stated after the 9/11 attacks, "the world changed that day," meaning that everything could justifiably be viewed as different from then on. This included control and surveillance.

Previous chapters referred to the massive changes in civil rights that occurred as a result of the USA Patriot Act and attendant legislation that accompanied the creation of the Department of Homeland Security. One of the big items was to increase surveillance along the U.S. borders, mainly in order to prevent terrorists from entering the United States. Tens of thousands of new jobs have been added to the Border Patrol (now Immigration and Customs Enforcement—ICE), and several hundred million dollars have been spent for more technologically enhanced security along the borders. And President Trump received enthusiastic cheers when he pledged to not only deport thirteen million undocumented people from the United States but to also build a wall along the Mexican border to be funded by Mexico. Very few—if any—bona fide terrorists have been captured as a result of this infusion of dollars and control along the border (although its proponents always argue the negative, which is basically that these expanded efforts have deterred numerous attacks). (Yet as the embarrassingly slow response by federal agencies to Hurricane Katrina's devastation of New Orleans in 2005 shows, there has been little attention paid to basic infrastructure repair and maintenance, emergency medical response, and systematic evacuation procedures.) But the security has had consequences. First, numerous foreign visitors, as well as U.S. citizens reentering the United States, have been checked and reminded again about the power of others over their bodies. Second, while drug arrests were common at the Mexican border for decades, the expanded surveillance approach did help nab people with criminal records. Thus, for all practical purposes, this portion of investment in Homeland Security—justified to keep us safe from terrorists—has provided us with more criminals. According to one report,

> About 30,000 of the 680,000 undocumented migrants who were arrested from May through December were identified as having criminal

records, compared with about 2,600 during the same period in 2002, more than an eleven fold increase. Criminal undocumented immigrants are those with past arrests or convictions for crimes ranging from shoplifting to murder. Since its start as a pilot program in 2003, the system has identified about 24 people suspected of homicide, 55 of rape and 225 of assault, according to Border Patrol statistics. (Marosi, 2005)

We also saw the abuse of surveillance from the information provided by Edward Snowden, Bradley Manning, and whistleblower information derived from WikiLeaks. But even WikiLeaks became corrupted and was used as a mere pawn by Russian computer hackers who released embarrassing digital information during the 2016 presidential campaign about Hillary Clinton and the Democratic National Committee (DNC).

The politics of fear exists and functions quite well even if each new control effort slips into virtual irrelevance for many members of society. The policies and procedures are still there, have symbolic clout, and become quickly reinforced when events—or skilled propagandists—call for them. Simply expanding the politics of fear via surveillance does not mean that all individuals are frightened to the point of inaction or that they tremble before those in power. To the contrary, like any negative reinforcement, surveillance and the tools of the politics of fear lose their effectiveness over time and with use. Children, prison inmates, students, and other creative citizens develop their own meanings about surveillance, most of which involve disrespect and combativeness. One of the ironies of expanded social control, then, is that efforts to regulate and protect at one point in time quickly become intrusions and obstacles to overcome at another point in time. This is particularly true when different audiences are involved at the different moments of control. Younger people, for example, may take for granted many of the original breaches of privacy by surveillance, but they are also likely to situationally disrespect the rules and the agents that enforce them. For example, many young people in the United States have violated rules (and sometimes state and federal laws) by taking contraband alcohol, drugs, weapons, or fireworks into protected places, such as stadiums, theaters, and commercial aircraft. Surveillance, then, does not always restrict activities; in some instances, it even promotes undesirable behavior. On the one hand, there are many instances where armed robbers "perform" before cameras. On the other hand, audiences, while aware of increased surveillance, may disregard it over time or develop various resistance strategies (e.g., covering faces while driving through intersections monitored by cameras, avoiding certain areas while driving drunk, or altering body language in retail stores).

These and other techniques of control that were examined in the previous chapters, including Internet surveillance, have social consequences even if individual actors adjust to them. It is the context of fear as the baseline, along with the expectation that authorities will constantly oppose it and protect us, that is important. This context involves an assumption of symbolic opposition to the sources of fear and other movements of change.

The discourse of fear permits widespread deviance from standard expectations of social control. Those who are really legitimate often believe that the rules do not apply to them in the same way. Indeed, many U.S. citizens support profiling of likely suspects (e.g., minorities). For example, as noted previously, many law-abiding citizens routinely speed, smuggle alcohol and drugs into secured environments, and complain bitterly when they are subjected to "security checks," often amounting to semi strip searches, pat downs, and shakedowns in airports. Many of these same people, particularly women, believe the extensive propaganda about the threat of terrorism to the United States and voted for a president who has pursued an imperial foreign policy. Few object to the profiling of Muslim and "Middle Eastern–looking" people in order to defeat the terrorists, yet they want to be treated with respect. Higher-status people are not accustomed to having their bodies treated as mere objects before a security agent who is perhaps a member of a minority group. The status quo is perceived by audiences accustomed to life framed as fear as protective and necessary in order to prevent the breakdown of social life. The fear shield that is erected becomes reified as the only reality possible rather than as an opaque shield covering possibilities.

The discourse of fear underlies modern propaganda. It comes from claims makers' construction of certain atypical events (e.g., the abduction of a child) as typical, common, and likely to happen to "you." These events are presented as symptomatic of all social life. These repeated propaganda messages are presented through mass media entertainment formats to draw on audiences' emotions of fear on the one hand while providing a refreshed perspective for framing and interpreting subsequent events as further examples of the need for more control on the other. Thus, propaganda involving symbols of fear and threat contributes to how situations are defined and shaped by the expanding symbolic fear machinery. Public expectations about order accompany the new symbolic frameworks, but this leads to more examples of disorder, which in turn call for yet tighter controls to protect the moral foundations from the dark forces of fear. So strong are these symbolic parameters that anyone who questions the process or challenges the assumptions is likely to be the most visible and easily targeted threat to order.

The politics of fear quickly transforms many people into politicians of fear. We begin to self-monitor our language, behavior, and perspective. I have in mind the way in which everyday life activities are monitored for compatibility with prevailing language, discourse, and assumptions underlying the politics of fear before they are carried out. One important consequence is that social actors become aware of this threat and begin to monitor their conduct through what Marx (1988) has referred to as auto surveillance. This may be done by simply refraining from certain activities (e.g., not renting pornographic videos because someone will find out or writing letters to the editor of a repressive newspaper) or not going to certain places or participating in activities that challenge official rulings and programs (e.g., protest marches and demonstrations). A Canadian commented on the implications of this expanding surveillance gaze:

> "At some point, you start asking yourself, as you do in societies that aren't free, should I do this particular thing or not?" says Radwanski. "Not because it might be illegal or wrong, but because of how it might look to watchers of the state." (*Toronto Star*, May 12, 2003, A01)

Altering language is one of the most important ways that people display the politics of fear. The use of disclaimers or amending the meaning of our words prior to uttering them is increasingly common (Hewitt & Stokes, 1975). For example, someone who opposes a foreign war might say to another whose views differ, "I support our troops, but I am not sure that this war was justified," or, "I am very patriotic and concerned about being attacked, but we need to plan our military action more carefully." Disclaimers enable us to maintain membership while skirting the edge of an issue that fundamentally challenges the very foundation and meaning of that membership. It is a covering device to protect us from outrage and scorn and, above all, from having our own legitimacy questioned by family, friends, peers, and fellows with whom we speak. Such caution is widespread in a world run on fear.

Citizenship is affected by the politics of fear. Successful politicians of fear obliterate the sanctity of citizenship, and they do this one case at a time. Bush administration officials engaged in numerous civil rights violations by arresting people and holding them without charge, denying access to attorneys, and conspiring with foreign governments to torture persons suspected of terrorism (Herbert, 2005; Jehl & Johnston, 2005).

> The unusually expansive authority for the C.I.A. to operate independently was provided by the White House under a still-classified directive signed by President Bush within days of the Sept. 11, 2001, attacks at the World Trade Center and the Pentagon, the officials said. The process, known as rendition, has been central in the government's efforts to disrupt terrorism, but has been bitterly criticized by human rights groups on grounds that the practice has violated the Bush administration's public pledge to provide safeguards against torture. (Jehl & Johnston, 2005)

Officials count on individual cases blowing over and not getting much attention, weakening the opposition, and, above all, silencing any news organizations that insist on publicizing such illegal conduct. These illegal acts are ensconced in the rhetoric of patriotism and moral justification, all wrapped up in the slogan *war on terrorism*. The Trump administration promised to increase torture, limit Muslim immigration, and deport millions of undocumented residents. The caustic reaction of some European countries to the influx of Syrian immigrants throughout Europe suggests that the politics of fear is gaining a renewed foothold on a continent devastated by brutal discrimination against others during World War II.

I have stressed throughout this book that citizenship all but disappears in our media age, where the emphasis is on marketing and efficiency. Members of our society are far more likely to be regarded as audiences than as individual citizens with rights who are part of a collectivity that shares certain assumptions and indeed is represented by those who place citizen values above that of the market or control or power. After all, citizenship involves the theoretical relevance of the symbolic uses of fear with audiences' everyday life. Note that I am stressing audiences rather than citizens because in our mediated age, all significant role relationships are governed by the market standard of justice by people in power. People simply make up the audiences for products and services. Politicians and corporate profits are turned on this basis, and even education and religion redefine students and congregations/parishioners/believers as clients and customers. Most of these relationships are shaped by mass media and popular-culture discourse about membership and eligibility. For example, medical insurance is connected to jobs, and adequate housing is a feature of income, as is education. Minimal health care for the elderly, provided by Medicare, does not even include dental coverage. What people receive is a feature of markets rather than rights. And we exist in markets as audiences and consumers.

The context for the politics of fear that I am presenting is quite different from the classical notion of citizenship. T. H. Marshall (1965) and others stressed that citizenship was constituted gradually by adding socially endowed rights to individuals, including civil rights (eighteenth century), political rights (nineteenth century), and social rights (twentieth century). Increasingly, citizen rights are subservient to market principles. This means that individuals, organizations, and agencies that control markets essentially control and regulate many aspects of everyday life. Conventional notions of inequality, freedom, and injustice fade in the dim neon lights of markets and cast faint shadows in the glare of economic utility. Increasingly, we regulate activities and attend to social problems insofar as they are critical for markets rather than for human needs and suffering. An exception is when natural disasters, disease, or conflict are amplified by the mass media. Federal and state aid (e.g., food, shelter, and even low-interest loans) will be given to all people if they are deemed to be victims of natural disasters. But the notion of disaster is short-lived, and when routine conditions return, the aid will be withdrawn no matter how bad those conditions may be. What makes these situations different is partly a collective sense that human suffering due to natural disasters should be avoided. The message is amplified when mass media images of suffering are carried into homes throughout the country. However, routine suffering and deprivation related to poor housing, health, education, and dim prospects for the future are by their very nature not sensational, are seldom stressed by the mass media, and therefore are tolerated (K. S. Newman, 1999).

There are ways to challenge the insidious effects of media culture promoting the politics of fear. The initial step is to expand awareness along with a reexamination of the role of media logic, mediation, and mediatization in social life (Adolf, 2013; Altheide, 2014a, 2016; Farré Coma, 2005; Hepp, 2012). The politics of fear is relevant for social life because it influences our activities, meanings, routines, and perspectives. An intensive focus on media literacy in education, as well as at home, is essential. It is difficult to undo the policies and procedures that expand control and fear, partly because, as I noted previously, it becomes taken for granted by the next generation. These effects can be reduced through critical thinking and awareness of the social changes and the implications of blanket adjustments in security and policy. This is especially challenging in our time of social media that are instantaneous, personal, and visual. Fake news and propaganda can only survive when users cannot think critically and are oriented to accepting brief, emotionally resonant messages.

Another important step involves journalism training, ethics, and responsibility. Since the first edition of this book (2006), there have been encouraging developments as journalists have become more critical and bold in refusing to report on blatant lies, or at least greatly qualifying the fallacious claims. The major problems of time and context remain, however: more time and space needs to be given to reports in order to provide more contexts to understand the meaning and significance of events. This includes journalists reflecting on coverage and narratives of prior events as things become clearer over time. Mistakes and errors should be acknowledged.

Journalists can also help audiences understand more about the context of risk, what is truly dangerous and threatening, on the one hand, from what is more speculative and anecdotal, on the other hand. Previous chapters discussed drug policies, mandatory sentencing, and foreign policy as examples. Another consideration is to recognize that very little of any consequence occurs in our society without popular culture. This is important to defuse harmful stereotypes, especially simplistic assertions about stronger social control to protect us from danger. I expect that we will see more investigative reports, movies, and television programs that dramatize the injustice and oppression that result from this expansive control. However, it is also likely that many people, at least in the United States, will object to such cultural wars material and reject it via their social media networks as propaganda promoting "political correctness."

This can be good, but it can also be harmful and used by propagandists to unjustly criticize efforts to protect at-risk populations from abuse and stigma. What we call things matters more than ever, particularly when politicians of fear seek more control by attacking safeguards of individual liberty and dignity.

Public civility is critical to protect individual freedoms. I also suggest that we continue to pursue international tribunals for redress against the illegal actions of the United States and others. Tyrants and madmen are not solely to blame for their mayhem; the challenge is to prevent crowds and voters from following them. Psychological perspectives can be useful in explaining how some individuals lack empathy, are cruel and sadistic. But sociological considerations must be drawn upon to account for the process that promotes the recruitment of masses of people who succumb to propaganda. Donald Trump's election cannot be blamed on him; sixty-three million people voted for him, so we must understand how so many presumably decent people could condone rants that were racist, bigoted, discriminatory, and destructive about fellow human beings, but also dismissive of basic scientific findings about critical developments such as global warming. This is why the media, especially journalism, is important, especially in a free society where they are often attacked for being biased. We should inform our students and citizens about a wide range of media literacy, and especially make them aware of war programming and terrorism programming and the deadly role it plays in darkening our future. We must tell the young people about another way, about the implications of social control and bad decisions. In addition, scholars and researchers of all persuasions should attend once again to the subtle forms of propaganda, deviance, and resistance. The relevance of these for all aspects of social life, symbolic communication, and moral conduct should be explored and promoted when morally justifiable. The foundation of this moral reasoning must be citizenship and civil rights, in addition to individual responsibility. In our endeavor, let us not become what we're trying to undo; let us not forget how moral absolutism and entertainment got us to this point. Above all, we must continue to tell our students and whoever will listen to be aware of the propaganda project, but to not be afraid.

The politics of fear has taken a toll on American life far greater than the normalization of massive surveillance and a herculean increase in the defense budget. Even in the United States of America, fear can win the day. Indeed, just a few days after winning the election, President Trump agreed with his advisor, Steve Bannon: "The media here is the opposition party. They don't understand this country" (https://www.nytimes.com/2017/01/26/business/media/stephen-bannon-trump-news-media.html). Two days later, on January 27, 2017, President Trump issued an executive order to close the U.S. borders to new immigrants and green card holders from Muslim countries, who had already been cleared to live and work in the United States. The edict called for an immediate ban on immigrants from seven countries: Iraq, Iran, Yemen, Somalia, Pakistan, Libya, and Syria. This order was overturned by three federal judges. The Trump team came back with a modified ban several weeks later that omitted Iraq and would not interfere with persons with visas and green cards. This ban was also challenged by several states as overreaching, especially since not a single person from these countries had been implicated in a terrorist attack in the United States. While the legal fallout on this was settling, there were more orders and seemingly spontaneous presidential tweets, including a systematic attack on the press, with President Trump proclaiming several times in February 2017 that the "press was the enemy of the people," accusing them of promoting "fake news" whenever journalists questioned his judgment or wrote critical analytical articles about shaky administrative behavior. The incendiary tweets and remarks sparked outrage within his own Republican Party when he accused President Obama of wiretapping his Trump Tower campaign headquarters prior to the election. Despite rapid denials by the FBI and other members of the intelligence community, the president's staffers continued to insist on the truthfulness of a report presumably gleaned from a less-than-reputable website. All of this within the first fifty days delighted his followers, and Fox News ratings soared.

While it is a cliché to argue that we are a product of our past, it is instructive to make specific connections with decisions, policies, and especially the role of propaganda and the politics of fear that have helped set the twenty-first-century agenda. To put it most directly, little of our misguided romp through the mushy quick sands of terrorism would have occurred without the misinformed stumbling into Afghanistan and Iraq that expanded the politics of fear and heightened Americans' anxiety about the future. This we must understand.

References

Aaronson, T. (2013). *The Terror Factory: Inside the FBI's Manufactured War on Terrorism*. New York: Ig Publishing.

ABA Journal. (2004, October). Another Close Call: George Bush and John Kerry Comment on Key Issues in the 2004 Presidential Election Race. *ABA Journal, 90*(10): 50–54, 75.

ABC News. (2003, March 5). *Nightline*: The Plan.

Adair, B., & Holan, A. D. (2010, December 16). PolitiFact's Lie of the Year: A Government Takeover of Health Care. Retrieved January 19, 2017, fromhttp://www.politifact.com/truth-o-meter/article/2010/dec/16/lie-year-government-takeover-health-care/.

Adams, W. C. (1981). *Television Coverage of the Middle East*. Norwood, NJ: Ablex Publishing Corporation.

Adams, W. C. (1982). *Television Coverage of International Affairs*. Norwood, NJ: Ablex Publishing Corporation.

Adams, W. C., & Schreibman, F. C. (1978). *Television Network News: Issues in Content Research*. Washington: Television and Politics Study Program School of Public and International Affairs, George Washington University.

Adolf, M. (2013). Clarifying Mediatization: Sorting Through a Current Debate. *Empedocles: European Journal for the Philosophy of Communication, 3*(2), 153–75.

Advertising Research Foundation. (2001, December). The ARF Supports Ad Council Coalition Against Terrorism. *Informed*. Retrieved February 27, 2017, from http://www.broadcastingcable.com/news/news-articles/ad-council help-combat-terrorism/90163.

al-Assad, B. (2016, October 21). Video: President al-Assad: "Fighting Terrorists Is the Way to Protect Civilians in Aleppo." Vicious, Shabby Interview by Swiss SRF-TV.http://www.globalresearch.ca/video-president-al-assad-fighting-terrorists-is-the-way-to-protect-civilians-in-aleppo-vicious-shabby-interview-by-swiss-srf-tv/5551942.

Alali, A. O., & Byrd, G. W. (1994). *Terrorism and the News Media: A Selected, Annotated Bibliography*. Jefferson, NC: McFarland.

Aldridge, M., & Hewitt, N. (Eds.). (1994). *Controlling Broadcasting: Access Policy and Practice in North America and Europe*. Manchester: Manchester University Press.

Altheide, D. L. (1976). *Creating Reality: How TV News Distorts Events*. Beverly Hills, CA: Sage Publications.

Altheide, D. L. (1981). Iran vs. U.S. TV News! The Hostage Story Out of Context. In W. C. Adams (Ed.), *Television Coverage of the Middle East* (pp. 128–58). Norwood, NJ: Ablex.

Altheide, D. L. (1985). *Media Power*. Beverly Hills, CA: Sage.

Altheide, D. L. (1987a). Ethnographic Content Analysis. *Qualitative Sociology, 10*: 65–77.

Altheide, D. L. (1987b). Media Logic and Social Interaction. *Symbolic Interaction 10*(1): 129–38.

Altheide, D. L. (1993). Electronic Media and State Control: The Case of Azscam. *The Sociological Quarterly, 34*(1), 53–69.

Altheide, D. L. (1994). Postjournalism: Journalism Is Dead, Long Live Journalism! In M. Aldridge and N. Hewitt (Ed.), *Controlling Broadcasting: Access Policy and Practice in North America and Europe* (pp. 134–70). Manchester: Manchester University Press.

Altheide, D. L. (1995a). *An Ecology of Communication: Cultural Formats of Control.* Hawthorne, NY: Aldine de Gruyter.

Altheide, D. L. (1995b). Horsing Around with Literary Loops, or Why Postmodernism Is Fun. *Symbolic Interaction, 18*(4), 519–26.

Altheide, D. L. (1996). *Qualitative Media Analysis.* Newbury Park, CA: Sage.

Altheide, D. L. (1997). The News Media, the Problem Frame, and the Production of Fear. *The Sociological Quarterly, 38*(4), 646–68.

Altheide, D. L. (1999). The Military-Media Complex. *Newsletter of the Sociology of Culture, 13*(3), 1 ff.

Altheide, D. L. (2000). Identity and the Definition of the Situation in a Mass-Mediated Context. *Symbolic Interaction, 23*(1), 1–27.

Altheide, D. L. (2002a). Children and the Discourse of Fear. *Symbolic Interaction, 25*(2), 229–50.

Altheide, D. L. (2002b). *Creating Fear: News and the Construction of Crisis.* Hawthorne, NY: Aldine de Gruyter.

Altheide, D. L. (2002c). Towards a Mapping of the "E" Audience. In J. A. Kotarba & J. M. Johnson (Ed.), *Postmodern Existential Sociology* (pp. 41–62). Thousand Oaks, CA: Sage.

Altheide, D. L. (2003). The Mass Media as a Social Institution. In L. T. Reynolds & N. J. Herman-Kinney (Ed.), *Handbook of Symbolic Interactionism* (pp. 657–84). Walnut Creek, CA: Alta Mira Press.

Altheide, D. L. (2009a). The Columbine Shootings and the Discourse of Fear. *American Behavioral Scientist, 52*: 1354–70.

Altheide, D. L. (2009b). Moral Panic: From Sociological Concept to Public Discourse. *Crime, Media, Culture, 5*(1), 79–99.

Altheide, D. L. (2009c). *Terror Post 9/11 and the Media.* New York: Peter Lang.

Altheide, D. L. (2013a). Media Logic, Social Control, and Fear. *Communication Theory. Special Issue: "Conceptualizing Mediatization," 23*(3), 223–38.

Altheide, D. L. (2013b). Shielding Risk. *Catalan Journal of Communication & Cultural Studies 5*(1), 97–120. doi: 10.1386/cjcs.5.1.97_7

Altheide, D. L. (2014a). *Media Edge: Media Logic and Social Reality.* New York: Peter Lang.

Altheide, D. L. (2014b). The Triumph of Fear: Connecting the Dots about Whistleblowers and Surveillance. *International Journal of Cyber Warfare and Terrorism, 4*(1), 1–7.

Altheide, D. L. (2016). *The Media Syndrome.* New York: Routledge.

Altheide, D. L., & Coyle, M. (2006). Smart on Crime: The New Language for Prisoner Release. *Crime, Media, Culture, 2*(3): 286–303.

Altheide, D. L., Gray, B., Janisch, R., Korbin, L., Maratea, R., Neill, D., . . . Van Deman, F. (2001). News Constructions of Fear and Victim: An Exploration Through Triangulated Qualitative Document Analysis. *Qualitative Inquiry, 7*(3), 304–22.

Altheide, D. L., & Johnson, J. M. (1980). *Bureaucratic Propaganda.* Boston: Allyn and Bacon.

Altheide, D. L., & Michalowski, R. S. (1999). Fear in the News: A Discourse of Control. *The Sociological Quarterly, 40*(3), 475–503.

Altheide, D. L., & Schneider, C. J. (2013). *Qualitative Media Analysis* (2nd ed., Vol. 38). Thousand Oaks, CA: Sage.

Altheide, D. L., & Snow, R. P. (1979). *Media Logic.* Beverly Hills, CA: Sage.

Altheide, D. L., & Snow, R. P. (1991). *Media Worlds in the Postjournalism Era.* Hawthorne, NY: Aldine de Gruyter.

Amis, D. (2002, May 4). Internet Anxieties. Retrieved June 14, 2002, fromhttp://www. netfreedom.org/news.asp?item=184.

Anderson, W. (1997). *The Future of the Self: Inventing the Postmodern Person.* New York: J. P. Tarcher.

Arendt, H. (1963). *Eichmann in Jerusalem: A Report on the Banality of Evil.* New York: Penguin.

Arendt, H. (1966). *The Origins of Totalitarianism* (New ed.). New York: Harcourt Brace & World.

Armstrong, D. (2002, October). Dick Cheney's Song of America: Drafting a Plan for Global Dominance. *Harper's Magazine*, 76–83.

Asher-Schapiro, A. (2016, October 17). How Many Civilian Casualties of U.S. Drone Strikes? The Deadly Results of President Obama's Endless Drone War. *The Washington Spectator*. Retrieved from https://washingtonspectator.org/drones-syria-obama/.

Associated Press. (2001, December 6). Gun Industry Uses Sept 11 to Sell Weapons; Gun Industry Watch to Launch Counter-Campaign. *U.S. Newswire, Inc.* Retrieved from Lexis/Nexis.

Baer, J., & Chambliss, W. J. (1997). Generating Fear: The Politics of Crime Reporting. *Crime, Law and Social Change, 27*(2), 87–107.

Baker, A. (2001). A Nation Challenged: Personal Security; Steep Rise in Gun Sales Reflects Post-Attack Fears. *New York Times*. Retrieved from http://www.nytimes.com/2001/12/16/nyregion/nation-challenged-personal-security-steep-rise-gun-sales-reflects-post-attack.html.

Barnes, B. (2012, November 7). Man Behind Anti-Islam Video Gets Prison Term. *New York Times*. Retrieved from http://www.nytimes.com/2012/11/08/us/maker-of-anti-islam-video-gets-prison-term.html.

Barnouw, E. (1990). *Tube of Plenty: The Evolution of American Television* (2nd rev. ed.). New York: Oxford University Press.

Baron-Lopez, L., & Waldron, T. (2015, November 4). Pentagon Paid Up to $6.8 Million of Taxpayer Money to Pro Sports Teams for Military Tributes. Honors Shouldn't Be "Taxpayer-Funded Marketing Gimmicks," Senators Say in New Report. *Huffington Post*.

Barry, E. (2017, January 3). India's Call-Center Talents Put to a Criminal Use: Swindling Americans. *New York Times*. Retrieved from http://www.nytimes.com/2017/01/03/world/asia/india-call-centers-fraud-americans.html?emc=edit_th_20170104&nl=todaysheadlines&nlid=27364645.

Barry, J., & Isikoff, M. (2004, May 24). The Roots of Torture: The Road to Abu Ghraib Began After 9/11, When Washington Wrote New Rules to Fight a New Kind of War. *Newsweek*.

Barson, M., & Heller, S. (2001). *Red Scared!: The Commie Menace in Propaganda and Popular Culture*. San Francisco: Chronicle Books.

Battaglio, S. (2016a, November 15). An Evening That Shocked Even the Pros: Trump's Stunning Win Stumped Anchors and Commentators at NBC Covering the Event. *Los Angeles Times*. Retrieved from http://eedition2.latimes.com/Olive/ODE/LATimes2/.

Battaglio, S. (2016b, December 29). Good Year for Cable News: Ratings Rise Thanks to Presidential Election, but Audiences Dwindle for Channels That Offer Entertainment. *Los Angeles Times*, B7. Retrieved from http://enewspaper.latimes.com/desktop/latimes/default.aspx?pubid=50435180-e58e-48b5-8e0c-236bf740270e&edid=2d71e1fd-329a-4032-8a83-ae4d51d49.

Bauder, D. (2016, June 30). Media Use in America Up a Full Hour Daily Over Just Last Year. *The Seattle Times*. Retrieved from http://www.seattletimes.com/business/media-use-in-america-up-a-full-hour-over-just-last-year/?utm_source=The+Seattle+Times&utm_campaign=450615b359-Morning_Brief_6_30_2016.

Beck, U. (1992). *Risk Society: Towards a New Modernity*. London; Newbury Park, CA: Sage Publications.

Becker, H. S. (1973). *Outsiders: Studies in the Sociology of Deviance*. New York: Free Press.

Beckett, K. (1996). Culture and the Politics of Signification: The Case of Child Sexual Abuse. *Social Problems, 43*(1), 57–76.

Belluz, J., & Resnick, B. (2015, November 16). Trump Understands What Many Miss: People Don't Make Decisions Based on Facts. Retrieved from http://www.vox.com/policy-and-politics/2016/11/16/13426448/trump-psychology-fact-checking-lies.

Beniger, J. R. (1986). *The Control Revolution: Technological and Economic Origins of the Information Society*. Cambridge, MA: Harvard University Press.

Bennet, J. (2001, September 16). Israel Wants Cease-Fire to Precede Truce Talks. *New York Times*, 1.

Bennett, W. L. (1988). *News: The Politics of Illusion* (2nd ed.). New York: Longman.

Benson, M. (2002). In the Name of Homeland Security, Telecom Firms Are Deluged with Subpoenas. Retrieved June 7, 2002, from http://www.newhouse.com/archive/story1a041002.html.

Bernton, H., Carter, M., & Miletich, S. (2011, June 26). FBI Says Terrorism Cases on Upswing. *Seattle Times*, A1. Retrieved from http://seattletimes.nwsource.com/html/localnews/2015427889_terror26m.html.

Best, J. (1995). *Images of Issues* (2nd ed.). Hawthorne, NY: Aldine de Gruyter.

Best, J. (1999). *Random Violence: How We Talk about New Crimes and New Victims*. Berkeley; London: University of California Press.

Bickley, D. (2004, May 4). Memorial Adds to Legend. *Arizona Republic*, C1.

Blume, H. (2016, December 17). How a Hoax Led to the Shutdown of L.A. Schools. *Los Angeles Times*, A1. Retrieved from http://eedition2.latimes.com/Olive/ODE/LATimes2/.

Blumer, H. (1962). Society as Symbolic Interaction. In A. M. Rose (Ed.), *Human Behavior and Social Processes* (pp. 179–92). Boston, MA: Houghton Mifflin.

Blumer, H. (1969). *Symbolic Interactionism: Perspective and Method*. Englewood Cliffs, NJ: Prentice-Hall.

Branson-Potts, H. (2016, November 27). Threatening Letters Are Sent to Mosques. Photocopied Missive States, "Your Day of Reckoning Has Arrived." *Los Angeles Times*, B5. Retrieved from http://eedition2.latimes.com/Olive/ODE/LATimes2/.

Bromwich, J. E. (2016, November 17). Trump Camp's Talk of Registry and Japanese Internment Raises Muslims' Fears. *New York Times*. Retrieved from http://www.nytimes.com/2016/11/18/us/politics/japanese-internment-muslim-registry.html.

Budzilowicz, L. M. (2002). *Framing Responsibility on Local Television News*. University of Delaware: Local TV News Media Project.

Burt, T. & Nichol, A. (2002, February 27). Action Stations: The US Defence Sector Is Attracting Renewed Interest from Investors as Contractors Race to Benefit from Sharp Increases in Pentagon Spending. *Financial Times*, 18.

Burton, J. (2002). The People versus Larry Matthews. Retrieved June 14, 2002, from http://www.netfreedom.org/news.asp?item=22.

Busmiller, E. (2002, June 2). U.S. Must Act First to Battle Terror, Bush Tells Cadets. *New York Times*, 1.

Calderon, R. V. (2003). The United States Invasion of Panama: A Tri-Dimensional Analysis. *Entrecaminos*.

Callimachi, R. (2015, June 27). ISIS and the Lonely Young American. *New York Times*. Retrieved from http://www.nytimes.com/2015/06/28/world/americas/isis-online-recruiting-american.html.

Campbell, D. (1998). *Writing Security: United States Foreign Policy and the Politics of Identity* (Rev. ed.). Minneapolis: University of Minnesota Press.

Carey, J. (1989). *Communication as Culture: Essays on the Media and Society*. Boston, MA: Unwin Hyman.

Carr, D. (2002, January 13). The Media Business; *Rolling Stone*, Struggling for Readers, Names Briton as Editor. *New York Times*, 5C.

Carr, D. (2003, March 11). White House Listens When Weekly Speaks. *New York Times*, 1.

Carroll, L. (2015, November 22). Fact-Checking Trump's Claim That Thousands in New Jersey Cheered When World Trade Center Tumbled. Retrieved December 10, 2016, from http://www.politifact.com/truth-o-meter/statements/2015/nov/22/donald-trump/fact-checking-trumps-claim-thousands-new-jersey-ch/.

Castells, M., & Himanen, P. (2002). *The Information Society and the Welfare State: The Finnish Model*. Oxford: Oxford University Press.

Cavender, G. (2004). Media and Crime Policy: A Reconsideration of David Garland's *The Culture of Control. Punishment and Society, 6*(3), 335–48.

Center for Human Rights and Global Justice. (2011). Targeted and Entrapped: Manufacturing the "Homegrown Threat" in the United States (p. 92). New York: NYU School of Law.

Cerulo, K. (1997). Identity Construction: New Issues, New Directions. *Annual Review of Sociology,* 385–409.

Cerulo, K. (2002). Individualism Pro Tem: Reconsidering U.S. Social Relations. In K. A. Cerulo (Ed.), *Culture in Mind: Toward a Sociology of Culture and Cognition* (pp. 135–71). New York: Routledge.

Cerulo, K., Ruane, J. M., & Chayko, M. (1992). Technological Ties That Bind: Media Generated Primary Groups. *Communication Research, 19*(1): 109–29.

Chaptman, D. (2002, January 7). State High Court Case Tests Child Enticement Law in Internet "Stings." *Milwaukee Journal Sentinel,* 1A.

Chen, D. W. (2002a, June 17). Lure of Millions Fuels 9/11 Families' Feuding. *New York Times,* A1.

Chen, D. W. (2002b, January 1). Many Relatives, Wary and Anguished, Shun Sept. 11 Fund. *New York Times,* B1.

Chen, D. W. (2002c, June 27). Struggling to Sort Out 9/11 Aid to Foreigners. *New York Times,* A1.

Chen, D. W. (2004, November 9). New Study Puts Sept. 11 Payout at $38 Billion. *New York Times.* Retrieved from http://www.nytimes.com/2004/11/09/nyregion/09victim.html?ex=1101020832&ei=1&en=0aa7354723c0205e.

Chermak, S. (1995). *Victims in the News: Crime and the American News Media.* Boulder, CO: Westview Press.

Chiricos, T., Eschholz, S., & Gertz, M. (1997). Crime, News and Fear of Crime: Toward an Identification of Audience Effects. *Social Problems, 44*(3), 342–57.

Chiricos, T., Padgett, K., & Gertz, M. (2000). Fear, TV News, and the Reality of Crime. *Criminology, 38*(3), 755–85.

Chomsky, N., National Film Board of Canada, & Necessary Illusions. (1992). *Manufacturing Consent: Noam Chomsky and the Media.* Montreal: Necessary Illusions.

Churchill, W., & Vander Wall, J. (1990). *The COINTELPRO Papers: Documents from the FBI's Secret Wars against Domestic Dissent.* Boston, MA: South End Press.

Cicourel, A. V. (1974). *Cognitive Sociology: Language and Meaning in Social Interaction.* New York: Free Press.

CNN. (2001, July 29). CNN Late Edition with Wolf Blitzer.

Cohen, P. (2016, November 4). Last Economic Snapshot Before the Election Shows Healthy Job Growth. *New York Times.* Retrieved from http://www.nytimes.com/2016/11/05/business/economy/jobs-report.html.

Cohen, S. (1980). *Folk Devils and Moral Panics: The Creation of the Mods and Rockers* (New ed.). Oxfordshire: M. Robertson.

Collom, L. (2004, May 9). Tillman's Character Is Celebrated. *Arizona Republic,* A1.

Comstock, G. A. (1991). *Television in America* (2nd ed.). Newbury Park, CA: Sage Publications.

Comstock, G. A., & Scharrer, E. (1999). *Television: What's On, Who's Watching, and What It Means.* San Diego; London: Academic.

Cooney, D. O. S. (2004, May 24). More Than 5,500 Iraqis Killed During 1 Year. *Arizona Republic,* A4. Retrieved from http://www.azcentral.com/arizonarepublic/news/articles/0524iraq-violent24.html.

Couch, C. J. (1984). *Constructing Civilizations.* Greenwich, CT: JAI Press.

Couch, C. J. (1995). Oh, What Webs Those Phantoms Spin. SSSI Distinguished Lecture, 1994. *Symbolic Interaction, 18*(Fall), 229–45.

Couch, C. J., Saxton, S. L., & Katovich, M. A. (1986). *The Iowa School.* Greenwich, CT: JAI Press.

Couldry, N., & Hepp, A. (2017). *The Mediated Construction of Reality.* London: Polity.

Crowley, M., & Pager, T. (2016). Trump Urges Russia to Hack Clinton's Email: The Campaign Later Attempted to Clarify Trump's Remarks, Saying He Wanted Russia to Hand over the Emails If They Had Them. *Politico.* http://www.politico.com/story/2016/07/trump-putin-no-relationship-226282.

Cunningham, B. (2003, July/August). Re-Thinking Objectivity: In a World of Spin, Our Awkward Embrace of an Ideal Can Make Us Passive Recipients of the News. *Columbia Journalism Review*, 24–32.

Curl, J. (2003, October 7). Press Corps Doyenne Gets No Notice. *Common Dreams Newscenter*. Retrieved from http://www.commondreams.org/headlines03/0307-07. htm.

Davis, J. C. (1986). *Fear, Myth, and History: The Ranters and the Historians.* Cambridge [Cambridgeshire]; New York: Cambridge University Press.

De Young, M. (2004). *The Day Care Ritual Abuse Moral Panic.* Jefferson, NC: McFarland and Co.

DeFleur, M. L., & Ball-Rokeach, S. (1982). *Theories of Mass Communication* (4th ed.). New York: Longman.

Denzin, N. K. (1995). *The Cinematic Society: The Voyeur's Gaze.* London; Thousand Oaks, CA: Sage Publications.

Denzin, N. K. (2003). Cultural Studies. In L. T. Reynolds & Nancy Herman-Kinney (Ed.), *Handbook of Symbolic Interactionism* (pp. 997–1019). New York: Rowman & Littlefield/Alta Mira.

Der Derian, J. (2002). The War of Networks. *Theory and Event, 5*(4).

Dilianin, K. (2013, June 30). The NSA Is Watching. So Are Google and Facebook. *Los Angeles Times*. Retrieved from http://articles.latimes.com/2013/jun/30/nation/la-na-consumer-tracking-20130701.

Doob, L. (1966). *Public Opinion and Propaganda* (2nd ed.). Hamdon, CT: Archon Books.

Douglas, J. D. (1970). *Deviance & Respectability: The Social Construction of Moral Meanings.* New York: Basic Books.

Doyle, A. (2001). *How Television Influences Social Institutions: The Case of Policing and Criminal Justice.* Doctoral Dissertation, University of British Columbia, Vancouver, BC.

Dreazen, Y. (2016, November 21). Michael Flynn, Trump's New National Security Adviser, Loves Russia as Much as His Boss Does. Retrieved December 20, 2016, from http://www.vox.com/2016/11/17/13673280/mike-flynn-trump-new-national-security-adviser-russia-isis-obama-clinton-turkey.

Edelman, M. J. (1985). *The Symbolic Uses of Politics* (Illini books ed.). Urbana: University of Illinois Press.

Editorial Staff. (2004, July 14). Spread the War Blame; The CIA Made Some Big Mistakes about Iraq, but It Should Not Be Made a Scapegoat for the Invasion. *Atlanta Journal Constitution*, 10A.

Eggen, D. (2002, March 2). Airports Screened Nine of Sept. 11 Hijackers, Officials Say; Kin of Victims Call for Inquiry into Revelation. *Washington Post*, A11.

Ekberg, M. (2007). The Parameters of the Risk Society: A Review and Exploration. *Current Sociology, 55*(3): 343–66.

Ekecrantz, J. (1998). Modernity, Globalisation and Media. *Sociologisk Forksning 35*(3–4): 33–60.

Electronic Privacy Information Center. (2002, May 19). Public Opinion on Privacy. Retrieved June 7, 2002, from http://www.epic.org/privacy/survey/.

Ellenius, A., & European Science Foundation. (1998). *Iconography, Propaganda, and Legitimation.* New York: Oxford University Press.

Ellin, N. (1997). *Architecture of Fear.* New York: Princeton Architectural Press.

Engel, M. (2002, May 17). U.S. Media Cowed by Patriotic Fever, Says CBS Star. *Guardian*, 4.

Ericson, R. V. (1993). Is Anyone Responsible? How Television Frames Political Issues (Book Review). *American Journal of Sociology 98*(6 May): 1459–63.

Ericson, R. V. (Ed.). (1995). *Crime and the Media*. Brookfield, VT: Dartmouth University Press.

Ericson, R. V., Baranek, P. M., & Chan, J. B. L. (1987). *Visualizing Deviance: A Study of News Organization*. Toronto: University of Toronto Press.

Ericson, R. V., Baranek, P. M., & Chan, J. B. L. (1989). *Negotiating Control: A Study of News Sources*. Toronto: University of Toronto Press.

Ericson, R. V., Baranek, P. M., & Chan, J. B. L. (1991). *Representing Order: Crime, Law and Justice in the News Media*. Toronto: University of Toronto Press.

Ericson, R. V., & Haggerty, K. D. (1997). *Policing the Risk Society*. Toronto: University of Toronto Press.

Espeland, W. N. (2002). Commensuration and Cognition. In K. A. Cerulo (Ed.), *Toward a Sociology of Culture and Cognition* (pp. 63–88). New York: Routledge.

Ewen, S. (1976). *Captains of Consciousness: Advertising and the Social Roots of the Consumer Culture*. New York: McGraw-Hill.

Ewen, S. (1999). *All Consuming Images: The Politics of Style in Contemporary Culture* (Rev. ed.). New York: Basic Books.

FAIR. (2003). In Iraq Crisis, Networks Are Megaphones for Official Views. Retrieved March 18, 2003, from http://fair.org/article/in-iraq-crisis-networks-are-megaphones-for-official-views/.

Farré Coma, J. (2005). Comunicación de riesgo y espirales del miedo. *Comunicación y Sociedad 3*, 95–119.

Ferraro, K. F. (1995). *Fear of Crime: Interpreting Victimization Risk*. Albany, NY: State University of New York Press.

Ferrarotti, F. (1988). *The End of Conversation: The Impact of Mass Media on Modern Society*. New York: Greenwood Press.

Ferrell, J., Hayward, K., & Young, J. (2015). *Cultural Criminology*. Los Angeles: Sage.

Ferrell, J., & Sanders, C. R. (1995). *Cultural Criminology*. Boston, MA: Northeastern University Press.

Fishman, M., & Cavender, G. (1998). *Entertaining Crime: Television Reality Programs*. New York: Aldine de Gruyter.

Flannery, P. (2004, May 4). Spirited Memorial for Athlete Turned Soldier. *Arizona Republic*, A1.

Fleishman, J., & Villarreal, Y. (2016, December 8). Will Hollywood Switch It Up or Dig in Its Heels? *Los Angeles Times*. Retrieved from http://ccdition2.latimes.com/olive/ode/latimes2/.

Fowler, R. (1991). *Language in the News: Discourse and Ideology in the British Press*. London; New York: Routledge.

Fox News. (2015, August 26). Gunman Who Killed 2 on Live TV Is Dead after Shooting Himself. *Fox News*.

Friedersdorf, C. (2016, March 14). The Obama Administration's Drone-Strike Dissembling. *The Atlantic*. http://www.theatlantic.com/politics/archive/2016/03/the-obama-administrations-drone-strike-dissembling/473541/.

Friesen, N. H. T. (2009). The Mediatic Turn: Exploring Consequences for Media Pedagogy. In K. Lundby (Ed.), *Mediatization: Concept, Changes, Consequences* (pp. 64–81). New York: Peter Lang.

Friess, S. (2012, July 31). Cruz's Secret: Mastering Social Media. Retrieved October 17, 2013, from http://www.politico.com/news/stories/0712/79213.html#ixzz2i17LhG5y.

Funt, D., Gourarie, C., & Murtha, J. (2016). *The New Yorker*, BuzzFeed, and the push for digital credibility. *Columbia Journalism Review*. http://www.cjr.org/special_report/newyorker_buzzfeed_trust.php.

Furedi, F. (1997). *Culture of Fear: Risk-Taking and the Morality of Low Expectation*. London: Cassell.

Furedi, F. (2005). *Politics of Fear*. London: Continuum.

Gabriel, T. (2017, January 12). In Iowa, Trump Voters Are Unfazed by Controversies. *New York Times*. Retrieved from https://www.nytimes.com/2017/01/12/us/donald-

trump-iowa-conservatives.html?emc=edit_th_20170113&nl=todaysheadlines&nlid=
27364645&_r=0.

Gale, P. M. (2002). *Hansonism, Howard and Representations: The Politics of Fear*. Paper presented at the International Sociological Association, Brisbane, Australia (ISA).

Gamson, W. A., Croteau, D., Hoynes, W., & Sasson, T. (1992). Media Images and the Social Construction of Reality. *Annual Review of Sociology, 18*: 373–93.

Gans, H. J. (1979). *Deciding What's News: A Study of CBS Evening News, NBC Nightly News, Newsweek, and Time* (1st ed.). New York: Pantheon Books.

Gantt, D. (2015, May 11). 14 NFL Teams Took Tax Dollars for Patriotic Pregame Displays. *NBC Sports*. Retrieved December 13, 2016, from http://profootballtalk. nbcsports.com/2015/05/11/14-nfl-teams-took-tax-dollars-for-patriotic-pregame-displays/.

Garfinkel, H. (1967). *Studies in Ethnomethodology*. Englewood Cliffs, NJ: Prentice-Hall.

Garland, C. A. (1997). *The "Context of Fear" as an Indication of Healthy Community Investment: 80 Low-Income Neighborhoods in Los Angeles*. Irvine: University of California.

Garland, D. (2001). *The Culture of Control: Crime and Social Order in Contemporary Society*. Chicago: University of Chicago Press.

Garland, D. (2008). On the Concept of Moral Panic. *Crime, Media, Culture, 4*(1): 9–30.

Gattone, C. (1996). Media and Politics in the Information Age. *International Journal of Politics, Culture and Society, 10*(1): 193–202.

Gerbner, G., & Gross, L. (1976). The Scary World of TV's Heavy Viewer. *Psychology Today* (April), 89–91.

Gerbner, G., Gross, L., Jeffries-Fox, S., Signorielli, N., & Jackson-Beeck, M. (1978). Cultural Indicators: Violence Profile No. 9. *Journal of Communication, 28*: 176–207.

Gerth, H. H. (1992). Crisis Management of Social Structures: Planning, Propaganda and Societal Morale. *International Journal of Politics, Culture and Society, 5*(3): 337–59.

Glanz, J., Larson, J., & Lehren, A. W. (2014, January 27). Spy Agencies Tap Data Streaming from Phone Apps. *New York Times*. Retrieved from http://www.nytimes. com/2014/01/28/world/spy-agencies-scour-phone-apps-for-personal-data.html?nl= todaysheadlines&emc=edit_th_20140128&_r=0.

Glassner, B. (1999). *The Culture of Fear: Why Americans Are Afraid of the Wrong Things* (1st ed.). New York: Basic Books.

Goodall, H. L., Jr. (2004). *Why We Must Win the War on Terror: Communication and the Future of National Security*. Unpublished manscript, Hugh Downs School of Human Communication, Arizona State University.

Goodykoontz, B. (2004, May 4). Emotional Words Have TV Stations Scrambling. *Arizona Republic*, A10.

Gorman, M. (2016, November 30). Sandy Hook Conspiracy Theorist Alex Jones Invites Slain School Principal's Daughter on Radio Show. *Newsweek*. http://www. newsweek.com/sandy-hook-truther-invites-principals-daughter-show-526908.

Graber, D. (1984). *Processing the News: How People Tame the Information Tide*. New York: Longmans.

Greenberg, J. (2012, September 6). Did President Obama Save the Auto Industry? Retrieved November 16, 2016, from http://www.politifact.com/truth-o-meter/ article/2012/sep/06/did-obama-save-us-automobile-industry/.

Griffith, R. (1987). *The Politics of Fear: Joseph R. McCarthy and the Senate* (2nd ed.). Amherst: University of Massachusetts Press.

Grimshaw, A. D., and Peter J. Burke. (1994). *What's Going on Here?: Complementary Studies of Professional Talk*. Norwood, NJ: Ablex.

Gronbeck, B. E., Farrell, T. J., & Soukup, P. A. (1991). *Media, Consciousness, and Culture: Explorations of Walter Ong's Thought*. Newbury Park, CA: Sage Publications.

Grossman, L. K. (1997, November/December). Why Local TV News Is So Awful. *Columbia Journalism Review*, 21.

Gunter, B. (1987). *Television and the Fear of Crime*. London: John Libbey.

Gutowski, S. (2016, November 2). October Gun Sales See Massive Spike, Set Yet Another Record. Retrieved November 18, 2016, from http://www.foxnews.com/

politics/2016/11/02/october-gun-sales-see-massive-spike-set-yet-another-record. html.

Hall, P. M. (1988). Asymmetry, Information Control, and Information Technology. In D. R. Maines & Carl J. Couch (Ed.), *Communication and Social Structure* (pp. 341–56). Springfield, IL: Thomas.

Hall, P. M. (2003). Interactionism, Social Organization, and Social Processes: Looking Back and Moving Ahead. *Symbolic Interaction, 26*(1): 33–56.

Hancock, L. (2001, May/June). The School Shootings: Why Context Counts. *Columbia Journalism Review,* 76–77.

Heath, L., & Gilbert., K. (1996). Mass Media and Fear of Crime. *American Behavioral Scientist, 39,* 379–86.

Hee, M. Y. (2015, July 8). Fact Checker Donald Trump's False Comments Connecting Mexican Immigrants and Crime. *Washington Post.* Retrieved from https://www. washingtonpost.com/news/fact-checker/wp/2015/07/08/donald-trumps-false-comments-connecting-mexican-immigrants-and-crime/?utm_term=.f5e9cf902778.

Hendershot, H. (2004). *Shaking the World for Jesus: Media and Conservative Evangelical Culture.* Chicago; London: University of Chicago Press.

Hepp, A. et al. (2011). *Mediatization, Media Technologies and the "Moulding Forces" of the Media.* Paper presented at the International Communication Association, Boston, MA. http://www.mediatisiertewelten.de/fileadmin/mediapool/documents/ Vortraege_ICA_Virtuelles_Panel/Hepp.pdf.

Hepp, A. (2012). Mediatization and the "Moulding Force" of the Media. *Communications, 37*(1): 1–28.

Hepp, A. (2013). *Cultures of Mediatization.* Cambridge: Polity Press.

Herbert, B. (2004, November 12). Death Comes Knocking. *New York Times.* Retrieved from http://www.nytimes.com/2004/11/12/opinion/12herbert.html?th.

Herbert, B. (2005, February 18). Our Friends, The Torturers. Editorial, *New York Times.* Retrieved from http://www.nytimes.com/2005/02/18/opinion/18herbert.html?ex= 1109394000&en=a84651749cc4f1d5&ei=5070.

Herman, E. S., & Chomsky, N. (2002). *Manufacturing Consent: The Political Economy of the Mass Media.* New York: Pantheon Books.

Hertog, J. K., and Fan, D. P. (1995). The Impact of Press Coverage on Social Beliefs: The Case of HIV Transmission. *Communication Research, 22,* 545–77.

Hewitt, J. P., & Shulman, D. (1991). *Self and Society: A Symbolic Interactionist Social Psychology* (5th ed.). Needham Heights, MA: Allyn and Bacon.

Hewitt, J. P., & Stokes, R. (1975). Disclaimers. *American Sociological Review, 40*(1): 1–11.

Higgins, A., McIntire, M., & Dance, G. J. X. (2016, November 25). Inside a Fake News Sausage Factory: This Is All About Income. *New York Times.* Retrieved from http:// www.nytimes.com/2016/11/25/world/europe/fake-news-donald-trump-hillary-clinton-georgia.html?emc=edit_th_20161126&nl=todaysheadlines&nlid=27364645.

Hirsch, P. (1980). The "Scary World" of the Non-Viewer and Other Anomalies: A Reanalysis of Gerbner et al. Findings, Part 1. *Communication Research, 7:* 403–56.

Hjarvard, S. (2013). *The Mediatization of Culture and Society.* London, England: Routledge.

Hoffman, C. (2004, September 1). As Anxiety Grows, So Does Field of Terror Study. *New York Times.* Retrieved from http://www.nytimes.com/2004/09/01/nyregion/ 01disaster.html?ex=1095428710&ei=1&en=ed0be3c7892d98c9.

Holstein, J. A., & Gubrium, J. F. (2000). *The Self We Live By: Narrative Identity in a Postmodern World.* New York: Oxford University Press.

Horowitz, J., & Cammarano, S. (2013, February 5). 20 Extraordinary Facts about CIA Extraordinary Rendition and Secret Detention. Retrieved December 12, 2016, from https://www.opensocietyfoundations.org/voices/20-extraordinary-facts-about-cia-extraordinary-rendition-and-secret-detention.

House, B. (2002). Bush Gives FBI New Domestic Surveillance Powers. *Arizona Republic,* May 31, 2002. Retrieved June 3, 2002, from http://www.arizonarepublic.com/news/ articles/0531fbi-ashcroft.html.

House, B. (2004, May 29). Tillman Killed by Friendly Fire. *The Arizona Republic*, 1.

House, B., & Shaffer, M. (2003, April 10). Mom, Hopi, Hero: Piestewa an Icon. *Arizona Republic*. Retrieved from http://www.azcentral.com/news/specials/iraq/articles/retro-piestewa.html.

Hunt, A. (1997). "Moral Panic" and Moral Language in the Media. *British Journal of Sociology*, 48(4): 629–48.

Hunt, D. M. (1999). *O. J. Simpson Facts and Fictions: News Rituals in the Construction of Reality*. Cambridge, UK; New York: Cambridge University Press.

Ignatius, D. (2015, October 29). How ISIS Spread in the Middle East and How to Stop It. *The Atlantic*.

Isikoff, M. (2008, December 22). The Fed Who Blew the Whistle. *Newsweek, 152*, 40–48.

Issenberg, S. (2008, October 11). Supporters Jeer as McCain Calls Obama "A Decent Person." *Boston Globe*, A1. Retrieved from http://archive.boston.com/news/nation/articles/2008/10/11/supporters_jeer_as_mccain_calls_obama_a_decent_person/.

Iyengar, S. (1991). *Is Anyone Responsible? How Television Frames Political Issues*. Chicago: University of Chicago Press.

Iyengar, S., & Kinder, D. M. (1987). *News That Matters*. Chicago: University of Chicago Press.

Jackall, R. (Ed.). (1994). *Propaganda*. New York: New York University Press.

Jackall, R., & Hirota, J. M. (1999). *Experts with Symbols: Advertising, Public Relations, and the Ethics of Advocacy*. Chicago: University of Chicago.

Jackall, R., & Hirota, J. M. (2000). *Image Makers: Advertising, Public Relations, and the Ethos of Advocacy*. Chicago; London: University of Chicago Press.

Jackson, R. (1946). One Hundred and Eighty-Seventh Day: Robert Jackson's Closing Speech (Part 6). Nuremberg, Germany.

James, D. (2004, October 9). Tillman Fliers Spur E-Mail Backlash. *The Tribune*. Retrieved from http://www.abor.asu.edu/1_the_regents/clips/100904.htm#Tillman%20fliers%20spur%20e-mail%20backlash.

Jamiesen, K. H., & Capella, J. N. (2008). *Echo Chamber: Rush Limbaugh and the Conservative Media Establishment*. New York: Oxford University Press.

Janofsky, M. (1999, May 9). Journalist Sentenced to 18 Months in Internet Pornography Case. *New York Times*, A17.

Jehl, D., & Johnston, D. (2005, March 6). Rule Change Lets C.I.A. Freely Send Suspects Abroad to Jails. *New York Times*. Retrieved from http://www.nytimes.com/2005/03/06/politics/06intel.html?ex=1110776400&en=e36cc36fc5ef2f81&ei=5070.

Jenkins, P. (1998). *Moral Panic: Changing Concepts of the Child Molester in Modern America*. New Haven; London: Yale University Press.

Jenkins, P. (1999). *The Cold War at Home: The Red Scare in Pennsylvania, 1945–1960*. Chapel Hill; London: University of North Carolina Press.

Johnson, J. M. (1995). Horror Stories and the Construction of Child Abuse. In J. Best (Ed.), *Images of Issues* (2nd ed., pp. 17–31). Hawthorne, NY: Aldine de Gruyter.

Jurkowitz, M., Mitchell, A., Hitlin, P., Santhanam, L., Adams, S., Anderson, M., & Vog, N. (2013). The Changing TV News Landscape 2013. Pew Research Center Project for Excellence in Journalism.

Kagan, R., & Kristol, W. (2000). *Present Dangers: Crisis and Opportunity in American Foreign and Defense Policy* (1st ed.). San Francisco: Encounter Books.

Kamalipour, Y. R., & Snow, N. (2004). *War, Media, and Propaganda: A Global Perspective*. Lanham, MD; Oxford: Rowman & Littlefield.

Kappeler, V. E., Blumberg, M., & Potter, G. W. (1999). *The Mythology of Crime and Criminal Justice* (3rd ed.). Prospect Heights, IL: Waveland Press.

Kappeler, V. E., & Potter, G. W. (2005). *The Mythology of Crime and Criminal Justice* (4th ed.). Long Grove, IL: Waveland Press.

Katz, J. (1987). What Makes Crime "News"? *Media, Culture and Society, 9*: 47–75.

Kellner, D. (1992). *The Persian Gulf TV War*. Boulder, CO: Westview Press.

Kellner, D. (2003). *From 9/11 to Terror War: The Dangers of the Bush Legacy*. Lanham, MD; Oxford: Rowman & Littlefield.

Kerr, D. M. (2000, July 24). Internet and Data Interception Capabilities Developed by FBI. Retrieved June 7, 2002, from http://www.fbi.gov/congress/congress00/kerr072400.htm.

Kimball, G. (2004, May 31). Bitter Twist to the True Story of a Hero's End. *Irish Times*, 24.

Kingston, A. (2002, April 20). You're a Goof. Buy Our Beer: What the Canadian Ad Awards Reveal About Us. *The Saturday Post*, SP1.

Kitroeff, N. (2016, November 15). The Promise of Bringing Back Jobs. Trump Won Over Many Rust Belt Voters with a Vow to Revive Manufacturing—a Task Experts Say Is Nearly Impossible. *Los Angeles Times*. Retrieved from http://eedition2.latimes.com/Olive/ODE/LATimes2/.

Klapp, O. E. (1962). *Heroes, Villains, and Fools: The Changing American Character*. Englewood Cliffs, NJ: Prentice-Hall.

Klasfeld, A. (2011). Terror Stings Breed Entrapment, Study Says. *Courthouse News*. Retrieved from http://www.courthousenews.com/2011/05/20/36745.htm.

Klein, E. (2016, November 7). Donald Trump's Success Reveals a Frightening Weakness in American Democracy. Retrieved November 10, 2016, fromhttp://www.vox.com/policy-and-politics/2016/11/7/13532178/donald-trump-american-democracy-weakness.

Klinkner, P. (2016, June 2). The Easiest Way to Guess If Someone Supports Trump? Ask If Obama Is a Muslim. Retrieved November 10, 2016, from http://www.vox.com/2016/6/2/11833548/donald-trump-support-race-religion-economy.

Knickerbocker, B. (2002, February 13). Return of the "Military-Industrial Complex"? *Christian Science Monitor*, 2.

Krakauer, J. (2010). *Where Men Win Glory: The Odyssey of Pat Tillman*. New York: Anchor.

Kristof, N. (2016, November 12). Lies in the Guise of News in the Trump Era. *New York Times*. Retrieved from http://www.nytimes.com/2016/11/13/opinion/sunday/lies-in-the-guise-of-news-in-the-trump-era.html.

Krugman, P. (2003, June 10). Who's Accountable? *New York Times*. Retrieved from http://www.nytimes.com/2003/06/10/opinion/10KRUG.html.

Lembcke, J. (1998). *The Spitting Image: Myth, Memory, and the Legacy of Vietnam*. New York: New York University Press.

Leonard, J. & Morin, M. (2002, January 17). Stalking the Web Predator. *Los Angeles Times*, A1.

Lewis, N. A. (2001, August 8). Rebels in Black Robes Recoil at Surveillance of Computers. *New York Times*, 1. Retrieved from http://www.nytimes.com/2001/08/08/national/08COUR.html.

Leyden, J. (2001, November 27). AV Vendors Split Over FBI Trojan Snoops. *The Register*. Retrieved from http://www.theregister.co.uk/content/55/23057.html.

Lichtblau, E. (2016, June 7). F.B.I. Steps Up Use of Stings in ISIS Cases. *New York Times*. Retrieved from http://www.nytimes.com/2016/06/08/us/fbi-isis-terrorism-stings.html.

Livingstone, S. (2009). On the Mediation of Everything: ICA Presidential Address 2008. *Journal of Communication 59*: 1–18.

Lopez, G. A., & Stohl, M. (1984). *The State as Terrorist: The Dynamics of Governmental Violence and Repression*. Westport, CT: Greenwood Press.

Lord, R. (2011, March 4). North Side Takedown: 29 Gang Members from Manchester Indicted for Drug and Gun Crimes. *Pittsburgh Post-Gazette*, B-1. Retrieved from http://www.lexisnexis.com.ezproxy1.lib.asu.edu/hottopics/lnacademic/?.

Lundby, K. (Ed.). (2009). *Mediatization: Concept, Changes, Consequences*. New York: Peter Lang.

Lyon, D. (2001). *Surveillance Society: Monitoring Everyday Life*. Buckingham [England]; Philadelphia: Open University.

MacArthur, J. R. (2003, May/June). The Lies We Bought: The Unchallenged "Evidence" for War. *Columbia Journalism Review*: 62–63.

MacKuen, M., & Coombs, S. L. (1981). *More Than News: Media Power in Public Affairs.* Beverly Hills, CA: Sage.

Maines, D. R. (2001). *The Faultline of Consciousness: A View of Interactionism in Sociology.* Hawthorne, NY: Aldine de Gruyter.

Manjoo, F. (2016a, November 2). How the Internet Is Loosening Our Grip on the Truth. *New York Times.* Retrieved from http://www.nytimes.com/2016/11/03/technology/how-the-internet-is-loosening-our-grip-on-the-truth.html?emc=edit_th_20161103&nl=todaysheadlines&nlid=27364645.

Manjoo, F. (2016b, November 16). Social Media's Globe-Shaking Power. *New York Times.* Retrieved from http://www.nytimes.com/2016/11/17/technology/social-medias-globe-shaking-power.html?emc=edit_th_20161117&nl=todaysheadlines&nlid=27364645.

Mann, J. (2003). A Look at the Failure to Find Any Weapons of Mass Destruction in Iraq. *Insight,* CNN.

Manning, P. K. (1998). Media Loops. In F. Y. Bailey (Ed.), *Popular Culture, Crime, and Justice* (pp. 25–39). Belmont, CA: West/Wadsworth.

Manning, P. K., & Cullum-Swan, B. (1994). Narrative, Content and Semiotic Analysis. In N. K. Denzin & Lincoln, Y. S. (Ed.), *Handbook of Qualitative Research* (pp. 463–78). Newbury Park, CA: Sage.

Margolis, H. (1996). *Dealing with Risk: Why the Public and the Experts Disagree on Environmental Issues.* Chicago: University of Chicago Press.

Marosi, R. (2005, February 20). Print System Nabs Migrant Criminals. *The Arizona Republic,* A12. Retrieved from http://www.azcentral.com/arizonarepublic/news/articles/0220border20.html.

Marshall, T. H. (1965). *Class, Citizenship, and Social Development: Essays.* Garden City, NY: Doubleday.

Marx, G. T. (1988). *Undercover: Police Surveillance in America.* Berkeley: University of California Press.

Marx, G. T. (2016). *Windows into the Soul: Surveillance and Society in an Age of High Technology.* Chicago: University of Chicago Press.

Massing, M. (2003, May 29). The Unseen War. *New York Review,* 16–19. Retrieved from http://www.nybooks.com/articles/16293.

Massing, M. (2009, January/February). Un-American: Have You Listened to the Right-Wing Media Lately? *Columbia Journalism Review,* 14–18.

Massumi, B. (1993). *The Politics of Everyday Fear.* Minneapolis: University of Minnesota Press.

McCoy, T. H. (2013, October 4). Facebook Moms. *Newsweek.*

McDonald, J. H. (1994). Te(k)nowledge: Technology, Education, and the New Student Subject. *Science as Culture,* 4(4): 537–64.

McQuail, D. (1983). *Mass Communication Theory: An Introduction.* London; Beverly Hills: Sage Publications.

Mead, G. H., & Morris, C. W. (1962). *Mind, Self, and Society from the Standpoint of a Social Behaviorist.* Chicago: University of Chicago Press.

Meyen, M., Thieroff, M., & Strenger, S. (2014). Mass Media Logic and the Mediatization of Politics: A Theoretical Framework. *Journalism Studies* 15(3) Mediatization of Politics: Theoretical and Empirical Perspectives): 271–88.

Meyer, T., & Hinchman, L. P. (2002). *Media Democracy: How the Media Colonize Politics.* Cambridge, UK: Polity Press; Blackwell.

Meyrowitz, J. (1985). *No Sense of Place.* New York: Oxford University Press.

Miller, G. (1999, September 25). Online Chat Is Sting of Choice in Illicit-Sex Cases. *Los Angeles Times,* AI.

Mills, C. W. (1940). Situated Actions and Vocabularies of Motive. *American Sociological Review,* 5: 904–13.

Min Kim, S. (2016, September 28). Congress Hands Obama First Veto Override. Retrieved November 28, 2016, from http://www.politico.com/story/2016/09/senate-jasta-228841.

Moehle, K. A. & Levitt, E. E. (1991). The History of the Concepts of Fear and Anxiety. In C. E. Walker (Ed.), *Clinical Psychology: Historical and Research Foundations* (pp. 159–82). New York: Plenum Press.

MSNBC. (2001, December 12). FBI Confirms "Magic Lantern" Exists. Retrieved June 7, 2002, from http://www.msnbc.com/news/671981.asp?0si=-&cp1=1.

Mueller, J., & Steward, M. (2016). *Chasing Ghosts: The Policing of Terrorism*. New York: Oxford University Press.

Muschert, G. W. (2007). The Columbine Victims and the Myth of the Juvenile Super-predator. *Youth Violence and Juvenile Justice, 5*(4): 351–66.

Muschert, G. W. (2009). Special Issue on "The Lessons of Columbine, Part I." *American Behavioral Scientist, 52*(9).

Naphy, W. G., & Roberts, P. (1997). *Fear in Early Modern Society*. Manchester; New York: Manchester University Press. Distributed exclusively in the USA by St. Martin's Press.

Nash, J. E., & Calonico, J. M. (2003). The Economic Institution. In L. T. Reynolds & N. Herman-Kinney (Ed.), *Handbook of Symbolic Interactionism* (pp. 445–69). New York: Rowman & Littlefield/Alta Mira.

National Public Health Service. (1995, February/March). Risk Communication: Working with Individuals and Communities to Weight the Odds. Retrieved from http://odphp.osophs.dhhs.gov/pubs/prevrpt/archives/95fm1.htm.

Newman, K. S. (1999). *No Shame in My Game: The Working Poor in the Inner City* (1st ed.). New York: Knopf and the Russell Sage Foundation.

Newman, R. (2001, October 1). The Day the World Changed, I Did, Too. *Newsweek*, 9.

Norris, P., Kern, M., & Just, M. R. (2003). *Framing Terrorism: The News Media, the Government and the Public*. New York; London: Routledge.

O'Neill, S., & Grynbaum, M. M. (2016, November 5). An Election Made for TV News. *New York Times*. Retrieved from http://www.nytimes.com/video/business/media/100000004731791/an-election-made-for-tv-news.html?emc=edit_th_20161106&nl=todaysheadlines&nlid=27364645.

Offe, C. (2002). Political Liberalism, Group Rights and the Politics of Fear and Trust. *Hagar: International Social Science Review, 3*(1): 5–17.

Palazzo, C. (2016, December 15). Twitter "Bounced" from Tech Meeting with Donald Trump over Anti-Clinton Emoji. *The Telegraph*. Retrieved from http://www.telegraph.co.uk/technology/2016/12/15/twitter-bounced-tech-meeting-donald-trump-anti-clinton-emoji/.

Patterson, T. E. (2016, December 8). Bash Both Sides Equally: Unrelenting Negative Coverage of Both Candidates Led to False Equivalency. *Los Angeles Times*. Retrieved from http://eedition2.latimes.com/Olive/ODE/LATimes2/.

Pearson, G. (1983). *Hooligan: A History of Respectable Fears*. London: Macmillan.

Perinbanayagam, R. S. (1974). The Definition of the Situation: An Analysis of the Ethnomethodological and Dramaturgical View. *Sociological Quarterly, 14*(4): 521–41.

Perinbanayagam, R. S. (1986). The Meaning of Uncertainty and the Uncertainty of Meaning. *Symbolic Interaction, 9*: 105–26.

Pew Charitable Trusts. (2002). Internet and American Life. Retrieved June 13, 2002, from http://www.pewinternet.org/reports/reports.asp?Report=32&Section=ReportLevel1&Field=Level1ID&ID=119.

Pfuhl, E. H., & Henry, S. (1993). *The Deviance Process* (3rd ed.). New York: Aldine de Gruyter.

Phelps, T. M. (2013, December 28). New Judge, New Ruling on Spying. *Los Angeles Times*. Retrieved from http://eedition2.latimes.com/Olive/ODE/LATimes/.

Potter, J., & Wetherell, M. (1987). *Discourse and Social Psychology*. Thousand Oaks, CA: Sage.

Powell, M. (1999, May 27). How to Bomb in Selling a War. *Washington Post*, C01.

Priest, D., & Arkin, W. M. (2010). *Top Secret America*. New York: Little, Brown & Company.

Pyszczynski, T. A., Greenberg, J., & Solomon, S. (2003). *In the Wake of 9/11: The Psychology of Terror* (1st ed.). Washington, DC; London: American Psychological Association.

Rand, J. (2004). *Fields of Honor: The Pat Tillman Story*. New York: Chamberlain Bros.

Ray, N. M. (2015, June 11). Frank Luntzisms: The Destruction of Meaning in Political Speech. Retrieved January 19, 2017, from http://www.dailykos.com/story/2015/6/11/1392544/-FrankLuntzisms-The-Destruction-of-Meaning-in-Political-Speech.

Reilly, R. (2004, May 3). The Hero and the Unknown Soldier. *Sports Illustrated*, 100, 80.

Risen, J., & Wingfield, N. (2013, June 19). Web's Reach Binds N.S.A. and Silicon Valley Leaders. *New York Times*, A1. Retrieved from http://www.nytimes.com/2013/06/20/technology/silicon-valley-and-spy-agency-bound-by-strengthening-web.html?pagewanted=1&nl=todaysheadlines&emc=edit_th_20130620.

Robin, C. (2002). Primal Fear. [Internet]. *Theory and Event*, 5(4).http://muse.jhu.edu/journals/theory_and_event/v005/5.4robin.html.

Robin, C. (2004). *Fear: The History of a Political Idea*. Oxford; New York: Oxford University Press.

Russell, K. K. (1998). *The Color of Crime: Racial Hoaxes, White Fear, Black Protectionism, Police Harassment, and Other Macroaggressions*. New York: New York University Press.

Rutenberg, J., & Carter, B. (2001, September 20). Draping Newscasts with the Flag. *New York Times*, C8.

Ryan, J. (2002, October 15). Media Feeding the Fear. *San Francisco Chronicle*, A23.

Saidi, N. (2004, November 1). Professor Under Investigation for Posters. *The State Press*. Retrieved from http://www.abor.asu.edu/1_the_regents/clips/110104.htm#Professor's%20art%20sparks%20public%20outcry.

Sanger, D. E., & Broad, W. J. (2016, September 5). Obama Unlikely to Vow No First Use of Nuclear Weapons. *New York Times*. Retrieved from http://www.nytimes.com/2016/09/06/world/obama-unlikely-to-vow-no-first-use-of-nuclear-weapons.html?emc=edit_th_20160906&nl=todaysheadlines&nlid=27364645&_r=0.

Savage, C. (2011, June 12). F.B.I. Agents Get Leeway to Push Privacy Bounds. *New York Times*. Retrieved from http://www.nytimes.com/2011/06/13/us/13fbi.html?_r=1&nl=todaysheadlines&emc=tha2.

Savage, D. G. (2002a, May 31). Response to Terror; Courts Likely to Endorse FBI Policy, Experts Say. *Los Angeles Times*, 22.

Savage, D. G. (2002b, June 1). Ruling Halts Internet Limits. *Los Angeles Times*, 12.

Schiller, D. (2011, June 24). Terrorism Suspect Not Going Quietly. *Houston Chronicle*, 1. Retrieved from http://www.lexisnexis.com.ezproxy1.lib.asu.edu/hottopics/lnacademic/?.

Schlesinger, P., Tumber, H., & Murdock, G. (1991). The Media Politics of Crime and Criminal Justice. *British Journal of Sociology*, 42: 397–420.

Schneider, C. J. (2016). *Policing and Social Media: Social Control in an Era of New Media*. New York: Lexington.

Schneider, C. J., & Trottier, D. (2012). *The 2011 Vancouver Riots and the Role of Facebook*. Paper presented at the Society for the Study of Symbolic Interaction Couch-Stone Symposium, Chicago.

Schneider, C. J., & Trottier, D. (2013). Social Media and the 2011 Vancouver Riot. In N. K. Denzin (Ed.), *Studies in Symbolic Interaction: 40th Anniversary of Studies in Symbolic Interaction* (pp. 335–62). New York: Emerald Group Publishing Limited.

Schneier, B. (2013, May 2). Why FBI and CIA Didn't Connect the Dots. Retrieved March 21, 2014, from http://www.cnn.com/2013/05/02/opinion/schneier-boston-bombing.

Schutz, A. (1967). *The Phenomenology of the Social World*. Evanston, IL: Northwestern University Press.

Schwalbe, M., Godwin, S., Holden, D., Schrock, D., Thompson, S., & Wolkomir, M. (2000). Generic Processes in the Reproduction of Inequality: An Interactionist Analysis. *Social Forces*, 79(2): 419–52.

Scott, M., & Lyman, S. M. (1968, February). Accounts. *American Sociological Review, 33*: 46–62.

Shales, T. (2001, December 30). Patriotism Advertising. *Washington Post*, 2. Retrieved from http://www.washingtonpost.com/ac2/wp-dyn?pagename=article&node=&contentId=A35030-2001Dec28.

Shapiro, M. J. (1992). *Reading the Postmodern Polity: Political Theory as Textual Practice.* Minneapolis: University of Minnesota Press.

Shapiro, M. J. (1997). *Violent Cartographies: Mapping Cultures of War.* Minneapolis: University of Minnesota Press.

Shapiro, M. J. (2002). Wanted, Dead or Alive. *Theory and Event, 5*(4).

Shaw, D. L., & McCombs, M. E. (1977). *The Agenda-Setting Function of the Press.* St. Paul, MN: West Publishing.

Shiffman, J. (2011, May 8). Philly's Terrorist Watch. *Philadelphia Inquirer*, A01. Retrieved from http://www.lexisnexis.com.ezproxy1.lib.asu.edu/hottopics/lnacademic/?.

Shirlow, P., & Pain, R. (2003). The Geographies and Politics of Fear. *Capital & Class, 80* (Summer): 15–26.

Signorielli, N., & Gerbner, G. (Eds.). (1988). *Violence and Terror in the Mass Media: An Annotated Bibliography.* New York: Greenwood Press.

Signorielli, N., Gerbner, G., & Morgan, M. (1995). Violence on Television: The Cultural Indicators Project. *Journal of Broadcasting and Electronic Media, 39* (Spring).

Silva, C. (2016, September 13). Syrian Civilian Death Toll 2016: ISIS, Assad Regime Fuel Refugee Crisis with Growing War. *International Business Times.* Retrieved from http://www.ibtimes.com/syrian-civilian-death-toll-2016-isis-assad-regime-fuel-refugee-crisis-growing-war-2415265.

Skogan, W., & Maxfield, M. (1981). *Coping with Crime.* London: Sage.

Skoll, G. R. (2010). *Social Theory of Fear: Terror, Torture, and Death in a Post-Capitalist World* (2010 ed.). New York: Palgrave Macmillan.

Smith, C. R. (2001, November 28). F.B.I. vs. C.I.A.: Battle in Cyberspace. Retrieved June 7, 2002, from http://www.newsmax.com/archives/articles/2001/11/28/142513.shtml.

Smith, G. (2004, May 3). Code of Honor: Pat Tillman 1976–2004. *Sports Illustrated, 100*, 40–46.

Smith, G. J., & Smith, D. (2016). Surveillance, Data and Embodiment: On the Work of Being Watched. *Body and Society*, 108–39.

Snow, R. P. (1983). *Creating Media Culture.* Beverly Hills, CA: Sage.

Solomon, S., Greenberg, J., & Pyszczynsk, T. A. (2004). Fatal Attraction. *American Psychological Society, 17*(10): 13–15.

Soothill, K., & Walby, S. (1991). *Sex Crime in the News.* London; New York: Routledge.

Sparks, C. (2003). Liberalism, Terrorism and the Politics of Fear. *Politics, 23*(3): 200–6.

Sparks, R. (1992). *Television and the Drama of Crime: Moral Tales and the Place of Crime in Public Life.* Milton Keynes, UK: Open University Press.

Spector, M., & Kitsuse, J. I. (1977). *Constructing Social Problems.* Menlo Park, CA: Cummings Publishing Company.

Spector, M., & Kitsuse, J. I. (1987). *Constructing Social Problems.* New York: Aldine de Gruyter.

Speier, H. (1969). *Social Order and the Risks of War: Papers in Political Sociology.* Cambridge, MA: MIT Press.

Staff. (2005, May 23). Tillman's Parents Lash out at Army. *Washington Post.* Retrieved from http://www.eastvalleytribune.com/index.php?sty=41825.

Staples, W. G. (1997). *The Culture of Surveillance: Discipline and Social Control in the United States.* New York: St. Martin's Press.

Staples, W. G. (2000). *Everyday Surveillance: Vigilance and Visibility in Postmodern Life* (Rev. ed.). Lanham, MD; Rowman & Littlefield.

Stelter, B. (2011, February 6). Al Jazeera Hopes Reports from Egypt Open Doors in U.S. *New York Times*, B1. Retrieved from http://www.nytimes.com/2011/02/07/business/media/07aljazeera.html?_r=1&pagewanted=all.

Stepanek, M. (2000, July 7). Now, Companies Can Track Down Their Cyber-Critics. Retrieved June 7, 2002, from http://www.businessweek.com/bwdaily/dnflash/july2000/nf00707g.htm?scriptFramed.

Stern, R. (2002, May 11). Sex Tour Sting in Arizona Nabs 10: Law Enforcement Uses Web to Battle Child Molestation. *Tribune*, 1.

Stone, G. P., & Farberman, H. A. (1970). *Social Psychology through Symbolic Interaction.* Waltham, MA: Ginn-Blaisdell.

Strom, S. (2002, June 23). Families Fret as Charities Hold a Billion Dollars in 9/11 Aid. *New York Times*, 29.

Sullivan, D. (2001, October 22). Washington Is Calling. Will Anyone Answer? *Newsweek*, 12.

Sullivan, T. (2004, June 23). Patriotism at Its Best Instinctive, Not Forced. *San Diego Union-Tribune.* Retrieved from http://www.signonsandiego.com/sports/sullivan/20040723-9999-1s23sullivan.html.

Surette, R. (1992). *Media, Crime, and Criminal Justice: Images and Realities.* Pacific Grove, CA: Brooks/Cole Publishing Company.

Surette, R. (1998). *Media, Crime and Criminal Justice: Images and Realities.* (2nd ed.). Belmont, CA: West/Wadsworth.

Surette, R. (2014). *Media, Crime, and Criminal Justice* (5th ed.). Belmont, CA: Wadsworth.

Surette, R. (2015). Performance Crime and Justice. *Current Issues in Criminal Justice, 27*(2): 195 ff.

Surratt, C. B. (2001). *The Internet and Social Change.* Jefferson, NC: McFarland.

Terkel, A. (2013, June 7). Watch the One Senator Who Voted Against the Patriot Act Warn What Would Happen. Retrieved from http://www.huffingtonpost.com/2013/06/07/russ-feingold-patriot-act-speech_n_3402878.html.

Tesler, M., & Sides, J. (2016, March 3). How Political Science Helps Explain the Rise of Trump: The Role of White Identity and Grievances. *Washington Post.* Retrieved from https://www.washingtonpost.com/news/monkey-cage/wp/2016/03/03/how-political-science-helps-explain-the-rise-of-trump-the-role-of-white-identity-and-grievances/.

Thiele, L. P. (1993). Making Democracy Safe for the World: Social Movements and Global Politics. *Alternatives, 18*(3): 273–305.

Thomaz, O. R. (1997). Bosnia-Herzegovina: The Victory of the Politics of Fear. *Novos Estudos CEBRAP, 47*: 3–18.

Tillman, P., Sr. (2004, May 31). Pat Tillman Sr. Thanks the Valley. *Arizona Republic*, B6.

Uberti, D. (2016). A New Normal in Journalism for the Age of Trump. *Columbia Journalism Review.* http://www.cjr.org/covering_the_election/trump_media_normalization_press_freedom.php.

USA Today. (2001, May 29). E-Monitoring of Workers Sparks Concerns. Retrieved June 6, 2002, from http://www.usatoday.com/life/cyber/tech/2001-05-29-worker-privacy.htm.

Uslaner, E. M. (2000). Trust, Civic Engagement, and the Internet. Retrieved June 13, 2002, fromhttp://www.pewtrusts.com/pdf/vf_pew_internet_trust_paper.pdf.

van Dijk, T. A. (1988). *News as Discourse.* Hillsdale, NJ: L. Erlbaum Associates.

Vasterman, P. L. M. (2005). Media-Hype: Self-Reinforcing News Waves, Journalistic Standards and the Construction of Social Problems. *European Journal of Communication, 20*(4): 508–30.

Velencia, J. (2016, January 12). Republicans Still Don't Think Obama Is American, But Don't Care Ted Cruz Was Born in Canada: Hypocrisy Much? Retrieved November 17, 2016, from http://www.huffingtonpost.com/entry/republicans-trump-cruz-canadian-birth-eligibility_us_56940e76e4b0c8beacf7fe2d.

Victor, J. S. (2006). Why the Terrorism Scare Is a Moral Panic. In B. Glassner, *The Culture of Fear: Why Americans Are Afraid of the Wrong Things* by Barry Glassner. [Internet]. *The Humanist.*

Vidich, A. J. (1991). Social Theory and the Substantive Problems of Sociology. *International Journal of Politics, Culture and Society, 4*(4): 517–34.

Vinograd, C., Jamieson, A., Viala, F., & Smith, A. (2015, January 7). Charlie Hebdo Shooting: 12 Killed at Muhammad Cartoons Magazine in Paris. *NBC News*. Retrieved from http://www.nbcnews.com/storyline/paris-magazine-attack/charlie-hebdo-shooting-12-killed-muhammad-cartoons-magazine-paris-n281266.

Voice of America News. (2014, March 23). Turkey PM Defiant over Twitter Ban. Retrieved March 23, 2014, from http://www.voanews.com/content/turkey-leader-defiant-over-twitter-ban/1877522.html.

Waite, C. K. (2003). *Mediation and the Communication Matrix* (Vol. 10). New York: Peter Lang.

Walker, J. (2002, March). Panic Attacks. *Reason, 33*: 36–42.

Warr, M. (1980, December 2). The Accuracy of Public Beliefs about Crime. *Social Forces, 59*: 456–70.

Warr, M. (1983, June 4). Fear of Victimization: A Look at the Proximate Causes. *Social Forces, 61*: 1033–43.

Warr, M. (1985). Fear of Rape Among Urban Women. *Social Problems, 32*: 238–50.

Warr, M. (1987, March 1). Fear of Victimization and Sensitivity to Risk. *Journal of Quantitative Criminology, 3*: 29–46.

Warr, M. (1990). Dangerous Situations: Social Context and Fear of Victimization. *Social Forces, 68*(3): 891–907.

Warr, M. (1992, December 4). Altruistic Fear of Victimization in Households. *Social Science Quarterly, 73*: 723–36.

Warren, M. (2016, August 12). Kristol: Trump Is "Discrediting Conservatism": "He Needs to Be Separated and Severed from Conservatism." *The Weekly Standard*.

Wasburn, P. C. (2002). *The Social Construction of International News: We're Talking about Them, They're Talking about Us*. Westport, CT; London: Praeger.

Weiler, M., & Pearce, W. B. (1992). *Reagan and Public Discourse in America*. Tuscaloosa, AL: University of Alabama Press.

Weiser, B. (2016, May 2). Departing Judge Offers Blunt Defense of Ruling in Stop-and-Frisk Case. *New York Times*. Retrieved from http://www.nytimes.com/2016/05/02/nyregion/departing-judge-offers-blunt-defense-of-ruling-that-ended-stop-and-frisk.html?emc=edit_th_20160502&nl=todaysheadlines&nlid=27364645.

Weisman, R. (2001, December 13). FBI Waves "Magic Lantern." Retrieved June 7, 2002, from http://www.newsfactor.com/perl/story/15301.html.

Werning, S. (2009). *Real Wars on Virtual Battlefields: The Convergence of Programmable Media at the Military-Civilian Margin*. New York: Transcript-Verlag.

Westfeldt, W. T. W. (1998). *Indictment: The News Media and the Criminal Justice System*. Nashville: First Amendment Center.

Westphal, D. (2001, October 8). Buildup Quickly Erasing Post–Cold War Peace Dividend; As the United States Mounts Its Campaign against Terrorism, Defense Spending Will Increase Rapidly. *Star Tribune*, 5A.

Whitaker, B. (2016, October 23). The Influencers: Social Media Stars Are Earning Big Money for Pitching Products in Short, Often Silly, Postings Seen by Millions of Followers. *60 Minutes*.

Williams, R. (1982). *The Sociology of Culture* (1st American ed.). New York: Schocken Books.

Williams, W. (2016, August 19). Column: Is Free Trade or Technology Causing Job Loss? *The Times News*. Retrieved November 18, 2016, from http://www.thetimesnews.com/opinion/20160819/column-is-free-trade-or-technology-causing-job-loss.

Willis, W. J., & Okunade, A. A. (1997). *Reporting on Risks: The Practice and Ethics of Health and Safety Communication*. Westport, CT: Praeger.

Wire Services. (2002, May 9). Web-Based Child Porn Sting Leads to Raids on 200 Homes. *The Record*, A4.

Wong, E. (2016, November 18). Trump Has Called Climate Change a Chinese Hoax. Beijing Says It Is Anything But. *New York Times*. Retrieved from https://www.nytimes.com/2016/11/19/world/asia/china-trump-climate-change.html?_r=0.

Wonneberger, A., Schoenbach, K., & Meurs, L. v. (2013). How Keeping Up Diversifies: Watching Public Affairs TV in the Netherlands 1988–2010. *European Journal of Communication, 28*(6): 646–62.

Wu, D. H. (2000). Systematic Determinants of International News Coverage: A Comparison of 38 Countries. *Journal of Communication, 50*(2): 110–30.

Wuthnow, R. (Ed.). (1992). *Vocabularies of Public Life: Empirical Essays in Symbolic Structure*. New York: Routledge.

Yan, H., Sgueglia, K., & Walker, K. (2016, November 17). "Make America White Again": Hate Speech and Crimes Post-Election. Retrieved November 17, 2016, fromhttp://www.cnn.com/2016/11/10/us/post-election-hate-crimes-and-fears-trnd/.

Yar, M. (2012). Crime, Media, and the Will-to-Representation: Reconsidering Relationships in the Social Media Age. *Crime Media Culture, 8*(3): 245–60.

Yavuz, M. H. (2002). The Politics of Fear: The Rise of the Nationalist Action Party (MHP) in Turkey. *Middle East Journal, 56* (2): 200–21.

Zagorin, A., & Burger, T. J. (2004, October). Beyond the Call of Duty. *Time*.

Zakaria, F. (2002, May 27). The Answer? A Domestic CIA. *Newsweek*, 39.

Zenko, M. (2016, January 12). Obama's Embrace of Drone Strikes Will Be a Lasting Legacy. *New York Times*. Retrieved from http://www.nytimes.com/roomfordebate/2016/01/12/reflecting-on-obamas-presidency/obamas-embrace-of-drone-strikes-will-be-a-lasting-legacy.

Zerubavel, E. (1985). *Hidden Rhythms: Schedules and Calendars in Social Life* (1st California pbk. ed.). Berkeley: University of California Press.

Zhondang, P., & Kosicki, G. (1993). Framing Analysis: An Approach to News Discourse. *Political Communication, 10*: 55–69.

Zillman, D. W. J. (1987). Fear of Victimization and the Appeal of Crime Drama. In D. Zillman (Ed.), *Selective Exposure to Communication*. Hillsdale, NJ: Elrbaum.

Zulaika, J., & Douglass, W. A. (1996). *Terror and Taboo: The Follies, Fables, and Faces of Terrorism*. New York: Routledge.

Index

About the Author

David L. Altheide, PhD, is Regents' Professor Emeritus on the faculty of Justice and Social Inquiry in the School of Social Transformation at Arizona State University, where he taught for thirty-seven years. His work has focused on the role of mass media and information technology in social control. His coauthored book with Robert P. Snow, *Media Logic* (1979), was foundational for more recent developments in mediatization and mediality. Some other recent books include: *The Media Syndrome* (2016), *Media Edge: Media Logic and Social Reality* (2014), *Qualitative Media Analysis* (2nd edition, 2012), and *Terror Post 9/11 and the Media* (2009). Dr. Altheide received the Cooley Award three times, given to the outstanding book in symbolic interaction, from the Society for the Study of Symbolic Interaction: in 2007 for *Terrorism and the Politics of Fear* (2006); in 2004 for *Creating Fear: News and the Construction of Crisis* (2002); and in 1986 for *Media Power* (1985). Dr. Altheide received the 2005 George Herbert Mead Award for lifetime contributions from the Society for the Study of Symbolic Interaction, and the society's Mentor Achievement Award in 2007. In fall 2012 he was a Fulbright Specialist in Germany (Zeppelin University) and a Distinguished Research Professor in Australia (Law Faculty, University of New South Wales). In spring 2017 he was selected as a Fulbright Specialist in Lisbon (Universidade Católica Portuguesa).